Reshaping Communications

Reshaping Communications

Technology, Information and Social Change

PASCHAL PRESTON

SAGE Publications
London • Thousand Oaks • New Delhi

First published 2001

SAGE Publications Ltd
6 Bonhill Street
London EC2A 4PU

SAGE Publications Inc
2455 Teller Road
Thousand Oaks, California 91320

SAGE Publications India Pvt Ltd
32, M-Block Market
Greater Kailash – I
New Delhi 110 048

British Library Cataloguing in Publication data

A catalogue record for this book is
available from the British Library

ISBN 0 8039 8562 2
ISBN 0 8039 8563 0 (pbk)

Library of Congress catalog card number available

Typeset by M Rules
Printed and bound in Great Britain by Athenaeum Press, Gateshead

CONTENTS

EC	European Commission
ECU	European Currency Unit
EU	European Union
G7	Group of Seven (leading industrial nations)
GII	Global Information Infrastructure
IC	Information and communication (industries, products, services etc)
ICT	Information and communication technologies
ISDN	Integrated Services Digital Network
ISH	Information superhighway
LFR	Less Favoured Region (official EU term)
MNTS	Major new technology system
NII	National Information Infrastructure
NTIA	US National Telecommunications & Information Administration
POTS	Plain old telephone service
R&D	Research and development
SEP	Socio-technical paradigm
SME	Small and Medium-sized Enterprises
TEP	Techno-economic paradigm

A book, like any text, is really the product of many minds, exchanges and formal and informal learnings. This book has been a long time in the making and reflects a large set of different influences within the professional and personal circles in which I have moved. Thus I must acknowledge many debts and influences beyond those formally listed in the references. These include exchanges with many colleagues and students over the past decade, as well as colleagues in various interdisciplinary and transnational research networks. I also appreciate the encouragement and support of former mentors and colleagues in PCL, UEL and in Reading University, especially David Marsh, Sophie Bowlby, Peter Hall, Ash Amin, Ruth Muller and Linda Peake. I acknowledge the support of DCU colleagues such as Farrel Corcoran, Barbara O'Connor, Stephanie McBride and the various formal and informal exchanges and 'learnings' derived from a great crew of past and current research students, including Roderick Flynn, Aphra Kerr, Des McGuinness and Michael O'Gorman.

Thanks too to Pauline Jones who has helped in the production of various drafts of the present text; to Julia Hall, Seth Edwards, Marion Steel and Rosie Maynard at Sage for their much-appreciated support and patience; and to two anonymous reviewers of an earlier draft.

In a real sense, authors of books, or any other text, bear the stamp of many extra-textual and extra-discursive influences. I also want to note the many special friends who have shaped 'the everyday life' and stimulated much more than the intellectual zones and all those who have made my adult life adventures, in London and Dublin, all the more vibrant, stimulating and often joyful. Here I should also express my appreciation to that special crew who have added the essential spices to life in the capital of the so-called 'celtic tiger', Europe's own would-be 'information age hub'. For their friendship craic and chats I want to express my thanks to: Kevin Maguire, Kozo Matsuda, Ruth Clarke-O'Daly, Miriam Lillis, Eilish Ward, Dennis Cahalane, Grainne Murphy, Stephen Sefton, Hitome Ebe, Clara Martin, Anne Tangy, Ana Pereda, Roisin Maguire, Angela O'Driscoll, Mary O'Sullivan, James Anderson, Roise Bhaoil, Lis Geary and Bernadette Clarke. And a special appreciation must go to Andrea Grisold for her very special friendship, support and intellectual exchanges.

This book is dedicated to my father, James Preston (1922–2000).

Part I

INTRODUCTION AND OVERVIEW

CHAPTER ONE

INFORMATION SUPERHIGHWAYS OR SUPERHYPEWAYS: IMAGES OF A NEW SOCIAL AND MEDIA ORDER

'To admire technology is all out of fashion . . .'

(Maddox, 1972: 15)

'No one can escape the transforming fire of machines. Technology, which once progressed at the periphery of culture, now engulfs our minds as well as our lives. Is it any wonder that technology triggers such intense fascination, fear and rage? One by one, each of the things that we care about in life is touched by science and then altered. Human expression, thought, communication, and even human life have been infiltrated by high technology . . .'

(Kelly, 1998:1)

DIGITAL DREAMS AND DELIRIA: ALL CHANGE FOR A NEW MILLENNIUM?

If in the early 1970s, one writer addressing social and political aspects of the then 'new' communication technologies could complain that 'to admire technology is all out of fashion' the situation has certainly changed a lot since then (Maddox, 1972: 15). By the 1990s, to 'admire' and indeed enthuse over new information and communication technologies had become highly fashionable and popular. So too had the perception that such new technologies are bringing about a rapid and fundamental change in the overall social, economic and cultural environment of the industrial world, if not globally.

We are currently riding along the crest of a new wave of interest in technological change and the promises it holds for a fundamental reshaping of social, political, economic and cultural affairs. The 1980s and especially the 1990s have witnessed a surge of excited discussion and anticipation concerning new information and communication technologies (ICT) and networks as powerful forces which are propelling us into entirely 'new times'. Thus much has changed since the 1970s. This is not only a matter of radical new technical innovations such as the rapid development of the Internet/World Wide Web and the prospects these afford for 'a new frontier' of downstream electronic commerce and digital multimedia services. Nor is it merely a matter of the widespread or 'pervasive' applications potential of recent advances in ICT devices and networks as platforms for a diverse set of emergent new communication networks, services and media for use within the workplace and inside our homes. We are not merely facing 'seismic shifts' in the nature of available technical infrastructures as we embark on the new millennium. What is also involved is nothing less than a major shift in the way we are supposed to think about the nature of such new technological developments and their implications for the social, economic and cultural order which has prevailed since the advent of the capitalist industrial era.

On one level, the surge of interest in new ICT matters in the 1990s might be viewed as a direct response to the emergence and adoption of a new cluster of radical technical innovations. By then, some of the earlier (1970s and 1980s) generation of 'new media' had become widely adopted throughout the developed world and even in many developing countries: cable and satellite television, video cassette recorders, mobile telephony, stand-alone personal computers and digital music systems. By the late 1990s, these had been complemented by a further layer or generation of radical new communication and media technologies. These comprise a further new cluster of advances in digital electronics and a growing technical 'convergence' of advanced telecommunications, computer and broadcasting networks. They are centred on a common digital mode of information processing and distribution, with the Internet, WWW and multimedia featuring prominently amongst the cluster of interrelated technical developments. In little more than a decade, telephony has become highly mobile in character and the personal computer has moved from a 'stand-alone' office tool to become an increasingly flexible terminal for various forms of communication and networking. The computer has also come to occupy a new role in the communication activities within a growing proportion of homes, at least in the advanced industrial economies. Indeed, for many commentators, the personal computer has now emerged as a competitor to the television set (and the telephone) as the key terminal for a growing range of communication activities in our homes and everyday lives. By the late 1990s, it was difficult to spend an evening grazing across the television channels without encountering stories telling you that you are engaged in a very old-fashioned activity, one which is rapidly becoming obsolescent in the face of new interactive, multimedia communication systems offering 'highly-immersive' cyber-worlds or virtual realities of limitless communication.

A historical perspective on technical innovation processes tells us that there have been prior shifts in the form and degree of attention accorded to the role of technology in public discourses concerned with the issues of social and economic change (Hall and Preston, 1988; Marvin, 1988). Around the turn of the twentieth century, the first modern multi-media technological 'revolution' (the invention of the telephone, movies, recorded music, etc.) certainly led to some excited discussions of their possible negative and positive 'effects' in the social and cultural domains. At the same time, the development of electrical power systems was accompanied by much fascinated speculation concerning the nature and impacts of this novel 'invisible fluid' and its pervasive applications potential. In the technical and trade press of the early electrical industry, there was much utopian speculation about the new types of economic 'abundance', decentralisation of industry, and other benign social benefits the new technologies might bring in their train. In certain respects, the content of such speculative responses to 'the shock of the new' a century ago can be taken as pre-figurative of many of the discourses surrounding new ICT, the Internet and 'cyberspace' in the 1980s and 1990s. But the latter differ greatly from those of a century ago when it comes to the degree of attention accorded to technology matters in public discourses and debates concerning the sources, direction and options for social change.

Thus at the outset, I want to register that something new is happening now besides the more visible technical inventions and innovations themselves and besides the surge of investments in their further development, diffusion and application on the part of economic and policy actors. Here I want to flag two other important parallel shifts which frame the agenda of this particular book. The first is a significant expansion in the degree of emphasis on technology matters in contemporary public discourses surrounding the origins, direction and processes of economic, social and cultural change. The second is a related tendency to assume and assert that new ICT implies a very specific and particular path of social, political and cultural change.

The recent surge of interest in new ICT and its perceived 'impacts' or 'effects' for economic, social and cultural affairs has been taking place across the whole spectrum of the media and fora of public communication. It has not been confined to the specialist media of a high-tech milieu of producers and users located at the leading-edge of these developments. Nor has it been confined to the various 'new media' and discussion groups which have emerged on the Internet. All the established 'mature' media of TV, newspapers and magazines now also regularly deliver excited messages about the 'impact' of one or other new communication technology whose emergence is seen to be catapulting us into a new digital, or atom-less 'information age'. Most 'serious' newspapers and television channels in the USA, Europe Union and elsewhere now have a regular weekly section or programming slot dealing with new developments in the fields of computing, electronic networking, digital broadcasting, or other digital multimedia fields.

The 1990s were also marked by a surge of popular books stressing the nature and meaning of this diverse cluster of new and emergent ICT. These publications tend to proclaim that new ICT is forging major changes in the social, cultural and communication processes and the very fabric of our everyday lives, both within and outside the workplace. Ideas and images such as 'cyberspace', 'information superhighways', the 'information society', the 'networked society' – which were largely confined to the realm of science fiction writing in the not so distant past – are now employed to describe significant social and cultural changes associated with new communication technologies. It seems as if McLuhan's old 1960s' vision of 'the global village' is at last being realised as we witness 'the death of distance' thanks to the wonders of new communication technologies and perceptions of their radical impacts on cultural, social and political affairs (Cairncross, 1997; Gates, 1995). Indeed, for some, the exponential diffusion of various forms of computer technologies into our everyday worlds at work and home now means that computing is no longer about computers but 'about living' and the very essence of experience and life itself becomes all about 'being digital' (Negroponte, 1995: 4–8).

Besides, one of the major growth areas within the magazine publishing industry in more recent years has been the spate of new titles dealing with aspects of new ICT for home as well as business users. One major feature of the increasing media coverage of ICT matters consists of advertising and promotional hype from the suppliers and retailers of new ICT-based media and services. These not only seek to encourage the further purchase and use of various new ICT-related hardware, software and services. They also extol the social and economic benefits of such new technologies for both business and home users. Indeed, it is notable that the most expensive marketing campaign ever in the history of product marketing was that launched in 1995 for a new computer operating system – one which prominently featured new computer-based networking and related communication services and their radical possibilities.

But the recent surge of promotional material for new ICT products has not been confined to the usual advertising and marketing activities of the corporations involved in the supply of commercial products and systems. Politicians as well as influential pundits, some with close links to the high-tech producing industries, have become prominent actors in the wider public discourses which propose exciting new social, cultural and media futures associated with the new communication technologies. There is a new fashion for techno-gurus, some of whom command truly super-star fees for conference sermons prophesying a shiny new 'promised land' based on ICT

Examples of perceived 'transformations'

'We now live in a new economy created by shrinking computers and expanding communities. This represents a tectonic upheaval in our common-wealth . . . We have seen only the beginnings of the anxiety, loss, excitement, and gains that many people will experience as our world shifts to a new highly technical planetary economy.' (Kelly, 1998:1)

'Electronic commerce . . . and the information technology industries that make "e-commerce" possible are growing and changing at breathtaking speed, fundamentally changing the way Americans produce, consume, communicate and play.' (US Dept. of Commerce, 1999: 5)

'By 1997, "community" had become one of the trendiest words around, both on and off the Internet . . . the Internet can be a powerful enabling technology fostering the development of communities because it supports the very thing that creates a community–human interaction.' (Dyson, 1998: 43–4)

'. . . I'm optimistic about the impact of the new technology. It will enhance leisure time and enrich culture by expanding the distribution of information . . . It will give us more control over our lives and allow experiences and products to be custom tailored to our interests . . .' (Gates, 1995: 250)

'A new, far richer range of novel services in the form of information, access to data-bases, audio-visual, cultural and leisure facilities will be opened up to everyone . . . it will be possible to gain access to general information directly, without any complicated technology . . .' (CEC, 1994a: 22)

'The information superhighway may be mostly hype today, but it is an understate-ment about tomorrow. It will exist beyond people's wildest predictions . . . The digital planet will look and feel like the head of a pin.' (Negroponte, 1995: 7, 231)

'Content is the key driver and the most important asset . . . the convergence of telecommunications and media industries and the resulting paradigm shift . . . has been enabled by the rapid development of digital technologies.' (CEC,1997: 6–7)

'The great irony is that the new media – the Web, cable, narrowcasting via satellite and all sorts of digital delights – could create a whole new range of public-service programming that includes, rather than edifies, the public.' (Wired, 1996: 59)

innovations. Influential sections of the global political and technocratic élites also advance grand visions of the universal benefits to be bestowed by new national, continental and global 'information infrastructures' or 'superhigh-ways' (e.g. USA-NII, 1994; Gore, 1994b; G7, 1995).

Prominent politicians, pundits and commentators regularly emphasise how new ICT and 'info-structures' are leading to a entirely new kind of 'information society' or 'digital economy' (CEC, 1994a, 1994b; US Dept. of Commerce, 1999). Even that hero of the long political struggle for change in South Africa, Nelson Mandela, has been occasionally mobilised to extol the promises of 'a world-wide information society' (1995). A core feature of the many national and global information society initiatives in the 1990s has been a universal stress on the pervasive benefits of new ICT. Irrespective of national origin, the pervasive prophesy is that we are entering an entirely new kind of 'information society'. Both new ICT and information are defined as increasingly central to all aspects of economic, political and cultural activity and the key drivers of radical social change.

Thus as we enter the new millennium, to admire and enthuse over technology and its presumed social or economic benefits has become highly fashionable compared to the 1970s. The dominant discourses favoured by the industrial and policy élites within the OECD countries converge around a number of core themes. We are on the way to a new economic and social system based on new ICT and information structures, one which is fundamentally different to the kind of social and economic order which has prevailed since the industrial revolution. These discourses adopt a very particular and flawed view of the historical significance of new ICT and changing information structures and define these as midwives for a transition to a radically new socio-economic order. More importantly, they tend to define these technology-based innovations as intricately linked to (determining) the adoption of a singular path of socio-economic development. Frequently, the perceived characteristics of new ICT are deemed to match or require a specific political economy and cluster of social values. These analyses tend to privilege a rather optimistic and one-sided view of prevailing socio-economic trends. For example, they stress a rapid growth in the number and range of 'high-level, grey-matter' occupations within the audio-visual, multimedia and other information or 'content-rich' industries. Many also prophesy a new 'communication revolution' deemed to take us beyond mere mass media to more interactive and personalised forms of digital multimedia, information services and cultural products – which will fashion a more participative polity and forms of community. Indeed a key element in these techno-pundits' forecasts is that the existing media, such as television, newspapers – and even books such as this – will soon become obsolete, to be replaced by radically new digital, multimedia or interactive systems of communication within a very short time (e.g. Toffler, 1983; Negroponte, 1995; Gates, 1995).

Alongside the growth of interest in technology matters within the media of public communication in the recent past, there has also been a parallel surge of academic writings with a specific focus on the role and impacts of new ICT and information structures. In keeping with the wider 'fashion' outlined above, the past decade has witnessed a striking increase in academic work which emphasises the role of new ICT and/or new information and communication networks in reshaping the contours of socio-economic and cultural development. Some of this academic work certainly presents a much less utopian or optimistic account of such developments compared to that originating in other spheres. But much of the recent academic literature, whether drawing on one or more of the competing or complementary models of postmodernism, post-industrialism, 'new economy', or the information society notion, also tends to assume or emphasise the 'strong' or revolutionary impacts of new ICT for socio-economic and cultural change. Many such contributions tend to focus on the distinctive technical characteristics of the new devices or systems, too often deriving ('reading-off') particular social, economic or cultural effects from the technical artefacts. This kind of approach has a prior history if relatively minor role within the social sciences and humanities. But on the whole, it is one which was much criticised and less influential in previous decades. It tends to ignore or deny the value of concepts and insights drawn from the wider social science research traditions as aids to a more grounded understanding of the nature and implications of new ICT as a distinctive new technology system. It also tends to exaggerate the dimensions change associated with new ICT whilst neglecting important aspects of social, economic and cultural continuities with earlier periods of industrial modernity.

One other related issue in the academic literature concerns the challenges involved in crossing the 'two cultures' divide which has developed and grown between the natural sciences and humanities over the past two centuries (Carey, 1995). Many of the academic contributions which have identified and emphasised the radical social and cultural impacts of new ICTs have been written by researchers based in technical disciplines such as computer science or computer applications, telecommunications or information systems fields. Unfortunately, despite (or because of) their detailed understanding and focus on the technical characteristics of new ICTs, many are stamped by the 'expert idiocy' which results from the deepening division of intellectual labour within the academy. They are marked by a weak theoretical and historical understanding of the complex interactions between technological change on the one hand and social, or economic or cultural and communication processes on the other. All too often they fail to engage with the considerable tradition of social science and cultural studies literature addressing questions of the interplay of technology and socio-economic and cultural change. One outcome is that many such media or technology-centred academic contributions to these debates simply end up reproducing the kinds of marketing and promotional hype advanced by very specific industrial interests and technocratic élites based in the high-tech sector.

Amongst technologists and computer specialists, the most popular and influential writings on the socio-economic and cultural dimensions of new ICTs are those which advance radical utopian (or, to a lesser extent, dystopian) lines of analyses. This has many parallels with the kinds of discourses favoured by the engineering circles involved in developing the electrical and electro-mechanical communication technologies around the turn of the twentieth century. One reason for the popularity of such categories of writing amongst this milieu may be that it supports an enhanced sense of self-importance, professional status or social relevance to those engaged in (the often mundane or highly-structured) work of producing and developing such new technologies. In addition, it is clear that such representations can deliver better psychic rewards as they certainly give more scope to the imagination. Both author and reader can be more easily 'seduced by the social simplifications of utopian romance' or less frequently, disturbed by dystopian nightmares (Kling, 1994: 168). In contrast, the social realist or more empirically-grounded approaches to the socio-economic implications of new ICTs are likely to involve more complex and subtle analyses. But, of course, these are precisely ones which 'have less rhetorical power to capture the imagination of readers' – whether located within the high-tech sector or without (Kling, 1994: 168). Given their own backgrounds and epistemological orientations, many technologists tend to dismiss the more social realist and empirically grounded analyses as irrelevant or anecdotal and have little tolerance for social or cultural theory. In certain respects, the utopian and anti-utopian analyses of new ICTs may represent useful genres for helping engineers and designers to imagine or understand how new technologies expand the limits of the possible (Marvin, 1988). But they provide poor maps to the social and economic implications of such technical advances, or the complex interplay of technical, social and economic forces shaping their application, adoption and diffusion.

All of this suggests that the challenge of an integrated and coherent interdisciplinary study of the socio-economic and cultural implications of new ICT and changing information structures is much easier to espouse than to achieve or implement in practice. But despite the undoubted difficulties, this remains a valid and important challenge if we are to better understand the present and the likely future prospects for a more benign and equitable social and communication order. The key aim of this book is to make a modest contribution to such an understanding, especially from the point of view and interests of the majority social groups, political and cultural interests located on the other side of the 'digital divide' from those whose version of the story tends to dominate contemporary discourses on such technology and information matters.

SO WHAT'S *REALLY* NEW?: THE 'WHAT?' AND 'WHY?' OF THIS BOOK

So what is the purpose and role of this particular book given the recent explosion of interest, debate and speculation concerning new information and communication technologies (ICTs), the information 'revolution' and their alleged impacts and implications? What is its distinctive story, purpose and justification given the real threat of a particular form of 'information overload' surrounding these kinds of issues?

The primary aim of this book is to advance a more grounded approach to mapping or understanding the complex interplay between new ICT and the changing role of information structures on the one hand, and significant trends of change (and continuities) in social relations and communication processes on the other hand. The present author believes that the dominant drift of recent discourses tends towards exaggerated accounts of emerging socio-economic and cultural changes and flawed accounts of the linkages between such changes and new ICT. This book challenges the dominant assumptions that new ICT (together with the accumulated layers of modern technological infrastructures) and/or the growing economic role of 'information' occupations, services or products are leading to a fundamental transformation of the social and economic order. The book develops an empirically-grounded model of the historical specificities of new ICT which aims for a more holistic account of the key features and implications of the changing institutional role of information and communication networks. In focusing on social and economic trends rather than a predominantly technology-centred analysis, it points to many significant, if negative, features of social development over the past two decades which are simply glossed away in other accounts. Thus this book tells a story of many important shifts and *changes* in socio-economic trends as well as in ICT technology fields, but it also points to the persistence of *continuities* in many important features of the socio-economic and communication order. Inevitably, this means that the book also engages with alternative models and ways of thinking about the implications or 'impacts' of ICT-based innovations for social, economic and cultural processes – not least those influential models informing the dominant discourses briefly described above. Along the way, this exploration will involve some original empirical work to map and assess the direction or extent of new socio-economic and communication trends. It will also involve a critical dialogue with relevant aspects of several influential and competing theories of contemporary social and cultural trends.

This book will develop a particular model of the historically specific technical features, innovation processes and current developmental trends directly surrounding new ICT and information structures. It defines new ICT as a cluster of inter-related radical innovations which comprise a major new technology system, and one that is historically rare (but not unprecedented) as it is marked by a pervasive applications potential. It will explore the interplay between new ICT and trends of change and/or continuities in the social and communication orders via what is primarily a social science-centred approach (rather than a technology-centred one). It will develop a particular model which draws heavily but selectively from the existing body of conceptual and empirical resources within sociology, communication and cultural studies as well as the field of evolutionary/institutional economics. It will further flesh out this initial conceptual map by engaging in empirical-level research focused on recent trends in socio-economic and cultural change, as well as addressing significant continuities within such change. This book also explores the manner and extent to which the communication services sector is changing. It will challenge flawed if influential theories which proclaim the rapid obsolescence of old media products, services or forms in the face of new media technologies and platforms. Here, thankfully, we will not have to engage in the convoluted, if amusing, acrobatics of some other accounts in the self-imposed effort to justify the use of an old medium (a book) to express such ideas (e.g. Negroponte, 1995). Besides, this book will also seek to avoid the pessimistic, apocalyptic approaches centred on the totalising vision of an all-powerful new communication and information order, the dystopian flip-side of the utopian perspective.

Thus the approach in this book does not dismiss new technologies, new digital modes of information production and distribution, as irrelevant to the study of socio-economic cultural change tendencies. On the contrary, it advances a theoretical framework which accords a high degree of importance to the cluster of radical innovations which comprise new ICT – defined as a historically rare, pervasive major new technology system. It also recognises that, compared to the eighteenth or nineteenth centuries, it is increasingly the case that the analysis of change in the overall social and economic fabric of capitalist industrialism cannot be understood in isolation from successive layers of innovation in the ICT or other technical fields and associated changes in the role of communication and information sectors.

One key aim is to directly challenge the now popular assumption that, as a major new technology system, new ICT is to be considered as an autonomous force determining a singular path of socio-economic change – or, indeed, continuities – in the key relationships and processes which characterise social, economic and cultural life in advanced capitalist industrial societies. In line with this, the book embarks on a specific interdisciplinary exploration of the historical specificities and role of new ICTs and their relation to shifts in information and communication structures. It examines key features of the 'I' and the 'C' of new ICT. It examines some key trends which are serving to reshape the role and features of different categories of 'information', their modes of distribution, flows and access. Here it will address some of the key stakes involved in the increasing commodification and commercialisation of diverse forms of information and knowledge, including (public) communication processes in advanced capitalist societies at this time.

THE STORY: CONTINUITIES AMID CHANGE

In essence, the present book aims to provide a more grounded understanding of the historical specificity of new ICTs and information structures and what these imply for both *change and continuities* in key social, economic and cultural relationships as we enter a new millennium. It will engage in critical dialogue with influential technology-centred and information-centred models of the contemporary. A key aim here is to by-pass the hegemony of technocratic and 'market-driven' discourses and re-insert the social and political back into the analysis (and process) of social and cultural development. This book advances an alternative social science centred model that is informed by empirical research on recent innovation processes in the ICT field and on relevant socio-economic trends and developments. The core aim is to develop a realist and grounded understanding of *changes* and *continuities* in the social and communication orders and their inter-linkages with new ICT-based innovations, shifts in the role of information structures and communication network developments. Clearly, innovation in the information technology and communication sectors is increasingly central to contemporary change in the overall social and economic order. In exploring these developments, the book adopts a holistic and interdisciplinary approach – one which engages with ideas and findings drawn from a constellation of research fields which do not always cross-communicate with each other.

To this end, Chapters Two through to Chapter Five investigate influential ideas concerning the implications of new ICT and the changing characteristics and role of information in the late twentieth century. This critical dialogue with competing theories will examine their key concepts, underlying assumptions, internal coherence and plausibility and their salience with respect to trends of change within the social and communications order. At the same time, this review will also prepare the ground for a particular theoretical perspective which challenges determinist views of technological innovations, but yet pays specific attention to new ICTs and changes in the information sector. In Chapter Six, I will move on to propose a more nuanced theoretical model for understanding the contemporary social order and the key characteristics of the processes of change and continuity in the sphere of public communication. I will then proceed to develop and refine this model in the course of a more grounded and empirically-orientated register of inquiry (Chapters Seven to Ten). Here the book will also seek to highlight the scope and importance of specific sets of actors and social forces in 'shaping' the very development and application of the new technologies and related innovations. In the final chapter, I will address the scope for alternative social and communication developments, and indicate the requirements for a more equitable social and cultural order.

Chapter Two commences this inquiry by turning to the most influential accounts of the historical specificity or significance of new ICTs and their presumed implications for change in social, economic and cultural processes as well as for reshaping the media and communications services sectors. Here I describe and evaluate key components of the transformative or 'third wave' perspective on current technological innovations. I critically interrogate its stress on the new technologies as drivers of a fundamental transformation in the social and economic processes of industrial capitalism. The core ideas underpinning this particular approach are not entirely new. They have been subject to much criticism in the past, yet they continue to be a highly influential perspective on the historical significance and specificity of new ICTs as we enter the new millennium.

The final section of Chapter Two considers one other recent stream of analysis which is labelled the 'post-Fordist' literature. This body of work advances a number of distinctive perspectives on the role and potential implications of new ICTs in the overall processes of economic, industrial and political change at the close of the twentieth century. In general, it is found to provide a much more robust conceptualisation of the historical specificity and implications of new ICT compared to the 'third wave' and some other influential theories. It is based on a more grounded and historically informed 'long waves' approach which helps to provide a more robust conceptualisation of new ICT and its implications within the overall dynamics of socio-economic change in the contemporary period. I selectively adopt and adapt elements of this body of work later in Chapter Six in order to develop a more grounded and rounded theory to address the implications of new ICT and changing information structures. Amongst the competing post-Fordist models, the neo-Schumpeterian approach is taken to offer particularly useful starting points for the analysis of major new technology systems (such as new ICT) and their implications for a more comprehensive theory of the contemporary. But it is one which must be further developed and augmented with concepts drawn from other theoretical traditions if it is to be rendered relevant to the overall concerns of this book. For example, many of these post-Fordist models are found to be highly functionalist and weak with respect to explaining the origins of long-run turning points in the accumulation process in the history of capitalist industrialism. They tend to neglect the role of social and political factors, as well as the specificities of information and communication as key factors in the contemporary restructuring of socio-economic and political order. They stress the material dimensions of restructuring and change (rather than the informational or symbolic) and, in this respect, they complement some of the other models addressed in Chapters Three through to Five.

For many theorists, as indicted above, the key to the contemporary centres around the 'I' and/or the 'C' components of the term new IT/ICT (as opposed to a focus on the 'T' dimension). Thus in Chapters Three through to Five, the attention shifts from technology-centred analyses to those which highlight the changing role of diverse forms of *information*, knowledge and communication within the advanced industrial world. These explore how, despite a long history of debates over the role of technology as a driver of social and cultural change, there was relatively little explicit attention to *information* as a major factor in the study of socio-economic or cultural processes prior to the 1940s. Indeed, despite their other differences, many recent theories have converged around the notion that increasing *informationalisation* of economic and social processes is one of the most distinctive and significant features of the contemporary. For example, many recent contributions which primarily focus on technology matters also give considerable weight to increasing informationalisation, often viewing such developments as determined by (or closely linked to) technical innovation in the new ICT field. Similarly, many recent models with a declared focus on information matters are found to place an equal stress on the perceived impacts of the emergence, application and diffusion of new ICT. Clearly then, the range and diversity of literature which highlights the changing role of information is very large indeed and so some selectivity is required for present purposes. Here I make a double distinction between the various streams of information-centred analyses of the contemporary. Despite some spillovers between the three selected clusters of concern and writings, each tends to display distinctive features concerning the nature and status of their claims as well as their particular focus on either socio-economic or cultural trends of change.

First, I distinguish between analyses which focus on the changing role and characteristics of information and knowledge in the sphere of production (and which largely address issues to do with the economic and social spheres) as opposed to those which primarily address the role of information within the sphere of consumption, including major shifts in the realm of the media and popular culture. Secondly, within the first of the above-mentioned categories, I draw a distinction between two separate sub-clusters of work often treated as similar in other accounts. In Chapter Three, I focus on the idea of an expanding 'information sector' (which draws attention to the changing economic and social roles of specific clusters of information or knowledge activities) and I also address the relatively recent origins of academic research fields or studies defined by the term 'information'. In Chapter Four, I examine the quite separate claim that we are moving into a distinctively new kind of 'information society' or 'information economy'. Finally, Chapter Five focuses on cultural and symbolic 'information' and communication matters more directly related to the sphere of consumption.

In Chapters Three and Four, I explore how, in many important respects, the emergence of distinct bodies of information-centred research and writing is very much a product of the late twentieth century. The growth of explicit information-centred analyses has been a feature of many new fields of technical inquiry as well as in more established social, economic and cultural fields of study. The further growth of such information-centred analyses has continued into the 1990s, not least because of the shifts in public discourses and policy debates, especially the notion that we are on the brink of some distinctive new 'information society' or global 'information age'. I will explore how this notion was first advanced in academic circles in the 1970s where it was largely greeted with strongly critical responses. Yet, it has become a core framing theme in high-profile policy initiatives launched by national governments and supra-national organisations such as the Group of Seven, the OECD and European Commission (e.g. CEC, 1994b, 1996a, 1996b; OECD, 1997; G7, 1995; Gore, 1994a; USA, 1999). Besides, most management 'gurus' and text books stress the importance of information resources, security and competencies as the cornerstone of commercial success in the contemporary economy (Negroponte, 1995; Kelly, 1998). Indeed many contributions to the literature on postmodernism have been strongly influenced, if not always explicitly, by the assumption that changes in the role and organisation of information is the key defining feature of change in contemporary social and cultural processes.

Here I also argue that, when viewed via the conceptual lens of structural shifts in the division of labour, the underlying phenomena and concerns of many information-centred analyses are often far from new. Indeed I provide a particular archaeology of the body of knowledge on 'information matters' which points to many fundamental continuities as well as changes in socio-economic processes. Although information society theory clearly appears to link up with certain contemporary concerns or 'the tempers of our times', the present author judges it to be fundamentally flawed as a way of understanding the sources, direction and implications of social and economic change. The information society/age models are found to be fatally flawed as they offer little by way of aiding grounded or material analyses of the contemporary. In summary terms, they are judged to be based on excessively abstract and misleading analyses of the autonomy, characteristics and role of information work, services and products in contemporary society. They are marked by idealised accounts of the inherent or intrinsic characteristics of information, and of the nature/origins of the promised new information-based economy of 'abundance'. They fail to recognise the manner and extent to which information work, products and services have become more and more 'thing-like' over time and subject to the similar types of instrumental rationality and commodification processes as apply to material goods production. In contrast, a more nuanced version of the information sector concept is found to be useful for mapping certain aspects of economic and employment change.

Chapter Five winds up the selective review by turning to analyses more specifically concerned with the changing role and features of information within the consumption sphere and the cultural realm. Many information society theories focus on producer and instrumental information of primary relevance to the economy, the workplace and organisational settings. Thus they neglect specific issues to do with information structures and activities more directly related to citizens and consumers in the realms of consumption or 'everyday life', including the media of public communication and related information 'content' services. In Chapter Five, I turn first to recent theorists who focus on aspects of information within the realms of consumption and culture. These provide an alternative, and in many ways complementary, set of perspectives on the changing role of information and/or new ICTs. In the first section I will focus on the writings of influential postmodernist theorists such as Jean Baudrillard and Fredric Jameson. These emphasise the expanding role of information flows and communication systems in the spheres of consumption and culture and they also advance distinctive theories concerning an associated radical shift in the social and cultural order of capitalist industrialism. Here I also examine the writings of another postmodern theorist, Jean-François Lyotard, which have closer resonances with the concerns of information society theorists such as Daniel Bell. Following the discussion of these postmodernist writers, I will move on to consider other streams of relevant work based in critical communication, social and cultural studies. These provide additional or complementary perspectives on the changing role of the media and other information activities. They also advance important conceptual and other challenges to many of the assumptions underpinning information society theories and the more recent rise of related policy initiatives. I borrow and adopt some key concepts from this literature in the analysis of recent developments in the media and public communications sector undertaken in Chapters Nine and Ten.

Chapter Six moves beyond the stage of critical review to outline a more adequate theoretical model which transcends some of the flaws and limitations identified in the influential accounts reviewed earlier. This exercise in theory construction commences from a particular long-wave approach and seeks to present a more realist, historically and empirically grounded account of the significance and specificity of new ICT as a major new technology system and its strategic implications for the analysis of the key trends and issues of concern in the remainder of this book. The proposed model takes explicit account of the development and implications of new ICT. It does so on the basis of a historically rooted 'long-wave' approach to major new technology systems and their interlinkages with organisational, institutional and social factors shaping long-run restructuring processes. Drawing on the historical evidence concerning the role of social and political movements in reshaping the long-wave transitions in the past, I will introduce the concept of a 'socio-technical paradigm' to take account of these processes. This concept compensates for some weaknesses identified in the existing neo-Schumpeterian accounts.

The adopted 'long-wave' approach locates new ICT as a major technology system in the context of a specific historical conjuncture or stage of capitalist industrialism. The latter is marked by the maturing or exhaustion of the Fordist/Keynesian mode of regulation and its associated socio-technical regime of accumulation which had sustained the long post-war boom in the advanced industrial economies. In essence, the period since the late 1970s has been stamped by an intensified process of crisis and restructuring, representing a long-wave 'downswing' phase marked by more than new technological developments. It has also featured relatively low productivity growth, the return of mass unemployment and low rates of capital profitability compared to the preceding post-war boom or 'upswing' era. The downswing is a (relatively long) period involving complex processes of search and struggle to establish a new cluster of related technical, political-economic and social conditions which can support a sustained virtuous cycle of accumulation and growth. In this long-wave perspective, new ICT is thus defined as a major new technology system, one that is rare but *not* unique or unprecedented in the history of capitalist industrialism. In the present historical context, new ICT can also be located as a key component in the system-wide struggles to establish a new techno-economic or socio-technical paradigm.

The dialectical long-wave model advanced in Chapter Six is applied and further elaborated in later chapters to interrogate and redress certain flaws in many influential analyses of new ICT in more recent times. First, most of the technology-centred analyses advanced by contemporary influential 'gurus' are stamped by a fatally flawed understanding of the historical specificity, significance and socio-technical characteristics of new ICT. They display a blissful ignorance or neglect of the historical dynamics of industrial, social, and institutional change processes linked to major or radical new technological systems in the past. As a result, they misrepresent or misinterpret the concrete challenges posed by new ICT today for a variety of economic, social and political actors, including the potential role of the state in shaping social development. Second, as a corollary (to the above), most of the influential technology-centred analyses are also flawed by a linear view of technological innovation processes. This is manifest in tendencies to greatly exaggerate or otherwise misrepresent the pace and patterns of particular technological innovation processes and of the patterns of economic and social change most directly linked to them. It is also manifest in very partial understandings of the interactions and trade-offs between

different strands of technical innovation or different generations of functionally similar systems – for example, the naïve and simplistic assumptions
that the newer technical systems will rapidly or predominantly replace the
more mature or established ones (e.g. Negroponte, 1995).

Third, this analysis points to the irony that the most excited descriptions
of the shiny new technologies are almost universally accompanied by fundamentally conservative and strikingly old-fashioned sets of policy
prescriptions and political values. On the one hand, we encounter digital
dreamware which, relying on the presumed power of purely technological
logics, delivers selective streams of images pointing to a radically new
utopian order. The essential story is that new technology and networks will
eliminate all kinds of social, gender or ethnic inequalities, provided everyone
buys or has access to computers and digital networks such as the Internet. If
social inequalities are explicitly recognised and addressed, they are defined in
terms of access to technology or information in isolation from any connection to the broader social relations of the capitalist industrial system.
According to the more extreme transformative theorists, such social inequalities are being eliminated from the political agenda by the progressive march
and sheer power of the new technological logics. Even where we find expres-
sions of anxiety concerning 'digital divides' or 'the information poor', the
problem and the solution are largely defined in terms of access to technologies and networks. In neither case do we find explicit recognition of the
growing polarisation of wealth and income which has been such a marked
feature throughout the industrialised world over the past two decades. On
the other hand, these presumed technological logics are frequently intricately laced (explicitly or implicitly) with strong prescriptions to embrace the
'invisible hand' of the market or the benign god of competition, the extended
individualisation and fragmentation of civil society or any collective forms of
social identity. The social and the political realms – and indeed communication processes – are eliminated in favour of the isolated individual or family
unit. Behind the 'born-again' rhetorics about the end of ideologies, the
absence of social identities and values in the contemporary world, or prescriptions to place our trust in the logics of technology (Toffler, 1983; Kelly,
1998) lies the full force of a very specific and terribly old-fashioned ideology
of market anarchism. Whilst such ideologies may well be compatible with
the interests of dominant corporate or oligopolistic actors, they are taken
here to provide poor guides to a better understanding of the stakes and
strategies of concern to the wider set of economic and social interests. They
also provide poor guides for pro-active policy-making aimed at shaping
such developments in the short and medium term.

This analysis also seeks to counter a fourth feature of the recent surge of
abstract fantasising about futures of (technology or information-based) universal 'abundance'. This concerns a fundamental failure of imagination on
the part of the mainstream political system when it comes to addressing the

actually existing material realities of socio-economic or other inequalities. In essence, they fail to engage (cognitively or imaginatively) with the necessity, possibilities or scope for progressive social movements or political reforms which might begin to deliver a more equitable and human-centred new socio-technical paradigm – or strategy for social and economic development. Fifth, this analysis challenges the view that the expanded production, adoption and diffusion of ICT (technological artefacts and systems) should be elevated and consecrated as the end of socio-economic and cultural development, rather than treated as a mere tool or means to such ends.

The alternative dialectical model advanced here challenges conceptions of the contemporary as the unfolding of a new social order based on technological logics, the changing economic role of information or some other linear long-run developmental tendencies ('progress'). Rather it defines the contemporary downswing as an era that is also marked by significant continuities with earlier epochs of capitalist industrialism. The empirical-level inquiry in later chapters indicates that the dominant drift of socio-economic development over the past two decades has been stamped by many continuities with earlier phases of capitalist development as well as by radical technological innovations, new communication networks and changes in the role of the information sub-sector. This analysis stresses a historical complex of change and continuities which largely fails to engage the gaze of the techno-gurus: intensified socio-economic pressures, extensions of social inequalities, high unemployment and relatively slow growth and other important social, economic and political tensions. In this author's view, this complex of continuities and changes cannot be grasped adequately by technology-centred analyses nor should they be treated as the accidental outcomes of quite separate and autonomous local processes, as the postmodernist temper of our times might suggest. Rather, these are systematically related and intricately linked to the usual 'downswing' developmental dynamics of long-wave movements in capitalist industrialism.

I also identify the information and communication services sectors as 'leading edge' new sites for economic growth and change associated with the diffusion and application of new ICTs. In this case, the analysis advanced in this book augments existing long-wave models by drawing on concepts and ideas derived from alternative research traditions. This is necessary to address the very particular challenges and stakes involved in the extended commodification of information and the reshaping of communications. Here the book aims at a more coherent understanding of the origins, nature and implications of the perceived growth of 'information' work, products and services since the early industrial era and the social and cultural stakes involved. I argue that if we are to understand this important dimension of the contemporary reshaping of the socio-economic order, it is necessary to address/embrace other crucial conditioning factors beyond the purely technological. First, it is important to recognise that the growth of specific kinds of industries and occupations now deemed 'informational' has long histori-cal roots in the ever-deepening *division of labour* which has been such a distinctive characteristic of capitalist industrialism from the outset. Second, the growing economic role of information industries, products and services has been rendered possible by a set of other political, economic and social (rather than purely technical) innovations.

Of key importance in this regard has been the framing and successful implementation of successive layers of enclosure or commodification of information (including the concept and policing of intellectual property rights) over the past two hundred years. In other words, instead of stressing 'the intangible' and elastic nature of information, this approach addresses and stresses the fundamental material processes by which information has become more and more 'thing-like'. It has been stamped by broadly the same industrialisation and commodification processes which characterise the production and distribution of physical goods. The book examines how the likely extended commodification of specific types (especially cultural/symbolic) of information 'content' services poses specific 'extra-economic' challenges which do not apply in the case of manufacturing or other sectors. It examines how such information services involve very par-ticular socio-political and cultural stakes which are largely ignored in the dominant discourses and most influential modes of contemporary analysis.

Chapters Seven through to Ten move on to a more empirical register of inquiry in order to further elaborate this particular theoretical model. They examine the relevant aspects of recent changes and continuities in socio-economic order as well as in the media and communication spheres. These chapters describe the nature and meaning of important recent developments, including specific attention to the implications for the media and cultural industries and the sphere of public communication. At the same time, these more empirical explorations are approached in a reflexive manner which aims to further develop and flesh out the initial theorisation advanced in Chapter Six.

Chapter Seven is focused on 'the *atoms and bits* of informational capital-ism'. It adapts a more nuanced version of the information sector concept to explore some of the strategic contours of the change in economic processes and everyday life at the edge of the millennium. It reports on the main find-ings of some original empirical research addressing relevant aspects of the changing industrial division of labour. This focuses on shifts in the respective roles of both the media/cultural information services and the specialised producer/instrumental information services in the USA over the past two decades. This chapter also addresses the role of paid employment in framing the everyday life of advanced industrial capitalism and explores some of the downsides of the recent trends of change including the return of mass unem-ployment and relatively slow growth compared to the post-war decades. Chapter Eight examines the increasing polarisation of wealth and income and life opportunities and related shifts in consumption processes over the recent history of capitalist industrialism and engages with the economic and political limits of recent 'information society' policy initiatives.

Chapters Nine and Ten turn to recent developments within the media and cultural (information) content sectors and the implications of the extended commodification of information. Chapter Nine explores the changing structures of the established or 'mature' media, describing some of the key recent trends emerging from the confluence of economic, policy and technological pressures. This chapter traces the genesis and rise of the Internet/WWW as a significant new digital communication network. It addresses a certain 'innovation deficit' with respect to the paucity of the much-heralded radical new product innovations in the media sector. It also points out how the mature media have quickly learned to love and embrace (appropriate) new digital media developments. Here, I also examine some key aspects of change in connectivity services such as telecommunications and Internet-based developments and the interrelations between them.

Chapter Ten addresses the changing role of the public communication sphere and the implications of the processes of extended commodification of media-based 'content' services. It addresses the non-technical factors and forces which are shaping the increasing concentration and globalisation of the media-based content industries and emphasises the special ('extra-economic') social and cultural roles and characteristics of such services. These considerations are neglected by the discourses and prescriptions underpinning recent industry and policy initiatives, pointing to specific implications for the future orientation and forms of the media and sphere of public communication. This chapter also considers some potential barriers to the pervasive visions of a major expansion in the overall economic role of the media 'content' sectors especially with respect to consumption norms and prevailing money-budget and time-budget norms.

The final chapter draws together some of the key implications of this inquiry for a more coherent understanding of the contemporary social and communication order as we enter the new millennium. This can be best characterised as the outcome of the complex interplay of three sets of movements or forces: changes, continuities, and (long-wave) cyclical factors. It reiterates the point that the turning to a long-wave upswing requires more than technological innovation and re-asserts the need to restore the social back into the analysis and process of social development. After more than two decades, the prevailing neo-liberal state regime has failed to redress the consequences of the downswing which have impacted so negatively on the material and other aspects of life facing large sections of the population. The chapter emphasises the relatively open and indeterminate process of long-run restructuring and change, pointing to the important role of social innovations and political movements in shaping new socio-technical paradigms in the past. It also seeks to explore some of the alternative prospects and scenarios for the construction of a more egalitarian and inclusive path of social and cultural development today – one which might ensure greater material security and equality for the majority in keeping with the cumulative productive capacities of industrial capitalism and its old and new technological infrastructures.

OTHER ELEMENTS OF THE APPROACH

Whilst examining and drawing on different theories of the nature and meaning of current transformations (originating in a number of different disciplines), the approach informing this book stresses the partially or relatively open nature of current transformations, defined as complex processes. For one thing, this points to the continuing role of empirical research when addressing questions about the continuities and discontinuities in the socio-economic or cultural trends. In rejecting a determinist or closed model, the book seeks to map the relevant trends of change in selected domains related to new ICT and information sector matters. In addition, this approach re-asserts the role of social action, seeking to provide a space which accommodates the (potential) scope for social movements, collective initiatives and public interventions in reshaping future social and communication developments. Hence it attempts to address the scope for alternative patterns of development, centred around the socio-economic and political shaping (or selection) of alternative new ICT-based socio-economic orders and communication systems. The approach here is concerned to explore the nature or possibilities of alternative strategies for the construction of more democratic and egalitarian new social and communication orders.

In the particular and restricted sense outlined above, the book aims to be *interdisciplinary* and *comprehensive* in its scope and approach. It aims at a coherent understanding of the key features of change and continuity in socio-economic, cultural and political affairs. It draws together and critically reviews key insights drawn from a complementary set of the relevant academic literature and policy research and relates these to empirical evidence when appropriate. It aims at a theoretically informed and an empirically rooted understanding of a broad range of overlapping and 'converging' issues relating to the implications of new ICT and the growth of the so-called 'information society'.

To these ends, I will address and seek to synthesise some of the key concepts and findings drawn from a spectrum of the recent academic, industrial and policy research literature. To an increasing extent, the boundaries between these domains of 'knowledge', research and debate are blurred and open. Thus, I will draw upon a wide variety of sources and research resources which fall outside the conventional parameters of academic sources. For sure, the relevant research resources here include work based in disciplines such as institutional economics, sociology, human geography, media and communications studies, information science and management studies fields, as well as cultural studies. But it should be noted that the more influential discourses, concepts, research (especially empirically-informed research) relating to the book's agenda originate outside of the academic realm. Much of it, for example, is rooted in industrial research networks and consultancy reports sponsored by government, corporations, trade associations and other private sector organisations based within the USA, EU and Japan. Some of it originates with semi-public international organisations such as the OECD, WTO, ITU and UN related bodies. Thus this book also engages in a dialogue with highly relevant non-academic discourses, including published and unpublished policy studies, Web sites and other 'grey literature' generated by such national and international government organisations, consultancy and policy research institutes.

Part 2

COMPETING THEORIES OF THE CONTEMPORARY

CHAPTER TWO

THIRD-WAVE VISIONS: TECHNOLOGY AS SOCIAL TRANSFORMER

'These changes are cumulative . . . they add up to a giant transformation in the way we live, work, play and think . . . what is happening now is nothing less than a global revolution, a quantum jump in history . . . It is the attempt to block such changes, not the changes themselves, that raises the level of risk. It is the blind attempt to defend obsolescence that creates the danger of bloodshed.'

(Toffler, 1980: 26, 452)

'It is ironic that computing, which is often portrayed as an instrument of knowledge, is primarily the subject of popular and professional literatures that are heavily weighted towards the less reliable utopian genres.'

(Kling, 1994: 168–9)

NEW ICT AND SOCIAL TRANSFORMATION

I want to start by examining one highly influential technology-centred stream of recent analyses which I define as *third-wave* models or transformative theories. These popular accounts are marked by a heavy reliance on the assumption that technological innovation is a powerful, autonomous force for change and their vision of the social implications of new ICT is heavily tinged with a utopian hue. In essence, they treat new ICT (and, in some cases, biotechnology) as the key 'driver' of a fundamental transformation of the core economic structures and social relations which have characterised the capitalist industrial societies for the past two centuries. They suggest that new

ICT is forging a radically new (third-wave) civilisation or mode of production, one which transcends or transforms the key social and economic relations of industrial capitalism. Besides a primary emphasis on the ICT (technology) factor, some of these analyses also refer to the transformative impacts of the expanding economic role of information and/or of the emergence and diffusion of digital communication networks (Kelly, 1998).

Before going on to explore these influential theories of the apparent revolutionary implications of new ICT it may be helpful to take a brief detour to explore the definitions and genealogy of key terms and the representation of new ICT as 'the most powerful technological juggernaut that ever rolled'. It is conventional and tempting to start this kind of story with a description of the relevant technological innovations. But here we should be mindful that the definitions attached to such key terms can be best understood in relation to the historical contexts which shaped their broader social meanings and marked the origins of the increasing emphasis on such technology matters since the late 1970s. In my view, there are a number of relevant contextual moments which stamped the original use, definitions and meanings attached to the term IT/ICT and this history continues to influence its broader role and meaning in industrial and employment policy circles and related public discourses today.

Firstly, this brief archaeology locates the initial use and popularisation of new information technology (IT/ICT) in Britain in the early 1980s. But in this case, however, it would be highly misleading to view this as some sort of logical or linear response to the stream of technological innovations which first emerged in this period. For there is one other important, if easily overlooked, contextual aspect which is quite distinct from the purely technical stream of innovation developments. Here I am pointing to the major crisis which was such a dominant feature of the overall social and political-economic climate in Britain in the early 1980s. This was most manifest in the huge surge in unemployment to levels which had not been experienced since the 1920s and 1930s and a related very low level of popular support for the government. Compared to the long boom of the 1950s and 1960s, the rates of economic growth and employment levels had begun to decline from the early 1970s in Britain (as happened in most other European countries from the mid-1970s). But the radical neo-liberal policies pursued by the Thatcher government in the early 1980s meant that this more generalised crisis was particularly pronounced in the case of Britain. This occurred despite the fact that the government party's main electoral slogan in 1979 ('Labour isn't working') promised to reduce the levels of unemployment.

The key point is that the emergence and rhetoric of this early British state-led project centred on new IT/ICT, especially its emphasis on the job creation potential of these new technologies, were not shaped simply by the stream of technological developments. These must also be understood as part of a very specific approach to the political management of a particularly acute social and economic crisis. Such rhetorics centred around the beneficial employment implications of new IT/ICT and formed an important element in this pioneering neo-liberal political project. The point applies notwithstanding the fact that the empirical evidence directly countered the optimistic claims made about the expansion of employment opportunities in the ICT-based 'high-tech' sectors of the British economy at that time (Preston, 1984; 1987).

Second, it is also worth noting that the early 1980s period also marked the beginning of the surge of popular media interest in technology matters already noted in Chapter One. The trend was manifest in the growing numbers of books and magazines concerned with (and, usually, enthusing over) the innovative characteristics, uses and beneficial impacts or effects of then relatively new ICTs such as personal computers, video recorders and cameras, etc. Such trends may be viewed as part of a wider cultural shift since the 1980s whereby the English language market for popular science writing was 'expanding as fast as the universe itself' (Tyler, 1997). This new phenomenon occurred despite many attacks on technology and rationalism, especially within the academic fields of social and cultural studies at this time. Thus the review of the relevant literature which follows below embraces some influential writers, sources and ideas which are frequently sidelined if not ignored in many academic treatments of ICT matters.[1] But first of all it is necessary to take a brief look at the role and meanings of the key terms.

FROM 'NEW IT' TO 'NEW ICT': ARCHAEOLOGY AND DEFINITIONS OF KEY TERMS

As noted above, the term 'information technology' (IT) first emerged within academic and more public policy debates in the early 1980s, a time when the first generation of personal computers were produced and marketed for use in the workplace as well as in the home.[2] Amongst other things, this was a time when the 1970s' generation of 'new media', such as cable and satellite-based television, video cassettes and recorders, teletext (and to a lesser extent videotex) were being more widely promoted and used in the household setting in the advanced industrial world. At this time there was a lot of emphasis on 'the mighty microchip' or 'the chip revolution' with many enthusiastic claims about the powers and socio-economic impacts of advances in microelectronics. These were strongly centred around the capability of the semiconductor industry to produce ever more powerful microprocessors at a rapidly decreasing cost per electronic function and in ever smaller size units, including their applications in new products such as micro and personal computers. Basically the term IT was coined as an umbrella term to refer to this cluster of interrelated computing, telecommunications, information and communication technologies linked to the advances in microelectronics.

It was also in the early 1980s, as a postgraduate research student in Britain, that I first came across the term 'information technology'. Indeed it was difficult to avoid the term at that time because the Thatcher government had officially designated 1982 as 'Information Technology' (or 'IT') year. It appointed a special Ministry for Information Technology and launched a wide series of public relations and other initiatives to promote 'public aware-ness' concerning a selective menu of the impacts and effects of IT. In 1982–3, the British Ministry for IT sponsored a series of major publicity campaigns all focused on the novel features of new IT, its potential to be used in many social as well as economic contexts, its capacity to create many new, clean, interesting and indeed pleasant forms of work. This major publicity cam-paign explicitly sought to promote 'awareness' and positive attitudes towards new IT within industrial workplaces, educational institutions at all levels and in wider public and media contexts. It explicitly promoted much media discussion of the new technologies and sought to stimulate a greater emphasis on information technology matters in the teaching and research agenda across the educational system[3] as well as in wider public debates.

This British government project involved the production of many glossy, if still print-based, booklets excitedly extolling the implications and wonders of new IT in the years 1982–4. According to one of these glossy booklets, new IT was defined as 'a startling blend of computers that can store huge quanti-ties of information and process it in split seconds, modern telecommunications that can transmit it almost instantaneously, and microelectronics that make it all neat, manageable and incredibly cheap'. It was stressed that 'the advances in telecommunications allied to computer technology are really going to bring the IT revolution to us all' and that 'IT is bound to become part and parcel of virtually every facet of living'. This early 1980s British government IT cam-paign placed great stress on how new IT had enormous potential to create new forms of employment and would have major impacts on the quality as well as quantity of jobs. It was stressed that new IT was not only leading to new high-tech jobs in new industries. In addition, 'IT is also transforming old industries, taking away boredom, removing danger, making factories cleaner, more pleasant places to work'. Besides, this powerful new technology would also improve efficiency and productivity, 'so enabling Britain to compete and create new wealth and higher standards of living' (UK, 1982a, 1982b: cited in Preston, 1984: 13–15).

These and other early 1980s discourses were strongly focused around the term *IT*. But from the mid-1980s, the term *ICT* (for information and communication technology) began to be used more widely to refer to broadly the same cluster of technical developments in the fields of comput-ing, telecommunications and digital electronics. It is evident that the latter term places a greater explicit focus on the *communicational* aspects of these new technologies and this has influenced its increasing usage compared to the older term over the past decade. Clearly this communicational aspect has been much more prominent in more recent years given the relatively high profile of technical developments such as the Internet and World Wide Web. However, such considerations were not entirely absent from the early 1980s literature, even if the main emphasis was on stand-alone rather than net-worked technologies (Preston, 1984; Hall and Preston, 1988).

Many of the core conceptions and claims found in this early 1980s 'wave' of enthusiastic discourses are strikingly similar to those that we find circu-lating today. One is the idea that new microelectronics and computer-based or digital technical innovations are *pervasive* in terms of their applications potential. This term is invoked to stress that this cluster of interrelated tech-nical advances could and would be incorporated in almost every kind of product and service and hence bring about a fundamental change in most if not all forms of economic, social and cultural activity. Another is the idea of *convergence*, which stresses that the new digital technologies and their appli-cations provide radically new opportunities for the handling, storing, distribution and processing of all forms of information (visual, audio, data, etc.) within 'a common digital mode'. Combined with the pervasive poten-tial of new digital techniques, these convergence tendencies at the technical level were deemed to imply an erosion of the inherited distinctions and industrial, regulatory and other boundaries between different information and communication activities such as broadcasting, telecommunications and computing (e.g. Pool, 1983). Another is the idea that this new cluster or system of interrelated innovations, precisely because they comprise *infor-mation and communication* technologies, will have major implications for change in the media and systems of communication. One other consistent strand over the past two decades is the explicit and implicit use of new IT/ICT as rallying points for the mobilisation of national/regional industrial and innovation projects directed at enhancing international competitiveness in the face of the perceived threats originating from similar initiatives else-where (Preston, 1984).

TRANSFORMATIVE VISIONS: THE 'THIRD-WAVE' THEORISTS

Alvin Toffler was one of the most widely read and influential writers on tech-nology as a driving force for socio-economic and political change in the 1970s and 1980s. His books, such as *Future Shock* (1970), *The Third Wave* (1980), and *Previews and Premises* (1983), have been international best-sellers, some reaching sales of several millions of copies, and they have been translated into many languages. Although dismissed and ignored by many academic social science researchers, Toffler has proved to be a major pioneer and populariser of a specific vision of the meaning and implications of new ICTs: the third-wave model. Certainly, many of his basic ideas have been echoed in popular accounts produced by other authors into the late 1990s (Negroponte, 1995; Kelly, 1998). Given the broad sweep of his concerns, his approach and his enthusiastic attempts at 'the big picture', Toffler's writings can be regarded as useful syntheses of the most influential third-wave ideas and popular claims concerning the revolutionary implications of new technologies. It should be noted also that false modesty is not one of Toffler's failings, as he and Heidi Toffler (his frequent co-author in more recent works), frequently proclaim his key role in identifying many new concepts and trends. They also proclaim their friendships and close associations with prominent figures amongst the industrial and political élites of the USA and other countries (e.g. Toffler, 1983; Toffler and Toffler, 1995a, 1995c; Moore, 1996). His enthusiastic writing style and content also very clearly bear the stamp of his time as associate editor of the élite business magazine *Fortune* as well as his consultancy work and other associations with large high-tech corporations such as AT&T.

The third-wave theorists emphasise that the new technologies are bringing about a number of fundamental changes in the overall socio-economic and political fabric of the advanced capitalist economies. The main theme is that the world industrial system is undergoing a process of restructuring or 'general crisis' and this is introducing a fundamentally new economic and social system. Such ideas were shared by a number of other early theorists, but Toffler was certainly the most influential exponent of such third-wave analyses of the nature and significance of new ICT in the 1980s (1980, 1983). This theme also pervades his subsequent work including his more recent collaborative writings with Heidi Toffler such as *Creating A New Civilization* (1995a). Similar ideas, concerning the revolutionary impact of new ICT on socio-economic and political developments, have been echoed in the work of many subsequent popular writings in the 1990s (e.g. Negroponte, 1995; Gates, 1995) as well as in some recent information society policy documents. Hence it is pertinent to indicate some of the key components of the most influential versions of the third-wave model at this point.

Third-wave theorists may be initially distinguished by a very particular and influential view of the historical significance and meaning of new ICTs. They claim that the implications of these technologies are of the same order and significance as the agricultural revolution of ten thousand years ago and the industrial revolution that first developed in Britain in the late eighteenth century. Each of these three major technological waves brought massive transformations to existing forms of social, economic, political and family life. In Toffler's account, 'a new critical transition' is upon us, as contemporary trends in technology, economics, politics, family life, energy use and other spheres usher in 'a third civilisational rupture' which he defines as a transition to third-wave social, economic and political forms (see Table 2.1).

TABLE 2.1   Summary of typical 'third-wave' model and periodisation

	The first wave	The second wave	The third wave
Timing	c8,000BC–1650/1750	1650/1750–1955/1965	1955/1965→
Period type	Agricultural civilisation	Industrial civilisation	The 'third-wave' era
Key features and progress of each wave or period	The rise of agriculture is taken as 'the first turning point' in human social development. The agricultural revolution diffused slowly across the planet spreading villages, settlements, cultivated land, and 'a new way of life'. Today, 'the first wave' has virtually subsided as only a few tiny tribal populations remain to be reached by agriculture. For Toffler, 'the force of this great first wave has basically been spent'.	From the end of the seventeenth century, the industrial revolution broke over Europe and unleashed 'the second great wave' of planetary change. The new process of industrialisation diffused much more rapidly across nations and continents. The 'second wave', 'having revolutionised life' in many parts of the globe in a few short centuries, continues to diffuse. According to Toffler, the momentum of industrialisation is still felt, 'it has not entirely spent its force'.	This period begins when 'the tide of industrialisation peaked' in the decades after World War Two. The 'third wave' begins when 'white-collar and service workers outnumber blue-collar workers for the first time'. It is also marked by the widespread introduction of computers, commercial jet travel, the birth control pill, and many other 'high-impact innovations'. The 'third wave' has begun to surge across the earth, 'transforming everything it touches'; it is likely to 'complete itself in a few decades'.

Note: The 'third-wave' theorists such as Toffler suggest that 'this latest historical turning point arrived in the United States during the decade beginning about 1955' and since then it has arrived, at slightly different rates, in most other industrial nations. Toffler also argues that today, all the high-technology nations 'are reeling from the collision between the third wave' and 'the obsolete, encrusted economies and institutions of the second' (1980: 28).

Source: Present author's schematic summary of the 'third-wave' model, based largely on the work of Alvin Toffler (1980: 24–30).

Third-wave theorists insist that we are fundamentally moving from a mass production, mass consumption economy to an essentially 'de-massified' economy. In Toffler's view, the traditional mass manufacturing factories pour out a stream of identical objects by the million. But in the emerging third-wave era, mass production is replaced by its opposite: demassified production – short runs, even customised, one by one production, based on computers and numerical controls. For Toffler, as indeed for Negroponte (1995) and many other 1990s theorists, the new technologies make diversity as cheap as uniformity. Toffler argues that for most industries, it is a question of 'customise or die' and that this is exactly the opposite of what was required in the second-wave' or industrial economy (Toffler, 1983:14).

With the growth of the Internet, the notions of de-massification, radical segmentation and individualisation have been applied to information and media services with particular force by many writers in the late 1990s (Negroponte, 1995; Kelly, 1998). Although the precise technological plat-forms may have changed, these 1990s visions largely echo Toffler's earlier claims about greater decentralisation and a rising level of social and indi-vidual diversity in the third-wave society. Thus these different generations of third-wave analysis both promise the end of mass media and centralised data banks in favour of a diversity of *ad hoc* networks, and de-massified, specialised small-audience, small-circulation media (Gates, 1995; Negroponte, 1995).

A feature of third-wave analysis is that the economic and industrial changes are global in scale – they affect most if not all countries and that national economies as such may be outmoded. Nation states are said to take less and less independent action, they are losing much of their previous sovereignty and national boundaries or identities are becoming less salient. Of course debate over the extent and meaning of globalisation has now become an almost pervasive theme in social and economic analyses. But in the 1990s, many third-wave theorists are amongst the vanguard of advocates for the 'strong globalisation' thesis, not least because of their determinist analyses of the expansion of the Internet and other new ICT-based net-works. These networks are viewed as 'boundless frontiers' which are intrinsically global in scope and in terms of most, if not all, of their potential applications. As such they are deemed to be major drivers of further inten-sified globalisation of economic, social and cultural relations and are bringing about 'the death of distance' (Cairncross, 1997; Negroponte, 1995; Kelly, 1998).

For Toffler (1980: 335), the presumed rapid decline in the role of the nation state and national boundaries or identities is not simply due to the growing role of transnational corporation but also arises from what he sees as a parallel shift from national to smaller-than-national production. He suggests that regional economies are growing more and more divergent. At the same time, it should be noted that Toffler and other third-wave theorists do not envisage or advocate the end of transnational corporations (TNC). Toffler suggests that 'the size, importance and political power of this new player in the global game has skyrocketed since the mid-1950s', the starting point of the third wave according to his own schema (1980: 330). But the TNCs are viewed as 'neither all good nor all bad' and he points to the

emergence of other new forces on the global stage. These include transnational trade union groupings and political, religious, cultural and ethnic
movements as well as a large number of other non-governmental organisations that flow across and establish links which transcend national lines
(Toffler 1980: 332).

These third-wave theorists are generally pro-active supporters of the 'revolutionary' social and economic trends they presume to describe. For
example, Toffler positions himself as an ardent advocate and promoter of
what he views as the inherent virtues of the new ICTs (alongside new
biotechnologies and energy technologies) and the expanding role of the ICT
and related information industries. He furthermore poses these as fundamentally distinct from, and opposed to, the activities, processes and cultures
of what he defines as the older 'rust-bowl' or 'second-wave' industries and
technologies. In this account, the intensified restructuring process or crisis
isn't capitalist or socialist – 'it is *industrial*' and/or technological (e.g. Toffler,
1983: 13, 83–103).

For 'third-wave theorists' one consequence of the perceived ICT-driven
socio-economic revolution is that the economic and social theories or concepts inherited from the capitalist industrial era are no longer valid. They
suggest that an entirely new or radically modified analytical framework is
required to make sense of it all (Kelly, 1998). For some third-wave accounts
new ICT and interactive networks are bringing about a significant decentralisation of decision-making and power, levelling or eroding established
hierarchies of economic, social and symbolic power (Toffler, 1980, 1983;
Kelly, 1998). According to one variant – authored by the chief executive of
a major corporation which has a commanding monopoly position in important segments of the global software sector – new ICT is leveraging in a new
era of 'friction-free' capitalism (Gates, 1995).

A further important change according to Toffler and later transformative
theorists (Kelly, 1998) is the demise or erosion of traditional social identities,
cleavages and conflicts – such as those of class, gender and race – which
characterised the old 'rust-bowl' era of industrial capitalism. Toffler explicitly insists that the fundamental social cleavages and political conflicts of
today are centred around what he defines as the divide between 'the second
and third-wave' forces in society. The essence of this narrative is that the
good guys and gals are those who are seeking to make a technology-based
revolution happen and the baddies are the enemies out there who do not
want this revolution to happen (Toffler, 1983; Toffler and Toffler, 1995a, c).
Toffler claims that the key focus of social conflict and political struggle has
shifted fundamentally away from 'left' versus 'right', socialist versus conservative, worker versus capitalist. He argues that the forms of interest
formation and social movements which emerged since the industrial revolution, such as those based around class, ethnic or gender inequalities, are now
redundant and anachronistic. He declares that the fundamental political

cleavages and conflict of interests have shifted to what he defines as a struggle between third-wave vested interests versus those of 'the second-wave' industries and their associated cultures (e.g. 1980, 1983, 1995a, 1995c).

In addition, the third-wave literature also claims a number of other social transformations, including increased leisure time. Toffler predicts a large-scale shift towards home-based work in the unfolding third-wave society, a big shift in typical male and female roles (e.g. 1983: 123–37). He also suggests that the emerging new economy involves a significant and growing sector based on what he calls '*prosuming*', whereby people are producing more goods and services, not for sale, or even for barter, but for their own use. He says this is not 'petty commodity production' but production for consumption by the producer and argues that this is an important shift in terms of altering the relationship of the consumer to the production process. In a rather weakly argued passage, Toffler claims that the rise of the prosumer comes at a time when 'the entire historical process of market-building' by the expansion of the capitalist economy has reached its limits (Toffler, 1980: 294–5). He is even less convincing in proposing that his observed shift towards increased prosuming marks nothing less than an erosion or termination of the processes of marketisation and commodification which have been key features of the era of capitalist industrialism since its infancy.

HEGEMONIC HYPE: TRANSFORMATIVE DISCOURSE IN THE 1990s

As indicated, the third-wave writers advance a number of central claims concerning the reshaping of the social, economic and communication orders which are deemed to be driven by new ICTs and other technologies, alongside the expanding role of information activities. In summary terms, the major claims include: (a) the emergence of fundamentally new forms of industrial production systems and employment; (b) a revolutionary new set of egalitarian social and political relationships, deemed to be essentially (or implicitly) post-capitalist in character; (c) a more decentralised and customised system of consumption, including the end of mass media systems and the emergence of more decentralised, individualised, interactive new communication networks and information 'content' media.

The overwhelming empirical evidence over the past two decades does not provide much support for most of the dominant trends of change promised by Toffler and other early proponents of a third-wave analysis. After two decades, there is little sign of a fundamental transcendence of the capitalist industrial order along the lines that they suggest (as I will indicate in greater detail in Part Three). But, such empirical challenges have not served as obstacles to the flow and gushing enthusiasm of such techno-utopianism in the

1990s (Negroponte, 1995; Kelly, 1998; Dyson, 1998). Indeed, as noted earlier, it is precisely this kind of analysis of the implications of new ICT that is most influential within scientific and technological circles. Besides, the information society discourses of the 1990s are also strongly laced with elements of the third-wave model.

It is also evident that the key themes of this 'third-wave' perspective are still central to influential and popular conceptions of the implications of new ICTs. At the end of the 1990s cosy images of an automatic transition to a post-conflict and more egalitarian social order of 'friction-free capitalism' pervaded many popular works (Gates, 1995; Kelly, 1998). Some of the third-wave model's set of values and ideas were also echoed in high-profile public sector 'information society' initiatives in the 1990s as will be indicated later. Indeed compared to the 1980s, the idea that the new ICTs were bringing about a social and political-economic 'revolution' – defined as inherently more egalitarian and decentralised – was more rather than less pervasive in the late 1990s. Within this genre, the story remained essentially the same although the particular fashionable technological artefacts under scrutiny could change their colours and shape.

The core common argument of third-wave writings in the 1980s and 1990s suggested that the economic or industrial system was undergoing a fundamental shift from the production and distribution of material goods towards a high-tech economy based on immaterial or information products and services. The sectors concerned with the production, distribution and consumption of 'bits and bytes' replaced or significantly diminished those involved in the production of material goods and products as the new technologies simultaneously transformed all the essential socio-economic and political relations associated with capitalist industrialism. In the 1990s, Toffler's vision of a third-wave economy comprising high-tech, software and service industries was not only advanced by himself and others with whom he had close associations (e.g. Dyson et al., 1996). It was also strongly echoed in the 'post-information age' vision of a borderless, globalised but decentralised world of bits (rather than of atoms) advanced by others. These included Cairncross (1997), Kelly (1998) and Negroponte (1995), an academic entrepreneur who appeared to be replacing Toffler as the technocratic elite's chief guru in the late 1990s (Shillingford, 1996).

The rapid disappearance or diminution of the material economy is the implicit if not explicit message of many recent works stressing the significance of the new and nebulous forms of 'cyberspace' and 'cyber-community' based on advanced ICT-based networks. Emphasising the economy or city of bits and bytes rather than of material production, many recent writings propose visions of a fundamental erosion of the material production, the decline of the specificity of place, space and geography and a significantly reduced reliance on 'bodily presence and material exchange' (Mitchell, 1995: 170). In addition, important elements of this kind of perspective also underpinned many national and global information superhighway or 'information society' initiatives advanced by governments in the latter half of the 1990s, as will be indicated later.

Similarly, in the late 1990s there were many new versions of the third-wave model's claims that new ICTs are leading to a much more egalitarian social, political and communication order. For example, it was often stressed that new ICTs have the power 'to change political institutions and mechanisms fundamentally' or 'to support real-time (or at least very fast) democracy on a large scale' (Mitchell, 1995:154). This was in keeping with the claim that new ICT is 'enlarging the scope of individual freedom and sweeping away many traditional underpinnings of centralised authority and control' (de Jonquieres, 1985). In 1996, for example, the editors of *Wired* magazine set out what they defined as a 'manifesto' for the digital age. They argued that the social and political revolution being wrought by new ICT is not only 'transforming society' but that it 'offers a new democracy dominated neither by the vested interests of political parties nor the mob's baying howl'; indeed they furthermore asserted that it 'can narrow the gap that separates capital from labour, it can deepen the bonds between people and the planet' (1996: 42–3). In somewhat similar vein, Esther Dyson and her three co-authors, including Alvin Toffler, proposed a 'Magna Carta for the Knowledge Age'. Amongst other things, this argued that new ICTs are 'turning the economics of mass production inside out' and driving the financial costs of diversity down towards zero and thus demassifying the institutions and culture of industrial society. They argued that this means the death of 'the central paradigm of modern life', the bureaucratic organisation, defined largely in terms of government or public sector bureaucracies (Dyson et al., 1996: 297).

Some of these popular themes in recent third-wave writings on the implications of new ICTs for socio-economic and political change will be the focus of more detailed empirical inquiry in later chapters. But at this stage it is necessary to take an initial critical review of some of the key tenets and components of Toffler's model and related third-wave analyses. This includes an evaluation of some of their basic assumptions or assertions concerning the meaning and implications of new ICTs for socio-economic and political change.

A CRITIQUE OF TRANSFORMATIVE VISIONS

In my view, the third-wave and other transformative models are fatally flawed as a guide to the meaning and implications of new ICTs. They are marked by a number of fundamental theoretical weaknesses and seem strikingly out of line with empirical observations of relevant socio-economic trends over the past two decades.

Firstly, these analyses rest on a fundamentally flawed conceptualisation of the historical significance and specificity of new ICT and thus they exaggerate its meaning and implications for socio-economic change. One key problem is that they fail to consider the role of prior major new technology systems within the history of industrial capitalism (not to mention adequate considerations of the key role of associated social, institutional and organisational innovations). These theorists' rather simplistic three-stage periodisation provides the key platform for their claims concerning a radical shift towards a new political-economic and social order. But this is achieved at the cost of deleting important historical complications which would certainly muddy this optimistic picture of the unfolding new order. A second related criticism is that Toffler and other transformative analysts assume and advance a very reductionist account of the long-term historical trends underpinning the development of an information or knowledge-based economy since the industrial revolution. The various 'long-wave' theories examined later provide a more historically grounded periodisation and a much more convincing starting point for the analysis of the meaning and specificities of new ICT. They are much more firmly grounded in historical and empirical terms compared to third-wave theorists' conception of new ICT as a unique and fundamentally 'revolutionary' technological revolution, as will be indicated more fully later.

Third, there is a distinct temporal ambiguity or inconsistency in many transformative analyses. One key problem here is that it is not always clear whether they are referring to changes that are already deemed to have taken place (i.e. by the late 1990s) or to those which are actually occurring now on the one hand, or whether they are referring to changes that are about to occur in the medium and longer term future on the other hand. For example, Toffler at times seems to suggest that some existing 'high-tech' economies have already become third-wave societies, whilst at other times it is obvious that he is referring to futuristic socio-economic-technical systems very far advanced from anything that exists today.

A fourth point of criticism is that third-wave analyses are often based on a very singular and partial consensual view of the current social and political order. In Toffler's case, certain cleavages are acknowledged to have existed in the past, but it is asserted that the basis of any such conflicts of interest has been fundamentally transformed, if not yet completely eliminated. But others too stress the emergence of a new 'frictionless' form of economy, where significant inequalities have disappeared thanks to the rise of electronic networking, or other specific ICT-based innovations (Gates, 1995; Negroponte, 1995; Kelly, 1998). I doubt that all readers will share Toffler's description of a potential new common internal 'enemy': those who do not wholeheartedly embrace ICT and the cluster of associated imperatives (social, political, ideological), and assumed benefits it brings in its train – as defined by Toffler or the powerful high-tech élites. Such prescriptions point to further analytical (and political) flaws based on rather radical/extremist 'abstractions' from empirical and historical realities. They make for a rather impoverished social theory, and eliminate the past and potential future role of social movements in shaping the trajectories of technological as well as socio-economic history.

The futuristic third-wave theorists, much like their techno-utopian predecessors in the early electrical era, pay scant attention to the most glaringly obvious and pressing trends of social and economic change in the here and now, and neither do they consider how these might affect the presumed or forecast beneficial socio-economic impacts of new ICT. Although Toffler, for example, occasionally mentions that immediate issues must not be ignored (e.g. 1983: 86), he never seems to confront them. Instead, he rather niftily sidesteps these awkward kinds of issues even in his more politically pointed writings. An additional related criticism, explored more fully in Part Three, is that many of the key transformative changes proposed by these third-wave theorists simply do not match up with the empirical evidence on recent socio-economic trends.

A final criticism is that most transformative theorists rely on a fundamentally linear technological determinist approach to social change, one which has long been criticised by other writers concerned with the social studies of technologic matters. For example, notwithstanding Toffler's own explicit rejection of this label, his work since the early 1980s at least has been strongly stamped by the key defining features of technological determinism (discussed later in Chapter Six). The new technologies are seen to possess an autonomous logic, teleology or trajectory of their own which is not only benign but quite divorced from any basis in existing socio-economic or political interests, relations or conflicts. Indeed, as we have seen, Toffler insists and stresses that new ICT represents an autonomous force which eliminates or transcends such relationships and interests. For Kelly and some other recent third-wave writers, new ICT represents the sole factor or force which is bringing about a fundamental change in economic and social structures (1998). Essentially, new ICT is treated as both the means and ends of social development and the just society. Furthermore, if social and political actors do occasionally fall within the gaze of these theorists, they must simply embrace the apparently benign logic and imperatives of the new 'sunrise' technologies (as defined by those in powerful positions) or else risk being branded an enemy of all that is progressive and good (Toffler, 1983; 1995c).[4]

POST-FORDISMS AND THE NEO-SCHUMPETERIAN MODEL

If we are to develop a better strategic starting point for a more robust theory of new ICT and the contemporary it is essential to transcend the types of linear, technology-centred and ahistorical analyses that characterise the transformative models which dominate contemporary discourse. Fortunately, as indicated earlier, there is one body of recent work which is particularly helpful in this regard: the post-Fordist literature. This comprises a large and growing body of writings whose concerns and approach are firmly based in the field of institutional or evolutionary economics. With a focus on fundamental or 'epoch-making' change, this work seeks to specify the key trends, causal mechanisms and tendencies involved in structural change in the general political and economic landscape of contemporary capitalism. It is also marked by a strong historical orientation in its examination of the manner and extent to which recent trends represent a radical break with the past or merely mark an extension or modification of older relations and processes.

In essence this work is centred around the idea that, since the industrial revolution and political upheavals from the late eighteenth century onwards, the history of capitalist industrialism has been marked by a series of transitions and distinct phases of development. It is argued that each of these historical phases of capitalist development is based on a specific set of economic, societal and political characteristics or norms. Most contributors to this literature stress that this kind of periodisation can only be approximate, that there will be significant variations between national, regional and sectoral developments, but most seem to concur that the duration of each phase has been of approximately forty to sixty years (Hall and Preston, 1988; Amin, 1994). They aim to identify the key set of economic, organisational, institutional and political factors shaping the rapid growth of output and productivity in each period and to theorise how these combine to form a distinct *paradigm* or system (or *regime of accumulation* for some writers) which is capable of sustaining economic stability and growth for a particular phase of capitalist industrialism. The dominant or 'leading-edge' industries will be marked and guided by a distinct set of guiding principles in each historical phase of capitalist development. Eventually, however, each particular paradigm or regime will exhaust its potential, reach the limits of its viability and relevance. This will lead to a period of transition and uncertainty (crisis and restructuring) during which there will be a struggle to devise and construct the elements of a new paradigm.

This field of academic work is perhaps best defined as the 'post-Fordist' *debate* (rather than 'theory' or 'school') as once again there are many important differences in emphasis and substance between the different contributors and even the very description 'post-Fordism' is disputed by some contributors. As one well-informed participant put it: 'arguments exist over the nature of the passing age, the origins of its crisis, the bearers of change, and the shape of things to come' (Amin, 1994: 3; see also Elam, 1994). Some of this work is marked by a distinct tone of social criticism, but the post-Fordist concept has also been widely adopted within many managerial, marketing, consultancy and applied policy research fields and it has influenced other administrative or instrumental discourses. A comprehensive overview of the different strands of the post-Fordist literature or research is beyond our scope here.[5] Instead, I will simply explore elements of one subset, the neo-Schumpeterian, which is judged to be most relevant to present concerns.

The neo-Schumpeterian model

Joseph Schumpeter, like Fritz Machlup, the pioneer of information sector studies (see Chapter Three), was a member of the later generation of the 'Austrian School' of economists who emigrated to the USA in the interwar years and went on to make a significant contribution to political economy fields somewhat distant from the orthodoxies of mainstream economic 'science'. Much of Schumpeter's work refuses to observe the conventional disciplinary boundaries between economic, political and sociological inquiry. It engages with the broader questions and methods of both the classical works of Smith, Ricardo, Marx and of more recent schools of institutional or evolutionary political economy (Schumpeter, 1939, 1943, 1954). Although Schumpeter's overall work is stamped by a strongly conservative political hue and a very positivist methodology, at times its more analytical concepts also suggest a strong, if generally unacknowledged, influence from the Marxist political economy tradition. He was generally relegated to the status of a footnote economist in the past, but his work has probably become much more influential since the 1970s (Freeman, 1982, 1984; Hall and Preston, 1988).

Schumpeter was one of the few economic thinkers of the early twentieth century to seriously address the role and implications of technological change and the multifaceted dimensions of the innovation process. He was also one of the first economists in the West to identify and analyse the idea of 'long-wave' cycles or phases of development in capitalist economies, a perspective which has clear links with that adopted in recent post-Fordist approaches. Borrowing an idea from the unorthodox Russian economist Kondratieff, Schumpeter argued that the short-run business cycles of concern to conventional economists were overlaid by longer cycles of approximately fifty years duration and these were divided into a first phase of relatively rapid growth followed by a downswing phase marked by slow growth (Schumpeter, 1939, 1943). He also suggested that the periodic clustering of interrelated new technological developments, in association with creative or 'heroic' entrepreneurship and other important aspects of the overall 'innovation' process, all combined to provide the basis for a new phase of sustained and relatively rapid growth (Freeman, 1982, 1984; Hall and Preston, 1988). The recent revival of interest in Schumpeter's notion of long-wave cycles of capitalist development and his stress on the important role of technological change and other types of innovations is in no small part due to the work of Christopher Freeman. Since his early writings in the 1950s, Freeman has himself proved to be one of the most influential recent researchers on the economic implications of technological change, tending to adopt a technological determinist approach in direct opposition to the traditional orientation of conventional economics to either ignore technological innovation altogether, or to concern itself merely with incremental technical changes (Freeman, 1982, 1984, 1985, 1987, 1994, 1995). Together with other colleagues such as Perez, Soete and Dosi, Freeman has made a major contribution to the development of the neo-Schumpeterian approach to long-wave cycles of approximately fifty years duration, each divided into sub-periods of 'boom and bust' (Perez, 1983, 1985; Freeman and Soete, 1987; Dosi et al., 1988).

New clusters of interrelated radical innovations (comprising *a major new technology system*), and especially their diffusion and application across the economy play a key role in explaining the shift to a long-wave upswing phase. The neo-Schumpeterians identify new ICTs as representing one of the 'historically rare' major new technology systems which have a 'pervasive application potential' in the sense that they can be applied and adopted in most economic sectors and indeed in many kinds of social and cultural activities. But the availability and emergence of such major new technology systems is only one essential part of the story in this approach, for its effective diffusion, applications and use to support a sustained phase of rapid economic growth requires a second set of conditioning factors. This refers to a set of 'matching' institutional and organisational innovations, including shifts in socio-institutional norms and regulations which will support and facilitate the adoption of the major new technology system and its potentialities. These are not pre-given or prescribed by the technology system itself, but require a process of search and discovery. The combination of these two sets of factors represents a new *techno-economic paradigm* which becomes a sort of universal standard or guide to 'best practices' across the economic system, as well as political and other institutions.

In this neo-Schumpeterian approach, the post-war boom marked the upswing of the fourth Kondratieff long wave and it was underpinned by electronic technologies, the extended diffusion of the automobile and other products of the mass consumption industries as well as petro-chemicals and oil as sources of relatively cheap energy. It also recognises standardisation, massification and scale economies, oligopolistic competition and mass consumption as key features of the post-war phase of economic growth. But it also places a strong emphasis on state welfare and education policies and the kinds of institutional innovations associated with Keynesianism in providing the basis for the virtuous link between low unemployment, high output and productivity growth. The crisis of the fourth long wave is often addressed here in terms of the dampening effect of oligopolistic competition in the face of maturing technologies and consequent upward pressures in wages and prices and the inefficiencies of large corporations which tended to exhaust the scope for productivity gains. But the crisis is also presented as a matter of a mismatch between the enduring social, economic and institutional framework of the old long wave and an emerging new technology system and techno-economic paradigm. There is a sort of inertia and time lag involved in changing embedded socio-cultural practices and norms across a wide range of institutions, and this may be exacerbated by the failure of neo-liberal policy regimes to provide the required direction in terms of industrial policy and co-ordination across other policy areas (Freeman, 1984, 1994; Freeman and Soete, 1987; Perez, 1983, 1985).

For some participants in the post-Fordist debates, the neo-Schumpeterian model has elements of technological determinism, with critics claiming that it places a dominant emphasis on technology-induced changes rather than social, organisational or economic factors which influence efficiency and growth trends (Elam, 1994). Certainly some leading exponents such as Freeman (1982, 1987) have explicitly favoured the virtues of viewing technology as a key determinant of economic growth and change, particularly in the context of criticising mainstream economists' neglect of radical technological innovations or major new technology systems. My own view is that this is a relatively flexible model which does not necessarily lead to a subordination of the 'socio-institutional' to the 'techno-economic' factors. For our present purposes, the neo-Schumpeterian model offers a number of positive features and advantages compared to other post-Fordist models as well as the other theories examined so far. It explicitly addresses the historical and technical specifics of new ICTs and their implications for social and institutional change without losing sight of the capitalist market system as a specific social form and product of a dramatic historical rupture. It is also able to accommodate the fact that capitalist development, by definition, involves a process of constant flux and change and that capitalism represents a system which is capable of many transformations in its modes of surface appearances (Wood, 1997).

For these and other reasons, the neo-Schumpeterian model is taken as very useful starting platform when addressing the potential for *change* associated with the production, adoption and diffusion of a major new technology system such as new ICTs (alongside distinct social and institutional innovations or initiatives). At the same time, it avoids the transformative rhetoric of third-wave models and remains sensitive to potentially important *continuities* with respect to the capitalist political-economic structures and social relations which characterise the system of accumulation. It thus avoids the hard technological determinist claims concerning a shift to a distinctively new socio-economic order, such as those advanced in various third-wave and information society theories examined elsewhere. The neo-Schumpeterian approach does not necessarily imply a singular shift towards 'flexibility', small-batch production and the end of mass production as celebrated in many recent theories of post-industrialism and postmodernity, including other contributions to the post-Fordist debate (Wood, 1997: 539–41). Besides, it is attentive to the continuing salience of the material realities and 'dull compulsion' of everyday life which absorb the bulk of the creative energies, not to mention the time and money budgets available to most people – whatever their engagement with the ephemeral pleasures and escapism of consumerist media culture. It refuses to subscribe to the postmodernist rants, however fashionable, concerning the 'disappearance of the real'. It also implies a holistic or systemic approach to the crisis/restructuring process which refuses the tendency to replace all other grand narratives with the singular meta-narrative of the end of meta-narratives. Rather, whilst marking the contemporary as a moment of long-wave crisis and restructuring alongside the potential new opportunities afforded by advances in ICTs, the neo-Schumpeterian approach remains relatively open as to the course and direction of future developments (Hall and Preston, 1988).

Notes

1 For example Toffler is not accorded any mention in the wide-ranging 102-page bibliography in the *Handbook of Science and Technology Studies* edited by Jasanoff et al., 1995.

2 The term IT only emerged in more public policy debates in Britain in the early 1980s, but some sources suggest that the term had been used since the late 1960s within a small specialist milieu. But even in Britain the precise choice of term and its definition varied according to the industrial configurations and interests of different institutional actors (Preston, 1984: 3). In the 1980s, the term 'information technology' was often used alongside other neologisms such as 'informatics', 'compunications' and 'telematics' which were coined elsewhere to describe broadly similar phenomena.

3 This government project has had no small role in shaping the subsequent research path of the current author. It can also be shown to have shaped the agenda of social science research on technology matters in British universities, including the establishment of the Economic and Social Research Council's major Programme on Information and Communication Technologies.

4 This matter of technological determinism and the choice of more appropriate alternative theories of the technology–society relation is a core issue in any work which attempts to address the strategic impacts or implications of new ICT for socio-economic, political and cultural change. Indeed it is one that cuts across concerns addressed in the subsequent

chapters of this book. Given the centrality of these issues, the competing general models of the relation between technological change and socio-economic change are considered in more detail in Chapter Six below. This will also help locate the model proposed by this author in the later chapters and its relation to third-wave and other alternative theories.

5   Ash Amin's *Post-Fordism: A Reader* (1994) provides an excellent introduction and overview of the field and is the main source for the summary review presented here. In addition, very useful critical reviews can be found in: Clarke, 1990; Elam, 1994; Lash and Urry, 1994; Sayer, 1989; Wood, 1996 and 1997.

CHAPTER THREE

AN ARCHAEOLOGY OF INFORMATION (SECTOR) MATTERS

> 'By examining white-collar life, it is possible to learn something about what is becoming more typically "American" . . . What must be grasped is the picture of society as a great salesroom, an enormous file, an incorporated brain, a new universe of management and manipulation. By understanding these diverse white-collar worlds, one can also understand better the shape and meaning of modern society as a whole, as well as the simple hopes and complex anxieties that grip all the people who are sweating it out in the middle of the twentieth century.'
>
> (Mills, 1956a: xv)

'OLD WINE IN NEW BOTTLES'?: THE RISE OF THE *INFORMATION* DIMENSION

Whilst there has been a relatively long history of concern with the role of technology, prior to the 1940s little explicit attention was paid to *information* as a major factor in the study of socio-economic or cultural change processes. In almost every research field, the very idea of *information* as a defining or core organising concept for the conduct of research and analytical activity is markedly a product of the latter half of the twentieth century. For example, before the Second World War, the concept of information did not serve as the organising principle for any distinctive field of academic research. Yet by the early 1980s, it was possible to identify as many as forty distinct sub-disciplines within the natural and social sciences with an explicit focus on information and communication (Machlup, 1980, 1983; Bell, 1980). Most recent contributions to the literature on social, economic and cultural change have been strongly influenced, if not always explicitly, by the notion that changes in the role and organisation of information is a key defining feature of the contemporary (Rose, 1991). This trend is also evident in the recent policy initiatives centred around the idea that we are on the brink of some distinctive new 'information society' or global 'information age'. Thus, at the beginning of the new millennium, it is clear that the category of *information* has become an increasingly important concern for economists, sociologists and cultural theorists as well as researchers based in many of the physical and biological sciences. So far, however, there is little by way of agreement on key concepts and no unified theories have emerged within these fields over the past fifty years. Nor, despite the efforts of some heroic pioneers, has there been any unified information theory which might receive consensual support across the traditional disciplinary boundaries (Schement and Curtis, 1995).

It will also be clear by now that the literature primarily focused on new ICTs on the one hand and that focused on information/knowledge on the other hand, are not at all mutually exclusive. There are many explicit and inevitable overlaps between these two bodies of work, if only because the dominant cluster of new technological innovations are precisely *informational* and *communicational* in character. But this, and the following two chapters, will engage with the growing body of work which places a primary focus and emphasis on shifts in the economic and social roles of *information* or *knowledge* and their implications. How can we understand the origins, meaning and extent of these apparent shifts in the role of information work, services and products in the history of capitalist industrialism? To what extent are they linked to clusters of technical innovation in the ICT field? What significance, if any, should be accorded to the perceived quantitative and qualitative changes in the role, flows and characteristics of different types of information, including shifts in its organisation, production, distribution or communication? Thus these chapters will engage with an important sub-set of recent research and writings which stresses fundamental changes in information or knowledge (rather than technology) and where the central focus of attention falls on the 'I' rather than the 'T' dimensions of new IT/ICT (ITAP, 1983).

I will start by examining the notion of an expanding *information sector* before moving on to explore the (for me) quite different idea that we are entering a distinctively new post-industrial or *information society* in the next chapter. I will adopt a distinctive archaeological route to address the key concepts and underlying issues involved in these information-centred models. The chosen route is rather different to the histories of relevant research adopted in other reviews of this literature as well as that adopted in some of the seminal substantive contributions to such information-centred analysis. It indicates that even if claims and research explicitly focused on an expanding 'information sector' or an emerging 'information society' are relatively new, the underlying phenomena of concern and issues at stake may not be as novel as frequently assumed. Rather they can be shown to have direct links with long-established concepts and prior lines of inquiry on trends of change within the social sciences.

For example, some have suggested that the roots of information-centred analysis of industrial and economic change may be traced to the closing decades of the nineteenth century, an era which witnessed the first modern 'communications revolution' centred around a cluster of radical technological innovations. These enabled the growth of telephone and radio broadcasting, they provided the means to capture and reproduce still and

moving images, voice and sound/music information 'content' and to distribute these to large-scale audiences for the first time. But this era also marked
the emergence of new approaches to the systematic application of science
and technology for industrial purposes. It also gave rise to a radical extension of earlier ways of thinking about information as though it were a
material object and greatly extended the role of various 'intellectual property
rights' (Machlup, 1980; Machlup and Mansfield, 1983; Schement and
Curtis, 1995: 2–20).[1] There are therefore strong links to be made between
the kinds of developments embraced by the old division-of-labour concept,
on the one hand, and more recent work which explicitly stresses the growth
of information industries and occupations in the twentieth century, on the
other hand. I will also explore further below some strong (if unacknowledged) links between the latter body of work and earlier sociological studies
of the changing socio-economic role of 'white collar' work.

Thus despite the relative novelty of information-centred categories of
socio-economic research, I want to suggest that some of the key concerns
and underlying phenomena were partly addressed (prefigured) in earlier
research and models. These were produced long before the emergence of new
digital technologies, the rise of explicit information-centred analyses or the
recent claims that we are moving towards distinctively 'new times' in terms
of socio-economic and cultural relations/processes. The outcome of this particular archaeological exploration is not necessarily a case of 'old wine in
new bottles'. But it does serve to underline the importance of attending to the
question of continuities as well as the changes with respect to the fundamental socio-economic relations of the contemporary.

'WHITE-COLLAR': THE DIVISION OF LABOUR AND INFORMATION WORK

I want to start with selective aspects of the long history of work in the social
sciences which has utilised the notion of the *division of labour*, a concept
which was accorded a central role in the founding texts of modern social and
economic studies. This provides a rich, if not essential, entry point for
exploring the sources and nature of change in occupational and work structures within capitalist industrialism. Yet this broader if older category is
often neglected or ignored in many contemporary analyses of socio-
economic change, not least those focused on technology or information
matters. Indeed, it represents an interesting alternative to the usual starting
point for reviews of the genealogy and state-of-the-art precisely because it is
more firmly rooted in the traditions of social and economic inquiry rather
than those which frame inquiry in terms of a technical focus on one or other
explicit 'information' concern/issue or technological factor. It also provides

a conceptual bridge between many of the contemporary debates over the social meaning or implications of changes in information (work, industries, etc.) and much older intellectual and political conflicts concerning the nature and sources of wealth, power and socio-economic 'welfare' and inequalities in capitalist industrialism.

The modern origins of the division of labour concept date back to the closing decades of the eighteenth century as capitalist industrialism began to emerge as the dominant social order in parts of Europe and the Americas. Many late-Enlightenment writers were concerned with both the sources of the increasing material wealth as well as descriptions and prescriptions as to the distribution of such increasing abundance. The pre-eminent seminal work here was Adam Smith's *The Wealth of Nations,* first published in 1776. Indeed one twentieth-century economic history text described it as 'the most successful not only of all books on economics, but, with the possible exception of Darwin's *Origins of the Species,* of all scientific books that have appeared to this day' (Schumpeter, 1954: 181–2). Whilst Schumpeter may overstate the case, it is clear that Smith's book provides a key starting point for subsequent work in the social sciences concerned with the specific economic, social and political features of capitalist industrial societies. This includes inquiries into the sources and distribution of material wealth.

In Smith's account, the major keys to understanding the expanding productive potential of capitalist industrialism lay in the deepening social and technical division of labour (between different industries and occupations) as well as the proportion of the workforce engaged in productive as opposed to unproductive labour. For Smith, the increasing division of labour was the major source of the rapid increase in output, especially within the expanding manufacturing sectors of late eighteenth-century Britain: the 'Silicon Valley' of that time. For him, the division of labour was the key to a new age of abundance afforded by the industrial revolution, a rising tide that lifted all boats. It was the key source of 'the superior affluence and abundance commonly possessed even by the lowest and most despised member of Civilized society, compared with what the most respected and active savage can attain to' (1776: cited by Schumpeter, 1954: 187). Smith emphasised the strong tendency for the division of labour to expand further within capitalist economies leading to an increasing specialisation of occupations and industrial activities. Ricardo and Marx expanded on this theme later, even if they were also more attentive to questions of capitalist property rights, class inequality and conflicts. The various forms of 'oppressive inequality' in the earlier stages of industrial capitalism were largely glossed away in Smith's vision of the new and universal abundance. Interestingly enough, Smith paid some attention to the role of specialised information and knowledge in increasing material wealth. But in the field of economic thought at least, 'nobody, either before or after Adam Smith, ever thought of putting such a burden upon the division of labour'. The concept was central to many subsequent analyses of capitalist industrialism, not least in the work of Durkheim and others in the new discipline of sociology – which had itself emerged as a part of the deepening division of intellectual labour since Smith's time (Schumpeter, 1954: 187).

This archaeology of information matters now cuts to the middle decades of the twentieth century, around the beginning of the neo-Schumpeterians' fourth long-wave upswing or the most sustained and rapid long-run boom of economic growth ever in the history of capitalist industrialism. By now sociology and economics were rapidly expanding distinct fields of inquiry and well established within the growing university sector. Many of the leading (information) workers in these fields were engaged in research and debates concerning the nature, extent and meaning of the major shifts in the division of labour since the early stages of capitalist industrialism. One important sub-theme centred on whether and how the 'mature' industrial capitalist society of the mid-twentieth century was different to that of Smith, Marx or Durkheim's times. Another closely related debate centred on the appropriate theories for the study of social class inequalities and conflicts given such perceived changes in the social order of the mid-twentieth century, not least the big shifts in industrial and occupational structures associated with the deepening division of labour.

By now, the hegemonic site of social and economic theory and writing had shifted from western Europe. The USA had assumed the role of the leading 'affluent society' as well as leader of 'the West' with respect to the ideological as much as the military battlefronts in the Cold War conflicts of that era. Here structural-functionalism dominated the field of sociological theory, marked by a strong orientation towards social order maintenance and a denial or downplaying of social inequalities and conflicts. The multidimensional processes of 'differentiation', not least in the division of labour, were deemed to have created multiple new structures of distributed social position, status and power which were radically de-linked from the distributional structures of wealth and income. Traditional sociological concerns with the distribution of wealth and power, including issues of class inequalities and conflicts, were deemed to be largely irrelevant in the face of the rise of the new managerial and professional occupations as well as the expanding ranks of clerical and more 'routine' white-collar workers. The hegemonic view suggested that the rise of the white-collar workforce was not merely an outcome of the deepening division of labour. It further suggested that the rise of the salaried white-collar workers (or, in 1980s-90s terminology, 'information workers') amounted to a profound change in the distribution of social position, power and status compared to earlier stages of capitalist industrialism.

It is in this context that we can identify the roots of the influential 'information society' theory to be explored in the next chapter. In this context, and in his 'first coming' as a prominent sociologist, Daniel Bell amended Weber's notions of bureaucratic rationality and 'the administration of things' in his first influential book, *The End of Ideology* (1960). Here Bell argued that the role of 'technical decision-making' had now come to displace social and political conflicts of values and norms based around class inequalities or other structural cleavages. For him, technical decision-making was directly opposed to ideology, in that the former was calculating and rational and the latter was essentially emotional and expressive. He proclaimed that 'the old political passions' had now become exhausted. He suggested that the working class 'whose grievances were once the driving energy for social change' were now fully met and satisfied by the prevailing social order. The (largely unspoken) sub-text was that the old cleavages of industrial capitalism had been eroded and transformed despite the contrary claims of a small minority of dissenting leftist or critical intellectuals (1960: 375; 1973: 34).[2]

The social meaning and rhetorical force of Bell's claims concerning the end of old political cleavages and conflicts can only be fully understood within their national and international contexts such as the post-war boom and Cold War. But despite the domestic 'fall out' from the Cold War in shaping the parameters of 'respectable' intellectual work in the USA in the 1950s and early 1960s, there were some dissenting and critical voices which are directly relevant to the concerns of this particular book. One such was C. Wright Mills, whose *White Collar* provides an extremely important, but usually neglected, starting point for any contemporary discussion of the origins and meanings of theories of an emerging 'information society' (1956a).[3] This is not least because the terms 'white-collar' and 'information' are so easily interchangeable with respect to the analysis of work, occupational and industrial change.

From the late 1940s, C. Wright Mills and others had begun to study the rapid growth of white-collar workers, comprising managers, salaried professionals, salespeople, clerical and other office workers and the related growth of new service industries and occupations. He found that they had grown from 15 per cent to 56 per cent of the middle class between 1870 and 1940 (Mills, 1956a). By the mid-1950s the number of white-collar workers outnumbered the blue-collar workers in the occupational structure for the first time in the history of capitalist industrialism in the USA. This ratio continued to widen steadily in subsequent years so that by 1970, the white-collar workers outnumbered the blue-collar by more than five to four.

However, what I wish to flag and stress here is that from the late 1940s, Mills and other sociologists had undertaken a series of research projects explicitly focused on this particular and important dimension of the changing division of labour. Mills' work was not simply concerned with measuring the quantitative changes in the white/blue collar divisions of labour. He also put a lot of emphasis on the 'social psychology' and subjective aspects of the growing ranks of white-collar workers, as well as their implications for political and social theory. He emphasised that the relative socio-economic status and political position of the majority of white-collar workers was not very different to that of the blue-collar working class. He argued that the growth of white-collar (information) work took place in the context of new corporate and bureaucratic structures of control and discipline and therefore did not necessarily bestow any greater autonomy or independence on the majority of such workers, nor did it imply any fundamental shift in power relations.

Mills' seminal work offers many critical challenges to several of the core assumptions, concepts and values underpinning Daniel Bell's later information society theory which (as I will argue in the next chapter) was based on the changing division of labour and new occupational and power structures in the US during the post-war period. It is also relevant to stress that Mills occasionally used the term 'white-collar society' in his book to emphasise the key role which information and related service work/workers had come to play in the USA of the 1950s. But he was also emphatic that this certainly did not imply the transition to some entirely new, post-capitalist or post-industrial social formation. As will be indicated later, this is in striking contrast to the key claims and implications advanced in Daniel Bell's subsequent analyses. It is also worth noting here that despite significant overlaps between the core concerns of Mills' book and that of Bell's later work announcing the advent of a new post-industrial or information society, the latter almost totally ignores the work of Mills and other relevant critical researchers. Indeed, it is quite striking that there are only two very brief and passing references to *White Collar* throughout the 490 pages of text in *The Coming of the Post-Industrial Society*. This archaeology of information matters suggests that such 'significant silences' speak very loudly indeed about the limits of Bell's own claims concerning 'objective' analysis. It also underlines the particular ideological characteristics of 'the end of ideology' thesis and other subsequent technocratic and information-centred analyses of the contemporary.

FRITZ MACHLUP: KNOWLEDGE PRODUCTION AND THE INFORMATION SECTOR

Thus, from the late 1940s, C. Wright Mills and other sociologists had begun to study the rapid growth of white-collar workers, comprising managers, salaried professionals, salespeople and office workers (Mills, 1956a). By the mid-1950s, an increasing number of social scientists were engaged in research on this particular dimension of the changing division of labour and related shifts in industrial structures. There was a growing dissatisfaction that the expanding 'services' sector was defined residually, embracing a very diverse set of activities in line with the basic three-sector model defined by

Colin Clarke (1940). This concern led to new efforts to define more nuanced and detailed typologies of economic activities (Preston, 1984, 1989). For example, Hatt and Foote (1953) sought to refine the three sector schema by proposing the introduction of quaternary and quinary sectors. They also pointed to the trend toward professionalisation of work and the growing importance of the quinary or intellectual sector. This was followed later by other contributions, largely from sociologists, which sought to disaggregate the traditional services sector into a number of more conceptually coherent categories (e.g. Singelmann, 1979; Stanback, 1979; Stanback et al., 1980, 1981; Gershuny and Miles, 1983).

More directly relevant to present concerns however, was the publication in 1962 of Fritz Machlup's seminal *The Production and Distribution of Knowledge in the United States* and his subsequent follow-up studies. This work is primarily concerned with an analysis of the changing economic role of knowledge and information in the sphere of production. But Machlup recognized that such a study must be multidisciplinary and that it is not possible to stay within the confines of conventional economics. This pioneering work opened up many interesting new avenues for research on social and economic aspects of information in contemporary society. Hence it is instructive to zoom in on selective aspects of Machlup's work, particularly since it is often poorly represented in many histories and reviews of the state-of-the-art in information-centred studies.

Unlike many subsequent theorists, Machlup starts from the view that knowledge or information is central to all human societies (by definition) and that information played a part in the analysis of many early political economists, such as Smith and List. However, he stressed that in mainstream modern economics, the role of knowledge or (productive/instrumental) information has been largely marginalised. Such an approach is fundamentally flawed according to Machlup, especially for any analysis of medium to long-term prospects or change (1962: 1-4). He went on to argue that the growth of technical knowledge and the growth of productivity that may result from it are vitally important factors in the analysis of economic growth and other economic problems. It was no longer valid, for example, to treat the stock of knowledge, and especially the state of technology, as exogenous variables or as trend functions in economic models (1962: 5).

Unlike many other information sector researchers, Machlup also sought to widen the prevailing agenda for the economic and social analysis of information. He explicitly recognised that besides technological or instrumental information directly designed to pay off in the future, there are many other important types of information or knowledge (1962: 6–7). Thus he recognised that there are types of knowledge such as that which give an immediate pleasure to the recipients as well as 'spiritual' and other types. He suggested that to limit study and research to the types of knowledge that are expected to yield a future return in terms of increased productivity would be unsatisfactory for two main reasons. First, it would not satisfy a 'transcendent intellectual curiosity'. Second, it is not possible to study 'productive' knowledge without paying considerable attention to 'unproductive' knowledge because they are quite often joint products. He argued that what is taught at school, printed in books, magazines and newspapers, broadcast over radio, or produced on television is also knowledge or information, and suggested 'that to study one is to analyse all' (1962: 6). Essentially, he opted for a contingent or subjective definition of knowledge, an approach criticised by some later information society theorists who favoured an apparently 'objective definition' (e.g. Bell, 1980: 517 and 548). Indeed, Machlup suggested that the scope of study should be extended to take account of the deepening division of labour between pure *brain work* and largely physical performance which has occurred in all sectors of economic and social organisation (Preston, 1989).

Machlup also discussed the particular conceptual and methodological problems involved in measuring the economic dimensions of information. He suggested that in any attempt to define economic activities in this way, the allocation can only be made on the basis of a conceptual scheme suitable for particular purposes. This may often involve a tension between theoretical clarity or consistency on the one hand and statistical convenience on the other. He also suggested that different purposes may often call for different conceptual schemes and he considered how the goals and tensions involved in such exercises relate to conceptualising in the field of knowledge production. Indeed, compared to many other information-centred analysts, I find that Machlup's work is exceptionally attentive to distinctions between different informational domains and types of activities. For example, he clearly distinguished between information content and its technological carriers – contrary to the readings suggested by Babe (1995) and other critics. He also distinguished between investment in knowledge and investment in durable goods needed for the production of knowledge.

Machlup's studies were also attentive to the important differences between an industry approach and an occupation approach and their implications for empirical studies of information in contemporary societies (Preston, 1989). On the basis of these and other conceptual and methodological considerations (beyond our scope here), Machlup largely concentrated on the industry approach (but he also undertook studies of information occupations). His schema for the industry approach divided the information industries into five major sub-sectors and he proposed an adjusted definition or measure of Gross National Product in line with his conceptual schema. His empirical findings underlined the growing role of these 'knowledge industries' in the USA. They suggested that approximately 29 per cent of GNP in the USA was accounted for by knowledge/information industries in 1958 and that these industries were growing at twice the rate of overall GNP growth in the years 1947–1958.

Machlup also examined the changing share of 'knowledge-producing occupations' in the total labour force in the USA as one other key measure of change in the division of labour in the twentieth century. In seeking to measure the growth of information occupations in all sectors of economic activity, Machlup recognised that it is not possible to draw a clear and incontrovertible line between 'physical' and 'mental' labour as almost every kind of operation requires both physical and mental effort. But he also argued that it was useful and justified (for both theoretical and practical purposes) to make a distinction between physical and mental operations, and between *predominantly* physical and predominantly mental labour. As part of his reasoning, he suggested that such distinctions are justifiable because the established and frequently used distinction between blue-collar and white-collar workers is largely designed precisely for this purpose (1962: 379). Machlup's empirical findings indicated that the number of white-collar workers increased steadily from five million in 1900 to 27 million in 1959. He estimated that by 1959, the number of white-collar workers had grown by 540 per cent since 1900, whilst manual and service workers had grown by 238 per cent, and the number of farm workers was only 59 per cent of that prevailing in 1900.

Machlup suggested that the distribution of the labour force among the three categories may be brought out in stronger relief if it is examined as a percentage of the total. Thus if all predominantly manual workers are taken together, their combined share in the labour force decreased from 82.4 per cent in 1900 to 57.9 per cent in 1959. On the other hand, white-collar workers increased from 17.6 per cent of the labour force in 1900 to 42.1 per cent in 1959. Machlup suggested that this uninterrupted trend for sixty years or more is the most impressive aspect of change in the labour force. Machlup defined the category of *knowledge-producing workers* as comprising 'transporters, transformers, processors, interpreters, analyzers, and original creators of communications of all sorts' and he distinguished these from *knowledge-using workers* (1962: 383). His early studies estimated that knowledge-producing occupations had increased from 10.7 per cent of the labour force in 1900 to 31.6 per cent in 1959.

Although it is often taken as 'self-evident' that advances in technology and shifts in demand lead to changes in the occupational composition of the labour force, Machlup was mindful that there was nothing necessary or self-evident about such changes. He rejected the technological determinist or linear view and suggested that it is conceivable that all sorts of technological changes might leave the occupational structure of the economy unchanged if occupations were not too narrowly defined (1962: 377–8). In interpreting the observed statistical trends of employment and technological change, he stressed the need to clearly understand the difference between what is logically necessary and what is logically probable. In the case of the USA, he suggested that the labour force had been adaptable to a high degree and that it had largely followed monetary and market incentives created by changes in relative earnings or the stimuli of open job opportunities.

Finally, it should be noted that Machlup launched a second phase of his research during the 1970s with the expectation that it would be completed and published in the early 1980s. Unfortunately, the research was interrupted with Machlup's death in 1983. However, the intellectual framework for the work had been laid down and two of his colleagues completed the quantitative work for publication. This included an account of the growth of the knowledge industry and its various branches over the period 1958–80 (Rubin and Huber, 1986). These researchers adhered to Machlup's definitions and selection of data sources. In absolute terms, they found that 'expenditures for knowledge production' in the USA increased steadily from 1958 to 1980, rising from $138,825 million to $967,909 million. But perhaps the key finding was that, according to Machlup's schema, the proportion of knowledge production in the (adjusted) GNP in the USA increased significantly from 1958 to the early 1970s but appeared to grow more slowly after that.

OTHER INFORMATION SECTOR STUDIES

After Machlup's pioneering work was published in 1962, some of its concepts, ideas and findings were clearly evident in a wide range of social science literature – particularly that relating to long-term or structural changes in the nature of employment and wealth-creating activities (e.g. the post-industrialism literature). In 1977, the Department of Commerce published the nine-volume report on *The Information Economy* in the USA based on research carried out by Marc U. Porat with Michael R. Rubin (1977). This report was linked to a large-scale research project which made use of the national income accounts produced by the US Bureau of Economic Analysis to create a computer model of the US economy for the year 1967. This report acknowledged its intellectual debt to Machlup but it adopted some very different definitions of the information sector and it adhered much more strictly to the categories of economic activities that are part of the conventional national income accounts scheme.

One notable feature of this study was its stress on the distinction between a *primary information sector* (PIS) and a *secondary information sector* (SIS). The idea of the SIS appears to have been influenced by the notion of the 'technostructure' advanced by Galbraith (Bell, 1980: 520). The distinction was made to take account of the fact that many of the elements of the information sector may be found both as separate industries and as adjuncts to other industries. For example, a print shop may be a separate operation

carrying out printing operations for the general public or it may be a component within a larger organisation (e.g. a motor manufacturer) that is not
a part of the primary information sector. The Porat and Rubin study
regarded the SIS concept as important in that a large proportion of information activities in the economy would remain hidden and unidentified if
not sought out in their typology. This study estimated that 25.1 per cent of
GNP in the USA could be attributed to the activities of the primary information sector in 1967 and an additional 21.1 per cent of GNP could be
attributed to the secondary information sector. It reported that the total
information sector accounted for over 46 per cent of GNP in the USA in that
year.

The OECD also conducted a study focused on the changing role of the
information sector in several of its member nations in the late 1970s, and the
results were published in 1981. In brief, this international study covered nine
countries and used very similar measures of the information sector to those
in the US study conducted by Porat and Rubin. In 1986 the OECD published
an update of its study of the information economy, using the same methodology and applying it to twelve countries. This provided estimates of a
continued growth in the importance of information activities for the later
period covered by the study, but this growth was less dynamic than the earlier period. The OECD authors also state that the term *information economy*
is used not because it describes a distinct socio-economic phenomenon, but
because 'it is clearly understandable in the present context' (1986).

Since the publication of Machlup's initial information sector work many
similar studies have been conducted in different national contexts. Some of
these have largely followed in the tracks of the Machlup, Porat and OECD
studies and/or have sought to develop more specific analyses of elements of
the information economy (Debons et al., 1980; Karunaratne, 1986). Some of
the studies have been commissioned by national government agencies with a
view to developing national policy strategies for both information technology and information industries (e.g. Nora and Minc, 1980). There has also
been a steady growth of academic and other publications over the past
twenty years which focus implicitly, if not explicitly, on the changing nature
and role of information and other service or 'intangible' activities (USA
Department of Commerce, 1999; OECD, 2000).

In the early 1980s, there was a marked increase in policy interest and
research focused on international trade aspects of the information industries
in countries such as the USA, UK and Germany. Some of this was stimulated
by the lobbying and other preparatory work for the 'Uruguay Round' of
GATT negotiations which sought to liberalise trade and investment flows
related to information and other services. For example, foreign policy
researchers in the USA were pointing to the strategic national economic
interests at stake in *The Coming Information Age* (Dizard, 1982). In the
UK, the government department previously concerned with the new IT

sector was also given responsibility for the co-ordination of policy for 'tradeable information' activities. This followed the publication of the report on *Making a Business of Information* produced by the Information Technology Advisory Panel (ITAP, 1983). This panel of experts was appointed by the Prime Minister. Its report stressed the importance of information ('the "I" of IT') and suggested that too much attention so far had been focused on the technologies and infrastructures (what it termed 'the "T" of IT'). It also stressed a close connection between new ICT hardware and infrastructures and new opportunities for harnessing the commercial value of information. This UK report divided the tradeable information sector into a number of component elements, adopting a more restrictive definition than that contained in the Machlup and OECD studies.[4] It also noted that, in the case of producer services such as banking and insurance, some important information-handling activities are carried out in order to provide an end service which is conceptually distinct from the supply of 'pure' information.

Most of the literature focused on the *information* sector or economy has tended to emphasise the production and distribution of specialised, producer or professional information services with relatively little explicit attention paid to the changing role of communication media and information services directed at final or household users.[5] However, there have been a number of studies which have adopted a separate or parallel focus on the media of mass communication and changes in the related information industries and flows. Some of these engage with traditional concerns in the fields of mass communication. One example was the attempt at a total census of national communication and information flows undertaken by Tomita and his colleagues at the Japanese Ministry of Posts and Telecommunications. Beginning in the late 1960s, they sought to develop indicators and collect data for the different forms and media of communication, in terms of a common standard (words supplied and consumed). They developed indicators for a number of different media of the volumes of information supplied, consumed, their costs of production, transmission and consumption. The methodology was changed and improved in at least two studies before the comparative study of communication flows in Japan and the US was conducted by Pool et al. (1984; see also Ito, 1981; Tomita et al., 1975). The study published by Pool and colleagues in 1984 sought to develop a standard methodology to measure communication flows in both the USA and Japan by using a revised version of the basic methodology pioneered by Tomita.

One other notable exercise in mapping change in the media and communication sectors was developed by French researchers, including some based in the IDATE research centre in Montpellier. This approach was based around the idea of the information sector as a *filière*, defined as a chain of activities which produces a given set of interlinked goods or services. It focuses attention on the structures and flow processes linking raw materials with final consumption through a set of interrelated and interdependent states. The coherence of the *filière* is determined by a shared technical system of production and related technical know-how and other competencies, a shared industrial structure, particularly of capital markets, a common product or services market and a coherent set of government policies or regulations. It is constructed as a 'structure in process' as each stage is subject to pressures for change related to shifts in technology, market and industrial structures and state regulation (Porter et al., 1987; Preston, 1989). This represents an alternative and conceptually coherent model in principle, but, in practice, the stages or categories will often appear blurred. Within this schema, the role of new ICTs and their implications for the editing, production, programming and distribution of different media information services can be mapped and measured with greater coherence. The model may be particularly relevant in studying certain implications of digital technologies and to map related developments in the emerging 'multimedia' arena – where new ICTs are facilitating complex process innovations, including the re-editing, re-mixing and re-packaging of traditional information material in new and saleable ways (Porter et al., 1987; Preston, 1989).

A CONTRIBUTION TO 'SOCIALLY NEW KNOWLEDGE'?

For Machlup, 'producing' knowledge meant, with respect to studies or books such as his own, not only discovering, inventing, designing, and planning knowledge or information but also its dissemination and communication (1962: 7). He used the term 'socially new knowledge' to refer to 'knowledge that is new, that has not been known by anyone before' (1962: 7–8). His own pioneering information sector study may be so described, even if the underlying phenomena and concerns are far from new as this particular history of information-centred studies serves to indicate.

That said, there are a number of important criticisms to be raised and considered with respect to Machlup's work. These also concern other information sector studies which have sought to map and measure empirically the changing role of information labour and industries. In addition, these same challenges also extend to information society theories insofar as the latter draw upon aspects of the former literature to support their theses.

The most fundamental criticism concerns the validity of defining and designating specific occupations, industries or sectors as 'information' and the consequent implication that other economic activities may be somehow designated as non-informational. The issues at stake here relate to the more fundamental point that by definition, all human communities or societies – whatever the technological or organisational base of the social system – are intrinsically and intensively informational. They comprise members who possess the capabilities for conscious and reflexive information-processing and communication. By definition all human and social communities depend upon distinctive sets of shared norms and values centred around both utilitarian/functional as well as symbolic/cultural forms of information or knowledge. The issues at stake here also touch upon the validity and coherence of the notion of an 'information' society (and indeed 'non-information' society) defined largely or primarily on the basis of perceptions of quantitative changes in information (Webster and Robins, 1986; Slack and Fejes, 1987; Lyon, 1988; Webster, 1995).

The particular problems with the studies which point to the changing role of the information sector or economy can easily be highlighted. For example, computer programmers or systems analysts producing ICT are readily considered to be in highly informational occupations whilst farmers or farm workers are by implication defined as essentially non-informational. For sure, the former work clearly requires modern high-tech competencies and 'theoretical knowledge' related to the production and/or application of the formal rules appropriate to a particular computer hardware and operating system environment. But it is highly questionable as to whether it should be assumed or implied that this kind of work necessarily involves a greater or more complex base of information compared, for example, to the work involved in the effective running of a small farm in the 'primary sector' of the late twentieth century.

Let us take the example of my own father whose formal schooling ended at the age of fourteen and whose subsequent working career included roles as labourer, manager and owner of small farms producing a diversity of vegetable and animal products in the west of Ireland. To function effectively in each of these successive stages of his work activity, it is clear that diverse and changing sets of knowledge or information were required. They included: i) a practical knowledge of the physical characteristics of different plants and animals with respect to their distinctive requirements for efficient growth and reproduction, ii) the appropriate matching of these with different types of 'natural' resource factors (soil, seasonal and weather factors) and manufactured commodities (fertilisers, food supplements etc.); iii) information related to the potential, application and maintenance of successive generations of mechanical and electro-mechanical technological artefacts to support production processes in keeping with rapidly changing efficiency norms for small farms in the national and European context (tractors, milking machines, cooling systems); iv) practical economic knowledge related to the rapidly changing market conditions and prospects of different kinds of farm products necessary to sustain or improve the viability of small farms within both short and longer term planning contexts; v) information concerning the practical implications of relevant national and European Union agricultural and food policies, including those which impinged upon food and health or safety standards, the policy incentives or disincentives related to different kinds of crop and animal products and so on.

This example helps illustrate that in many respects, the effective conduct of such work in the 'primary sector' environment of industrial economies involves a great diversity of information and knowledge. It also serves to challenge the assumption that such work is somehow less information-intensive compared to that involved in the production of computer software products. The latter category of work may well require a high level of more theoretical knowledge and formal rules-based procedures related to particular computing system environments. But it certainly does not appear to require the same diversity of information related to a wide range of natural, economic and policy environments involved in the farming example illustrated above.

The issues raised here are not entirely new and have echoes with more traditional debates in the social sciences (as well as long-established conflicts in the wider industrial relations realm). These concern the classification of specific types of jobs with respect to their skill-intensity and appropriate remuneration or 'value', as well as status position. Adam Smith, for example, pointed to the relatively low value placed on farm workers even two hundred years ago – despite the fact that 'after . . . the fine arts, and the liberal professions . . . there is perhaps no trade which requires so great a variety of knowledge and experience' (1776: 143). Essentially, the conventional categories of skill differentials have tended to relegate most of the fundamental forms of human work to the status of 'unskilled' as Braverman (1974) has stressed. Indeed, Raymond Williams also pointed to a 'fantastic distortion' whereby the category of 'semi-skilled' has been used to support a quite false assertion of an increase of skilled labour in industrial production whilst 'the deep skills of tending land and growing food are categorically reduced' (1983: 89–90).

Only some of the researchers engaged in information sector studies have explicitly addressed the problems involved in selecting certain occupations or industries as informational. We have seen how Machlup suggested that it was often a question of making a distinction between 'predominantly' mental or information labour and 'predominantly' physical labour. He argued that such a distinction was valid for certain theoretical and empirical purposes in economic and sociological inquiry, pointing out that the earlier division between white-collar and blue-collar workers had long been designed and used precisely for similar purposes (1962: 379). Machlup explicitly recognised many of the conceptual and operational problems involved in defining certain industries or occupations as informational and expressly recognised that it entailed many judgements and arbitrary decisions. Nevertheless, it must be borne in mind that his work, no less than that of the other information sector researchers, still fundamentally depended upon the highly problematic designation of certain activities as information and by extension, the implicit conception of others as non-information. At the very least, it suggests the need to be mindful that any such quantitative measures are far from 'objective' or value-free (despite some of Bell's claims to the contrary) and that they are highly dependent upon discretionary judgements and evaluations which may not always be made explicit.

A second and related set of criticisms suggests that the information sector or economy is an incoherent concept which lumps together a very diverse set of industries, occupations and economic activities. Some suggest that an information sector approach fails to redress many of the problems inherent in the 'residual' definition of the services sector (in the traditional three-sector division of the economy) compared to alternative and more detailed typologies of services developed in the 1970s and 1980s. For example, Gershuny and Miles (1983) adopted and developed one such alternative typology. They declared that concepts such as information sector or work are misleading and represent 'anodyne aggregations' of diverse activities which serve to hinder understanding of the processes of social change and the prospects for social choice. They criticised the information sector approach for failing to address the distinctive and changing socio-economic roles of different service industries or activities within the overall division of labour, or their relation to changes in consumer demand and consumption trends within the advanced industrial economies.

Information sector studies have also been criticised for their failure to address the distinctive economic characteristics of different information commodities and markets. Critics have argued that such studies tend to treat data, information, knowledge and wisdom as a singular thing and as a mere commodity (Roszak, 1986; Webster, 1995). In his communicational approach to economic theory, Robert Babe has criticised various efforts within conventional economics to treat information as a commodity on the grounds that information is non-quantifiable, suggesting that commoditisation pertains mainly to artefacts that 'contain' information not to information *per se* (1995: 3–4, 29–33). He and others have argued that the attempts of Porat and others to quantitatively measure the value of information are fundamentally flawed because information is essentially heterogenous and hence lacks the equivalences or standards which are required for measurement and comparison. The information sector approaches have also been criticised for failing to take due account of the role of tacit knowledge and other informal information resources which may be very important in shaping economic growth. Besides, they generally fail to address the qualitative values of diversity and pluralism when it comes to the cultural and symbolic realms of information.

Babe has also argued that whilst new technological platforms change the capacity for storing and transmitting symbols and may facilitate the

increasing commoditisation of symbolic artefacts, few if any of the quantitative measures used by economists touch directly upon the informational
content which gives the 'hardware' most of its value (Babe, 1995). This
overlaps with the criticism of Roszak and others concerning the tendency of
many quantitative approaches to reduce information simply to whatever
can be encoded for transmission through a channel or carrier (1986). The
result is that information is emptied of any actual semantic content or meaning and that many of the most important social and cultural dimensions of
information production and exchange are simply ignored or dismissed from
consideration altogether (Boulding, 1971; Roszak, 1986; Babe, 1995). The
crucial social, economic and labour processes involved in the production,
distribution, communication and consumption of information simply disappear from the equation. For many types of social and economic inquiry, these
quantitative efforts at 'valuing the invaluable' may simply replicate the errors
of the counting of bits and bytes inherent in quantitative engineering models
of communication. Whilst these may be useful for electronic communications engineers or corporate planners, they end up defining and measuring
information in essentially non-social terms and non-economic terms. In this
sense, there is a danger that information (and not simply technology) tends
to end up being reified, defined as a thing or autonomous force for change,
in response to which society must simply adjust to its consequences (Webster,
1995: 25–8; Schement and Curtis, 1995). In the end, it is simply a case of
reinventing anew the old problem of crude economistic thinking which, to
echo the words of Oscar Wilde, 'knows the price of everything but the value
of nothing'.

INFORMATION-TEMPERED TIMES

As noted above, Machlup used the term 'socially new knowledge' to refer to
'knowledge that is new, that has not been known by anyone before' (1962:
7–8). In terms of this criterion, his own conceptual and empirical work on
the changing role and organisation of information work and services merits
the academic equivalent of an 'Oscar' for the production of 'socially new
knowledge'. Since its publication, a very large and diverse number of theories and studies of socio-economic change have been influenced, either
directly or indirectly, by readings of this pioneering information sector study.
Machlup's original work remains a key starting point for many of the subsequent 'information society' theories, including the more recent spate of
related policy and research initiatives which have been such a prominent feature in the latter half of the 1990s. But Machlup's work merits this particular
'Oscar' for reasons other than its blockbuster (in academic terms) influence

on subsequent work. For one thing, much of the latter make claims and assumptions which fit very uneasily with those advanced by Machlup himself. This suggests that the majority of both proponents and critics simply read the reviews rather than attended to the original production. More importantly, his work is informed by a breadth of interdisciplinary perspectives, intellectual rigour, challenging ideas and nuanced analysis which few other subsequent information-centred studies begin to approximate. For these reasons, it was and remains a genuinely seminal work. Alongside Mills' *White Collar*, it merits an important place in the history of ideas relevant to the changing organisation and role of information in contemporary society, not least because it stimulates many negative as well as positive responses to the multitude of ideas it contains.

Drawing towards a conclusion to this chapter, I would suggest that the above-mentioned criticisms raise important flaws and objections with respect to the coherence of the information sector studies examined. But I would suggest that they are less valid in the case of Machlup's contribution which advances a much more nuanced approach to knowledge production and the diversity of information work and its outputs compared to many subsequent works. His writings are much more explicitly sensitive to the diversity of information flows, forms and their roles. His typologies deserve closer attention than hitherto from researchers concerned with understanding changes in (instrumental and symbolic) information activities and communication processes. Even if he does not place much emphasis on public communication activities, Machlup's concepts, typologies and attempts to map the many other types of knowledge and information have the potential to complement the traditional concerns of institutional political economy and critical theories of communication such as those of Habermas. Thus in sum, Machlup's work, like that of Mills, deserves much closer attention than it has received in subsequent contributions to the literature on information-centred analyses of the changing division of labour.

This particular archaeology of information-centred approaches to the changing division of labour suggests further that Machlup's work resonates much more closely with the dominant tempers and perceptions of our own times than was the case when he first launched his pioneering studies four decades ago. Indeed viewed from the perspective of the new millennium, it is remarkable how the core idea of a shift towards increasingly information-intensive economic and social structures has become so pervasive and normalised over the past thirty to forty years, even amongst writers who give Machlup's work little more than a passing mention. Here I have in mind the recent work of many postmodernist and other cultural theorists, including those discussed in Chapter Five, as well as work of other writers advancing intellectually challenging analyses of social and economic change who, however, refuse to embrace the information society thesis to which I now turn in Chapter Four.

1 This was the period which marked the emergence of organised industrial 'research and development' laboratories and other aspects of a new systematic approach to the application of science and technology for industrial purposes. This was linked to new ideas and practices centered around the 'enclosure' of scientific and technical and other forms of information as 'private' (intellectual) property. Secondly, it should be noted that this was also the period when electricity first emerged as a major new technology system with pervasive applications potential (Hall and Preston, 1988). It is worth noting briefly some parallels between the prevailing conceptions of electricity and information in both periods. In some influential contributions to the more recent literature which focuses on information as a key feature and driver of social change, information (and its new supporting networks and infrastructures) is often endowed with more than technical properties or functional powers. Indeed, as Kumar and others have pointed out, in some of these influential accounts, not only is information treated as an abstract force which is independent of the institutional context of its production and use, it is accorded some bizzarely mystical or magical qualities with respect to its implications for all pervasive social and cultural change (1996: 14–16). But the point I wish to make here is that it is done in a manner that has many echoes, if not direct parallels, with certain conceptions of electricity as an omnipotent 'invisible', 'ethereal' or 'etheric' fluid with major ramifications for social and cultural change which were advanced on the eve of the twentieth century.

2 Unfortunately, space will not permit the exploration of one other fruitful sub-plot in the narrative at this stage. This concerns the short duration of Daniel Bell's 'first coming' as a prominent social theorist and the nature and reasons for his retreat from this role with the (relatively brief) rise of the fashion for more critical sociological theory later in the 1960s and the ensuing attacks on his core claims and assumptions. A close reading suggests that aspects of this experience inform the content and sharpness of some critical passages in the key texts produced during the period of his 'second coming' which was centred around his post-industrial and information society theories (1973 and 1976).

3 Mills' *White Collar* was originally published in 1951.

4 The ITAP report was also a major factor shaping the development of the Programme on Information and Communication Technologies (PICT), the major UK research programme focused on the economic, social and policy aspects of new ICT which was launched by the Economic and Social Research Council in the mid-1980s. The PICT programme was based around interdisciplinary research centres in six UK universities and a central co-ordinating unit. Some of my research and ideas which inform this book originated during a two-year period as a Research Associate to the founding Director of the Programme, Professor William H. Melody.

5 Conceptually at least, Machlup's work is an exception to this general tendency.

CHAPTER FOUR

'INFORMATION SOCIETY' THEORIES

> 'The axial principle . . . is the centrality of theoretical knowledge and its
> new role, when codified, as the director of social change . . . If one com-
> pares the formal properties of postindustrial society with those of
> industrial and preindustrial society . . . the crucial variables . . . are
> information and knowledge.'
>
> (Bell, 1980: 501 and 504)

FROM INFORMATION 'SECTOR' TO 'SOCIETY'

Not least because of the complex role of formal and informal communication processes which underpin any scientific or sociological research
endeavour, the initial temporal and spatial origins of the information society
idea are a matter of some dispute. In any case, given the varying uses and definitions of the key term, not to mention those of parallel notions such as
informatisation or indeed *post-industrialism*, any linear search for the precise
origins is somewhat pointless. Thus for present purposes, we may simply note
that the idea of an information society appears to have emerged simultaneously in North America, Western Europe and Japan between the late 1960s
and the late 1970s. It builds upon the empirical studies of quantitative
changes in the role of information work and knowledge production which
were examined in the last chapter. But it borrows and amends the more
descriptive analyses to argue that such quantitative trends in the division of
labour imply qualitative shifts towards fundamentally new social forms and
political-economic structures. It also shares many common features with the
'third-wave' technology-centred theories which became popular at this time
as described earlier.

A considerable body of new work emphasising the disruptive impacts of
the changing role and organisation of knowledge began to emerge in Europe
from the 1960s (Bohme, 1997). Here the term *informatisation* was occasionally used to describe shifts in socio-economic structures similar to those
proposed by information society theorists (e.g. Nora and Minc, 1980;
Altenpohl, 1985). In the USA, management guru Peter Drucker suggested in
The Age of Discontinuity (1968) that the modern economy had evolved
into a distinctively new kind of knowledge economy and that information

and organisation are the prime creators of wealth (Drucker, 1968). By the late 1970s and early 1980s the information society notion had entered the discourses of industrial, research and policy circles in the USA (Dizard, 1982; NTIA, 1988). In Britain, Tom Stonier's *Wealth of Information* (1983) advanced a rather utopian vision of a radically new social and economic order based on the synergy of new knowledge and information structures alongside new ICTs and biological technologies. Umesao was one of the earliest writers to advance an explicit notion of 'informatisation' in Japan and the Japanese government quickly popularised the idea (Ito, 1981, 1991; Braman, 1997: 16–17). Another more widely-known Japanese proponent of the information society was Yoneji Masuda whose work was published widely in Europe and North America (1980, 1985). Like others, he adopted an evolutionary approach to the emergence of an information economy, viewing it as the latest stage in the development of advanced societies, following the agricultural and industrial stages.

In the Anglophone world, Daniel Bell emerged as one of the more influential early writers to advance a comprehensive theory of fundamental change in social and industrial structures focused on the changing role and characteristics of knowledge and information. Already an established and prominent sociologist in the USA, his was clearly the most formidable, coherent and articulate account of the information society with respect to the traditional concerns of the social and cultural studies disciplines (Schement and Curtis, 1995; Webster, 1995; Kumar, 1996). Unlike that of Masuda, Stonier or other advocates of the information society thesis, his work explicitly engages with the theories, concepts and methods directly related to the study of socio-economic change since the Enlightenment era and therefore could be considered the most 'intellectually robust'. With this in mind, I will zoom in on his work in order to explore the key claims, concerns and merits of the information society thesis. However, in addition to the academic theorists, this chapter will also briefly consider the surge of interest in notions of 'an information society' which has been such a prominent feature amongst influential sections of the political and industrial élite since the early 1990s.

DANIEL BELL'S 'INFORMATION SOCIETY' THEORY

In a major and influential work published in 1973 – and which he defined as an 'essay in social forecasting' – Daniel Bell claimed that 'in the next thirty to fifty years we will see the emergence of what I have called "the post-industrial society"' (1973: x). Although Bell here used the term 'post-industrial' to describe what he viewed as an emerging new social order, he later used the term 'information society' to describe these very same phenomena. For him, both concepts were interchangeable and addressed the sense that in Western society we are 'in the midst of a vast historical change' in which old social relations (which were property bound), existing power structures (centred on established élites), and bourgeois culture (based on notions of restraint and delayed gratification) 'are being rapidly eroded' (Bell, 1973: 37). Bell claims that, irrespective of the particular term used, the sources of the perceived historical upheaval in social and economic processes are scientific and technological, but he adds that they are also cultural. He stresses that culture has achieved autonomy in Western society (1973: 37) and this became the central theme of his next major work (1976).

In discussing the origins of his ideas and key influences, Bell generally constructs a very specific account of the relevant literature, one that is fully in keeping with his role as an influential and politically conservative social theorist in the USA context, as noted earlier (Frankel, 1987: 5). He indicates that his key concern with the changing role of technical decision-making in society was implicit in his first major work, *The End of Ideology* (1960). Other intellectual influences cited by Bell himself include the work of Joseph Schumpeter which he reads as emphasising 'technology as an open sea'. One other major work in Bell's acknowledged inventory of influences was an essay by the physicist and historian of science, Gerald Holton. For Bell, this essay illuminated the significance of theoretical knowledge in its changing relation to technology, and the codification of theory as the basis for innovation not only in science but also in technology and economic policy as well (Bell, 1973: 35).

Although much of Bell's empirical references centre on the US developments, the stated object of his analysis is 'Western' industrial society and its emerging transformation. Indeed, he suggests that 'industrial society' is a concept that embraces the experiences of a dozen different countries and one which cuts across the contrasting political systems of such different societies as the United States and the Soviet Union. For Bell, industrial society has been essentially organised around the axis of production and machinery, for the fabrication of goods. He contrasts this with pre-industrial society which was dependent on raw labour power and the extraction of primary resources from nature. He suggests that in its 'rhythm of life' and organisation of work, *industrial society* is the defining feature of the social structure of modern Western society. For starters then, we may note that this particular periodisation is similar to that of third-wave theorists, and represents a much reduced historical schema or typology of social systems compared to that of Adam Smith and Karl Marx.

In Bell's schema, modern society is divided into three parts and each is ruled by a different axial principle. First, there is the social structure which comprises the economy, technology and the occupational or stratification systems[1] (Bell, 1973: x–xi, 12–13). He says that in modern Western society,

65

the predominant axial principle of the social structure is *economising* – a way of allocating resources according to principles of least cost, substitutability, optimisation and maximisation. The second part is the polity, which in Bell's schema regulates the distribution of power and adjudicates the conflicting claims and demands of individuals and groups. He says that the axial principle of the modern polity is *participation* and this may be sometimes mobilised or controlled and sometimes subject to demands and pressures from below. The third part in Bell's schema is 'the culture' which refers to the realm of expressive symbolism and meanings. He says that the axial principle of the culture is the desire for the *fulfilment and enhancement of the self.* He further claims that in the past these three areas of society were linked by a common value system (and in bourgeois society through 'a common character structure') but in more recent times there has been an increasing disjunction of the three, emphasising that this is widening (Bell, 1973: 12–13). Thus, despite his frequent stress on 'axial principles' of the industrial and information social formations Bell declares his opposition to a holistic view of society. Furthermore he repeatedly stresses that the social structure is analytically separate from the two other dimensions of society, the polity and the culture.

Moving on to more substantive elements, Bell's model of an emerging post-industrial or information society suggests a change in the social structure, the consequences of which will vary in societies with different political and cultural configurations. But he also claims that as a social form, this will constitute a major feature of the social structures of the United States, Japan, the Soviet Union, and Western Europe over the following thirty to fifty years (Bell, 1973: x). According to Bell, the most significant characteristics of the emerging information society comprise the following:

a) The change from a goods-producing to a service society; including a particularly rapid growth of 'health, education, research and government services' and high-tech industries.

b) The centrality of the codification of *theoretical knowledge* as the source of innovation in technology and policy formation; IBM is 'the paradigmatic corporation' of the science-based industries at the end of the twentieth century; the university is 'the primary institution of the post-industrial society'.

c) The (related) creation of 'a new "*intellectual technology*" as a key tool of systems analysis and decision theory' based on new theoretical knowledge, computerisation, formal rules and procedures; it involves new methods which 'seek to substitute an alogrithm (i.e. decision rules) for intuitive judgements'; it involves the codification of knowledge into abstract systems of symbols and the primacy of theory over empiricism (in addition, the computer has made new economic models, large-scale planning and conscious decision-making more possible: the 'management of complexity').

d) The strengthened role of science and cognitive values as a basic institutional necessity of the society.

e) The tendency to make decisions more technical brings scientific or economic experts more directly into the political process; the growing role of service professionals favours a declining role of the market mechanism and the negative effects of its fluctuations and insecurities; shifts from an 'economising' towards a 'sociologising' ethos.

f) The deepening of existing tendencies toward the bureaucratisation of intellectual work may create strains for the traditional definitions of intellectual pursuits and values.

g) These changes are further promoting a more meritocratic system, where rewards and power are based on merit (due to the erosion of the importance of wealth or property based inequalities).

h) The creation and expansion of a technical intelligentsia raises crucial questions about the relation of the technical to the literary intellectual. (Bell, 1973; 43–4)

For Bell, one of the key changes in social structure concerns the rapid growth of professional and technical employment in recent decades. Jobs which usually required a college education grew at a rate twice that of the average since the early 1950s and he suggests that this will continue. He particularly emphasises the changing role and influence of the scientists and engineers whose rate of growth has been triple that of the working population. He further suggests that the significance of this group's changing role is not simply a matter of quantitative growth, but that these form 'the key group in the post-industrial society' (Bell, 1973: 17).

Bell argues that in a post-industrial society the emphasis is on a specific set of services: health, education, research, and government services. It is precisely the growth of this fourth services category 'which is decisive for post-industrial society'. This is 'the category that represents the growth of a new intelligentsia – in universities, research organisations, professions and government' (Bell, 1973: 15).

Bell recognises that knowledge has been necessary in the functioning of any society, but what is distinctive about the post-industrial or information society for him is 'the change in the character of knowledge itself' and especially the growing role of *theoretical knowledge*. This new society is increasingly organised around knowledge, especially for the purpose of social control and the directing of innovation and change. He claims that this in turn gives rise to new social relationships and new structures which have to be managed politically. He suggests that in contrast, industrial society has been centrally concerned with 'the coordination of machines and men for the production of goods' (Bell, 1973: 20). Bell stresses that since the information society increases the importance of the technical component of knowledge, 'it forces the hierophants of the new society' (the scientists, engineers, and technocrats) either to compete with politicians or become their allies (Bell, 1973: 13).

One feature of industrial society is the increasing bureaucratisation of science and the increasing specialisation of intellectual work into minute parts. For Bell, it is unlikely that individuals entering science will accept this segmentation and he claims that this is unlike the individuals who entered the factory system a hundred and fifty years ago (Bell, 1973: 13). His model asserts that the inequalities of wealth or power previously associated with capitalist property relations are becoming of much less significance in a knowledge-centred meritocratic order. Furthermore, Bell argues that new modes of life, which depend strongly on the primacy of cognitive and theoretical knowledge, inevitably challenge the tendencies of the culture sphere which strives for the enhancement of the self. He suggests that the culture sphere turns increasingly antinomian and anti-institutional – the central theme of his later work *The Cultural Contradictions of Capitalism* (1976).

Bell points to new aspects of space/time compression and its relation to the themes of knowledge and new (especially transportation and communication) technologies in the emerging information society (1973: 165–200). He suggests that there is much confusion about these questions, including issues to do with the pace of change in these two variables. Rather surprisingly, perhaps, he suggests that in terms of technology, many of the more substantial changes were introduced into the lives of individuals in the nineteenth century (by the railroad, steamship, electricity, and telephone), and in the early twentieth century (by radio, automobiles, motion pictures, aviation, high-speed vertical elevators). He suggests that these earlier technologies may be more important than television or computers – the main new technological items introduced in the twenty-five years prior to his writing the book (Bell, 1973: 42). This claim runs counter to those advanced by many other writers, not to mention his own stress on the important role of computers in this same book and elsewhere. For example he has claimed that the computer is the key symbol of the information society and that 'the computer has been the "analytical engine" that has transformed the second half of the twentieth century' (1980: 509).

'THE CULTURAL CONTRADICTIONS OF CAPITALISM'

According to Bell's three-part schema, 'the culture' refers to the realm of expressive symbolism and meanings where the axial principle is the desire for the fulfilment and enhancement of the self. He also repeatedly insists that the three spheres are to be viewed as largely autonomous and he pointed to an increasing disjunction of the three spheres, emphasising that this is widening

(Bell, 1973: 12–13). In *The Cultural Contradictions of Capitalism* (1976), Bell focuses on contradictions or disjunctions between the kind of organisation and the norms demanded in the economic realm or social structure, on the one hand, and the norms of self-realisation that are central in the culture sphere, on the other. In essence, this book explores Bell's concerns about growing tensions between the principles underlying the economic realm and those informing the realm of culture which, he claims, lead the actors and social groups involved in contrary directions (1976: 13–15).

Bell believes that in nineteenth-century bourgeois society, the culture, character structure and economy were integrated and infused by a single value system. But all of this had now changed: 'ironically, all this was undermined by capitalism itself' *(1973: 477)*. Through mass production and mass consumption, capitalism had destroyed the Protestant ethic by zealously promoting a hedonistic way of life. He suggested that by the middle of the twentieth century, capitalism sought to justify itself not by work or property but by the status badges of material possessions and by the promotion of pleasure. Rising standards of living and the relaxation of morals had become ends in themselves and the very definition of personal freedom and achievement. For Bell, this had resulted in 'a disjuncture within the social structure itself' (1973: 477). He suggested that contemporary culture, in its concern with the self, combines the 'deepest wellsprings of human impulse' with the modern(ist) antipathy to bourgeois society. He is worried that 'the lack of a rooted moral belief system' is the cultural contradiction of the society; the 'deepest challenge to its survival' (Bell, 1973: 480).

Bell insists that culture is now autonomous and has 'clearly become supreme' and he suggests that what is played out in the imagination of the artist 'foreshadows, however dimly, the social reality of tomorrow' (Bell, 1976: 33). He also stresses the fundamental changes in the relation of the artist to the public, claiming that the *avant-garde* artist usually now dominates the cultural scene: 'it is he who swiftly shapes the audience and the market, rather than being shaped by them' (Bell, 1976: 39). He suggests that culture (more specifically its predominant current, modernism) has triumphed over a society that in its social structure (economics, technology and occupational bases) remains bourgeois: 'the culture has become detached and self-determining' (1976: 40). In Bell's account, the advocates of this adversary culture now constitute a distinct cultural class, due to a number of extraordinary changes. Bell adds that 'what is singular about this "tradition of the new" . . . is that it allows art to be unfettered, to break down all genres and to explore all modes of experience and sensation' (Bell, 1976: 34).

In a section on postmodernism, Bell states that it has carried the logic of modernism to its farthest reaches. He suggests that against the aesthetic justification for life, postmodernism has 'completely substituted the instinctual' so that only 'impulse and pleasure' are real and life-affirming; and all else is neurosis and death (1976: 51). He suggests that 'postmodernism overflows the vessels of art' as it tears down the boundaries and insists that *acting out,* rather than making distinctions, is the way to gain knowledge (Bell, 1976: 52) . One effect of all this is that the traditional bourgeois organisation of life, its rationalism and sobriety, now has few defenders in the culture (realm). Besides, Bell is also concerned about the perceived absence of an established system of cultural meanings or stylistic forms with any intellectual or cultural respectability (Bell, 1976: 53).

A BLURRED AND OUTDATED TECHNOCRATIC VISION

The more utopian information society theorists such as Masuda, and to a lesser extent Stonier, tend to treat information in terms of its abstract inherent characteristics, in total isolation from the institutional context in which it is produced, distributed or consumed. The emphasis falls on the 'public good' characteristics of information (non-exclusivity of consumption, etc.) in a manner which simply ignores the concrete economic and political context of its production, accessibility and regulation. There is a total failure to address the long-run tendencies in capitalist industrialism to 'enclose' information behind intellectual property rights, to treat it as a privately owned and controlled resource or to regulate (or restrict) access via commodity exchange relations. They also neglect the major extension of such tendencies in more recent times, marked by the increasing stress on 'making a business of information' on the part of the economic and political élites internationally. Thus the key sources of the increasing market/exchange 'value' of information (increasing commodification, intellectual property rights, new subscriber payment systems, technology-carrier obsolescence, etc.), which are highlighted in the 1990s information society policy initiatives, are simply assumed away in the mystical haze surrounding the crystal ball of Masuda and Stonier and other such information theorists. In essence, these theorists (and some of this applies to Bell too) neglect the processes of expanded commodification of information – the very trends which have made the information economy and communication industries such a 'sexy' area for investors in recent decades.

Daniel Bell certainly advances a much more grounded and challenging theory compared to Masuda and Stonier or third-wave theorists. He is the most formidable and informed proponent of the information society thesis with respect to engagement with the established social science methods, concepts and literature concerning the dynamics of social change. These and other considerations mean that Bell does not soar to the utopian and mystical dreamware of fellow travellers such as Toffler and Masuda. But his essay in 'social forecasting' nevertheless paints an extremely optimistic and positive picture of the new socio-economic and political order that he claims to be emerging out of the capitalist industrial order at the close of the twentieth century. The overall image is one of ever-increasing material abundance and welfare for all sections of a meritocratic society where the old inequalities and privileges associated with ownership and control of property have somehow disappeared. At times however, he strikes a highly conservative and pessimistic tone concerning the realm of culture and its perceived threats to a new increasingly rational and knowledge-based socio-economic order.

So the key question is whether all of this amounts to an adequate theory of social change and development to support the significant claim that we are moving to a new information society that is not only post-industrial but also post-capitalist. Like many earlier critics of Bell's work, I think the answer to this question must be firmly in the negative. For in every usual sense of the word, this is a very partial analysis of both the essential features of capitalist industrialism as a distinct mode of production as it emerged from feudalism in the European context, and of the key trends and counter-tendencies evident in its development in the latter half of the twentieth century. Not only do most of the distinctive social relations of capitalism disappear from the technocratic vision of the new post-industrial information society but they are also glossed out of this version of the preceding industrial and social orders. What disappears is the complex mosaic of forces and conflicts involved in the extension of capitalist property rights, the cycles of competition and 'gales of creative destruction' involved in periods of intensified crises and a restructuring of the industrial and occupational division of labour. The focus on selective aspects of the organisation and forces of production eliminates the social relations of production, as described not only by Marx and other critical political economists but also by Joseph Schumpeter. Bell cites the latter as a major intellectual support for his own work, yet Schumpeter's works and key concepts are barely mentioned, let alone explored and harnessed throughout the 489 pages of Bell's *The Coming of the Post-Industrial Society* (1973). A fuller engagement with Schumpeter's might have led to a much more historically grounded and less dramatic or 'apocalyptic' vision of change[2] and served to modify the heavy hand of Saint-Simon in guiding this thesis.[3] After all, Bell has declared his desire to oppose 'apocalyptic' approaches in favour of more empirically testable alternatives (Bell, 1976).

To a great extent, Bell's thesis about the coming of a qualitative new social form rests on the quantitative growth of rational/instrumental information occupations and services, especially the expansion of professional occupations and functional roles in scientific and engineering fields. But as argued earlier, such trends of change in the division of labour do not provide anything like sufficient grounds for claiming a shift to a new social order. His thesis also depends on idealistic assumptions concerning the autonomy of specific forms of theoretical knowledge and the insulation of information work from the economic and political setting in which it is located. In this regard, his assumptions about the declining salience of the market (economistic rationality) seem not only misguided, but quaintly old-fashioned and dated when viewed from the vantage point of more than two decades of neo-liberalism. Besides, Bell's notion of the rise of a new form of 'theoretical knowledge' has also been subjected to criticism. One matter here is the uncertainty as to what precisely this key term means for him. The problem is that Bell appears to utilise the notion of new 'theoretical knowledge' with three very different meanings or implied definitions, which is no small matter as it renders comprehension as well as evaluation of his thesis more difficult (Webster, 1995). One can also point to some other problems with the historical basis of Bell's theory, including its historical account of shifts in the role of scientific and technological knowledge (1973: 501–2). For example, the important shift from 'talented tinkering' did not begin in the last half of twentieth century as his work assumes.

To sum up, Bell's one-sided account of how the quantitative growth of specialised technical knowledge and other information services serves to transform the capitalist socio-economic order simply ignores another, at least equally logical and feasible possibility. It neglects the possibility that what has been happening is precisely the extended industrialisation and commodification (as well as bureaucratisation) of knowledge functions and services. Indeed, as Mills suggested in *White Collar* (1956a) and as the discussion in later chapters will argue further, the society that is now embarking on a new millennium 'is in no sense post-industrial'. Rather it is best viewed as 'a specific and probably absolute climax of industrialism itself' (Williams, 1983: 93).

It should now be clear too that in identifying Bell as the most intellectually challenging theorist of the information society, it is not possible or viable to consider only the force of his more 'technical' arguments as a prominent and well-read social scientist. In evaluating his work, one must also explicitly recognise that any 'essay in social forecasting' is as much concerned with prescription as with description. Furthermore it is clear that, despite all his declarations about 'the exhaustion of political passions' in *The End of Ideology* (1960) and later work, Bell is neither a value-free technical analyst nor some kind of political eunuch (as his own model of the theory production might seem to imply). For one thing, as Jameson reminds us, in the social and cultural/linguistic context of the 1950s, the term 'ideology' meant socialism or Marxism or any other attempt to create a radically different social order in the USA (1991: 159–60). For another, Bell has been an extremely influential as well as 'emotional and expressive' participant in the key political disputes and conflicts of our time. In particular, he has been an active participant in the intellectual endeavours which have informed and sustained the neo-liberal or neo-conservative political project for almost three decades.

By way of conclusion, it is relevant to note here that there is nothing really new in pointing to the key role of knowledge and learning in capitalist economic development. This applies to Smith's *Wealth of Nations*, the foundation work on the sources of material abundance in capitalist industrialism, just as it was also a key theme in debates about the conditions and sources of 'progress' throughout the nineteenth century (Freeman, 1995). Besides the division of labour, Smith saw very clearly that the major sources of the increase in the productive powers of labour, 'which is what we mean by economic development . . . all involve the knowledge process' (Boulding, 1971: 27). Information society theorists tend to pay passing references and homage to *The Wealth of Nations* as an intellectual support for their own endeavours. Yet, they essentially ignore this particular reading of Smith's seminal political economy text, much like the now dominant neo-classical and neo-liberal schools of economic theory. This little history lesson may serve to question not only the need for 'a new information theory of wealth creation' or any new 'knowledge theory of value' (Bell, 1980; Stonier, 1983; Kelly, 1998). It also questions the potential of such information society theorists to provide convincing maps that can sketch the key contours of capitalist economic and social developments as we enter the new millennium.

THE SURGE OF 'INFORMATION SOCIETY' POLICY INITIATIVES IN THE 1990s

Notwithstanding the above (and the many prior) criticisms of information society theory, there has been a surge of interest in the idea of an emerging 'information society' amongst influential segments of the industrial and political élites throughout the advanced capitalist world since the early 1990s. As noted earlier, national governments in every continent as well as the European Union and other international policy organisations (such as the Group of Seven and the OECD) have launched countless research and policy initiatives centred around the notion of an information society over the past five or more years.

The growing popularity of the 'information society' idea in the international policy realm in the 1990s must be addressed as an important contemporary development and one whose origins, meaning and implications deserve some attention from social and cultural theorists. This recent surge of interest on the part of industrial and policy élites is often seen to have been triggered by the Clinton/Gore national information infrastructure initiatives of the early 1990s. But the diffusion and popularity of this notion in so many national settings cannot be understood as simply a matter of the US government's belated success in 'exporting the information society' idea internationally to meet economic policy goals. For sure, some US foreign policy strategists in the early 1980s argued that this would serve to 'amplify

American ideas and values in a more forceful way than has ever been done before' (Dizard, 1982: 148–9). But an understanding of the origins and meaning of this universal phenomenon must move beyond conspiracy theory to embrace a more sociologically grounded approach. Such an analysis needs to address the *internal* political shifts and changing economic conditions affecting so many different national or regional settings in the 1990s (to which I shall return).

In the practical policy realm, the notion of an 'information society' has been adopted by certain industrial and policy élites to describe a set of policy initiatives which appear to be more directly concerned with technology, or infrastructures, than they are with information or social issues. These strategies generally involve a primary emphasis on the inherent technical benefits of new ICTs and on promoting the maximum use and adoption of such technologies for industrial or individual 'competitiveness'. They also involve a familiar if very particular and technocratic vision of society and the processes of change. Their understanding of what constitutes 'information' (as goods, service and resource) and knowledge and its relation to socio-economic wealth, welfare and well-being is very partial and specific. As attempts to theorise socio-economic and cultural change, they are stamped by a certain failure of intellectual rigour or imaginative flair compared to the earlier academic theories.

Essentially, they start off and end up confusing ends with means. They are usually framed in instrumental economistic fashion as serving the strategic goal of increasing international competitiveness at a time of 'profound' technology-driven transformations, including the new god of 'globalisation'. In terms of practical action, they are predominantly focused on increasing the pace and scale of production and adoption of new ICT products and services. This may well help to further expand the profits, sales and markets of new ICT industries and the related high-tech sectors, whose industrial élites, it just so happens, have played a key role in many national 'information society' policy-making bodies. But it fails to address the wider public interest issues involved in developing a progressive strategy for social and economic development at the close of the twentieth century.

The utterly impoverished and narrowly conservative 'vision' of these information society policy initiatives is marked by one key irony: on the one hand they extol the revolutionary power or potential of new ICTs to transform social and economic relations; yet, on the other hand, they combine this 'vision' with an extremely conservative set of 'market-driven' political-economic and cultural orientations and values (Preston, 1994, 1995, 1996a).

This feature, more than the intellectual rigour of Daniel Bell or any other information society theorist, provides a more grounded understanding of the origins and meaning of the popularity of information society discourses in the 1990s, as we will see later. In essence these information society initiatives provide a happy meeting ground, or an especially convenient 'strategic alliance', between the specific economic interests and élites of the ICT-producing sectors and 'leading- edge' industrial users (such as financial firms) on the one hand, and the narrowly economistic orientations and productivist values of the neo-liberal political élites on the other hand. The result is an inversion of the progressive modernist visions of the relationship of technology to social and economic 'progress'. The latter viewed technology as an important support or means to the realisation of politically or collectively defined social and economic goals. In contrast, the production, diffusion and consumption of new technology-based commodified products becomes the singular end and measure of progress and social development in such visions of 'the information society'.

Indeed, despite (and precisely because of) the current fashions for such information society discourses, the academic theories must also be held up to further critical scrutiny in terms of their adequacy both as guides to understanding and action, whether by politicians, ordinary citizens, workers, consumers or other interests. For one thing, it should be stressed that since the notion of the 'information society' was first advanced more than twenty years ago, it has been very widely and sharply criticised by academic researchers. This critical response came from those located on Bell's disciplinary home turf (sociology) and from those based in the political economy of communication and critical cultural studies fields (Garnham, 1981; Williams, 1983; Melody, 1985; Bannon et al., 1981). Indeed, the overwhelming drift of academic debate on the matter was highly critical of the kind of information society thesis advanced by Bell, Masuda and others.

Hence, the current keen interest in the concept of an information society notion amongst influential industrial and policy élites has emerged despite (rather than because of) the general thrust and trends of 'theoretical knowledge' production in these particular domains. Ironically, its popularity invites further challenges concerning the substantive adequacy of the original academic information society theories. The rise of the information society idea in the face of a major stream of criticism poses interesting questions about the power and force of (at least, some) 'theoretical knowledge'. This failure might be taken to indicate that, despite Bell's assertions, the degree of autonomy and 'power' possessed by the relevant knowledge workers in the so-called information age is relatively minor. Alternatively, it suggests that some varieties of 'theoretical knowledge' or 'information' power are more autonomous, powerful and influential amongst the political and economic élites who count. These suggested alternatives, in turn, point to doubts about the 'the end of ideology' theses which have underpinned Daniel Bell's work from the outset.

This chapter has largely been devoted to theories of an emerging information society, in particular that advanced by Daniel Bell. These have been criticised for failing to provide a convincing account of a supposed transition to a post-capitalist and post-industrial social order. These information society theories have been almost exclusively focused on scientific, technical and other specialised information; they have relatively little to say about the consumption sphere, or the changing role and characteristics of cultural or symbolic information structures and flows. Indeed, the changing role of information services related to final consumers or citizens receives little attention compared to technological and other specialised (producer) information services in the work of most prominent information society theorists. For example, analysis of the changing roles and functions of the mass media is confined to two pages in the almost five hundred pages comprising Daniel Bell's *The Coming of the Post-Industrial Society*, and the nine pages of its subject index do not contain any listings for key terms such as advertising, television, newspapers or telecommunications. The situation is only marginally better in the 280 pages of text in his subsequent work explicitly focused on the realm of culture. By any standards, it is quite remarkable that any serious study focusing on an expanding information sector or emerging information society should neglect this dimension and it is a particularly noteworthy *lacuna* given the concerns of this particular book.

This neglect is in strong contrast to the spate of parallel studies in communication and cultural studies fields which have focused precisely on the rapid growth of information goods and services in the sphere of everyday life outside the workplace setting. As indicated in the next chapter, this body of writings, especially those of a postmodernist persuasion, have stressed the pervasive growth of the mass media, the growing informational and symbolic content of all sorts of consumer goods and services and pointed to a veritable explosion of *signification* or information in the sphere of consumption or everyday life. Whilst many of these may tend to neglect the kinds of specialised, producer information activities stressed by Bell, he in turn neglects the issues highlighted in these more media-centric approaches. Yet as we will see, both Bell and some of these other theorists arrive at some remarkably similar ideas concerning the emergence of a new information-based social and economic order.

Notes

1   Bell also suggests that 'when used statically', the phrases 'industrial society' and 'capitalism' may be inadequate, because they do not refer to fixed social forms. For example, he says that the industrial society of the twentieth century, with its dependence on technology and science, is very different from the manufacturing society of the previous two centuries (Bell, 1973: x).

2   However, by the mid-1980s, Bell seems to have been more willing to acknowledge the value of the neo-Schumpeterian long-wave perspective (personal communication with the present author).

3   After all, although not cited as an intellectual guide, Saint-Simon gets more citation in Bell's index of names than Schumpeter, for example.

CHAPTER FIVE

CULTURE AND INFORMATION: POSTMODERNISMS AND THE PUBLIC SPHERE

> 'We might speak here of a kind of "event strike" . . . That the work of history has ceased to function . . . That the information system is taking over the baton from History and starting to produce the event . . . This is the point . . . where events do not really take place precisely because they are produced and broadcast "in real time", where they have no meaning because they can have all possible meanings. We have, therefore, to grasp them now . . . *at the point where they become lost in the void of information.*'
>
> (Baudrillard, 1998: emphasis in the original)

THE 'POSTMODERN TEMPER' IN SOCIAL AND CULTURAL REALMS

Although Daniel Bell's information society theory was very much focused on changes in the scientific and specialised instrumental information sectors, in *The Cultural Contradictions of Capitalism* he addressed the cultural ramifications of 'a powerful current of postmodernism' which was carrying the logic of modernism 'to its farthest reaches' (Bell, 1976: 51). For him, postmodernism represented a cultural tendency which went 'against the aesthetic justification for life' and tended to completely replace it with 'the instinctual', celebrating the view that impulse and pleasure alone are real and life-affirming, all else being defined as neurosis and death. In Bell's view, even the most daring stream of 'traditional modernism' had played out its impulses in the imagination, within the constraints of art and within the ordering principle of aesthetic form. Although it might be subversive of society's prevailing norms, it 'still ranged itself on the side of order' and implicitly, of a rationality of form if not content (1976: 51–2). But, for Bell, postmodernism 'overflows the vessels of art' as it tears down the boundaries and insists that *acting out*, rather than making distinctions, is the way to gain knowledge (Bell, 1976: 52).

For Bell, 'the postmodern temper' in the cultural realm may be defined as a set of loosely associated doctrines, which generally moves in two opposing directions. One is a type of 'negative Hegelianism' in philosophy which, for Bell, was represented by the works of Michel Foucault. The second has a more social or popular form which provides 'the psychological spearhead' for an onslaught on the values and motivational patterns of 'ordinary' behaviour in the name of liberation, eroticism, 'freedom of impulse and the like'. This second more popular form means that a crisis of middle-class values is imminent as there is no longer an *avant-garde*, because 'no one' in postmodern culture is on the side of order or tradition (Bell, 1976: 52–3). In Bell's conceptualisation, this postmodern temper has links to significant changes in the social structure which cancel the traditional sociological assumption that variation in the behaviour of groups of persons is linked to their class or other strategic position in the social structure. In Bell's view, this no longer holds true in many respects.

Bell was not the only early sociological writer to refer to new developments or trends as postmodern. For example, Mills had earlier pointed to an emergent 'postmodern' period but in his account, the term referred to an era marked by a 'retreat from history' (1959: 173–4). Contrary to Bell's concerns, Mills invoked the term to refer to a tendency (in the USA) whereby historical explanation was becoming 'less relevant than for earlier periods' and this would make it more difficult to understand the features of society and social processes. Here, again, Mills strikes a chord which has many direct resonances when it comes to analyses of the contemporary, as his historical amnesia theme crops up in Jameson's characterisation of postmodernism. But the differences between Bell and Mills in this particular matter can be taken as an initial signal of the extreme variations and flexibility of the 'postmodern' label in contemporary discourse.

Of course, much has changed since the publication of Bell's work in 1976 and not only with respect to the fate of the peculiar late-1960s/early 1970s culture of 'happenings' and 'permissive' sexual behaviour and the other social and cultural currents which caused this conservative-minded author so much concern. On the global stage, the Cold War has ended with the demise of the bureaucratic state socialist regimes in Eastern Europe and the internationalisation of capital, corporate structures, trade and cultural relations as well as the migration of people entering a new phase of expansion. But, since then too, the post-war 'great boom' of sustained capitalist economic growth has petered out into a period marked by more erratic but relatively slow growth and mass unemployment has returned to the core capitalist economies on a scale not witnessed since the pre-war era. Many working people now face temporary and increasingly 'flexible' employment contracts as well as stagnant or declining levels of incomes in real or relative terms, reflecting a trend of increasing polarisation of social inequalities in many capitalist industrial economies. Since then too, the post-war Keynesian welfare-state regime has been abolished and replaced by neo-liberalism as the hegemonic practical political economy guiding state policies and the meta-narrative of 'the market' and its mystical 'invisible hand' has been reinstated throughout the capitalist industrial world with all the totalising zeal appropriate to a 'born-again' dogma. Of course, since then too, new 'high-tech' industries have emerged to supply a range of new communication networks, technologies and services and there has been a cluster of new media platforms, consumerist practices and lifestyle trends. There has also been an apparent decline in the legitimacy of the official political institutions and in traditional forms of citizenship identities and practices (e.g. rates of participation in elections). At the same time, a variety of new social movements have emerged and asserted an important role especially in the spheres of feminist, ecological, ethnic and sexual politics.

But this brief, if crude, snapshot of some key changes in the terrain of socio-economic, political and cultural experience is only one dimension of what it means to say that 'much has changed' since Bell authored his account of a new 'postmodern temper' in the 1970s. Of equal if not greater importance in the context of present concerns with the term 'postmodern' is the fact that there has also been a major change in the register of epistemological, methodological and conceptual codes deemed appropriate to address the issues of social and cultural change in the late twentieth century. For the term 'postmodern' poses as many issues about *the how* (how to describe, represent, etc.) as it does about *the what* (the key content or contours or facts) of social and cultural change. In the 1980s and 1990s, postmodernism emerged as a significant term and idea to define both an intellectual movement or particular forms of intellectual practice on the one hand, and changes in the objects or phenomena of concern to intellectual work in many fields, on the other hand. Even if some of the earliest uses of the term referred to the social field (Harvey, 1989; Rose, 1991) it really began to be widely used in the 1960s and 1970s to refer to particular types of artistic and architectural forms or currents. But since the 1980s there has been a veritable explosion of ideas and practices, explicitly defined as postmodern, which have been adopted by a growing number of academic disciplines, a fashion not confined to the social science and humanities fields. These postmodernist ideas have been explicitly mobilised to support some of the technology-centred transformative accounts of the contemporary, including that of Kevin Kelly:

> '. . . as networks rise, the center recedes. It is no coincidence that global networks appear at the same time as the postmodern literary movement. In postmodernism, there is no central authority, no universal dogma, no foundational ethic. The theme of postmodernism in the arts, science and politics . . . results in fragmentation, instability, indeterminacy and uncertainty. This also sums up the net.'
>
> (Kelly, 1998: 159)

In what follows I will not seek to summarise the key contours of either of the two dimensions of the expanding postmodern terrain identified above or the wider 'truly motley crew of strange bedfellows' who have populated it

(Jameson, 1991: xiii).[1] Instead I will zoom in on aspects of the work of a select few influential postmodernist theorists: Jean-François Lyotard, Jean Baudrillard and Fredric Jameson. These are chosen not only because of their prominence as influential postmodernist theorists. They have also made specific analyses of the changing role of information, mass media and communication technologies and their implications for the study of contemporary social and cultural change. I start with Lyotard as he has the closest links with the work examined in the preceding chapters. Besides, Baudrillard and Jameson place a stronger focus on the changing role and place of mass communication flows and the public information sphere. They help us get a better fix on what it means to say that information has become more 'thing-like', especially in the media and cultural sectors since the first 'multi-media revolution' which occurred in the late nineteenth and early twentieth century. Thus their work serves to alter but complement the focus on technology or specialised producer information and the production sphere in the literature examined so far.

Following an explanation of these postmodernist writers, I will move on to the work of Jürgen Habermas who advances a distinctly alternative viewpoint in stressing modernity as an 'incomplete project'. The last section of this chapter will turn to a closely related set of writings focused on the political economy of communication and mass media. Like many recent 'information society' policy initiatives the authors that I highlight have also tended to address the changing economic role and characteristics of the mass media and communication industries. But they are also informed by an explicit social and political perspective which, in sharp contrast to most recent policy approaches, is highly critical of the increasing commodification of information and communication services. These writings also serve to complement the 'post-Fordist' literature which was introduced earlier. This was found to provide a useful initial model in addressing the role of new technologies in the overall processes of economic, industrial and political change in recent decades. But whilst it stresses the more material dimensions of restructuring and the role of instrumental knowledge in this process, it tends to neglect other categories of information. Indeed most of the work considered so far tends to be focused on technology or knowledge in the sphere of production. Thus there is a consequent neglect of the major changes in the character and role of cultural/symbolic information and the domain of consumption. In essence, this chapter seeks to remedy this neglect of the symbolic or cultural dimensions of information and thus much of the work considered here provides important complementary concepts and concerns which are central to the agenda of the present book.

POSTMODERNISMS: A 'MOTLEY CREW OF STRANGE BEDFELLOWS'

Jean-François Lyotard: meta-narratives as 'terroristic'

Prior to his death, Lyotard had published widely in fields ranging from lin-
guistics to psychoanalysis, and in his later work he focused on the issues of
cultural politics where he tended to position himself as a philosopher. But it
was *The Postmodern Condition: A Report on Knowledge* which established
his reputation in the English-speaking world (1984, originally published in
French in 1979) and this is the main work which I will consider here. This
book established Lyotard as one of the most influential French thinkers
(next to Baudrillard) on the postmodernist turn in social and cultural studies in the Anglophone countries.

As its subtitle suggests, *The Postmodern Condition* is focused on the
changing role and characteristics of scientific and technological knowledge in
the twentieth century, rather than on the mass media or cultural information
services. It addresses many of the same phenomena as Bell's *The Coming of
the Post-Industrialist Society*, stressing changes in the roles and structures of
knowledge even if it sometimes presents a different interpretation. Yet,
despite its heavy reliance on familiar post-industrial society notions,
Lyotard's work has had a remarkably strong influence on subsequent work
in relatively distant cultural studies fields. This may be because of its attempt
to draw together strands emerging from the founders of the three most influential ways of thinking about modernity: Marx, Nietzsche, and Saint-Simon
(Callinicos, 1985: 85). Connor, following Jameson, suggests that this may be
because Lyotard's book is positioned at 'a crossroads' where debates surrounding politics, economics and aesthetics intersect (Connor, 1989: 28). But
in my view, the widespread influence of Lyotard's work in the cultural and
social studies arena is due to its particular reading of developments in scientific knowledge which in turn serves to imply additional legitimacy to the
discursive turns in the area of social analysis.

According to Lyotard, 'the status of knowledge is altered as societies
enter what is known as the post-industrial age and cultures enter what is
known as the postmodern age' (Lyotard, 1984: 3). He dates this transformation from the end of the 1950s, but like Bell he states that the pace differs
according to country and sector. For Lyotard, postmodernism is the cultural correlate of a post-industrial society, as capitalist industrialism has
shifted to a post-industrial society in which knowledge has become the prin-
cipal force of production (1984: 5). In Lyotard's work, scientific knowledge
is treated as discourse and this is the key feature which sharply distinguishes
it from Bell's treatment of the post-industrial knowledge structures. Indeed
Lyotard's approach to scientific knowledge as 'a kind of discourse' allows

him to treat it in a deconstructionist manner like other forms of literary or philosophical discourse. In addition, Lyotard also occasionally mixes his deconstructionist view of science (as a form of discourse) with the notion that discourse is something which can be commodified and alienated from its producer. This latter position is not consistently held in Lyotard's analysis, but it occasionally suggests that the analysis sometimes borrows more from Marx than from Bell's depiction of the role of theoretical knowledge as a sort of 'axial principle' for his post-industrial/information society. Besides, Lyotard also occasionally uses other concepts from Marx (such as the distinction between use value and exchange value, alienation and reification) and his complex arguments interweave these with concepts more familiar to liberal and conservative post-industrial social theory (Callinicos, 1985; Rose, 1981).

Lyotard uses the term *modern* to 'designate any science that legitimates itself with reference to a metadiscourse . . . making an explicit appeal to some grand narrative' (1984: 71–2). In this context, Lyotard identifies amongst the 'metanarratives of modernity' the philosophies of Hegel, Marxism, capitalism and the more recent work of Habermas (Connor, 1989; Rose, 1991). For Lyotard, meta-narratives or 'grand narratives' are 'terroristic' as they comprise those narratives which subordinate, organise and account for other local or micro narratives.

Thus Lyotard primarily defines the 'postmodern' in terms of an *incredulity towards meta-narratives*. His approach is strongly marked by a scepticism towards what are termed the 'meta-narratives' of the modern period. Secondly and relatedly, Lyotard also insists that the term postmodernism is to be used to describe 'the condition of knowledge in the most highly developed societies' (Lyotard, 1984: xxiii). Lyotard asserts that the period since World War Two has witnessed a terminal decline in the power of grand narratives to provide a legitimating frame for scientific work. But as many critics have noticed, Lyotard is 'infuriatingly vague' about what he sees as the causes of this important element of his argument (Connor, 1989; 31). Lyotard suggests that postmodernism proceeds by introducing new moves into old games, or inventing new games, so that they can be evaluated not from the standpoint of some uniform truth, but on the basis of a pragmatics which is concerned with utterances' effects, not their conformity to some overarching philosophical discourse. He claims that postmodern science and knowledge may be characterised by incomplete information, 'fracta' or 'little narratives', difference, catastrophes, the maximisation of language games, a focus on producing the unknown rather than the known or knowledge. Lyotard argues that postmodern science depends not upon logic but upon the 'quest for paralogy', faulty, incomplete or deliberately contradictory reasoning. The concept of 'paralogy' is apparently taken from Kant to name any procedure which seeks to maintain or extend the discontinuities and differences in science. In these respects, several critics have pointed to Lyotard's many affinities with the work of Feyerabend (Callinicos, 1985; Rose, 1991; Hollinger, 1994). In my own reading, Lyotard's arguments in this respect also have some interesting, if largely unnoticed, affinities with some of Marshall McLuhan's earlier work on the sway of instrumental reason and his discussions of the limits of discursive closure (1962: 266–78). But whatever the precise confluence of prior influences, Lyotard often appears much less enchanted with the benign features and role of theoretical knowledge compared to the modernist vision of Daniel Bell.

At times, Lyotard acknowledges that the discourses of the 'post-industrial' society are strongly influenced by narratives such as 'performativity' . This might point to the possibility of turning the goals of science ever more towards the centres of economic and political power and the extension of the principles of rationalisation which have long been the nightmare of critical theorists. But Lyotard suggests a more optimistic and utopian vision based on the assertion (dreamware) that computerisation may open up a situation of truly 'perfect information'. He suggests that it may also encourage unorthodox thinking and the opening up of existing paradigms, especially if it is somehow redirected from 'performativity' to the 'opening up' of all memory and data banks to the public (Rose, 1991; Connor, 1989). Lyotard is as 'infuriatingly vague' in terms of how such a truly revolutionary situation might be brought about as he is ambivalent, if not contradictory, in his brief discussions of the impacts of computing (Poster, 1990). Here he also directly echoes some of the more mystical and idealised notions in the information society theories advanced by writers such as Masuda which totally abstract from (i.e. ignore) the secular increase in the commodification and enclosure of information behind intellectual property rights. It is also difficult to reconcile this claim with Lyotard's own accounts of the increasing tendency for scientific work and technological activity to take place in corporate and government organisations and outside the traditional academic setting.

It should be clear by now that Lyotard's account of the shift to postmodernism in the sciences, or the social or cultural studies fields, is very closely dependent on the presumed development of post-industrial or information societies in advanced capitalist industrialism and related shifts in the way that knowledge is now legitimated (Lash, 1990: 93; Rose, 1991). In many respects, Lyotard has performed better than Bell in rescuing science from its traditional characterisation in cultural studies as the servant of tyranny by repositioning it into the role of potential *avante-garde* liberator. But, it is noteworthy that although his work has been widely read and influential within literary and cultural studies it has had relatively little impact amongst scientists themselves. In part this may be directly caused by tensions between Lyotard's work and the accounts provided by more established philosophers and historians of science.[2] For one thing, Lyotard paints a particularly one-sided picture of the tendencies towards an interpretative or discursive turn, the inevitable 'diaspora' of knowledge or the pervasive abandonment of the universal perspective within contemporary science compared to my own account in the later chapters of this book and that of others (e.g. Gillott and Kumar, 1995). For another, his own model has been criticised as doubly totalising because it not only assumes or asserts the total collapse of meta-narrative everywhere for all time, it also depends upon the totalising assertion or simplistic assumption of an absolute domination of meta-narrative and universal truth claims before the postmodern moment (Habermas, 1985a, 1985b; Connor, 1989; Bennington, 1988).

From the point of view of a materialist or institutionalist approach, how-ever, Lyotard provides a very partial, incomplete and contradictory account of the conditions of scientific and technological practices in the contempo-rary world, not to mention those governing the production and distribution of other kinds of information. As with Bell, his account ultimately rests upon the autonomy of the scientific worker as author of his/her own pro-ductive activity and texts. These optimistic moments are difficult to reconcile with the changing political-economic and social contexts shaping contem-porary scientific practice, even as described in Lyotard's own partial account of such developments. Such optimistic moments sit very uneasily with the pessimistic tone in many other aspects of Lyotard's complex and contradic-tory account of postmodernism.

The political implications of some of Lyotard's more recent work have drawn fairly direct and trenchant criticism from writers as diverse as Richard Rorty and Jürgen Habermas. Rorty has criticised Lyotard's neglect of a long tradition of more pragmatic thought and his inability or unwillingness to conceive of anything in between absolute and dogmatic adherence to uni-versals on the one hand and absolute delegitimation on the other hand. In denying all universal theories or principles and in stressing the play of dif-ference and the quest for cynical forms of illogic, Lyotard assumes and asserts that individualistic dissension and conflict will necessarily lead to innovation and more open prospects for scientific or cultural diversity. He fails to offer any grounds on which to distinguish between language games and individualised strategies which may be functional for the system or those which may be linked to projects opposed to dominant powers, inter-ests or discourses. His account places a singular stress on a 'war on totality' whilst neglecting the role of 'decentred' profit-seeking and greed, which (given the peculiar economic characteristics of information and cultural products) generally leads to increasing concentration of control and homogenisation in contemporary market economies.

Essentially, Lyotard's is a conservative vision which suggests that there is no point in proposing or imagining any collective response or alternative to the system we now know. All that remains is to 'activate the differences' especially within the sphere of scientific practice, to promote the lines of indi-vidual resistance to the existing form of domination rather than seek any fundamental change at a social or system level. This strategy is similar to that of Baudrillard, Foucault and Deleuze in that it presupposes a theory of power whose fundamental assumption, that domination is omnipresent, either makes of resistance a mystery or collapses into Nietzschean metaphysics (Callinicos, 1985). One example of Lyotard's totalising view of domination is his suggestion that political conflicts over cultural diversity may be meaningless now because cultural differences are in fact encouraged even more by multinational capital by virtue of the whole range of tourist and culture industries. Essentially, Lyotard's stress on indeterminacy and pluralism represents a kind of libertarian individualism which, in a capitalist market economy context, seems to end up sharing many commonalities with highly conservative thinkers such as Popper and Hayek (Connor, 1989: Hollinger, 1994).

As will be indicated in more detail below, Habermas has provided some formidable criticisms of postmodernist writings including that of Lyotard. With its stress on the unfinished project of modernity, the possibilities of communicative action and the search for a social ethics based on reason, Habermas' work directly challenges many aspects of Lyotard's writings. For the latter, aspects of Habermas' theory of communicative action pose a threat to the types of dissent at the root of invention and the heterogeneous play of language (Lyotard, 1984). In turn, Habermas has criticised what he finds as the strong convergences between the postmodernists' rejection of any notion of substantive rationality or justice on the one hand, and neo-conservative political and social theories such as those of Daniel Bell, on the other hand (Habermas, 1985a, 1985b). Indeed many recent writers have also criticised Lyotard and other French deconstructionists in similar vein. Harvey, for example, argues that, in challenging all consensual standards of truth and justice, of ethics and meaning, deconstructionism has ended up 'in spite of the best intentions of its more radical practitioners', reducing meaning and knowledge to 'a rubble of signifiers' (1989: 350; see also Lash, 1990).[3] It has thereby inspired a condition of nihilism which may have encouraged or prepared the ground for the re-emergence of charismatic politics and even more simplistic, if not politically dangerous, propositions than those which were the object of 'deconstruction' in the first place.

Jean Baudrillard: 'lost in the void of information'

Jean Baudrillard's early published work focused on the growth of consumerism and was rooted in neo-Marxist political economy (1981; 1988). But from the early 1970s his work was marked by a striking postmodernist turn and since the early 1980s, he has emerged as one of the most influential 'high-priests' of postmodernism in the Anglophone world (Kellner, 1989).[4] Indeed for many media and communication scholars, he is viewed as providing 'the most sophisticated postmodern critique of mass communication' currently available (Stevenson, 1995: 144).

The work of Roland Barthes represents an important influence and entry point for Baudrillard's postmodernist turn, alongside that of Marshall McLuhan, Louis Althusser and Situationists such as Guy Debord. Indeed Barthes' work has been widely recognised as an important influence on the overall growth of postmodernist approaches in the literary, media and cultural studies fields, and in analyses of digital (multi)media developments (Kearney, 1991; Webster, 1995; Landow, 1997). In the 1960s, Barthes challenged the prevailing conventions in literary studies by stressing that the meaning of words and writings (such as classic French literary texts) were inherently unclear to contemporary critics. He stressed that all critical approaches were frustrated in any attempts to make clear the text's (and author's) original meaning, particularly because they were crucially dependent upon *meta-languages* (such as Freudianism, Marxism, structuralism). In essence, Barthes claimed that language is not some transparent medium through which external phenomena or realities may be described or analysed. Instead he stressed that all forms of authorship are solely or primarily a matter of languages and not about engagements with some external phenomena or realities.

Barthes argued that this approach could be applied to a great variety of fields in the contemporary world, so that movies, radio, fashion and politics could be discussed or read as texts or types of languages and discourses. He suggested that there is no fundamental reality outside of language and discourse. Thus everything which we encounter or experience as 'reality' is only (or primarily) a matter of languages or texts or discourses – that is essentially forms of information – rather than external things (there is no 'out there', as it were). In some of his 1970s writings, Barthes claimed that all of language is inherently 'mythical' and he suggested that there is no real hope of getting outside 'the postmodern labyrinth of the imaginary'. Barthes also claimed that the quest to describe or analyse a fundamental reality or 'true' meaning is pointless, because all we are left with are different interpretations (*polysemous* views of different texts). Barthes emphasised the role of the reader/consumer in the production of the meaning of texts, stressing that the goal of literary work (of literature as work) is to make the reader no longer a consumer, but a producer of the text. Thus for Barthes, modernism's ideal of an autonomous imagination, whether focused on literary, political or scientific endeavours, is essentially de-centred and de-psychologized. The resulting implication is not only that 'the death of God is now supplanted by the death of the author' (Kearney, 1991: 174). It also implies the death of modernism's conception of reason and any empirically informed efforts at 'scientific' understanding of the world, and by extension, any project aimed at fundamental social and political change. Many echoes of these ideas pervade Baudrillard's later work.

Since the 1970s, Baudrillard has argued that there has been a complete rupture between the current situation and the previous stage of society and that this rupture involves the *'end of political economy'*. Baudrillard's methodological approach is one which rejects the validity of political economy or indeed any sustained sociological or empirical research aimed at exploring socio-economic trends or developments. Instead he suggests that political economy and all other dimensions of concrete, empirical historical reality have all essentially disappeared in the mutation into a postmodern society. Baudrillard takes the linguistic turn in contemporary philosophy to mean that there is no longer an extra-discursive (material) reality which language or any symbolic code (such as Marxist or liberal political economy) can concretely represent. For example, writing about the 1987 stock market crash, Baudrillard asserted that there cannot be a 'real catastrophe' of the economy today because the economy has become purely 'fictional', no more than a circuit of imaginary, fictive capital. He argues that political economy has now expired, disappearing by its own self-mutation into a speculative transeconomy which undermines its productivist logic. In his view, political economy no longer has anything to do with either the economic or the political; rather it is 'a pure game' of floating and arbitrary rules. Indeed in keeping with this methodological approach and particular 'meta-theory', Baudrillard was later to make the notorious suggestion that the Gulf War was merely a media event which had little or nothing to do with real events or lives.

Baudrillard's emphasis on the de-centred subject and his treatment of ideology frequently points to close links with Barthes' work and to the writings of Situationists such as Guy Debord. But there are many twists of emphasis in his work, including influences from his associations in the late 1960s with Louis Althusser's structuralist approach to socially constituted and ideologically interpellated subjects (Levin, 1981: Stevenson, 1995). In contrast to his more popular texts, much of Baudrillard's earlier work was focused on rethinking the relations between production and consumption, the material and the symbolic, the economic and the cultural (1981; 1988). But beginning with his distinctive postmodern turn in the early 1970s, Baudrillard's work has increasingly emphasised the changing role and forms of information as key factors shaping change in the socio-economic and cultural realms in the late twentieth century.

Unlike Lyotard or Bell, Baudrillard focuses attention on mass communication processes related to the sphere of consumption and everyday life. His emphasis turns on the characteristics and role of new communication technologies, the expanding media, cultural and heritage industries, the proliferation and circulation of signs associated with consumer goods, advertising and the media, consumerist culture and lifestyles and their impacts in transforming the experience of the late twentieth century. In essays such as *The Mirror of Production* (originally published in 1975)[5], Baudrillard signalled a major distancing from his previous positions. From now on, he argues that, at best, the Marxist (and indeed any) political economy model can only offer a theory of economic production as it tends to reduce or subordinate a range of non-economic activities to purely economic categories. Here he is not merely reflecting the critique of crude economism advanced by many other leftist cultural theorists. Baudrillard argues that political economy is unable to account for social practices which do not mirror the logic of production and that, for him, is now a fatal flaw. This, he suggests, is because the production and consumption of all kinds of commodities (not just media-based texts) has now come to involve all-important significatory or symbolic dimensions (which were less significant in earlier stages of capitalist industrialism). For him, the analysis of signs and cultural codes has become the key challenge for critical theory in the contemporary world.

Having made this initial break, Baudrillard's subsequent work turns its back on the material dimensions of production as well as consumption and the focus turns exclusively towards the symbolic and an overriding emphasis that everything experienced in the economic, social and cultural realms is a matter of signification. In his view, the mode of production, long the important starting point for critical social and cultural theory, is now redundant. Contemporary capitalism has transcended any connections with the material dimensions of production and consumption processes and is now primarily a system of circulating signs, codes and consumer identity formations. For Baudrillard, the expansion and internationalisation of financial flows marks a radical detachment of money from any material production processes just as the expanding symbolic significance of commodities detaches them from any connection with material processes, use values and biological or other utilitarian needs. The circulation of commodities and objects is intensified by the rapid turnover of fashion trends and the ever-shorter life cycles engendered by the cultural processes of obsolescence as well as the explosion of the mass media of communication. In Baudrillard's view, the proliferation of signs and signification is not confined to the mass media; they saturate every commodity and object. In his essay, *Symbolic Exchange and Death*, he proposes a three-stage periodisation of the modern age of signification and simulations, dating from the Renaissance. The final and current stage of *simulation* is one where culture no longer copies the real but produces it, postmodern culture is viewed as largely an effect of electronic technologies and networks such as television, computers, stereo head-sets and so on (Baudrillard, 1988: 119–48).

With the ceaseless circulation of signification, signs have lost all connection with any external signified or referent; reality begins and ends with the signs conveyed via commodities and the mass media. If it was possible in the past to think that the images and signs received via the television or radio set were *representational* (in the sense that they pointed to some external reality), for Baudrillard this is no longer the case as they have become nothing more than mere *simulations*. The quantitative explosion and accelerating circulation of signs results in the qualitative decay and a 'collapse' or 'death of meaning'. For one thing, the overproduction of signs and information results in an overloading of the interpretative capacities of the subject. For another, we are surrounded by an explosive profusion of constructed images in which there is nothing to see, a seething sea of 'spectacular' signs without meaning. The new millennium marks the point where reality no longer exists, 'this is the point where . . . events do not really take place precisely because they are produced and broadcast "in real time", where they have no meaning because they can have all possible meanings' (Baudrillard, 1998: 7). At times, Baudrillard takes licence from his 'poetic theory' to make apparently contradictory assertions, suggesting that *everybody* knows and realises the lack of meaning and authenticity embedded in the profusion of media signs.

Welcome to the society of the spectacle and simulation where signs are increasingly pervasive, empty, meaningless but also devoid of any connection to a 'reality' beyond themselves or possibilities for authentic communication. Welcome to the postmodern society where distinctions between the authentic and the inauthentic, true and false, the real and unreal reality have collapsed. Welcome to the world where 'the real is abolished' and events have 'become *lost in the void of information*' (Baudrillard, 1998: 7; emphasis in the original).

Notwithstanding the many contradictory twists in his 'poetic' theory, there is little doubt that Baudrillard's work, especially his earlier writings, contains many stimulating and provocative suggestions concerning the implications of electronic communication technologies and networks for the media and cultural realms of contemporary capitalism. Ultimately however, his postmodern turn simply ends up as a reverse caricature of the economism of the base/superstructure model he originally set out to critique: signification is everything and the symbolic is everywhere as the material dimensions of capitalist production and consumption processes simply disappear in Baudrillard's meta-narrative. We are presented with an overdetermined and extended one-dimensional – if now culturalist – logic of a seamless media-centric system without limit. It's a story lacking any sustained attention to the existence or possibility of contradictory trends or counter-tendencies, not to mention material ecological limits. It amounts to a media-centric vision which dreams away many of the most significant material challenges and struggles which pervade the 'dull compulsion of everyday life' for the unemployed and marginalised as well as many segments of the working population. This is especially the case in the context of a socio-economic system which has been marked by increasing insecurities, polarisations of incomes and life opportunities since the 1970s, precisely the period since Baudrillard adopted his postmodern turn.

Despite their apparently contrasting self-conscious perspectives, images and 'subversive' posturing, in political economic terms, influential postmodernists such as Baudrillard appear to end up making very happy political bedfellows with conservative thinkers such as Daniel Bell or techno-gurus such as Toffler. For example, Baudrillard has often declared that the traditional categories of the political left and right no longer hold any meaning in his vision of media 'simulation' in contemporary postmodern times. Yet his particularly sharp and consistent criticisms of the political left, feminism and the peace movements are very much in keeping with the 'humours' of the neo-liberal orthodoxy. More detailed studies of the trajectory of his work indicate that ultimately it amounts to a 'capitulation to the hegemony of the right' and a striking complicity with élitist 'aristocratic conservatism' (Kellner, 1989: 215). Indeed, there are many resonances of deep affinities in the thinking and ideas underpinning the writings of Baudrillard and Bell.

Some cultural theorists have suggested that Baudrillard's work offers a fruitful source for developing progressive social movements to deal with the pressing political issues of our times (e.g. Stevenson, 1995: 151). However, it is difficult to reconcile Baudrillard's nihilism and cynicism with feminism or any other progressive social project, not to mention his celebration of commodified sexual relationships. Besides, there appears to be a particularly shallow if not cynical aura surrounding the authoring, content and marketing strategies of his own texts in recent times, one which strongly echoes the worst excesses of the communication order he describes. There is no doubt that his international fame as a high-priest of postmodernism soared to dizzy heights from the late 1970s and into the 1990s. But it is precisely over this period that 'in its use of slogans, its hard-sell rhetoric and its attacks on competitors' products' his work has become more and more like advertising and the consumer society which was the original object of its critique (Kellner, 1989: 202; Stevenson, 1995).

Fredric Jameson: 'the cultural logic of late capitalism'

Fredric Jameson has proposed a highly complex and dialectical version of postmodernism theory to account for the changing role and features of the cultural sphere in contemporary capitalist industrialism. He places a lot of emphasis on new tendencies or an emergent order where culture has become a veritable 'second nature' and the short-term calculus of market consumerism has exploited 'heritage' but marginalised history. Unlike other postmodernists such as Baudrillard, or post-industrial theorists such as Bell, he also insists that these shifts cannot be conceived as transcending or as autonomous from the material processes of capitalist accumulation and production. Indeed his account of postmodernism is distinctive in that it explicitly seeks to relate changes in the cultural and consumption spheres to traditional political economy questions concerned with shifts in the organisation of industrial production processes, the role of markets and the state. As noted above, Baudrillard shared some of these concerns in his early work, but since the mid-1970s, he has largely relegated them to the dustbin.

In Jameson's work, a key theme is that postmodern consciousness expresses (or is strongly influenced by) the contemporary context of accelerating socio-economic and cultural change and postmodernism represents an attempt to theorise its own conditions of possibility or existence. He emphasises that modernism thought compulsively about the new and tried to observe and register the new coming into being, whilst postmodernism is focused on breaks, discontinuities and on events rather than new worlds. With echoes of Mills (1959), Jameson both emphasises and questions the tendency in much postmodern social and cultural theory to focus on surface phenomena and to neglect history or any search for 'deeper logic'. This is marked by what he views as a concomitant frenzy whereby 'virtually anything in the present is appealed to' and pressed into service as a symptom or index of the deeper logic of postmodernism (1991: xi–xiv). He suggests that (his own) postmodern theory may be grasped as 'an attempt to think the present historically in an age that has forgotten how to think historically in the first place' (1991: ix).

In defining postmodernism as 'the cultural logic of late capitalism', Jameson suggests that the task of postmodernism theory is to explore and co-ordinate new forms of practice, social and mental habits which may represent what Raymond Williams defined as 'a structure of feeling'. Contrary to Bell and Baudrillard, he suggests that the interrelationship of cultural and the economic realms must not be viewed as separate or a one-way street. Rather it must be conceived as a process involving continuous reciprocal interaction and feedback loops. He suggests that postmodernism may well lead to whole new perspectives on subjectivity as well as on the object world. Jameson proposes that postmodernism is a situation where the modernisation process is complete, 'nature is gone for good' and culture has become a veritable 'second nature'. Indeed, he occasionally suggests that changes in culture provide the more important clues for tracking the features of the postmodern condition (1991: x). Like many other postmodernists, he stresses that the contemporary is marked by 'an immense dilation' of the sphere of culture and commodities, 'an immense and historically original acculturation of the Real' and a quantum leap in the 'aestheticisation' of reality (Jameson, 1991: x). At times he is close to aspects of Baudrillard's account as when he suggests that 'culture' has not merely become a product in its own right, but also that 'the market has become a substitute for itself and fully as much a commodity as any of the items it includes within itself'

(1991: x). Indeed on occasion he directly expresses the influence of Baudrillard in shaping some of his ideas and approach (e.g. 1991: 399). But unlike Baudrillard, Jameson is also concerned not to overinflate the cultural sphere in his account of postmodernism. He therefore stresses the importance of continuing to address changes in the realms of the economy, the social and the cultural as a series of semiautonomous and relatively independent traits or features, even if the nature of the interrelationships between them may change over time.

In Jameson's account, the postmodern is clearly stamped by the pervasiveness and centrality of the media of mass communication, and the ever more 'intimate symbiosis between the market and the media' (1990). Jameson's main concerns lie with postmodernist cultural styles and forms, where the key themes revolve around the tendencies towards pastiche, the multiplication and collages of styles, the fragmented or 'schizoid' nature of identity, the loss of a firm sense of self or individual subject and the fading of a sense of history. He emphasises the flatness and deathlessness (and 'superficiality in the most literal sense') together with 'the waning of affect' and an emptying-out of feeling, emotion and subjectivity in postmodern cultural forms and theories (1991: 9–12).

Whilst *Postmodernism or The Cultural Logic of Late Capitalism* (1991) is largely concerned with the formal features and stylistic currents in the cultural realm, it also attends to specific political, economic and social dimensions of 'the transformation of the lifeworld' in recent decades. It often expresses exasperation at the 'historical deafness' which often marks contemporary efforts to take the temperature of the age or zeitgeist. He explores how the ongoing tendencies of change in the economic system *and* the cultural 'structure of feeling' somehow crystallised in the early 1970s. Unlike many other postmodernist writers, Jameson is explicitly concerned to address the continuities as well as breaks in the contemporary social and cultural orders. He emphasises that postmodernism is not the cultural dominant of a wholly new socio-economic order or a rumoured 'post-industrial' society; rather he suggests it is 'only the reflex and the concomitant of yet another systemic modification of capitalism itself' (1991: xii). At other times he is at pains to stress that in his definition and use of the term, 'postmodernism' is not an exclusively aesthetic or stylistic term or a specifically cultural category. He uses the term to name a mode of production in which cultural production finds 'a specific functional place and whose symptomatology is in my work mainly drawn from culture' (1991: 406, 399).

Given the concerns of this book, it is important to note that Jameson not only rejects the post-industrialism of Daniel Bell and all other accounts which suggest a waning or transcendence of capitalism. Rather, he points to continuities as well as changes by addressing the restructuring and intensification of capitalist socio-economic relations and emphasising that cultural changes cannot be understood as totally separate from social and economic processes as Bell had suggested. In contrast, Jameson recommends that cultural shifts be understood as interlinked with changes in the social and economic spheres. Instead of any rigid separation of realms, his account stresses how there has been 'an explosion' and a 'prodigious expansion of culture throughout the social realm' to the point at which everything in our social life – from economic value and state power to the very structure of the psyche itself – 'can be said to have become *cultural* in some original and yet untheorised sense' (1991: 48). For Jameson, the realms of culture and representation themselves, including the mass media and advertising as well as less popular forms, have become significant new areas for commodification and colonisation by capitalist relations and forms.

Jameson's many stimulating challenges to the currently fashionable taboos against most forms of holistic inquiry, whether those advanced by postmodernists such as Lyotard and Baudrillard, or the more explicitly conservative theorists such as Daniel Bell, are particularly noteworthy, even if his own accounts of certain contemporary socio-political and economic currents can be challenged in important respects. For these and other reasons, I regard Jameson's as the most compelling postmodernist theory of contemporary developments and I will draw on some of his concepts in framing the more empirical explorations in later chapters. It is interesting to note, however, that Jameson's version of postmodernism is particularly marked by the influence of early critical theorists such as Benjamin and Marcuse, as is the self-defined modernist work of Habermas, to which I will now turn.

JÜRGEN HABERMAS: MODERNITY AS 'INCOMPLETE PROJECT'

'The demand for reason simply means, resonating indeed to an ancient truth, a demand for the "creation of a social organisation in which individuals can collectively regulate their lives in accordance with their needs".'

(Jurgen Habermas, citing Herbert Marcuse, Habermas, 1985a: 72)

Many contributors to the postmodern literature are clearly informed by ideas drawn from the Frankfurt School of critical theory. Indeed in some respects, the totalising negativity of some postmodernists appears to echo and extend that of earlier critical theorists such as Adorno and Horkheimer. The latter had suggested that as a result of the continued expansion of capitalism, instrumental reason was tending to shape the entire universe of experience, discourse and action and to produce an omnipresent system which swallowed up or repulsed all alternatives (Habermas, 1985a: 74). In contrast, Habermas has been particularly concerned to retain 'the dialectical trust in determinate negation, in the disclosure of positive alternatives' which was evident in the work of other critical theorists such as Walter Benjamin and Herbert Marcuse (Habermas, 1985a: 67).

Habermas' early and perhaps best-known work concerned the development of the bourgeois public sphere from the late Enlightenment period and its subsequent 'structural transformation' over the past two centuries (1992, originally published in 1962). For Habermas, the bourgeois public sphere is conceived as a sort of 'ideal type' which represents the historically unique, progressive and potentially liberatory aspects of the democratic thrust of 'the unfinished project' of modernity. The bourgeois public sphere created a new space for public debate (where eligible participants were able to engage in the exchange of ideas and opinions, for example in saloons and coffee houses). In Habermas' account, the 'literary' dimensions of the public sphere reflected a new sense of interiority or social psychology associated with the growing role of individual identities in the modern period. In addition, the 'political' dimensions of the public sphere reflected a novel democratic role for public discussion of conflicting political ideas and a new legitimacy of public opinion in resolving political disputes and in shaping the paths of social and political developments. As an 'ideal type', the bourgeois public sphere is an arena autonomous of government and partisan economic interests which is, in principle, dedicated to rational debate and argumentation. It is the space where public opinion is formed which provides ready access and is open to inspection by all qualifying citizens. It is clear that in Habermas' account, information and communication processes lie at the heart of the public sphere, for example, the production, exchange and distribution of idea and opinions, literary and political criticism, etc.

Whilst fully recognising its selective and limited membership, Habermas emphasises that the bourgeois public sphere was a central element in the hesitant and partial shifts towards more democratic forms of modernity. It involved a historically new and democratically important principle of individuals coming together as equals in a forum for public debate around such matters. The principles and potential of the early bourgeois public sphere have been undermined by subsequent developments, including the increasing role of large-scale or monopolistic economic institutions and the changing functions and role of the state. The transforming forces also included the commercialisation of the mass media and cultural industries, the shifting emphasis from information to mass entertainment, the stage management of contemporary politics in the media and parliament, the rise of advertising and the dominance of commercial interests over those of the public or citizenry. The role and orientation of the mass media change as they become increasingly orientated towards the marketing requirements of the capitalist system and towards the formation of public opinion rather than the role of information provider. Thus the public sphere has today become something of a sham or shadow of its former potential as 'public opinion' is no longer formed through open rational debate but through manipulation and control strategies, for example those inherent in the expansion of advertising and public relations activities.

Habermas suggested that the early public sphere provided a space for certain professional groups to occupy a position between the market/economy and government/polity (1992). These and other aspects of Habermas' work have been taken to explain the creation and role of a certain type of *public service ethos* in modern society, not least in the sphere of public communication. They also lend themselves to a particular conception of the creation and role of public broadcasting corporations which were founded in many European countries with the advent of radio in the interwar years and adopted later with the advent of television. Institutions, such as the BBC in Britain and RTE in Ireland or their equivalents in other European countries, were established out of particular constellations of social and political interests and cultural movements which prevailed in these countries at that time. These were not the result of any inherent technological logic, as the more 'market-driven' approach to broadcasting in the USA clearly illustrates. Whilst public service broadcasting cannot be conceived as some sort of direct equivalent to Habermas' ideal-type public sphere, it suggests that, in some important respects, these institutions were created in order to protect such communicational functions from dominance by capitalist economic interests or other partial interests. Moreover, there was often a peculiar unity of radicals and conservatives involved in these projects. Indeed, this same orientation towards supporting a public sphere defined as democratic and accessible to all – and thus protecting public information infrastructures from domination by sectional economic or other interests – is not confined to broadcasting. It may also be extended to other cultural and communication institutions such as public libraries, government statistical services, museums and art galleries (Garnham, 1990; Schiller, 1981; Curran and Seaton, 1988; Webster, 1995).

Since his early work on the public sphere, Habermas has continued to address the unfinished business of a more democratic modernity by developing a model of 'communicative action' and a modern ethical system based upon the principles of reason, justice and democracy which both avoids the oppression of false forms of consensus and is attentive to conflicting and minority voices and interests. He has sought to establish the grounds for justice based on free, undistorted communication and to discover the kinds of guarantees required to accommodate the multiplicity of competing voices and interests in any situation rather than simply trusting in goodwill or enlightened self-interest. Habermas advances a notion of reason, defined in terms of 'the ideal speech situation' whereby individuals seek consensus by adhering to 'universal validity claims' such as 'truth, rightness and truthfulness' within the context of equal relationships. Like Marcuse before him in the Frankfurt School tradition of critical theory, he recognises that the abstract concept of reason, the fundamental category of philosophical thought, lends itself to all forms of ideology. But he also recognises that the abstract ideals of cognitive and moral universalism and of expressive sub-jectivism 'carry also a utopian content which transcends the limits of false consciousness' (1985a: 72). For Habermas no less than the later Marcuse, humanitarian and moral arguments are not merely deceitful ideology, rather 'they can and must become central social forces' (Habermas, 1985a: 76). Thus, he clearly adopts a more affirmative and positive attitude to the devel-opment of universal concepts of reason and principles of justice compared to the absolute scepticism and dismissal of such concepts on the part of post-modernists such as Lyotard. Indeed, Habermas has criticised the postmodernists' attack on reason and abandonment of the principle of jus-tice as essentially irrationalist and based on the resort to the mere play of language games. For him, such arguments converge with politically neo-conservative thought which advocates that politics must be kept as distant as possible 'from the demands of moral-practical justification' or which seeks to limit the aesthetic experience to privacy (Habermas, 1983: 14; see also: 1985a, 1985b; Lash, 1990).

Habermas' work also challenges much of the 1990s techno-centred and individualistic analysis of communication processes, not least the excited cel-ebrations of the Internet's possibilities to extend individualised connectivity. In contrast, Habermas' work stresses the fundamentally *social character* of communication processes. He argues that the processes of cultural repro-duction and social integration as well as socialisation are inextricably linked with the existence of a communicatively structured life-world. This life-world provides the basis for the continuity of tradition and the coherence of knowledge, it shapes the coordination of action and the stabilisation of group identities. It also ensures that individual life histories are, to some extent, in harmony with collective forms of life (Habermas, 1985b). Here Habermas' work may be taken as a sort of benchmark for other more recent accounts in which 'everyday life' is defined as the site for a (nostalgic) cri-tique of contemporary culture (Maffesoli, 1996: Crook, 1998).[6] He advances the notion of *communicative rationality* as the basis to counter the tenden-cies towards relativism (and individualism) in much recent philosophical, social and cultural studies literature. According to Giddens, this aspect of Habermas' theory of communicative action builds on Mead's distinctions between a philosophy of consciousness and a philosophy of language centred around the role of symbolic interaction. It begins from the idea of 'a sym-bolically structured life-world in which human reflexivity is constituted' and thus it avoids the assumption of a self-sufficient subject confronting an object world (Giddens, 1985: 105).

The theory of communicative action advanced by Habermas is very complex and dense but, like his earlier work on the rise of the public sphere, it provides many critical alternatives to the core claims of postmodernist work and other techno-centred analyses of public communication. It also provides important corrections or complements to the recent accounts of knowledge domains and forms of information, such as those suggested by Machlup. In more recent times, according to Habermas, new tendencies have emerged whereby the comunicative basis of the life-world is failing to provide the kinds of supports which the economy and polity require. These new tendencies involve a process of 'internal colonisation' of the life-world such as the destruction of tradition which threatens the reproduction of the overall social and economic order. It may be noted briefly here also that although Habermas' language and approach are quite distinctive (as is his evaluation of the technicisation of politics), his treatment of these tendencies often evokes strong echoes of Daniel Bell's concerns with 'the cultural contradictions of capitalism' (Bell, 1976), a work to which he appears to have paid close attention (Habermas, 1985b).

Habermas opposes the recent tendencies to aestheticise politics, or to replace politics by moral rigours or to submit it to the dogmatism of a doctrine. He rejects any (postmodernist) characterisation of the intentions of the surviving Enlightenment tradition as being rooted in a sort of 'terroristic reason' (1983: 12; 1985b). Here he appears to object not only to neo-conservative writers but also to more poststructuralist and postmodernist writers, including Lyotard, who have thrown out the more liberating (moral rights) aspects of the Enlightenment baby with 'the statist bathwater' as Lash put it in another context (Lash, 1990: 106). For Habermas, any radical new relinking of modern culture with an everyday praxis that depends on vital heritages drawn from the three spheres of European cultural traditions can only be established if societal modernisation is also steered in a different direction. Even if the chances of this are not good today, he suggests that the life-world must become able to develop institutions out of itself which set limits to the internal dynamics and imperatives of 'an almost autonomous economic system and its administrative complements' (1983: 13). These ideas have a particular resonance when it comes to considering the key features of recent information society discourses in Europe and elsewhere as I will indicate later.

However, it may be noted that, in common with Lyotard, Habermas' model pays relatively little attention to the dynamics of class, gender or other social movements and related struggles in shaping the path of capitalist development. This failure to directly address changing class and gender relations and more recent shifts in the distribution of wealth and power corresponds to a neglect of the labour, women's or green or other new social movements as agents for an emancipatory social project. In important respects, the relevant work of Habermas and Lyotard, alongside that of many other contemporary theorists, is marked by a certain parochialism, if not élitism, whereby concerns at the analytical or aesthetic realms are poorly articulated with those of the social and economic struggles or processes of everyday life. This distancing is marked in Lyotard's and Baudrillard's frequent dismissals of popular culture in Adorno-like vein, but it is also a feature of Habermas' 'seminar model' of social change (Lash, 1990).

Another notable weakness in Habermas' work is that, despite his emphasis on the historical processes of an unfolding rationalisation of the life-world, he pays remarkably little attention to the technological and other socio-technical changes which have strongly impacted on communication practices in everyday life since the nineteenth century. Is this the inevitable price of 'heavy-duty global theory' in the contemporary intellectual division of labour? In certain respects, it seems that Habermas' own writings often directly (if non-reflexively) reflect the very problems of detached 'expertism' addressed in his model of communicative action. Essentially, the accounts of 'everyday life' or the life-world provided by Habermas, and other recent social theorists such as Giddens, are marked by a very broad brush approach to pervasive activities such as watching television, listening to the radio, using the telephone, going to movies and so on (e.g. Crook, 1998). Here Habermas' model of the public sphere may be fruitfully augmented, if not amended, by the work of communication researchers who are more attentive to the changing role of the media in everyday life and social experience. For example, Negt and Kluge (1993) examine television and other electronic media and emphasise the need to understand postliberal, postliterary public formations in terms other than those of disintegration and decline. This kind of work also rejects any singular definition of the public sphere and stresses its heterogenous character as an accumulation or aggregation of phenomena which have quite different characteristics and origins. Negt and Kluge pay much attention to the 'industrial-commercial' publicity of late capitalism which, they argue, has been founded with the explicit purpose of making a profit. Although their approach is more dialectical than many postmodernists, they also suggest that modern communication has as its object of appropriation, the very 'life context' of its consumers.

Despite these and other criticisms, it is difficult to resist the breath and power of Habermas' command of social theory and the modernist democratic concerns underpinning his critical perspective. His work certainly provides many helpful insights in assessing the implications of a deepening commercialisation of public information and communication services. But in my own reading of his work, a key weakness is a tendency to imply a certain separation of the realms of the political and the economic, in turn based on an underlying assumption of progressive social evolution. This may well have been justified in the context of the conditions of the post-war boom and Keynesian social democratic settlement in which he first developed his public sphere thesis. But this position now seems less tenable given the direction of key socio-economic and political developments over the past two decades, not least the universalisation of the neo-liberal project, and also given the thrust of many recent analyses in the fields of institutional political economy. These suggest that the economic 'core' of the capitalist system has more visibly and significantly increased its penetration of the political and indeed other seemingly differentiated spheres in recent decades (Wood, 1997: 556–8). In these respects Habermas' work can be complemented fruitfully by insights drawn from post-Fordist and other critical political economy approaches as well as from cultural theorists such as Jameson.

COMMODIFICATION AND THE POLITICAL ECONOMY OF COMMUNICATION

In contrast to the work of Baudrillard, Lyotard, or indeed that of Bell and other information society theorists, the writings of Jameson and Habermas have many direct links to another relevant body of literature to which I will now turn. This is a field of work which is also explicitly focused on the changing role of information and the communication industries involved in the packaging, publishing and distribution of information products and services to final users (citizens and consumers). It has been concerned with questions of how successive layers of media-based information infrastructures, content and flows (together with other public communication services) are shaped by wider social and economic forces. It has also focused on how such communication systems, services and related practices in turn play an increasing role within the overall social, economic and political fabric of modern societies. To a limited extent, this field shares some of the same concerns with the quantitative growth of information which is central to the social theorists examined in Chapters Three and Four. But it tends to place a much greater emphasis on the *qualitative* rather than quantitative aspects of the changing role and forms of information. It also tends to focus more on those information and communication services which are directed at final/household consumers and citizens (rather than specialised scientific and 'producer' information).

This literature comprises the work of a particular set of researchers and writers who have sought to develop *political economy theories* or models of communication media and institutions and of related information activities. Primarily based in the expanding interdisciplinary fields of media and communication studies in universities, it comprises a very diverse set of contributions. Given its distinctive concerns, this field certainly represents a further complementary body of work of direct relevance to the concerns of this present book, but once again space will only permit a very brief, thematic and selective review here.[7]

This is a dispersed and relatively young field of inquiry which has emerged and grown in parallel with the expanding role of the media and cultural industries, telecommunications and the newer electronic communication services (and the academic study of the same) in recent decades. The very term *political economy* itself suggests a certain distancing from any specialised or autonomous 'economic' science approach such as that which unpins the boundary walls of mainstream neo-classical economics. Indeed, it marks a refusal to separate out the political from economic concerns and favours alternative institutional or holistic approaches to the study of any phenomena in line with the methodological traditions established by earlier writers such as Smith, Marx, Veblen, Innis and the Frankfurt School. It also borrows from that long, if often subsidiary stream of cultural studies which has been attentive to the processes by which the expression and flows of oral, literate and audiovisual stories (or 'content') have been shaped by socio-economic and political forces.

In keeping with these methodological principles, this field is marked by a major concern with the changing structural role and characteristics of the media and the *systemic* features of communication and information in advanced capitalist economies. As such it seeks to develop an explicitly *holistic* approach to the study of the changing features and role of the media and other communication or information activities and how these in turn are linked to broader patterns of change in social, economic and political processes.[8] Some of these authors have sought not merely to develop a regional political economy theory of communication and information. Rather, following the innovative lead of Harold Innis (1950, 1951) and the Frankfurt School, many also seek to develop a more adequate institutional political economy model of contemporary capitalism which takes appropriate account of the changing role of communication and information in capitalist industrialism.[9] Thus much of this work is focused on exploring how technological, economic and political factors have brought about fundamental but interrelated sets of changes in both (i) the media of public communication and (ii) in the broader/overall fabric of socio-economic and political processes in contemporary capitalist industrialism.

Contrary to most of the technocratic and economistic approaches mentioned earlier, the sources, forms and implications of the extended *commodification of information* have been a central concern for many contributions to the political economy of the communications (Mosco, 1996). In its approach to these issues, this body of work has also been strongly and clearly influenced by critical theory and some contributors explicitly acknowledge the importance of Habermas' work (e.g. Garnham, 1990). Certainly, Habermas' notion of the public sphere, with its attendant emphasis on the factors shaping the quality and availability of information and its modes of communication, has influenced many recent contributions to the political economy of communication (Mosco, 1996). It has also served as a resource or influence on strands of more empirically orientated research focused on changes in specific information and communication services, whether in the realm of print media, broadcasting, the Internet, public libraries, government information services, or museums and art galleries.[10]

In contrast to information society theorists' celebrations of the quantitative growth in the economic significance of information and communication services (i.e. as sources of wealth and profits) many political economy writers provide alternative concepts and more critical perspectives, including a stress on final users, defined as citizens as well as consumers. Here too, many contributors tend to be highly critical of the commodification process and growing tendency to treat information as a commodity or 'thing' to be enclosed behind property rights as a result of successive shifts in national and international industrial and trade policies.[11] Many also provide empirically based explorations of the specific economic characteristics and changing institutional contexts of information production, distribution and control processes which directly deflate and contradict the optimistic projections and abstract analyses of abundant and freely available information resources proposed by information society theorists such as Masuda and Stonier.[12]

Another key concern in much of this work centres on the patterns of ownership, funding, control, and regulation (in the broad sense) of the media and other information services, the conditions of access to such information and their relation to competing conceptions of democracy, citizenship and consumer identities in contemporary societies. One research theme has been the growing concentration and centralisation of ownership of media and communication services. A related theme has been the investigation of the dominant forms of *structural transformation* in the information and communications sector, such as tendencies towards increasing integration of communication business and control functions across traditionally separate industrial and technological boundaries, and tendencies towards outsourcing of certain (often high-risk) activities and functions to smaller 'independent' networks of firms. This stream of work often overlaps with the concerns of post-Fordist approaches to contemporary restructuring processes (Askoy and Robins, 1992; Banks, 1992; Robins, 1992). A related concern centres round the institutional factors shaping the diversity of information and the more qualitative features of the forms and flows of information content associated with different funding, ownership and regulatory regimes. Here some studies have addressed the implications of the growing concentration and centralisation of ownership and control of media at the national and international spatial scales and on the erosion of the public service regimes of regulation in the case of radio and television broadcasting.[13] Others still have focused on the impact and implications of the growing role of advertising and sponsorship expenditures and related public relations activities in reshaping the forms and content of the mass media.[14]

The political economy of communication fields provides a rich research tradition centred on international dimensions of the organisation and control of information infrastructures, 'content' and flows, including the related issues of appropriate strategies for the regulation of increasingly global communication networks. In contrast, the role of communication technologies, media and information services has been a much neglected theme within the overall field of international relations studies until relatively recent times. But it is one which has become increasingly prominent in relation to the overall debates over new forms of globalisation and regulation of trade and investment in the 1990s (see, for example, Strange, 1994, 1996). Thus, despite the relative neglect of such issues in the wider international relations literature, this field provides a rich and long-established tradition of research on international aspects of communication and information. It includes a long tradition of work specifically focused on the role of communication technologies and media in fostering the development of less developed countries, the specific economic characteristics and policy factors shaping the international structure and flows of (both producer and final consumer/citizen) information and media services, and the relative merits of the 'free flow of information' versus more structured and regulated approaches.[15] This tradition provides many challenges to some of the ahistorical if optimistic attempts to address these questions in the recent surge of technology-centred and/or information society discourses.

Some researchers have drawn on the political economy tradition to provide more grounded accounts of the specific features and issues associated with the newer ICT-based communication networks (such as the Internet/WWW) and related services. Here again these tend to provide much more nuanced accounts of the issues and challenging stakes involved compared to the dominant discourses discussed earlier. For example, some have explored communicative aspects of the new networks and the manner or extent to which aspects of their design and regulation may contribute to the construction of new social spaces (Samarajiva and Shields, 1997; Mansell and Silverstone, 1996). Other contributions have examined comparative aspects of recent national and global information infrastructure policy initiatives, including the implications for convergence and the smaller and less developed economies (Drake, 1995; Melody, 1997; Preston, 1996a). One other important sub-field has been focused on the rapid changes taking place in the scale, structures and regulation of the telecommunications services sector and the emergence of new 'convergent' electronic communication services such as the Internet and World Wide Web. Some have investigated the factors and forces shaping the re-regulation of the telecommunications sector and questioned the distributional consequences of the emerging new services and policy regimes. Others have interrogated the material and symbolic implications of recent changes in the policy practices and discourses surrounding telecommunications services.[16]

In general, such work in the political economy of communication field places a central focus on the many important distributional concerns (who gains, who loses) which are ignored or marginalised in the more dominant discourses surrounding new ICT and the expanding economic role of information. They provide many useful insights as to how and why new information infrastructures and the flows and content of public communication are shaped by wider social and economic forces in advanced capitalist societies. It is notable that much of this academic work based in the political economy of communication tends to be influenced by critical theory and to adopt a 'public interest' stance. This has usually involved a critical stance towards the processes of increasing commodification and the particular forms of re-regulation of the communication industries associated with the hegemony of neo-liberalism over the past twenty years. Ironically, explicit neo-liberal political economy approaches have occupied a relatively small role in this academic field – at least compared to their dominant role in the fields of applied industrial research and consultancy as well as policy practices. It is also relatively small compared to the dominant international position of neo-liberal ideas and discourses in shaping and framing information and communication industry and policy practices in recent times.[17] For these reasons, the political economy of the communication field can be defined as an important resource for a more rounded understanding of the stakes and interests involved in the changing role of information and communication processes today.

Notes

1   The following provide accessible and useful reviews of this terrain: Harvey, 1989; Rose, 1991; Norris, 1990; Featherstone, 1991; Connor, 1989; Hollinger, 1994.
2   This is beyond our scope here, but for a useful summary, see for example Connor, 1989: 35–7.
3   Again space will not permit a discussion of these questions here, but see the useful summaries available in Rose, 1991: 55, 60–63 and 85–94; Connor, 1989: 38–43; Callinicos, 1985.
4   Douglas Kellner (1989) provides a comprehensive and fascinating account of Baudrillard's intellectual concerns and their relation to changing political and cultural currents in France and elsewhere.
5   Reproduced in the collection of Baudrillard's earlier works edited by Mark Poster (Baudrillard, 1988).
6   See Gregory (1994) and Crook (1998) for useful discussions of 'everyday life' and recent social theory.
7   The most comprehensive recent overview of the work in question here can be found in Golding and Murdoch (1997) but Vincent Mosco (1996) provides a very accessible and useful introduction to the field. Important examples of contributions to this field include Curran and Seaton, 1988; Garnham, 1990; Habermas, 1992; Hamelink, 1994; Melody, 1997; Melody, 1981; Mattelart, 1979 and 1991; Schement and Curtis, 1995; Schiller, 1981 and 1986; Smythe, 1983; Wasko, 1993. Some seminal early attempts to outline the scope of this particular field include Murdoch and Golding, 1974; Garnham, 1979; Schiller, 1981.

8   For key examples of this work see: Murdoch and Golding, 1974; Garnham, 1979, 1990; Guback, 1969, 1979, 1993; Schiller, 1981, 1986; Smythe, 1981, 1983; Mosco and Wasko, 1988; Mosco, 1996; Golding and Murdoch, 1980, 1997; Wasko et al., 1993; Curran and Seaton, 1988; Curran et al., 1987; Collins, 1990.

9   The pioneering work here was that of the Frankfurt School and the Canadian political economist Harold Innis. Significant recent contributions to this sub-field include: Dallas Smythe, 1981 and 1983; Melody et al., 1981; Melody, 1996 and 1997; Lamberton, 1971; McBride Commission, 1980; Wasko et al., 1993; Babe, 1995.

10 Amongst the examples of such work, see: Schiller, 1981, 1986; Golding and Murdock, 1980; Garnham, 1990; Curran et al., 1987; Miege, 1989; Mattelart, 1991, 1996; Webster, 1995.

11 See, for example: Schiller, 1981, 1986; Garnham, 1981, 1994; Slack and Fejes, 1987; Salvaggio, 1989; Schement and Lievrouw, 1988; Mosco and Wasko, 1988; Schement and Curtis, 1995; Streeter, 1996.

12 Examples here include the work of Miege, 1989; Banks, 1992; Askoy and Robins, 1992; Robins, 1992; Schement and Curtis, 1995.

13 Examples of this kind of work include: Garnham, 1990; Curran et al., 1987; Curran and Seaton, 1988; Chomsky and Herman, 1992; McQuail and Siune, 1998; Downing et al., 1995; Corcoran and Preston, 1995; Preston and Grisold, 1995.

14 Examples here include: Curran and Seaton, 1988; Mattelart, 1991; Jhally, 1991.

15 Again Harold Innis' writing represents a pioneering attempt to sketch out some of the issues relevant to this field. Other select examples of this stream of work include: Schramm, 1964; Rogers, 1983; Mattelart, 1979, 1991; Nordenstreng and Schiller, 1993; McBride Commission, 1980; Melody et al., 1981; Smythe, 1983; Rosenberg, 1982; Hamelink, 1994; Sussman and Lent, 1991; Wasko et al., 1993; Mody et al., 1995; Braman and Sreberny-Mohammadi, 1996; Gerbner et al., 1996; Mowlana, 1997; Sinclair et al., 1995.

Part 3

MAPPING A NEW MILLENNIUM AND MULTIMEDIA ORDER

CHAPTER SIX

CHANGES, CONTINUITIES AND CYCLES: TOWARDS A MORE REALIST(IC) THEORY

'The essential point to grasp is that in dealing with capitalism we are dealing with an evolutionary process . . . a fact which was long ago emphasised by Karl Marx . . . Capitalism then, is by nature a form or method of economic change and not only never is, but never can be, stationary . . . This process of Creative Destruction is the essential fact about capitalism.'

(Schumpeter, 1943: 82–3)

'. . . the full economic and social benefits (including employment generation) of information technology depend on a . . . process of social experimentation and learning which is still at an early stage.'

(Freeman and Soete, 1994: 41–2)

CRISIS AND RESTRUCTURING: CHANGES VERSUS CONTINUITIES?

In the preceding five chapters I have reviewed a number of important but competing theories which emphasise particular facets of change in the socio-economic and cultural order at the end of the twentieth century. Each highlighted specific aspects of the role, characteristics and socio-economic or cultural implications of new ICTs and/or shifts in the role and forms of information and communication.

However, despite the multiplicity of competing concepts, ideas and terminologies in the theories reviewed earlier, there are also some remarkable overlaps and commonalities between what, at first sight, seem quite separate approaches. For example, although they may do so in different ways, the majority of these theories have tended to emphasise new ICT and the increasing importance of information and communication flows and institutions. Some highlight changes in the role of specialised, scientific or other types of instrumental knowledge, others stress the media and cultural industries as well as the changing role of symbolic and cultural information flows and processes in every sphere of social and economic activity. Almost all of these theories pay particular attention to the pervasive implications of new information and communication technologies and related new networks, systems or media of communication, even if they differ significantly in their periodisations and definitions of the historical specificity and importance of these technical developments.

Yet, many of these apparently quite different theories are marked by a common tendency to neglect the most significant social and economic trends which have emerged over the past couple of decades, not least the return of mass unemployment and widening socio-economic cleavages. Despite many other apparent differences and emphases on particular new technological, informational or cultural developments, most contributions tend to assume a continuation of the distinctive kinds of social and economic conditions which prevailed during the long post-war boom era. But as I will demonstrate in later chapters, there have been many significant shifts in these socio-economic conditions over the last two decades. These shifts are associated with the turn to a long-wave downswing phase and must be fully addressed in any adequate theory of the contemporary. As we will see, many of these changes cannot be addressed as the effect of any specific technological or information centred development. Rather, they can be best understood in terms of continuities of deeper structural features and the long-wave dynamics of capitalist industrialism.

The key purpose of this present chapter is to move beyond the stage of review and critique of existing theories and approaches. It will outline a more robust theoretical model for understanding the dynamics of change and continuities in the socio-economic and cultural realms of late capitalist industrialism, with particular attention to the changing role of the media 'content', communication and cultural industries. This combines what I consider to be the most compelling ideas and concepts in the competing models focused on recent developments in ICTs and in the production, distribution or communication of information. The initial model sketched out in this chapter will then be adopted and further developed in relation to a more concrete and empirical level of inquiry which follows in the subsequent chapters.

As already flagged in Chapter Two, this integrated theory-building exercise initially draws upon the author's interpretation of the long-waves approach derived from recent neo-Schumpeterian and neo-Marxist theories, in particular the work of Perez, Freeman and his various collaborators as well as Mandel.[1] The proposed approach views the history of capitalist development as comprising successive long-wave movements, of approximately fifty years' duration. Each long wave comprises an upswing period of relatively rapid growth followed by a downswing of relatively slow growth. This approach was found to provide the most fruitful and coherent starting point for understanding the nature of fundamental transformations as well as the continuities which define contemporary capitalist industrial societies. This approach is potentially holistic and interdisciplinary in the sense that it can provide a multidimensional approach to innovation, stressing the inter-linkages between the processes of technical, social, organisational and institutional innovation. It is attentive to strategic changes in the economic, social, political and cultural realms, including the importance of interconnections between long-term changes in the spheres of production and consumption. But to fully address the key contours of contemporary change of concern in this book, this basic long-wave model must also be adapted, refined and augmented. I will do so by incorporating important concepts and insights derived from selected theories which stress the changing role of information and non-technical knowledge, including the mass communication and cultural industries.

THINKING THROUGH THE TECHNOLOGY–SOCIETY/CULTURE RELATION

A Spectrum of Approaches

So to begin this task of theory-building, one must address the question of how we define the historical importance, specificities and implications of new ICTs. To do so, I will draw on concepts from two different fields of research focused on the social role and implications of technology but which, as indicated earlier, do not often cross-refer to each other. The first is that based in the communication and media studies disciplines, the second is the 'science, technology and society' studies (STS) literature based in the fields of sociology and institutional political economy.

By definition, technology has always been present in human society, even from its very origins. For example, there is a considerable body of archaeological research which suggests that the silica axe was one of the first tools which facilitated co-operation and communication in the act of hunting. Moving to more recent times and the rise of social and cultural 'modernity' in Europe, some (a minority) historians and other social and economic theorists have emphasised that modern institutional and social structures have been shaped or strongly influenced by technological developments. One frequently mentioned example is the introduction of printing to Europe by Gutenberg in the mid-fifteenth century. For some, the printing press not only helped disseminate ideas and aspects of culture which were previously largely enclosed within the medieval monasteries and royal courts. It is also deemed to have played a major role in helping to reshape the social, political as well as communication and cultural orders which we take as typical of modernity. Marshall McLuhan represented one prominent exponent of this approach to the study of communication technologies and their social and cultural implications. He argued, for example, that the introduction of 'typography ended parochialism and tribalism . . . [and] had psychic and social consequences that suddenly shifted previous boundaries and patterns of culture' (1964: 170–1). By the criteria of other accounts, this represents a much reduced and overly technology-centred approach to the complex array of socio-economic, political and military factors which shaped the forms and boundaries of cultural and social 'space' in contemporary Europe (Lefebvre, 1974). Yet the impoverished McLuhanite or technological determinist version of historical change processes has become highly fashionable in the 'postmodern' (a-historical) culture of the 1990s. Mills' old definition of the 'postmodern' as a tendency to 'retreat from history' certainly rings with greater validity today given the rising new fashion which reduces the complexities of social, political or media history to a singular technological 'lever'.

Thus the recent contributions, which emphasise the role and impacts of the cluster of new ICTs (or sometimes, one component new technology such as the Internet or WWW) as independent variables in bringing about fundamental changes in the socio-economic or cultural structures of capitalist industrialism are not novel or unique. They can be viewed as part of a well-established, if relatively recent tradition of thinking and debate about the technology–society relation. The fundamental issues at stake concern competing conceptions of the autonomy of technological innovation and its role in shaping the past and future patterns of socio-economic and political development. A full review of the competing theories or models which pervade the different disciplinary fields is not possible here for reasons of space. But it is useful, and indeed necessary, to address the major competing theories in summary form in order to indicate the present author's particular approach to a more adequate understanding of the meaning and specificity of new ICT.

For these purposes, it is useful to identify a basic typology consisting of two sharply polarised models of the technology–society change relation, with technological determinism on one side and social shaping (or economic or cultural shaping) approaches at the other extreme. This very basic typology is probably best imagined as a continuum or spectrum of possible approaches to the technology–society change relationship, with

FIGURE 6.1   Contrasting models of the technology–society change relation

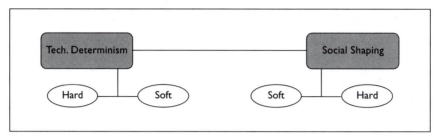

Source: The author

many actual contributions falling somewhere between the two extremes (see Figure 6.1). Within this crude typology, it is also important to recognise that there are 'soft' and 'hard' variants of both these extreme models (Pool, 1983).[2]

Technological determinist views

Technological determinism is probably the most popular and influential model of the technology–society change relationship. As indicated earlier, it is the one that most frequently informs popular and journalistic accounts of the effects or impacts of new ICT, even if it is generally viewed in a very negative light (and often invoked as a term of abuse) amongst academic writers (Bijker, 1995; Heap et al., 1995). The basic assumption of technological determinism is that a new technology, such as the printing press, television or the Internet, 'emerges' from technical study and experiment. This is then treated in terms of the changes that it is deemed to bring about in the society or the sector into which it has 'emerged' or 'diffused'. It is also assumed that social actors will or must adapt to it in a specific fashion because it is the 'modern' way (Williams, 1983: 130). It is also usually assumed that the procedures and processes shaping the emergence and design of the new technology are based in a special realm of scientific activity, viewed as semi-autonomous or external to the social and economic spheres. In a strict sense, technological determinism is based on three sets of ideas or assumptions: that technological development is autonomous, that societal development or history is determined by technology and that the patterns of technological diffusion, applications and use are linear or predictable. A number of different versions of technological determinism are identified within the technology–society studies literature (see Jasanoff et al., 1995; Bijker, 1995; Heap et al., 1995). It is often recommended that the term be reserved for approaches which assume that technology is autonomous and which advance the idea of technology determining change in society, or culture, the economy or history.

In this light, we can clearly locate many of the third-wave and transformative models (see Chapter Two) in the technological determinist school (Toffler, 1980, 1983; Toffler and Toffler, 1995a; Negroponte, 1995; Kelly, 1998). Despite Toffler's own explicit rejection of the label, his work since the early 1980s at least, has been strongly stamped by the key defining features of technological determinism as described above. His protests to the contrary simply indicate that technological determinism is one of those analytic errors or 'sins' that is more frequently condemned than it is avoided. In the transformative and 'third-wave' accounts, new ICT is configured as an independent force which is bringing about or demanding a fundamental change in economic and social structures. New ICT is viewed as possessing an autonomous logic or trajectory of its own which is not only benign but quite divorced from any basis in existing socio-economic or political interests, relations or conflicts. Indeed, Toffler insists and stresses, in true determinist fashion, that new ICT represents an autonomous force which eliminates or transcends the 'old' conflicts or interests based on social class or gender cleavages. The result (and message) is that new ICT and other 'third-wave' technologies are to be regarded as nothing less than both the means and ends of social development and the 'just society' (e.g. Toffler and Toffler, 1995c).

Social shaping approaches

At the other extreme of the spectrum (as indicted in Figure 6.1), the *social shaping* (and/or economic or cultural shaping) approaches reject the idea that technological change is an autonomous process or that it represents some kind of independent variable or force causing social change. Social shaping models stress that technology is not following its own momentum or a sort of rational, goal-directed, problem-solving path. Instead, it is suggested that every moment or stage of the technological innovation process (from design, development, adoption, application and use or consumption) is largely or overwhelmingly shaped by social factors. This approach stresses the role of socio-economic or cultural forces in effecting change – even when change coincides with the emergence or adoption of new technologies. Technological innovations are seen to 'embody social arrangements' and must always be viewed as part of larger social processes (Williams and Edge, 1996).

The social shaping approach tends to stress that new technologies are not designed or created exogenously. Rather they must be understood as the product of a specific socio-economic, institutional and cultural context.

Thus technological innovations have little or no status as independent forces driving socio-economic change and they should not be reified or deified in the manner characteristic of most technological determinist accounts. The social shaping approach suggests that the very origins, design and adoption of new technologies are part of wider social relationships and processes and they do not have separate or fixed 'impacts' in themselves. It is also suggested that a new technology is not itself something fixed or determining in any of its given forms. Rather it is relatively 'open' and adaptable to its surroundings and context, i.e. with respect to users' application or adoption or adaptation of any new technological innovation (Heap et al., 1995; Jasanoff et al., 1995; Bijker, 1995).

The social shaping model has been developed by an influential school within the academic fields of social studies of technology since the 1980s. For example, writers such as MacKenzie and Wajcman (1985) adopted and developed this model in a number of studies which directly refuted the technological determinist model head on. Another example of this model (inspired by Marx and Braverman) was advanced by Noble (1984) in his study of the automation of machine tools. He argued that the social shaping of this technology and the choice of particular types of automation can be best understood in terms of management's concerns about control over the labour process (Williams and Edge, 1996).

But again, the idea that technology is socially shaped, rather than an autonomously developing force in society (or a primarily cognitive development) is far from new or novel (Bijker, 1995: 241). For example, Lewis Mumford argued (1934) that socio-cultural conditions precede the development of specific technologies. Raymond Williams, a key figure in the development of cultural and media studies in Britain, was another early advocate of this kind of model. Williams consistently rejected the ideas of technological determinism with respect to the media and the sphere of popular culture. In particular he rejected many of the ideas advanced by Marshall McLuhan and other technological determinists, both of the optimistic variety as well as the cultural pessimists (Williams, 1974, 1983). Against the ideas of technological innovation as an autonomous, accidental or external process, Williams stressed that virtually all technical study and experiment are undertaken within already existing social relations and cultural forms, typically for purposes that are already in general foreseen. In addition, he argued that a technical invention as such has comparatively little social significance. It is only when it is selected for investment towards production, and 'when it is consciously developed for particular social uses', that is, when it moves from being a technical invention to what can properly be called an available technology, 'that the general significance begins' (1983: 130). Williams stressed that these processes of technology selection, investment and development are clearly of a social and economic kind and must have a prior location within existing social and economic relations. Within a specific social order, new communication or other technologies do not simply emerge, rather they are designed for particular uses and the particular patterns of their application and use will be strongly shaped by the existing social and cultural contexts (Williams, 1974, 1983).

The earlier work of Raymond Williams and others has been further developed by a number of subsequent writers in the sociological, communication and cultural studies fields. Much of the recent work has placed a major emphasis on the active role of consumption processes and of socially situated users in shaping the appropriation, meaning and use of domestic technologies. Although this work is often neglected in many typologies of sociological studies of technology, it can be classified as an important stream within the social shaping approaches of the typology identified above.

Particularly in relation to the consumption and use of communication and other technologies in the household or domestic setting, this work draws on valuable concepts in the media and cultural studies fields as well as the literature on consumption practices. At its best, this stream of work indicates how the design and development processes may encode preferred forms and types of use/deployment of new technology. It furthermore suggests that these tend to be reinforced by the more symbolic forms of encoding advanced by the marketing and promotional activities of the producers and distributors. Some of this work treats any new consumer technology as a text or commodity which can be 'read' and decoded in different ways. It also stresses that the way in which any such technology is deployed or used is not inherent or built into the artefact or fixed by its marketing and promotional characteristics. Rather this approach not only suggests that technology may lead a 'double life', it also argues that users are active and socially situated decoders of technologies (Sørensen and Berg, 1990; Silverstone and Hirsch, 1992; Cawson et al., 1995; Mansell and Silverstone, 1996; Williams and Edge, 1996). Furthermore, it draws on the idea that the consumption processes are highly symbolic rather than utilitarian, as emphasised within recent literature on consumerism such as that of Miller (1987).

Much of the recent social shaping work tends to focus on detailed, micro case studies of particular technologies and users' responses to 'the menu' constructed by the producers. This means that they often fail to engage with the cumulative implications of a clustering or system of interrelated new technologies (such as new ICTs) or with the more macro forms of socio-economic interests and related political stakes or the potential mobilisation of alternative collective strategies. Much of this recent social shaping work does not engage with structural questions of competing socio-economic interests or distributional issues. Nor does it provide any direct route to engagement with pressing political questions that informed earlier social studies of technology. In many recent social shaping (and indeed other) approaches to technology, 'the toll of academic respectability threatens to produce politico-cultural irrelevance' (Bijker, 1995: 255). Another result is that some recent strands of social shaping research frequently pay too little attention to the specific nature and functions of the technology under study and/or they fail to address the implications for broader patterns of social or cultural change (Bijker, 1995; Heap et al., 1995).[3]

NEW ICT AS A MAJOR NEW TECHNOLOGY SYSTEM: A 'LONG-WAVES' APPROACH

This brief consideration of competing general models of the technological/socio-economic change relation immediately leads to one crucial set of questions for this book: what is the most appropriate model for understanding the significance and implications of new information and communication technologies in influencing socio-economic and cultural change today? What are the respective merits and limits of the technological determinist or social shaping models for understanding the significance and implications of new ICTs for socio-economic and cultural change at the close of the twentieth century?

Posed in this way, these debates and the choices at stake remain very abstract, indeed they often take on the character of an absolutist theological struggle between contending belief systems. Thus at this point we can usefully begin to explore these questions via one other short detour which will help us move beyond the arid debates concerning the most appropriate model of the technology–society relation. This involves an explicit attempt to identify and specify different types of technological innovation which may provide a more grounded guide to theory-building and selection. It is a step which helps identify distinctive features and stages in the emergence, construction and firming up of major new clusters of technological innovations (such as new ICT today), their diffusion, use and their implications for the shaping and firming up of associated social and institutional practices.

Thus, for these purposes, I will first of all specify a number of different types of technological innovations which served as implicit guides in the analysis in earlier chapters. This typology, summarised in Table 6.1, is developed from categories suggested in the prior work of Chris Freeman and other neo-Schumpeterian theorists. It is also firmly grounded in a historical understanding of technological and industrial innovation processes. It suggests that it is possible to identify four distinctive types of technology-centred innovations. All of these vary significantly with respect to their importance for socio-economic and cultural change. Although frequently neglected in much of the literature, I believe that this kind of typology can help us move

TABLE 6.1   Typology of technology-based innovations

Categories	Characteristics and socio-economic implications
1) Incremental Innovations	• Minor improvements or functional extensions to an existing technology. • Account for vast majority of patents and economic research on 'demand-led' innovation is heavily focused on this category of innovative activity. • Usually 'market-led' technical innovations which take place continuously within the production process. • Relatively minor socio-economic impacts/implications, largely confined to one industrial sector; some have big impacts on productivity, product quality or reliability.
2) Radical Innovations	• Important and distinctively new/novel devices, systems or other technologies. • These are unevenly distributed over industries and time. • Since the late nineteenth century these usually result from deliberate R&D. • Less 'market-led' compared to incremental ones, but R&D workers responsible for inventing/developing them are guided or influenced by considerations of a potential market and by the values and goals of their funding organisation. • Some may provide opportunities for the growth of new industries/markets. • Important radical process innovations can lead to major improvements in the cost and quality of many existing products. • Whilst some are deemed to have dramatic impacts (e.g. television) in general their economic impacts are sectorally confined or localised.
3) Major New Technology Systems (MNTS)	• These comprise a family or cluster of radical and incremental innovations which are technically and economically interrelated. • They often involve organisational innovations affecting many firms or industries. • MNTS stimulate significant socio-economic changes, including the rise of entirely new industrial sectors. • Some of the most important (and historically rare) MNTS have a 'pervasive applications potential': they can be adopted in most sectors of economic activity, and social and cultural realms (e.g. electricity in the late nineteenth century; new ICT today).
4a) New 'Techno-Economic Paradigm' OR	• For neo-Schumpeterians, the shift to a new long-wave upswing involves more than the supply, adoption and diffusion of (especially pervasive) MNTS. • It requires related or 'matching' innovations in other fields (i.e. organisational, institutional innovations) to form a new 'techno-economic paradigm' (TEP). • Each pervasive new MNTS leads to a 'paradigm shift' in terms of the appropriate range of 'best practice techniques' across a range of managerial, organisational and indeed other (non-technical) fields, including the policy fields. • This concept is linked to gales of 'creative destruction' in Schumpeter's model. • The crystallisation and diffusion of such MNTS and matching sets of innovations in the paradigm may take decades to occur. It involves a process of economic and managerial selection from a range of technically feasible combinations of innovations which takes time to emerge.
4b) New 'Socio-Technical Paradigm'	• The TEP is taken as an important concept (helps avoid a crude technological determinism). But it is often linked to an excessive stress on economic, managerial and organisational processes and/or functional/instrumental analysis.

TABLE 6.1 *cont.*

Categories	Characteristics and socio-economic implications
	• The neo-Schumpeterian approach must be augmented by a stronger emphasis on the wide range of social forces and institutional factors, which have shaped the strategic features and direction of long-run upswings historically. These include the role of social movements and state or policy innovations shaping the norms underpinning production and consumption practices.
	• The 'socio-technical paradigm' (STP) concept is proposed instead of TEP to more fully reflect the significant role of social, political and cultural movements in both the sphere of (economic) production and consumption.

Notes:
a) This typology refers to 'technological' or 'technology-based' innovations; Schumpeter and some neo-Schumpeterians emphasise that there are many other important types of innovations besides the purely technical.
b) In the present work, the concept of new 'socio-technical paradigm' is preferred to that of new 'techno-economic paradigm', for reasons indicated in the text.

Sources: Devised by the present author, inspired by the earlier work of writers such as Chris Freeman and his various collaborators.

beyond the more abstract debates concerning the impacts of technological innovation. Each category raises quite specific stakes or challenges and very particular implications with respect to the question of the influence/autonomy of technological change. For example, each of these categories of techno-logical innovation is clearly of a very different order. Each of these types poses very different sets or registers of issues with respect to its historical importance and hence poses specific challenges for any consideration of the potential 'impacts' or implications of technological innovation on society, economy or culture.

Thus, in this sense, *incremental innovations* (for example, some minor improvement in the functions of say, radio or television receivers) raises issues and stakes of a very different order to those posed by *radical techno-logical innovations* (such as the development and diffusion of the motor car, personal computers or the Internet). They are also quite distinct from *major new technology systems* (MNTS) which comprise clusters or families of closely related radical technical innovations. In turn, even more distinctive stakes are involved in the case of those, historically rare, major new tech-nology systems with *pervasive* applications potentials. The latter take a relatively long time to 'firm up' and link up with related 'matching' innova-tions, not only in the technological domain. More importantly, they involve much more than technical innovation as they comprise an associated set of social, institutional and organisational (including 'managerial') innovations or best practices (which amount to a new 'techo-economic' or 'socio-technical' paradigm, as I suggest later).

In line with this typology, major and pervasive new technology systems (MNTS) are taken to pose very different and distinct sets of questions and stakes compared to the first two categories of technology-based innovation identified above. Here I wish to propose that, in a certain sense, the initial development and diffusion stages of pervasive MNTS have certain 'disruptive' impacts, at least in terms of industrial restructuring and the division of labour. They open up bounded but historically distinctive incentives and pressures, as well as significant new opportunity frontiers or possibilities for the restructuring of economic, social as well as spatial structures and processes.

Thus, to address this dimension of the contemporary technical and industrial change processes, there has to be some recourse to the (soft) determinist model. This is not to revert to any transformative or crude/hard determinist logic. For a start, the historical approach adopted here clearly insists that the origination or 'emergence' moments of all types of technical innovations have, over time, become increasingly subsumed under the sway of the logics of capitalist industrialism. The 'disruptive' impacts referred to here involve important changes in incentives and pressures for change in productivity frontiers, industrial structures and the division of labour. But these do not imply any shift or transcendence of the core structures of socio-economic relations which have typified capitalist industrialism from the outset. Besides, these disruptive effects are viewed as highly uncertain and relatively open with respect to social, economic or cultural outcomes. Major new technology systems, such as new ICT, are highly malleable in terms of how they may be adopted, applied and used or consumed by user industries, social groups or in the household setting. Hence, they must be addressed within a social shaping perspective which takes adequate account of the full range of socio-economic and political forces which influence all moments or stages of their trajectory.

In essence, then, the approach adopted here comprises *a dialectical model*, which embraces elements of both the soft technological determinist and social shaping perspectives. Such a dialectical model is required in order to embrace the most important dimensions of the complex and intensified forms of restructuring associated with pervasive major new technology systems in capitalist industrialism.

This particular approach is partly based on my reading of the historical evidence on the economic and industrial implications of MNTS in the past, such as the electrical technology system around a century ago (Hall and Preston, 1988). In the economic sphere, this earlier MNTS provided a direct stimulus to the emergence of significant new industrial sectors involved directly in the supply of electrical power systems as well as in the supply of a plethora of 'downstream' innovative products and services. In addition, the diffusion and application of this pervasive new technology system also provided an important stimulus and novel set of economic incentives for a range of process and other technical innovations in almost every other major industrial sector (Hall and Preston, 1988). In many cases, the diffusion path and dynamic role of MNTS on industrial structures and processes may extend across two long-wave eras. This is clearly the case with the railways (van Geldern, in Freeman, 1996: 30–1), electrical technologies, automobiles. In my reading, this is the most compelling account of the economic implications of electrical power as a major new technology system. It is drawn from the relevant historical and innovation literature, whether more rooted in technological determinist (e.g. Freeman, 1982, 1985, 1987; McLuhan, 1964) or social shaping theoretical traditions (Hughes, 1983). Thus, I draw on the historical case of electrical technology in order to support my point about the advantages of the dialectical approach to the selection of theoretical models appropriate to these particular categories of technology-related innovations. But the case of the (then minor) cluster of new media innovations in the 1880–1920s period also underlines the disruptive impacts on industrial structures and the division of labour. By permitting cultural expression to be 'fixed' or 'frozen' in new media systems, these technical innovations created both powerful incentives and opportunities for industrial innovation along the lines hinted by Adam Smith more than a hundred years before their development. They provided a distinct impetus on the supply side towards the extended industrialisation of culture and related shifts in the division of labour.

Thus whilst recognising that historical (no more than any other) 'facts' do not possess an independent existence outside theoretical constructions, I will draw upon the electrical technology case as support for the following proposal: when it comes to the strategic economic or social implications of the emergence and diffusion of MNTS, a (very) soft technological determinist model is required in order to address certain aspects of the innovation process. This applies whether one is addressing electrical power in the past, or new ICTs today. At the level of the economic or industrial system and the division of labour, pervasive MNTS have distinct 'disruptive' effects in terms of what (products or services) are produced as well as how goods or services may be produced. They are socially and consciously constructed systems which introduce distinctively new opportunities and incentives for profit-making and the enhancement of productivity gains which are system-wide and which, by definition, did not exist before. They also introduce new incentives for the deepening of the social and technical divisions of labour.

However, I want to stress that a 'soft' rather than a 'hard' technological determinist approach is being proposed in this case. The new possibilities for economic and social change opened up by such MNTS are, of course, not completely open but bounded in many respects. They are bounded by the technical features of the major new technology system, by particular technological dependencies which may pre-determine the 'trajectory' of its applications or diffusion, and by distinctive new sets of economic incentives and opportunities. Even more importantly, however, they are bounded by the very specific political-economy culture and social relationships of capitalism, not least its inherent drive to expand commodification ('the naked cash nexus') into every sphere of social relations and cultural processes. In more sociological terms, they are bounded by the prevailing configurations of 'power and domination' in the structuration of allocative control (over the material world) and authoritative control (over the social world), to use Giddens' terminology (1995). Yet it must also be recognised that the precise forms and range of new possibilities remain relatively fluid and open, especially in the early (emergence) stages of a major new technology system compared to the later stages. In the early stages, there is a necessary process of experimentation and trial-and-error procedures with respect to the most appropriate configuration of the technical components of a major new technology system as well as its associated social and institutional innovations. Any such window of technical and socio-economic experimentation is limited and finite in the case of major new technology systems, however. Eventually there is a firming up and consolidation of a specific configuration of technological forms and associated 'best practice' techniques in the economic and social realms to form a new techno-economic and social paradigm. But the precise form and extent of such new norms or practices will vary according to specific national or regional settings (Hughes, 1983).

Indeed, in terms of both classical and contemporary social theory, the approach adopted here is one which suggests that major and pervasive new technology systems tend to be 'disruptive' of the prevailing norms and factors conditioning the levels of economic productivity and industrial best practice (Freeman, 1996). At least in the economic realm, they disturb the boundaries of the prevailing equilibrium, not least by offering the potential of a 'free lunch' via significant new product innovations and productivity gains. But such gains are not automatic; their realisation requires a cluster of innovations along a series of micro and macro social, political and institutional dimensions. Thus MNTS open up strategic new possibilities in terms of both components of (any) agency-structure theory, and in ways which have not yet been fully explored or integrated into social theory.[4] Especially since the nineteenth century, the origination of all technological innovations has become more and more integrated into the logics and sway of capitalist development. But the construction of a major new technology system, together with the firming up of the optimal technical configurations and the associated struggles to establish new socio-economic paradigms, favourable to their application, diffusion and use all have important 'downstream' disruptive impacts and effects. In important ways they provide novel options, as well as new incentive structures and means which are mobilised or 'appropriated' by different social forces. In other words, they disturb in significant ways the prevailing 'circumstances' element within Marx's pithy and much-cited maxim that 'men make history, but not in circumstances of their own making'. Even for many critics of Marx, this is 'still the most evocative encapsulation of the agency-structure relation in social theory' (Soja, 1989: 141). To put this in the terms of more contemporary social theory, such as Giddens' theory of structuration, MNTS tend to disturb the existing 'social systems' defined as comprising 'patterns of relationships between actors or collectivities reproduced across time and space'. Indeed they may also be seen to disturb 'the structuration of social systems' defined as 'the conditions governing their continuity, change or dissolution' (Giddens, 1995: 26–7).

Where does this lead us with respect to the debates and discourses surrounding the meaning and implications of new information and communication technologies (ICTs) or indeed, new communication systems such as the Internet/WWW or the 'information superhighways'? Here, it is now possible and useful to specify a number of key defining features and implications which are largely drawn from the literature on long-wave restructuring and change and earlier work on the history of electrical and electronic technologies (Hall and Preston, 1988).

In the first place, new ICTs can be defined as a socially produced MNTS, with a pervasive application potential. As such, it represents a historically rare, but not unique, major new technology system. It is one of a series of MNTS which have been developed since the advent of capitalist industrialism. As such new ICT heralds not the transcendence of the key features of capitalist industrialism, but important transformations and change *within* this system. This implies a certain continuity of key social, economic and political relations as well as changes in certain aspects.

However, more generally it must be stressed that new ICT (including its component new media technologies or information infrastructures) represents more than a major new 'technology' system with a pervasive applications potential. Indeed as the currently predominant major new technology system, new ICT also represents an important stimulus and site for the contestation and/or negotiation of future social, political and cultural developments in addition to the more strictly 'economic' processes of change and continuities. New ICT involves a historically significant set of new incentives or structured/channelled opportunities to produce novel goods and services as well as 'mature' ones in new ways (a cluster of product and process innovations). It brings in its train a pervasive and persuasive (productivity + profit-enhancing) set of incentives for intensified change or restructuring at least in terms of the given 'instrumental reason' and expansive economic calculus underpinning all material processes in industrial capitalism. Thus new ICT represents a strategic stimulus and site for efforts to reshape the characteristics and range of industrial products and services produced by the economic system (including their modes of distribution). It also serves to reshape many aspects of the social, political, and cultural practices and relationships which have been inherited from the past. But the precise forms of such current or of future developments will not follow some predetermined singular 'trajectory'. Nor are they to be viewed as solely determined by the characteristics of this major new technology system. They will be shaped in important respects by organisational and managerial innovations in the economic realm as well as by wider social, political and cultural initiatives or innovations/processes.

Thus, in economic terms, new ICT represents a major new technology system, the adoption and diffusion of which has the potential to enhance profits and productivity as well as stimulate both the emergence of significant new industrial sectors and wider patterns of economic growth in the long term. The former include both the sectors directly involved in the supply of the new ICT hardware, software and systems as well as 'leading-edge' application or user industries involved in the supply of a plethora of 'downstream' innovative products and services. In addition, the diffusion and application of this pervasive new technology system also provides an important stimulus and novel set of economic incentives for a range of process and other technical innovations in almost every other major industrial sector.

Not least, precisely because it comprises new information and communication technologies, the currently predominant new MNTS involves particularly significant implications for the diverse range of communication, mass media and cultural industries. It is likely to stimulate important new product and process innovations within these sectors and neighbouring fields, including some expansion in their overall shares of employment, economic output and growth in the advanced industrial world. According to many accounts, the further development and diffusion of advanced ICTs towards 'a common digital mode' will stimulate tendencies towards a 'convergence' between previously separate information and communication industries and activities and promote the development of new kinds of 'multimedia' products and services. But the theoretical model proposed in this chapter, together with the now long history of flawed technology-centred forecasts, alerts us to the many barriers or limits to such convergence tendencies. Besides, the failure of many related corporate investment initiatives in the past also serves to underline the fact that non-technological factors play an important role in any such process of change. They indicate that there are many non-technical considerations which block or delay the transitions to a singular convergent or seamless 'multimedia' communications sector. Despite the further developments in digital and multimedia technologies, the continuing salience of non-technical factors (e.g distinctive industrial cultures, core organisational competencies, regulatory conditions, etc.) represent important barriers or delays to any rapid erosion or blurring of the existing boundaries between different communication or media industries.

Again, precisely because it comprises new information and communication technologies, new ICT is likely also to stimulate significant changes in the overall role and characteristics of specialised information services and knowledge production as well as in their modes of distribution. This refers to the sectors involved in the production of specialised or 'producer' information services or products and related forms of instrumental or functional knowledge. It includes the kinds of activities which were so central to the analyses advanced by information sector theorists such as Machlup or the OECD researchers and by information society theorists such as Bell, as well as other theorists reviewed in previous chapters. Here we are pointing to not only specialised scientific and technical knowledge, but also financial, legal, economic and marketing information. This category also embraces the specialised information or knowledge activities related to advertising, public relations and the increasing role of visual design aesthetic and other symbolic dimensions underpinning much of the material or economic relations in the contemporary world. Here it may be helpful to recall the distinctions between the primary and secondary information sectors which were noted earlier in Chapter Three. In this view, new ICTs will also have major implications for secondary information sector – for the production, access and use of such specialised information within all sectors of the economy.

The newer 'broadband' electronic information (or communication) infrastructures (the so-called new information superhighways) can be identified as advanced core network technologies or systems lying at the heart of new ICT (conceptualised and defined as a pervasive major new technology system). Besides the 'I' and the 'T' components of the term ICT, it is also important to emphasise the 'C' component here. This serves to highlight the central role of the new 'communication' and networking features inherent in this pervasive new technology system. It highlights the new structural incentives or opportunity channels provided by broadband systems to reshape the nature, role and scale of the division of labour based on diverse forms of networking relationships. This may be especially marked in the case of the sub-sets of primary and secondary information services which can be delivered remotely via the ever more rapid, reliable and cheaper distribution (communication) systems. The extended or neo-Fordism of telecentres and other telematics-based white-collar 'factories' are examples of these developments.

Lastly, since the industrial revolution, successive new communication and transportation technologies have played an important role in fostering the increasing density and intensification of economic, social and cultural exchanges across space. They have contributed to what Marx called the increasing tendencies towards the 'annihilation of space by time' and what Giddens refers to as the process of 'space–time distanciation'. Their adoption and diffusion in particular modes and contexts has enabled and contributed to the construction of new forms of economic, social and cultural 'spaces'. The novel communicational and networking possibilities afforded by new ICTs today are likely to provide new incentives or competitive 'opportunities' to stimulate a further extension or intensification of these long-established tendencies. This includes new forms of the much-heralded 'globalisation' of economic, social and cultural relationships, including a significant extension or deepening of the particular forms of the international division of labour which emerged in the fourth long-wave era. But, again, the precise extent and forms of such potential developments will be shaped by socio-economic forces as well as by the crucial role of state policies, not least those steering the spatial contours of information, financial and other services sectors.

THE 'SOCIO-TECHNICAL PARADIGM' CONCEPT

'At the same time that capitalism is tending to drive forward the development of productive forces, it is doing it on the basis of a tendency to keep wages down. This is one of the central contradictions of capitalist development.'

(Chesnais, 1986: 186)

For many subsequent theorists, Schumpeter failed to provide a clear account of how a major cluster of new technological innovations translates into a sustained long-wave 'upswing' of relatively rapid economic growth. Indeed, notwithstanding their other differences, the explanation of such 'turning points' remains the key challenge for both neo-Schumpeterian and neo-Marxist long-wave theorists (Freeman (ed.), 1996; Mandel, 1982, 1984, 1985, 1996). For some of the former theorists, it appears that the diffusion trajectory of pervasive, major new technology systems stimulates quantum leaps in productivity in leading sectors, and this may be sufficient to tilt the overall economy towards an upswing. But others remain unconvinced by this particular version of hard technological determinism. As indicated earlier, the concept of 'technico-economic paradigms' is central to many of the recent neo-Schumpeterian long-wave approaches. Here the development of major new technology systems is viewed as only one, if essential, part of the story of long-run capitalist development and change because their effective diffusion, application and use to support a sustained new phase of rapid economic growth require a second set of conditioning factors. This refers to a set of 'matching' managerial, organisational or institutional innovations, sometimes including appropriate shifts in 'socio-institutional practices', norms and regulations which will support and facilitate the adoption and diffusion of the major new technology system and its potentialities. These are not pre-given or prescribed by the technology system itself, but involve a process of search and discovery, especially a process of economic selection from a range of technically feasible combinations of innovations. The combination of these two sets of innovation factors has been defined as *a new techno-economic paradigm* and characterised as a standard or guide to 'best practices' across the economic system, if not more widely (Freeman, 1984, 1985, 1986, 1994; Perez, 1983, 1985).

In principle, the techno-economic paradigm notion is potentially very useful for present concerns. It opens the way for a more holistic and socially grounded approach to such long-term phases of socio-economic change and development in capitalist industrialism. It moves beyond any fixation on technology matters to account for the structuring of strategic new opportunities afforded by the productivity gains and associated 'free lunches' linked to major new technology systems. It appears to open the way for an approach to the major historical turning points in capitalist industrialism which takes account of the interplay of social, institutional and policy forces as well as technological change. In many respects, it seems to borrow from Schumpeter's own tendency to adopt a wide definition of what constitutes 'innovation'. But in practice, this concept has been very loosely defined and it is interpreted or applied in quite different ways by its by neo-Schumpeterian proponents, including the pioneering and prolific work of Christopher Freeman. Sometimes the non-technological components are confined to the conventionally defined realms of the economic and managerial discourse where the salience of the social and institutional innovations, not to mention the cultural, disappear from view. All too frequently, the concept is used in a highly selective and restrictive manner, with the stress on managerial and organisational innovations. When addressed, explicitly, the role of state policies or socio-political movements, whether those of the past or the present, tends to be treated in a highly technocratic or abstract mode.

Hence I want to propose the alternative concept of a 'socio-technical paradigm' (STP). The new concept proposed here explicitly draws upon the ideas inherent in the work of neo-Schumpeterians such as Freeman and Perez, but it involves more than a mere change in terminology. It is proposed in order to highlight and more consistently emphasise the centrality of social, political and institutional forces in shaping the nature and direction of long-wave turning points in the development of capitalist industrialism. The notion of a 'socio-technical paradigm' can embrace the important kinds of managerialist and organisational innovations which have been highlighted by proponents of the techno-economic paradigm concept. It also embraces important strategic changes in production and consumption spheres also addressed in some other post-Fordist accounts. But it has the advantage of locating them within the wider set of extra-economic processes of negotiation, conflict and learning which shape the overall trajectory of historical change. It also has closer resonances with the older notion of 'socio-technical systems' which provided an earlier route towards an alternative to hard

TABLE 6.2 Summary: four long waves of capitalist development

		LW1: 1790s–1840s	LW2: 1840s–1880s
1)	New technology systems and infrastructures	Water and steam power Early mechanisation of textile etc. production New iron production techniques Canals and (turnpike) roads	Railway transport Steam power in factories, shipping, etc. Precision engineering, machinery and tools New steel and coal production processes
2)	'Leading-edge' growth sectors	Iron works and casting Cotton textiles, Textile machinery Potteries Wholesale and retail trade in consumer goods in expanding urban centres	Railways and equipment Steam engines/precision machinery Coal/steel-based industries
3)	Organisational, managerial innovations; typical production/labour processes	Growth of the factory system and utilisation of detailed division of labour Small firms managed by individual owners and families	Growing role of large firms Joint stock companies and new forms of investment, control and ownership Steam energy increases locational flexibility, and scale of production units
4)	Social, institutional and political innovations/shifts	Shift to liberal laissez-faire principles via dissolution of old guilds, monopolies, restrictions on trade, travel, etc. Suppression of early trade unions Secret societies to promote interests of lower classes in urban and rural contexts	Growing pressures 'from below' for social and political reforms Craft unions gain some legal rights Minimal regulation of work-time/hours, women's and children's work Consolidation of the 'nation-building' project in some countries Growth of formal education and technical training
5)	Innovation in consumption and sphere of everyday life	Rapid shift from rural to urban living Decline in working and living conditions and life opportunities of working classes Growth of commodity markets in expanding urban centres	Rapid growth of large cities and 'urbanism as a way of life' New water/sewerage systems, sanitary and pollution regulations Growth of domestic servants in new urban middle class households

Notes:
a) As in any such summary schema, the treatment of key aspects is necessarily selective (e.g. no attention is given to the important role of international developments and there is little reference to changing spatial forms and divisions of labour in different long-wave periods).
b) The idea of specialised R&D departments is adopted by large and medium-sized firms in many if not most industrial sectors in the post-war (4th LW]) era. This upswing era was also marked by: (i) relatively high levels of state funding for (S&T and) R&D activities in civilian and often military fields; (ii) rapid expansion of secondary and tertiary education and industrial training; (iii) some limited transfers of technology via licensing agreements, investments by multinationals, etc.
c) In most cases, successive MNTS tend to develop complementary rather than replacement/substitution relations with earlier technological systems.

LW3: 1890–1940/45	LW4: Late 1940s→
Electrical engineering and machinery Chemicals and dyes Steel and heavy engineering	Mass diffusion of motorised transportation Electronics Aerospace Artificial fibres
Electrical and heavy engineering industries Chemicals and dyes Consumer durables sectors Growth of 'white collar' services/occupation SEC: New mass media and leisure sectors (Automobiles – USA)	Automobiles Electronics Aerospace, Chemicals Growth of producer/specialised information, electronic media, etc. and cultural industries Growth of women's paid employment
Growing scale/concentration of capital units Era of 'monopoly' or finance capitalism Electric power used to increase flexibility in factory location and layout Early Fordism and 'scientific management' in new 'mass production' sectors New role of in-house R&D depts 'Sloanism': new marketing, advertising, obsolescence, consumer credit strategies	Growing role of (industrial) MNCs Extension of Fordism to many sectors Managerialism and professional expertise Growth of state and private R&D activity Strong role of trade unions (1945–1975) Extension of Sloanist marketing, advertising, obsolescence strategies, targeted around diversified 'life-styles'
Major expansion of trade unions and more politicised labour movement Growing pressures for extension of citizenship and political rights Reshaping of 'time/money budgets' Liberal reforms: insurance and pension schemes for workers (W. Europe) New roles/forms of R&D activities, patents and other IPR protections State industrial policies, regulation role Publicly owned utilities /natural monopolies	UPSWING:1940–70s: 'We're all Keynesians now' with 'full employment' as priority policy goal, major welfare state reforms Shift to 'mixed-economy' with new social citizenship rights DOWNSWING: c1975–1990s Rising hegemony of neo-liberalism High unemployment and slow growth Increasing social inequalities Some weakening of labour movements New social movements (feminism, greens)
Growth of rail and other mass transit systems for increasingly large conurbations Beginnings of sub-urbanisation process New mass markets for consumer durables Growth of mass media and increasingly privatised consumption practices	Mass extension of surburbanism, privatised individualised lifestyles and media-orientated consumption practices Expanded flows of commodities: diverse consumer durables and symbolic goods Growing use of credit facilities for housing and consumer durables Rise of self-servicing – only in upswing?

d) In many cases, the diffusion path and dynamic role of MNTS may extend across two long-wave eras. This is clearly the case with, for example, the railways (van Geldern, in Freeman, 1996, pp. 30–1), electrical technologies, automobiles.

Sources: Summary of author's model; inspired by the previous work of long-wave theorists (e.g. Freeman, 1984, 1985, 1996; Freeman and Perez, 1988; Freeman and Soete, 1994; Mandel, 1972, 1995; Hall and Preston, 1988)

technological determinism and also stressed the interplay of technological, social and institutional innovations in the past (e.g. Cherry, 1978). In addition, I believe that the term 'socio-technical paradigm' also serves to challenge the tendency to neglect or ignore social and political forces (compared to technological, technocratic and managerial factors) in shaping historical change. As the earlier chapters indicated, this was a prominent and common feature in most of the existing theories of contemporary socio-economic and cultural change. I believe that the SEP concept serves to highlight the important role of such forces in shaping developments in the past and, potentially, in shaping the future direction of social, economic and cultural developments linked to the application and diffusion of new ICTs.

The implications of the 'socio-technical paradigm' across the four successive long waves are briefly (if somewhat schematically) indicated in Table 6.2 which aims to summarise key features of the overall model. Rows one and two (only) describe the more purely technological and industrial moments of the innovation process. Row three describes the moments usually highlighted by the new socio-technical paradigm concept. Rows four and five highlight some of the key dimensions I wish to emphasise by proposing the concept of the socio-technical paradigm.

THE MODEL IN 'THE REAR-VIEW MIRROR': THE THIRD LONG-WAVE ERA

By way of illustration, I can briefly indicate the merits of stressing the role of social and political forces with respect to the third long-wave upswing of capitalist development which emerged at the close of the last century. In many neo-Schumpeterian models, aside from the technological innovations in the chemicals and electrical engineering fields, the emphasis tends to fall on the managerial and organisational innovations associated with the introduction of Fordist mass production and labour processes together with Sloanism in the sphere of consumption and marketing. Yet, it seems clear that both these types of non-technical innovations, as well as other aspects of the structures of everyday life both inside and outside the workplace, were themselves strongly shaped by distinctive social and political movements, especially in the case of West European industrial societies.

Here I have in mind the growth of trade unions and labour movement political organisations on the one hand and in the official political arena, the democratic movements to widen the base of electoral participation rights and conceptions of citizenship on the other. The combined effects of the labour movements and these various 'historical and moral elements' led to a significant shift in the distribution of income and a reduction in average working hours. They influenced the particular path taken by Fordist and scientific management innovations in the sphere of production or labour processes in the third long-wave era and later (Braverman, 1974). Moreover, these social movements also consciously sought and wrought fundamental changes in time and money budget norms which were far from insignificant. Indeed, these may be defined as prior conditions for the expanding markets for the new mass-produced consumption goods. These as much as any purely technological, managerial or organisational innovations, provided the prior conditions for the first emergence of newspapers as a truly 'mass medium' and the subsequent development of the 'new media' industries. The social struggles which established the new time and money budget norms critically shaped the 'first communications technology revolution' (film and recorded music), as well as other cultural and 'leisure' service industries in the early decades of the twentieth century (the third long-wave era).[5] Indeed in some European countries, they also provided the impetus for the development of important forms of collective consumption in the third long-wave era which were distinct from the more individualised forms which characterised the USA (Preston, 1996d).

In addition, the associated movements concerned with widening the social basis of political participation were critical in expanding conceptions of citizenship, including the introduction of elementary social insurance and pension schemes. In important respects, these political innovations extended the role and functions of the state into the previously defined 'private sphere'. Even if they only temporarily or partially favoured the weaker social strata, they 'succeeded in translating economic antagonisms into political conflicts' (Marshall, 1950; Habermas, 1992). In combination, these social and political innovations were highly significant in shaping the contours of the third long-wave upswing. In essence, they indicate that the subsequent trajectory of capitalist development, whether in relation to mass production or consumption, cannot be reduced to any interlinked combination of technological, managerial or organisational innovations, especially in Western Europe.

It must also be recognised that in important respects, such social and political forces or innovations transformed the essential features and direction of capitalist development from the closing decades of the nineteenth century. They not only transformed the 'opportunity structures' in an economic sense, but they also made the 'conditions of life' of the majority of the wage-earning population more tolerable by extending the functions of the state, including its role in the redistribution of income, as Habermas (1992) notes.[6] But in a more significant way than the purely managerial or organisational innovations (whether Sloanism or Fordism), these social and political initiatives established new social and cultural norms or 'paradigms'. They 'constructed' the new time and money budgets which were the preconditions for the new mass consumption norms of the third long-wave upswing. This was no minor social innovation for it opened up 'that indispensable market for the final product which the self-destructive drive of capitalism towards a more and more inequitable distribution of national income would otherwise have closed' (Strachey, 1956: 185; cited in Habermas, 1992: 146). These 'actions' or social innovations 'structured' the material preconditions for the mass consumption and diffusion of the new electrical products and media products (e.g. the cinema and gramo-phone records) of that era as much as any technological or managerial developments.

Whilst Schumpeter stresses the role of 'heroic entrepreneurs' or the 'swarming' of imitation innovations, he neglects these equally heroic social and political movements. These must be considered as part of the 'action' as well as the 'structures' in any long-wave story of new upswings and socio-technical paradigms or distinct regimes of accumulation. That is one reason why long-wave movements cannot be defined as regular cycles (Mandel, 1996). Another is that key features of the long-wave downswing include a general slowdown in economic growth (despite rapid growth in some new technology-based sectors) and low rates of profitability as well as high levels of unemployment (Mandel, 1996; Freeman, 1996). The working through of such complex crises and associated restructuring processes necessarily involves more than mere adjustments in technological, managerial or organ-isational processes. Hence the stress here on the actual or potential role of social and political movements in the past as well as in the contemporary moments of these long-wave movements.

IMPLICATIONS AND SOME QUALIFIERS

Compared to many of the other theories of socio-economic change and restructuring, the neo-Schumpeterian approach has been taken as the most useful starting point for a more adequate theory of the contemporary. It provides an initial set of concepts for a more historically grounded and com-prehensive multi-factor approach to understanding key aspects of the contemporary and the kinds of continuities and changes (dis-continuities) involved in the dynamics of capitalist development. Of particular note here is the fact that it highlights the importance of a long-wave cyclical dynamic in order to understand the key features of the contemporary processes of change and restructuring. This aspect of the neo-Schumpeterian approach suggests that the contemporary should not be understood merely in terms of a linear historical trajectory (or in terms of a break in long-run secular trends), but also as a particular moment or phase in a 'long-wave' cycle of development within the capitalist industrial system. This is an important fea-ture of the neo-Schumpeterian model and one which it has in common with a few of the other theories reviewed (e.g. some other post-Fordist models and Jameson's adoption of Mandel's schema of crisis and restructuring in his version of postmodernism).

The modified long-wave cyclical perspective is important for more than methodological reasons. It also helps to focus attention on a more rounded understanding of contemporary social and economic developments which tend to be neglected in other technology-centred approaches. Many of the apparently quite different theories reviewed earlier are marked by a common tendency to neglect the most significant social and economic trends which have developed over the past couple of decades. For example, most third-wave, information society and postmodernist theories tend to totally neglect important social and economic developments since the 1970s, not least the return of mass unemployment, widening socio-economic cleavages and the slowdown in economic growth compared to the post-war upswing era. Thus despite other apparent differences and emphases on particular new technological, informational or cultural developments, they tend to highlight or assume (if only implicitly) the kinds of social and economic conditions which prevailed during the long post-war boom era. The cyclical perspective inherent in this approach helps to focus attention on these recent developments and stresses their importance in understanding the dynamics of contemporary social developments and their potential implications for the future direction of change.

But, as we have seen, the neo-Schumpeterian model only represents a starting point for a more adequate theory of the contemporary restructuring process. It represents an important entry point for present concerns but one which must also be complemented by ideas and concepts drawn from the critical social theory traditions and cultural studies fields explored earlier. It tends to favour a rather restrictive account of the non-technical dimensions of the innovation processes associated with the turning points from one long-wave of capitalist development to another.

This chapter has outlined some of the foundations or components of a more adequate theory of new ICT and the key tendencies promoting change in industrial structures and division of labour. It has indicated their strategic implications for an intensified socio-economic restructuring process, including further shifts in the role of the media and other information services sectors. In the following chapters I will move on to elaborate and further develop this initial theorisation by exploring some more concrete trends, stakes and tendencies. I will move to a more empirical register to examine the key trends or tendencies of socio-economic change as well as identifying important continuities. I will also examine the trends which are serving to reshape the role and characteristics of information and communication sectors in the shift towards a new long-wave phase of capitalist development: informational capitalism.

I want to stress again that the long-wave model and the dialectical approach proposed here are far from technologically determinist. Neither a new long-wave upswing nor extended commodification of the information sector, nor a more or less egalitarian social or political order necessarily follow from the development of new ICTs as a historically rare major new technology system. There is no linear technological trajectory which drives the form and pace of capitalist development. The long-wave turning point involves a complex process of interlinked innovations including social learning and struggles along many dimensions. For example, it may be that dynamic developments on the technology supply side remain relatively localised within certain sectors and in combination with the 'spontaneous' or inherent imperatives of the accumulation process, they may fail to tip the overall economy into a new long-wave upswing.

Our unfolding social, economic and cultural 'future(s)' are not inscribed in the new communication technologies but depend upon the complex of forces covered by the STP concept. Here, it is important to stress that since the ending of the great post-war boom (the fourth long-wave upswing) the contemporary period has not only been marked by the development of a major cluster of new ICTs and the potential expansion of a specific type of increasingly information-intensive economic and social order. It has also been marked by a profound social and political crisis and restructuring process whose key features and tendencies require further interrogation (a task to which the following chapters will turn). The contemporary may also be characterised as a (typically long) period of economic and social experimentation. It involves the search for the complex institutional matrix and an appropriate mix of economic, social, and political innovations which might lead to a sustainable new upswing of economic growth and development. In this sense, the contemporary is also marked by a fundamental 'process of social experimentation and learning which is still at an early stage' (Freeman and Soete, 1994: 41–2). Thus the precise components or configuration of any new long-wave socio-technical paradigm are not predetermined by technology, rather they can be strongly shaped by the initiatives of diverse economic and political interests, including the potential role of established and new social movements.

In addition, it should be noted that the neo-Schumpeterian research tradition has had relatively little to say about the specific role and characteristics of the information and communication services. This is especially marked in the case of the cultural industries sectors which appear to be so central to the overall process of restructuring and change in the contemporary period. Here in particular, the long-wave model must be augmented further by concepts and insights drawn from the writings of Habermas and various contributors to the political economy of communication and cultural studies fields, including the work of less apocalyptic postmodern theorists such as Jameson. I will turn to these important challenges in the following chapters.

Notes

1 It should be noted that there are many other recent models of technology, such as those focused innovation networks and actor-network approaches, which cannot be discussed here for reasons of space.

2 Space will not permit any detailed discussion of the relations between Shumpeterian and Marxist approaches to long-wave cycles here. But it can be briefly noted that despite his vehement opposition to Marx's political agenda and values, Schumpeter frequently acknowledged his debt to Marx. Indeed there are many commonalities between Marx's accounts of capitalism's crises and restructuring processes, its inherently expansionary tendencies, etc., and Schumpeter's ideas of long-wave cycles and 'gales of creative destruction'. There are also many distinct echoes between Marx's work and some of the key ideas informing later neo-Schumpeterian notions of new techno-economic paradigms (for a brief account see Chesnais, 1986). In the present author's view, both neo-Marxist and neo-Schumpeterian approaches to long waves are in many respects quite complementary and the approach adopted here draws on elements of both traditions.

3 An important exception here is the work of Tom Hughes (1983).

4 Giddens is widely recognised as the major contemporary social theorist but, perhaps understandably, much of his work is focused on a very high level of abstraction. Indeed in much of his work he pays only fleeting attention to the historical role of major new technology or communication systems, despite his concern with 'time–space distanciation' (e.g. 1995: 38, 188–9; 199). See also Soja (1989) for a sympathetic critique of this aspect of Giddens' work.

5 As McLuhan notes in one of his more compelling sections of *Understanding Media*, electrical power also provided a necessary precondition (if not novel stimulus) for the subsequent development of cinema as an important new cultural industry in the early part of the last century as well as the new flexibility of time use afforded by the electrical lighting (McLuhan, 1964).

6 As Habermas notes in his early work (1962), which was more attentive to 'action' and the role of social agency and hence the more 'messy' and complex processes of historical change compared to his later work.

CHAPTER SEVEN

THE 'ATOMS AND BITS' OF INFORMATIONAL CAPITALISM

'I'm optimistic about the impact of new technology. It will enhance leisure time and enrich culture by expanding the distribution of information . . . It will relieve pressure on natural resources because increasing numbers of products will be able to take the form of bits rather than manufactured goods. It will give us more control over our lives . . . Citizens in the information society will enjoy new opportunities for productivity, learning and entertainment.'

(Gates, 1995: 250)

'Despite universal primary and secondary education in OECD countries, one person in six is functionally illiterate – unable to fill out a job application, excluded from the rapidly changing world that demands new skills in processing information.'

(UNDP, 1999: 37)

'IT'S THE ECONOMY STUPID!': PRODUCTION, CONSUMPTION AND THE RHYTHMS OF 'EVERYDAY LIFE'

The theoretical model sketched earlier suggests that the contemporary can be best understood in terms of the complex interplay of three different movements: *changes, continuities and cyclical turbulences*, a cluster of restructuring processes associated with a long-wave downswing.[1] Here I will both apply and further elaborate this model to explore aspects of the long-wave crisis/restructuring processes since the late 1970s. This will also involve an examination of the complex interplay of factors and forces involved in the search for, and construction of, a new socio-technical paradigm (SEP).

This approach suggests that the new emphasis on diverse forms of information should not be taken to imply the erosion or transcendence of the fundamental features of a specifically *industrial* or capitalist form of society. Rather we are dealing with important long-run or strategic *changes* in certain of its structures and forms as well as *continuities* or extensions of certain other longer-term tendencies in society.[2] In most respects, we are dealing with the extension of developments in the functions and roles of the division of labour, including intellectual labour, which were first identified by Adam

Smith, and developed further in the nineteenth century by Marx, Durkheim and Simmel.[3] Hence, the industrialisation of various kinds of information work, including the commodification of the media and cultural industries sphere, is far from novel, even if the prospective extension of such tendencies raises quite distinct political and cultural questions besides those that may be defined as economic in scope.

In attending to cyclical dynamics and the complexity of forces involved in the construction of new socio-technical paradigms, the adopted long-wave model opens up new avenues to examine the contemporary condition. In particular, it counters some of the inadequacies and blindspots, concerning the material realities of everyday life, which characterise many of the other models explored in earlier chapters. These tend to focus on the implications of new technologies, accelerating change, the presumed de-materialisation of the economy or the increasing cultural freighting of capitalist industrialism. Yet, ironically enough, many recent accounts of social and economic conditions fail to support their arguments with relevant empirical evidence. One result is that they appear to be stuck in a sort of time warp, one which has not moved on to take account of significant social, economic and cultural developments over the past two decades (Wood, 1996; 1997).

This chapter therefore considers selective aspects of the multi-directional 'gales of creative destruction' which have fanned the crisis and restructuring process, including shifts in the industrial division of labour, since the end of the fourth long-wave upswing. It will shift to a more empirical register in order to critically interrogate the manner and extent to which there has been a profound 'de-materialisation' of economic and social life over the past two decades associated with the much-heralded changes in technological infrastructures and the expanding role of diverse types of information and knowledge activities. It considers the changing employment and economic profiles of the contemporary 'leading edge' or 'high-tech' growth sectors including those involved in the supply of new ICTs and other information and communication industries.

I will also apply a nuanced version of the information sector concept to explore the changing respective roles of information and material production activities and related shifts in consumption processes in contemporary societies. I use this to investigate whether and how certain tendencies of change in the production and consumption of information and communication services have been increasing in importance in more recent decades. This work touches upon some of the important assumptions of socio-economic trends which have underpinned many of the information society, postmodern and other theories reviewed earlier. This chapter also highlights some of the downsides, including 'downsizing', linked to the prevailing gales of creative destruction. It describes the return of mass unemployment, new patterns of work and much-neglected new trends in social inequalities including the polarisation of rich/poor, inclusion/exclusion cleavages which have emerged in more recent years.

In this and the following chapter, I will address empirical evidence related to important trends of change in the spheres of production and consumption in everyday life over recent decades which many of the alternative theoretical perspectives have tended to neglect, if not totally ignore. This inquiry constructs a very different version of the contemporary condition compared to the glossy landscapes portrayed by the many recent information society or technology-centred accounts. It explicitly departs from many postmodern and self-defined critical 'readings' of the contemporary, where, following Baudrillard, the focus of attention falls almost exclusively on a presumed shift towards consumption-based and/or media-centred life. For sure, the consumption of (relatively inexpensive) media and other culturally freighted commodities has increased in the long run in some respects (for example, as measured by time spent on consumption). But I will seek to emphasise how, for 'the masses' (that majority, the secrets of whose daily life Baudrillard so frequently presumes to describe and understand so well), the material realities of everyday life and/or political economy have not disappeared into some *void of information* or jungle of detached signifiers. On the contrary, in the downswing years since the 1970s, there has been a series of important 'shocks' and twists in the long-run trajectories of development in the realms of consumption as well as in the production sphere. This account of such shocks also calls into question some of the claims underpinning influential versions of 'risk society' and 'reflexive modernisation' theory which also presume that the contemporary may be defined by a shift away from economic scarcities and other material considerations which informed sociological analysis in the past (e.g. Beck, 1992).

To start with the production sphere and the material aspects of everyday life, it is important to note that the fourth long-wave upswing represented the longest and most extensive period of capitalist industrial development and growth ever. This upswing period, between the late 1940s and the mid-1970s, was organised around a particular configuration of Fordist mass production techniques, Keynesian state policies and a distinct set of institutional arrangements and practices. As indicated earlier, these comprised important components of a distinctive socio-technical paradigm. The 'great post-war boom' was characterised by relatively high annual rates of growth in economic output and productivity as well as low levels of unemployment throughout the advanced capitalist industrial world. The result was, of course, a significant growth in the real wages and material living standards for the majority of the population and a concomitant increase in average and *per capita* personal consumption expenditures. The post-war upswing was also formed around new modes of collective consumption in the form of expanded welfare state regimes throughout the core capitalist world and beyond.

But this sustained virtuous circle of expanding output, productivity and consumer spending capacity during the post-war upswing period was no 'free lunch'. It was only made possible by a significant extension of the industrially organised and collective labour of the population, usually under the direct sway of capitalist production relations. It was also linked to important changes in the occupational and industrial structures and in the social and technical divisions of labour. Another important aspect has been the increased rates of participation of women in the paid workforce since the 1940s, both in the core capitalist economies and beyond and these trends continued up to the late 1990s (see Table 7.1).

TABLE 7.1   Change in the economically active:
North America, Europe, Japan and Asia, 1950–95

	Economically active population					Crude activity rates (%)		
	Total	Males		Females		Total	Men	Women
	Millions	Millions	Per cent	Millions	Per cent	Per cent	Per cent	Per cent
North America								
1950	72.9	52.7	72.3	20.1	27.6	42.5	61.4	23.4
1970	98.2	62.9	64.1	35.2	35.9	42.4	55.3	30.0
1995	151.1	82.9	54.9	68.1	45.1	50.9	56.7	45.3
N. Europe[1]								
1950	36.0	25.0	69.6	10.9	30.4	46.1	66.3	27.2
1970	40.5	25.5	63.1	14.9	36.9	46.3	60.0	33.3
1995	47.2	26.2	55.6	20.9	44.4	50.9	57.5	44.0
W. Europe[2]								
1950	65.0	42.5	65.3	22.6	34.7	46.2	63.8	30.3
1970	71.7	45.6	63.6	26.0	36.4	43.4	57.4	30.4
1995	85.9	49.7	57.8	36.2	42.2	47.5	56.2	39.1
Japan								
1950	36.7	22.6	61.6	14.1	38.4	43.8	55.0	33.0
1970	53.3	32.5	61.0	20.7	39.0	51.0	63.4	39.1
1995	66.8	39.6	59.2	27.2	40.8	53.4	64.4	42.8
Asia[3]								
1950	709.5	448.3	63.2	261.3	36.8	50.61	62.4	38.2
1970	991.1	612.9	61.8	378.2	38.2	46.2	55.9	36.0
1995	1711.1	1029.7	60.2	681.3	39.8	49.8	58.6	40.6

Notes:
1 Northern Europe covers Denmark, Estonia, Finland, Iceland, Ireland, Latvia, Lithuania, Norway, Sweden, and UK.
2 Western Europe covers Austria, Belgium, France, Germany, Luxembourg, Netherlands, Switzerland.
3 The data for Asia include Japan as well as China, India and 47 other countries.

Source: Author's estimates based on data in ILO (1997) The Economically Active Population, 1950–2010. Vols. I and IV, Table No.1.

The key point here is that for an ever greater proportion of 'the masses', both men and women, active engagement in the official economy of production and paid work has become an increasingly important feature of their everyday life.[4] This, of course, has also been an essential prerequisite for admission to the carnival of commodity consumption. I am emphasising this precisely because within much of what passes for contemporary social and cultural theory, there has been a significant turning away from considerations of work and productive activity as key aspects of social processes and everyday life experience. The trends summarised in Table 7.1 clearly indicate how productive activity (usually in the form of commodified labour), not simply commodified consumption, absorbs a considerable portion of the creative energies and time resources of an increasing proportion of the population in the advanced capitalist world and beyond. They illustrate the fact that access to, and engagement in, employment within the official (and, in most cases, market) economy is part of the daily life and experience of an increasing absolute number and percentage of the citizens in these and all other major world regions covered by the dataset. They also remind us of the continuing, indeed increasing, importance of what Marx long ago referred to as the 'dull compulsion of economic relations' in regulating the economic regime, social processes and in disciplining the routines and rhythms of everyday life.

TABLE 7.2   Estimates of annual working hours and time spent on use of selected media, USA, 1994–5[1]

(Hours per person per year)

Average annual total time use in hours		TV and video		Print media			On-line media
Average working hours[2]	All listed media	Total TV	Home video[3]	Daily news	Consumer magazines	Consumer books	On-line[4]
2,126	1,970	1,560	52	169	84	102	3

Notes:
1 Media use estimates refer to adults aged 18 or older, except where estimates include persons aged 12 or over in 1994.
2 Average yearly working hours of persons working full-time, USA, 1995: 2,126 hours.
3 Playback of prerecorded tapes only.
4 Consumer on-line/Internet access services.

Sources: Author's calculations from data in US Dept. of Commerce, Statistical Abstract of the US, 1996, pp. 562 and 402.

In qualitative terms, the intensity of attention and creative energy expended during paid-work time is generally much more concentrated than that spent in the more passive activities of media consumption. But in this particular context, it may be worth noting too that the average annual time spent at work by full-time employees in the USA (2,126 hours) far exceeds that spent viewing television and video programming, for example (1,612 hours) (see Table 7.2). Since the early stages of capitalist industrialism, the length of the working week or year has declined significantly, but this was not the automatic outcome of any technological logic nor of any autonomous economic trend (such as productivity gains). Rather, thanks in large part to the pressures exerted by the trade union and related political and social movements in earlier periods, the average annual number of working hours declined significantly in the advanced capitalist economies during the second and third long-wave eras. It declined from an approximate average of 3,000 hours per year in 1870 to 2,100–2,300 hours in the late 1930s. Since the late 1940s, there has been some (not always voluntary) increase in part-time work and 'early retirement'. But the available indicators suggest that the standard for 'full-time' workers' annual hours has been subject to very little change. It had declined to approximately 1,890 hours in the EC countries by the mid-1990s, but it had remained fairly static in the case of the USA (around 2,126 hours per year). The US case reflects a particular national form of institutional continuity linked to 'the overworked American' syndrome as described by Juliet Schor (1991).

This elementary point about the role of work-time and productive activity in contemporary social and everyday life is worth emphasising at the outset as it is a basic fact of social life and everyday experience that is often ignored or simply assumed away by so many theories of the contemporary. It is one which has been largely neglected by various generations of participants in the literature on 'workless capitalism' beginning with the 1950s automation debates. This neglect continues right down to many of the recent transformative discourses centred around new ICTs or media consumption practices and the changing role of information work. This includes the glossy technocratic accounts of an impending information society of automatic or universal abundance. The more material aspects of everyday life being highlighted here serve to challenge those many theorists, however self-defined as critical or radical, who advance consumption, leisure and media-centric analyses of the contemporary. They point to major weaknesses inherent in the discursive turn and the fashion for predominantly consumption-orientated analyses of everyday life within sociology and cultural studies. The resulting agenda of concerns, together with their mode of treatment, are all too often defined in blissful isolation from any consideration of the time, energy and discursive resource implications of work-time or of other productive or material activities.

Thus here, as elsewhere in these more concrete and empirically orientated sections of this book, it proves necessary to step outside the terms of reference set by this discursive turn and mindset. Whatever its relative strengths in the past, this has now become 'dangerously disengaged' from the everyday challenges and problems confronting the majority of citizens and consumers (Rorty, 1998). In much of what follows I will sidestep the challenge of extended gladiatorial contests centred around language games or tilting lances at 'theoretical hallucinations' (Rorty, 1998). Instead, I will have occasion to recall one successful recent political slogan which simply stated that 'it's the economy stupid' and, to support my arguments, I will also resort to one all-too-frequently neglected resource, empirical evidence concerning the phenomena under study.

GALES OF CREATIVE DESTRUCTION'?: CRISIS AND RESTRUCTURING PROCESSES

Many alternative accounts of the contemporary are essentially linear in that they tend to emphasise the progressive march of the technological or other singular trajectories of social and economic development. They generally stress the novel aspects of change such as the emergence of new industrial innovations and related 'sunrise' sectors of economic and employment growth. In contrast, this approach suggests that the contemporary is also fundamentally marked by a 'downswing' moment of the long-wave movements of capitalist accumulation. Not only has this moment had historical precedents, in many aspects it also represents a 'break' from what immediately preceded it. It involves a complex web of shifts and changes including low profitability, relatively slow growth of output and productivity, and high levels of unemployment compared to trends in the upswing phase of the long wave. It is also marked by certain *continuities* with previous downswing periods as well as distinctively new technological and socio-economic developments or *changes*. Within the expansive logics of capitalist industrialism, the continuities dimension of the long-wave downswing moment include the re-assertion of accumulation imperatives, the return of high levels of unemployment and the struggle to restore rates of profitability and productivity growth. The pressures, trends and dynamics involved here may be best examined by firstly, attending to empirical inquiry on contemporary socio-economic developments, and secondly, by focusing the rear-view mirror on previous downswings rather than technology-centred futuristic gazing or speculation.

This perspective on the contemporary does not seek to deny the emergence of major technological innovations nor the potential expansion of major new sectors of industrial activity and employment growth which are celebrated in other models. But it does suggest that such positive trends of change represent only one important dimension of the current processes of intensified industrial and economic restructuring. Indeed, they constitute the more positive aspect of what, following Schumpeter, we may refer to as 'the gales of creative destruction' which are generated during the downswing phases.

The image of creative gales of destruction is, I believe, particularly useful and evocative in referring to the processes of crisis and intensified restructuring in the capitalist economic system that have usually been associated with the downswing phases of development. It evokes the deep nature of the politico-economic crisis, stresses and shock waves within the older established regime and the intensified, if still uncertain and unstable search for new sectoral sites and spatial centres of accumulation which are typical of such downswing moments. It also invokes the instability of the prior spatial environment and the fevered construction of often temporary or unstable new landscapes and spatial forms of accumulation, as well as deepened forms of time-space compression as Harvey (1989), Gregory (1994) and other geographers have suggested. This phrase also helps to evoke the relative complexity and openness of the constellations of forces which serve to shape the turning point from a long-wave downswing to a new upswing of relatively rapid growth. As indicated when proposing the notion of a socio-technical paradigm in the previous chapter, much more is involved than the development, adoption and adaptation of major new clusters of technological innovations or technical systems.

TABLE 7.3   Productivity and output growth in OECD countries, 1960–96

(Percentage changes at annual rates)

	1960–73	1973–79	1979–86	1979–96
Output	5.2	2.9	2.3	2.7[3]
Total factor productivity[1]	3.1	0.8	0.6	0.9
Labour productivity[2]	4.6	1.8	1.4	1.6
Capital productivity	−0.5	−1.5	–	−0.7

Notes:
1 TFP growth is equal to a weighted average of the growth of labour and capital productivity.
2 Output per employed person.
3 This output estimate refers only to 1986–96 inclusive (based on 'Real GDP' data series).

Sources: OECD (1989), pp. 48–9; OECD (1997) and OECD Economic Outlook 62., 1998, Tables A66 and A4.

Besides the rise of new technologies and industries, there is another, more negative dimension to the downswing phase which has received remarkably little attention in much of the literature reviewed earlier. This concerns the relatively slow rates of overall growth in terms of economic output and productivity. For these and other purposes, it is necessary (and today, more than ever before) to address the capitalist economic system on a global rather than national scale. This may be illustrated by reference to the key economic trends within the twenty-five leading capitalist economies comprising the member states of the OECD.[5] The main points highlighted in

Table 7.3 are that the annual rates of growth in output across the OECD bloc declined from the mid-1970s to almost half of those which prevailed during the post-war long-wave upswing phase. At the same time, the annual rates of productivity growth dwindled to less than one-third of those prevailing in the earlier period.

These indicators refer to the general trends which are observable across the twenty-five economies at the core of the global capitalist system. But as in previous long-wave downswings, there are important variations and differences in economic performance along the sectoral and spatial dimensions. In sectoral terms, the telecommunications sector (alongside other ICT-related supply sectors) has been marked by very high rates of economic and productivity growth in recent decades. But these changes have been relatively localised or confined to a few sectors and have not had major economy-wide impact. National and regional economies articulate with the global system in very different ways, and so the precise patterns of output and productivity growth of any single economy may be more or less in line with such long-wave fluctuations or other global economy trends. A few, often smaller, newly industrialising countries (NICs) have experienced relatively rapid economic and productivity growth since the late 1970s, especially the four 'Asian Tigers' along with Ireland, the so-called 'Celtic Tiger' of the 1990s.

However, the growth rates and prospects of major economies like Japan remain pretty dismal at the close of the 1990s and those of the EU remain very much below those of the post-war boom period, whilst the US economy stands out as an exception to the overall growth performance of the major OECD economies, especially in the late 1990s. The USA was the only G7 country to manage a growth rate above two per cent in real terms in the 1990s, and it achieved a growth rate of four per cent in the 1996–99 period (*OECD Observer*, November 1999). There has been much discussion of the 'boom' in the US economy in the late 1990s, including some excited talk about the beginnings of a new economy or long-wave turning point but this has also been countered by some concerns about its sustainability. But even if the US economy was booming in the late 1990s for the wealthy élite, 'it is definitely not booming for the majority of US workers, especially those with the poorest jobs' (Moseley, 1999: 32).

These general trends of relatively slow rates of economic growth and productivity since the late 1970s should be viewed as the fans or stimulants of the recent gales of intensified industrial restructuring rather than the effects. Indeed, when viewed from the experiences of, or impact on, the working class or other major sections of society, this process of intensified restructuring is far from benign or creative. These trends also directly challenge the assertions or assumptions of contemporary theories which celebrate new ICTs and communication networks as direct sources of a new abundance of wealth, economic growth and material welfare. Indeed, such trends pose fundamental questions for the discourses favoured by the suppliers of new ICT-based systems and services, and by national and supra-national public policy agencies. For two decades now, these discourses have energetically marketed and promoted the purchase, use and diffusion of new ICTs precisely on the grounds that they will enhance economic perfor-mance, productivity, competitiveness and material welfare. Yet after massive investments in successive generations of such new systems and related edu-cation and training services, on the parts of firms, governments, citizens and final consumers, the question arises: Why are there still so few visible gains by the conventional measures of economic growth and welfare?

In response to the *productivity paradox* problem, those involved in the promotion of new ICTs have stressed that the conventional indicators may tend to underestimate the extent of achieved productivity gains since in 1980s. They suggest that this is due to measurement problems linked to the changing industrial structures and the more elusive or qualitative character of the productivity gains in services-based new growth sectors. There is no clear empirical test that can be applied to this claim, but even if one permits that this may well be a valid response in the case of growth trends in some sectors, it only represents one component of any adequate overall explana-tion of the productivity paradox.

Turning to the work of neo-Schumpeterian theorists such as Freeman and Soete (1987) and Perez, a number of other factors may be mobilised to offer a more satisfactory explanation. One is that the synergetic and cross-sectoral economic benefits of major new technology systems are generally relatively slow. It is suggested that such lags in the diffusion of the new sys-tems and related best practices in managerial and organisational techniques across sectors arise precisely because of the radically novel nature of new technological innovations. A second is that radically new technology systems may produce temporary disequilibrating or unstable effects in the relations between international trade, regional development and industrial structures which may serve to retard the realisation of the new systems' potential to deliver economic benefits. A third explanatory factor, and one that partly links with the concept of the socio-technical paradigm outlined earlier, cen-tres around the inherently slow process of devising or constructing institutional and organisational forms which are appropriate to the new technological systems. In other words, there may be a bad 'fit' between the organisational and institutional forms which were constructed around the now mature technology and production systems, therefore the search for 'matching' new forms may take a relatively long period. Writing in 1994, Freeman and Soete suggested that '. . . the full economic and social benefits (including employment generation) of new information technology depend on a . . . process of social experimentation and learning which is still at an early stage' (1994: 41–2). This kind of explanation is, in my view, much more important than that centred on mere measurement problems. But, the former explanation also needs to be extended to address the role of social and political movements in line with the concept of the socio-technical paradigm outlined earlier.

One reason for doing so is that the key investment decisions in the capitalist economic system continue to be made on the basis of the private profit-generating calculus of competing blocs of the owners and controllers of capital. Hence any wealth or job generation impacts of these decisions are merely the effects of the operations of such private calculus as are a wide set of other more public and social effects. The downswing era of the long wave is marked by many dimensions of uncertainty, instability and risk associated with the transition from one regime of accumulation to another. Yet there is no reason to assume that the combination of the private and dispersed decisions of the economic élites will readily combine or co-ordinate to produce the new patterns of interlinked industrial innovations, or related job and wealth generation impacts which might be deemed necessary and desirable from a broader social and political basis of calculus and decision-making. This raises the potential role of novel social innovations arising from more broadly based political initiatives or social movements. As indicated in the previous chapter, these played a major role in the construction of new socio-technical paradigms in previous long-wave turning points. At the very least, this approach also poses the question of the potential role of the state as the second 'key steering mechanism' of the capitalist system. But, as we will see later, far from adopting a pro-active role in seeking to shape and steer techno-economic developments along lines more in keeping with post-war employment and social equity policy goals, throughout the capitalist world, the state has generally taken a quite different turn since the 1970s.

MASS UNEMPLOYMENT: THE 'EXCLUSIONS' OF ENFORCED LEISURE

'Up to one-third of the world's three billion workers will be either without a job or under-employed by next year with the growing global recession . . . the number of jobless will reach 150m by the end of this year, with a further 750m to 900m people under-employed . . . 60 million young people aged between 15 to 24 are searching for work but cannot find any.'

(International Labour Organisation, 1998)

This long-wave approach emphasises one other negative feature of the prevailing gales of intensified restructuring. Like others before, the current downswing era is marked by the return of high levels of unemployment, especially by comparison with those which prevailed during the upswing phase from the late 1940s to the early 1970s. Mass unemployment has risen to levels which have not been experienced since the bad old days of the inter-war years in many of the advanced capitalist economies (Table 7.4). Indeed, unemployment has become a pressing problem at the global level and some of its major impacts are directly experienced by much more than 150m people – as is made abundantly clear in the quotation from the ILO, cited above.

TABLE 7.4   Estimates of unemployment levels: selected years 1933–98

(As percentage of total labour force)[1]

	1933	1950	1959–1967[3]	1973	1982–1992[3]	1992–1997[3]	1998	1998: number unemployed (millions)
France	4.5	2.3	0.7	2.7	9.5	11.8	11.8	3.1
Germany[2]	14.8	8.2	1.2	1.0	7.4	9.5	11.2	4.3
UK	13.9	2.5	1.8	2.2	9.7	8.8	6.2	1.8
USA	24.7	5.2	5.3	4.8	7.1	6.1	4.5	6.2
Japan	–	1.9	1.5	1.3	2.5	2.9	4.1	2.8
OECD total	–	–	–	–	7.0	7.6	7.1	35.0

Notes:
1 Data are percentage of the total labour force; the rightmost column gives the absolute numbers unemployed for 1998. The official unemployment data have long tended to present a 'consistent understatement' of the absolute numbers of jobless. This problem has been exacerbated since the 1970s as the definitions on which such official estimates are based have been revised many times in Britain and other countries.
2 Data for 1950–1992 refer to the Federal Republic.
3 Data in this column are averages over the period of years indicated.

Sources: Freeman and Soete (1994), p.5, (data for 1933, 1959–67, 1982–92); OECD (1989), Table 2.4 (1950, 1973); and OECD Economic Outlook 62. Table A24, (1992–97 data); OECD Employment Outlook, June 1999, Table 1.3.

The return of mass unemployment in the core capitalist societies does not only impact upon those directly unemployed and their dependants. It is also accompanied by the revival of old risks, threats and fears amongst many sections of the employed population, whose ramifications go beyond the purely economic. As in the past, it acts as a major disciplining factor in the practical conduct of power relations between employers and employees which is probably more pronounced in contemporary consumerist capitalism than in previous eras. Besides this, unemployment also brings in its train many costs in terms of social and psychological pressures which tend to be differentially distributed across social groups and tend to amplify the more visible material inequalities of income and wealth. Of course the material and psychological effects of unemployment, the growth of part-time and temporary working contracts hit hardest those directly involved (Freeman and Soete, 1994). But they also have much wider indirect effects on the families, colleagues and the communities of those most directly concerned, not least a greater sense of insecurity, social exclusion and related social identity crises. In an important sense, the pressures and insecurities of the downswing crisis and restructuring process may represent an amplification of key features of the social psychology of late capitalism, including heightened experiences of the self as battered by social and institutional processes. This remains a tentative suggestion because the traditional tools and language of sociology and political economy of unemployment tend to focus on institutional and structural levels of analysis. They do not easily lend themselves to the exploration of such experiences and related developments in the lifeworld. In this sense, the academic division of labour seems to replicate the wider institutional mechanisms whereby interiorised stresses and strains of lived experience which often have clear social origins are allocated to the private realm and treated as individualised crises. This aspect of the intellectual division of labour results in a knowledge gap or language deficit which hinders the development of more social forms of understanding and resistance to such developments, as Mosco suggests in another context (1996: 166–7).

The period since the mid-1970s has also been marked by increasing inequalities, as the official measures of income and wealth in most of the advanced industrial economies have indicated, and by a significant expansion in the rates of poverty. Whilst the level and distributions of income cannot be mechanically explained by the return of mass unemployment (Mandel, 1996), it is important to consider them in relation to other features of the downswing phase since the mid-1970s. These material inequalities represent important new phenomena of central relevance to the agenda of social and cultural studies and any adequate theory of the contemporary. For example, the return of high unemployment has been accompanied in the late 1990s by the return of important, if sporadic, new mobilisations of unemployed workers and trade union organisations in France and elsewhere. But it has also been marked by a significant increase in support for extreme racist political parties in certain regions of France and Germany and other parts of Europe.

These developments highlight the complexity of the current intensified restructuring processes and the important role of social and political movements in any search for a new socio-technical paradigm in the contemporary period. They also serve to question the validity of the overwhelming stress on the newer social movements within most of the recent literature considered earlier, especially that which seeks to go beyond the mechanical or technocratic visions of socio-economic change. Here I am not seeking to dismiss the historical importance of feminist or ecological movements or their critical political relevance for a more democratic and accountable social order. But

I am questioning the relative neglect of the rise of racist movements in Europe. I also want to question the tendency of many self-defined critical theorists to relegate the 'old' social class-based movements, such as trade unions, to the dustbins of history. Indeed, this is often carried out with a totalising force which exceeds that of neo-conservative thinkers or even the practices of many 'leading edge' high-tech industrial élites. This is yet another form of the end of history thesis which seems as premature as it is wrong-headed. For sure, trade unions have been the subject of extreme external and internal disciplining pressures since the 1970s. However, in most countries, they have not experienced the same kinds of defeats as those inflicted on working-class organisations in the downswing era between the two great wars (Mandel, 1996).

The return of mass unemployment alongside other features of the downswing (which include increasing income inequalities and relatively slow rates of economic growth) in so many countries over the past twenty years clearly poses significant new challenges for social, political and cultural analysis. This cannot be simply ignored as is so often the case in many technology and media-centric theories of the contemporary. The pervasiveness of such developments cannot be explained as the inevitable outcome of technological change, but they clearly have important connections with the shift from a long-wave upswing to a downswing phase. They certainly serve to highlight the continuing salience of older bases of economic and power relations beyond those of knowledge/information or even the cultural domains stressed in much of the postmodernist literature. They directly point to the implications of significant shifts in politico-economic and social power associated with a downswing, the abandonment of the Keynesian welfare state and the increasingly hegemonic role of neo-liberalist ideas and policy practices over this period.

The abandonment of the commitment to a 'full employment' economy is a highly significant development. This was the key policy priority and foundation stone for the post-war social-democratic settlement in Europe and elsewhere, and its abandonment represents more than a purely economic phenomenon. It marks a major diminution of the social rights dimensions of citizenship and a historically significant reversal of the long-standing struggles (waged since the early stages of modernity) to construct a more comprehensive conception of democracy. The key social innovation of the post-war era involved a commitment to a 'full employment' economy in the advanced industrial economies. However temporary, this historically significant reform extended a semblance of democratic regulation to a core aspect of the economic realm (the right to work for those seeking work), one which still exerts a central influence on the material realities of everyday life in contemporary societies. This settlement was the outcome of many prior struggles even if its realisation was made possible by the conjunctural balance of social power during and after the second major 'total system' war of the century. It cannot be reduced to the logical outcome of some new leap in intellectual technology or economic modelling (or even economic theory) capacities as the technocratic musings of Daniel Bell (1973) amongst others, would have us believe.

NEW FRONTIERS? MAPPING INFORMATIONAL CAPITALISM

Long-wave dynamics of industrial restructuring, innovation and growth

The gales of destruction accompanying the long-wave downswing restructuring process have their more positive or 'creative' aspects as well and these must be addressed alongside the more negative aspects. One important dimension here is the development and expansion of entirely new industrial sectors, generally those based on the production and application of major new clusters of technologies. In basic terms, new technology systems provide opportunities for the opening up of entirely new frontiers for profitable capitalist investment, product development and hence job creation. For example, a century ago, the development of the technical means to produce and distribute 'heavy-current' electricity led to the expansion of significant new industries and sources of employment. This was manifest not only in the sectors producing and supplying the flexible new energy source, but more significantly in a whole range of *downstream* sectors involved in the supply of new appliances or devices which plugged into and harnessed the 'invisible power'. As a major new technology system, the new networks of power provided the necessary resource for a wide set of process innovations across many other sectors, of which Henry Ford's moving assembly line and electric motor powered mass newspaper presses are but two examples.

I have already mentioned the significant growth in the overall numbers of people engaged in paid work in the industrial economies since the beginning of the fourth long-wave upswing in the late 1940s. According to the conventional sectoral categories, it is also clear that the distribution of such growth in paid work has varied considerably across different sectors and that this reflects major shifts in the industrial and social division of labour. In the case of the USA, for example, the relevant indicators suggest that the trends in employment and economic growth rates have varied considerably across sectors during both the upswing and downswing periods of the fourth long-wave era. Taking 1950 as the base year, we find that overall numbers of paid workers had grown by 243 per cent by 1996. Whilst the numbers employed in the manufacturing grew by only 122 per cent, the number of workers engaged in the various 'services' sectors grew by 510 per cent throughout this 46-year period. But even within this crude 'services' umbrella category, there were important sub-sectoral variations in the trends of growth in paid work with the conventional categories of 'business services' and 'miscellaneous professional services' registering particularly high rates of growth. There is perhaps little that is new or surprising in such indicators of change in the division of labour based around the conventional sectoral indicators. As they stand, they do not directly link up with the key concepts or concerns advanced in the new ICT or information-centred literature on contemporary change examined earlier nor do they engage empirically with the presumed shifts in the division of labour and economic role of information activities. This suggests that some conceptual innovation may be useful in order to map and describe the contours of recent industrial and employment change (see Table 7.5).

The majority of the discourses surrounding new ICTs, including the various national and global information infrastructure/society initiatives, tend to emphasise the positive or 'creative' dimension of the contemporary restructuring process. My main concern in this section is not to deny the potential for significant product and process innovation or the growth of new industrial sectors and occupational groups. Rather, I wish to address the challenge of how to map and measure their scale and significance, not least with regard to shifts in the industrial division of labour. In so doing, I will also redress the significant absences in currently influential models and discourses when it comes to the question of empirical supports for their particular visions of change trends in the contemporary era. This applies particularly to models centred on the expanding role or 'explosion' of information, whether their focus falls on instrumental and performative or symbolic and cultural forms of information.

It may be worth noting here that, at the turn of the last century, the term 'second industrial revolution' was sometimes used to refer to the prevailing major technological changes in the fields of electrical power, chemicals and related downstream innovations. All of these, as we have seen, helped foster 'mass' production processes and the 'mass' consumption society which developed from the early part of the twentieth century. Yet, most present-day technology or information-centred discourses tend to ignore the history of major new technological systems. The role of 'downstream' innovations in supporting important features of change *within* the capitalist industrial system in the past are largely ignored. Even when such moments are occasionally recognised in the more historically grounded treatments of our own new times, the general tendency is to assert or imply that the centrality of information in the present-day restructuring process renders any such historical parallels redundant. Thus, to borrow some of Negroponte's terms, a common strategy is to claim is that we are at the dawn of an entirely new social, economic and political era as the multiplying 'bits' of information overwhelm the 'atoms' and other material features of the old material, capitalist industrial world. It is further argued that this revolutionary shift requires entirely new conceptual and theoretical schema. In my own reading, such characterisations of the contemporary are fundamentally flawed but they reflect highly influential views and 'the tempers of our times' amongst the hegemonic industrial and political élites. As such they demand that explicit attention be paid to the changing institutional base and forms of information in any attempt to map or describe the emerging new frontiers of capitalist accumulation and growth.

TABLE 7.5   Modified primary information sector (PIS): typology and description

PIS sub-sector and description	Examples of relevant products types/services
1) Supply of ICT Devices, Systems and Networks The industries supplying devices, systems, networks and services for the storage, processing, retrieval and communication of information	
1a) *Mature ICT manufacturing industries* The supply of (mainly) manual, mechanical and electro-mechanical information storage, processing and communication equipment.	*Writing and drawing paper; pens, inks, drawing implements, printing presses, typewriters; cameras and photographic equipment; clocks*
1b) *New ICT manufacturing industries* Industries producing new ICT-based (predominantly hardware) devices, systems and equipment, microelectronic components.	*Telecoms and computer equipment; radio/TV recoding, delivery and receiving devices; VCRs, audio recording/playback devices*

1c) *New ICT software, DP and connectivity services*
Industries involved in the design and production of:
   i) Telecoms and (predominantly) 'contentless' infrastructures, networks and connectivity services;
   ii) Computer etc. software, DP and computer services.
	Telecoms services: (telephone, fax, cellular and data communications) ICT (computer, etc.) software, DP and computer services

1d) *Mail, courier, etc. connectivity services* Industries involved in the common carriage of (largely paper-based) mail, packages and related information goods.	*Postal services; air courier services; earth-based messaging and courier services*
1e) *Wholesale/retail of ICT and IC products* Components of the wholesale and retail trades concerned with the distribution, sale and maintenance of ICT devices, systems and IC goods and commodities.	*Bookshops; newsagents; computer and office equipment shops; radio, TV and electronic stores; recorded music and camera stores*
2) Core Info-Intensive and Communication Industries	
2a) *Consumer/citizen media, information and cultural industries* Industries involved in the origination, production and communication of information services orientated towards consumers and citizens; includes media-based information; other cultural, entertainment, recreational and amusement services; one new/emergent segment = production of ICT-based computer games and multimedia cultural 'content'.	*Print-based newspapers, books, magazines; radio and TV services; motion pictures; museums and galleries, etc.; theatre and music concerts; commercial sports and dance; digital multimedia content*

TABLE 7.5   *cont.*

PIS sub-sector and description	Examples of relevant products types/ services
2b) *Instrumental/producer IC services* Industries involved in the provision of specialised information and knowledge-based services; mostly orientated to business or other organisational users and with provision of producer or instrumental forms of information/knowledge.	*Engineering, research (R&D) and test laboratory services; business info services; management and PR services; commodity and insurance brokers; legal services; advertising services*
2c) *'Mixed' producer-consumer IC services* Industries involved in the provision of information and knowledge-intensive services which cut across categories 2a) and 2b) above.	*Education services; membership organisations (business, professional, civic, spiritual, etc.); diagnostic health offices/services*
3) Selected State-Government-based IC Services	*Research and education; legislative, judicial, regulatory and related state-based IC services*

Source: Author's model (c 2000)

However, as I suggested in earlier chapters, this orientation does not necessarily imply a rush to embrace some of the more chaotic concepts or outlandish claims advanced by information society or other third-wave based models. On the contrary, what I am proposing here is the potential value of conceptual schema and related empirical work which may directly engage with such currently influential concepts and claims. It implies the rejection rather than the embrace of the flawed assumption that 'information' or knowledge represents some special sort of autonomous force and novel type of 'immaterial' resource and source of power. Arguments centred on the inherent immaterial and other characteristics of information are no more convincing than claims that the then new 'invisible liquid' of electricity augured the end of the social and economic relations of capitalist industrialism a century ago. In sum, such information or knowledge-centred determinism is no less flawed than the more established analytical mode of technological determinism (to which the former is usually very closely linked in any case).

The 'atoms' and 'bits' of informational capitalism

How then, can one apply and elaborate the long-wave model to develop a more plausible map or description of the more 'creative' or positive dimensions of the current downswing, one which takes account of both the new ICT or technology component and the changing industrial and employment roles of certain forms of information-intensive sectors? How best to set about defining and mapping the emerging and expanding new frontiers for capitalist accumulation and hence industrial and employment growth? For the most part, there has been very little by way of systematic empirical analysis of such issues within the vast array of documentation produced by the various information infrastructure/society policy initiatives since the early 1990s.[6] What little there is tends to be solely focused on measuring the production, adoption and use of specific new ICTs and network services. Despite its widespread influence in recent publications in sociological, media and cultural studies fields, there is a similar dearth of sustained empirical analysis in recent academic work for or against the information society thesis. Even the original empirical research underpinning Daniel Bell's post-industrial/information society thesis is heavily centred around measures of scientific and technological knowledge production and related occupational groups. Much like Lyotard's work, it ends up as a highly technology-centred analysis, focusing on one sphere of information activity and neglecting other aspects which appear to be so central to the concerns and underlying assumptions of much postmodernist and other recent social and cultural theory.

In this light, I now propose that a specific version of the primary information sector (PIS) concept may be useful to describe and map the presumed expanding new frontiers of capitalist accumulation and growth at the turn of the millennium. Here I am proposing a modified version of the information sector model first advanced in the work of Machlup, Porat and the OECD. The adapted model concentrates on a core set of ICT, communication and information-intensive industries which are common to all three studies – and indeed several subsequent studies along similar lines in other national settings. It also embraces most of the specific information-centred developments of (direct or implicit) concern to many other recent theories of the contemporary addressed earlier. The model proposed and adopted here excludes some of the minor activities which these earlier studies defined as information or communication (IC) industries as well as some of the more peripheral ones which they described as joint or hybrid information industries. It focuses on private sector ICT and IC industries but includes state-based education services and selected other information-intensive industries in line with earlier definitions. Thus this PIS model includes the key industries supplying ICT hardware and software devices, systems, infrastructures and networks, as well as most of the core information-intensive industries emphasised in much of the literature reviewed earlier. The result is, I believe, a model which directly connects with the often quite different concerns of several of the major theories of contemporary change addressed in earlier chapters. It can be applied to map and describe some major aspects of change in the industrial division of labour which is my main concern here.

This modified model of the PIS is disaggregated into a number of component elements. On the one hand, these seek to better reflect contemporary industrial innovation and developmental trends than is the case with earlier typologies. On the other hand, the aim is to link up with some important theoretical concerns, including distinct differences in emphasis on (and distinctions between) various types of information or knowledge which were encountered in the literature explored in Part Two of this book. Another consideration which has shaped its construction is the limited availability of empirical data series. In advancing this model, I recognise that there are usually problems of leakage and spillover between categories in such conceptual schema. I also fully acknowledge that these are especially compounded when such typologies are applied to more concrete empirical levels of analysis and when the object of study is that of 'information' or knowledge. Yet, the predominance of speculative discussions more than justifies any such ventures seeking to develop empirically grounded descriptions of the complex processes of change (or continuity) within the restructuring processes of the current downswing. The proposed model of the primary information sector (PIS) and its component sub-sectors are described in Table 7.5.

THE 'LEADING EDGE': CONTOURS OF CHANGE IN THE US PRIMARY INFORMATION ECONOMY

Having developed this model, the next obvious step (even if a more challenging and hazardous one) was to operationalise it as a framework to assemble a complex patchwork of empirical data and to arrive at a more grounded map of the relevant contours of the current long-wave downswing restructuring process. Thus I applied the model in order to map some key features of the new frontiers of industrial and employment growth over the past two decades in the USA, the country generally taken as at the 'leading edge' of ICT and information-centred accumulation processes. In this exercise I have focused on private sector industries (apart from government-based educational services) and, for reasons of data availability, have excluded the sub-sector (1e) which covers employment in the wholesale and retail trade industries dealing with the distribution of ICT and information products. I will now proceed to summarise some of the highlights emerging from this particular empirical exercise, the key results of which are summarised in the accompanying Tables (7.6 and 7.7).

First, the findings suggest that this core primary information sector (PIS) represents an expanding 'new frontier' for economic growth at the close of the twentieth century, at least as measured in terms of the changing industrial division of labour. They indicate that the PIS has indeed been the site of employment growth in the period since 1980, whether measured in terms of

TABLE 7.6   Numbers employed in selected PIS industries, USA 1980–98

(FT and PT employees, in 000s and percentages)[1]

Industry and PIS sub-sector[2]	1980	1990	1995	1998	1998 as % of 1980
TOTAL – ALL SECTORS	98,408	117,639	125,171	131,463	133.6
ALL MANUFACTURING	20,437	19,141	18,592	18,772	91.8
1) SUPPLY OF ICT DEVICES, SYSTEMS AND NETWORKS					
1a) *Mature ICT manufacturing industries*	1,378	1,349	1,281	1,275	92.5
1b) *New ICT manufacturing industries*	1,890[3]	1,677	1,467	1,589	84.1
1c) *ICT Software, DP and connectivity services*	1,460	1,683	1,980	2,606	178.5
• *ICT Software, DP, computer etc. services*	305	773	1,085	1,599	524.3
• *Telecoms: telephone, teleg., fax etc. services*	1,155	910	895	1,007	87.1
1d) *Sel. Mail/courier etc. connectivity services*	679[4]	818	843	867	127.7
Sub-Total:	5,407	5,527	5,571	6,377	117.9
2) CORE PIS INFORMATION INDUSTRIES					
2a) *Consumer Media and Cultural Industries*	2,588	3,586	4,122	4,320	166.9
2b) *Instrumental/Producer IC Services*	4,333	7,216	8,123	9,404	217.0
2c) *'Mixed' Producer-Consumer IC Services*	10,626	13,494	15,005	16,240	152.8
Sub-Total:	17,547	24,296	27,250	29,964	170.8
TOTAL ALL SUCH PIS INDUSTRIES					
1) **Sub-Total: ICT Devices, Systems etc. Supply**	5,407	5,527	5,571	6,377	117.9
2) **Sub-Total: Sel Core Info-Intensive Inds.**	17,547	24,296	27,250	29,964	170.8
Total Employed in these PIS Industries	22,954	29,823	32,821	36,341	158.3
As Percentage of Total Employment	23.32	25.35	26.22	27.64	

Notes:
1 Full-time and part-time employees.
2 Due to incomplete data at relevant detailed industry levels, this table does not cover two sub-sectoral components of the PIS: first, wholesale and retail trade activities for information products; second, government information services other than education.
3 Author's estimate, based on RUIT and Co-Com databases.
4 These data refer only to the US Postal Service, as detailed time series data for private courier services are not available.

Source: Author's model and calculations. Data extracted from Co-Com datasets.

absolute numbers of employees, rates of growth or percentage share of total employment. Aggregate employment in these PIS industries expanded from 22.9 million employees in 1980 to 36.3 million in 1998 whilst total employment in the USA grew from 98.4 to 131.4 million over the same period. Taking 1980 as the baseline, the PIS industries are found to have grown by 158 per cent compared to a figure of 134 per cent for the growth of employment in the US economy as a whole. This moderately higher rate of growth in the PIS industries relative to the overall US economy is reflected in the fact that the their combined share of total industrial employment (division of labour) increased from 23.3 per cent in 1980 to 27.6 per cent in 1998.

These particular findings only relate to the primary information sector. Ideally, they should be complemented with measures of the secondary information sector, a task beyond my resources. But they are highly relevant to contemporary debates concerning the pace and direction of emerging shifts in the industrial structures of the advanced capitalist economies. They clearly suggest that the overall growth of employment in the primary 'information' economy or sector has been relatively slow or gradual over the past couple of decades, at least in terms of key assumptions and ideas underpinning much recent policy and industrial discourse. These findings, based on trends in the 'leading edge' information economy in global terms, provide further empirical evidence to challenge many of the fashionable assertions of a radical or rapid shift in industrial structures or divisions of labour. They point to a very minor or gradual shift towards a 'weightless' or 'de-materialised' economy – one concerned with the production and distribution of 'bits' as opposed to 'atoms' – over the past two decades.

Second, the findings also point to significant variations in the changing employment roles of the various (largely private sector) industries comprising the core primary information sector examined in this empirical exercise. For one thing, they indicate that the direct employment role of the 'high-tech' manufacturing industries producing new ICT-based devices and systems (row 1b. Table 7.6) has declined since 1980. This declining trend is evident whether measured in terms of absolute numbers of employees or in terms of shares of total employment (similar trends are evident in the 'mature' ICT manufacturing industries). This is also a notable finding in that the prior generations of such 'high-tech' manufacturing industries, producing devices or other goods based on major new technology systems, were always the direct sites of significant employment growth in the core industrial economies during previous long-wave downswings. This shift in the spatial contours of industrial innovation reflects the sector's pioneering role in establishing a new international division of labour since the 1970s. At the global level, the most rapid centres of direct employment growth within such new ICT manufacturing industries are located in a small number of newly industrialising countries. Thus this experience is not peculiar to the USA as it is also one shared by many of the other advanced capitalist economies. The explanation lies in the fact that the new ICT manufacturing industries are structured around complex new forms of (intra-industry) international divisions of labour. Of course, in the US case, this declining employment role of ICT manufacturing industries has been compensated for by a relatively rapid growth of all other PIS sub-sectors within the industrial division of labour. For example, the ICT software and other 'services' industries involved in the supply of ICT systems, infra-structures, networks and connectivity services generally experienced relatively rapid employment growth (apart from telecommunications). The data findings summarised in this table clearly indicate that the US domestic economy has continued to experience relatively strong growth in all the major information-rich or content-producing and distribution services over the past two decades.

TABLE 7.7 Percentage shares and changes in PIS employment, USA 1980–98[1]

PIS sub-sectors' shares of total employment[2]	1980	1990	1995	1996	1997	1998
1) SUPPLY OF ICT DEVICES, SYSTEMS AND NETWORKS						
1a) Mature ICT manufacturing industries	1.40	1.15	1.02	1.00	0.98	0.97
1b) New ICT manufacturing industries	1.92	1.43	1.17	1.19	1.21	1.21
1c) ICT SW, DP and connectivity services	1.48	1.43	1.58	1.68	1.86	1.98
1d) Mail, courier etc. connectivity services[3]	0.69	0.70	0.67	0.67	0.66	0.66
2) CORE INFO-INTENSIVE AND COMMINICATION INDUSTRIES						
2a) Media/cultural industries	2.63	3.05	3.29	3.34	3.28	3.29
2b) Instrumental/producer IC services	4.40	6.13	6.49	6.57	6.89	7.15
2c) 'Mixed' IC services	10.80	11.47	11.99	12.08	12.15	12.35
All PIS as percentage of Total Employment[4]	23.32	25.36	26.21	26.53	27.03	27.61

Notes:
1 Based around the 1987 Standard Industrial Classification.
2 Due to incomplete data at relevant detailed industry levels, this table does not cover two sub-sectoral components of the PIS: first, wholesale and retail trade activities for information products; second, government information services other than education.
3 These data refers only to the US Postal Service, as detailed time series data for private courier services are not available;
4 Author's estimates, based on RUIT and Co-Com databases.

Source: Author's model and calculations. Data extracted from Co-Com datasets.

Third, the empirical data also highlight relatively rapid change in the role of the specialised instrumental/producer information sub-sector (row 2b, Table 7.6) within the changing division of labour compared to the consumer media and cultural industries sub-sector. The former sub-sector accounted for 4.3 million employees in 1980 and for 9.4 million in 1998, so that the employment provided by these industries in the late 1990s was some 217 per cent higher than that recorded for this sub-sector in 1980. The consumer media and cultural industries sub-sector accounted for 2.6 million employees in 1980 and for 4.3 million in 1998, resulting in an employment level some 165 per cent higher than that recorded for this sub-sector in 1980. Thus in terms of both absolute numbers and growth rates, the PIS industries engaged in the provision of specialised instrumental or producer information services are growing relatively rapidly. They have accounted for a much more significant and expanding share of the primary information sector in the USA compared to the media and other cultural industries. This is confirmed by trends evident at a more detailed or dis-aggregated industry level than those reported in these summary tables. Some component industries within this sub-sector experienced very rapid rates of employment growth over the past two decades compared to those registered by the total economy or indeed by the overall primary information sector. These included 'management, consultancy and public relations' services, 'security and commodity broker services', and information-intensive 'business services' as well as those providing specialised services for the agricultural sector.[7] The stand-alone R&D related industries (engineering, research and testing industries) grew less rapidly than those just mentioned above. A separate analysis centred on occupational dimensions of change in the division of labour in the USA indicates that such scientific and technical functions increased in importance across many industrial sectors in this period. But at the same time, business, managerial, marketing, legal and other information service occupations grew even more rapidly. This suggests that the latter types of instrumental/producer information services now account for increasing shares of both the primary and secondary information sectors.

Overall then, the findings of the empirical inquiry summarised here point to a number of significant shifts in the division of information or white-collar labour in the USA case. They underline the growing importance of various types of specialist/instrumental business, management and marketing information services, at least in terms of the industrial division of labour. They also point to the growing role of particular types of specialised/producer information services which are, in many respects, quite distinct from the kinds of scientific and engineering (intellectual technology) services which were most emphasised in Daniel Bell's seminal works.[8]

A fourth implication of these findings is that the emerging economic system may be much less culturally-laden or 'freighted' than many recent cultural studies versions of the contemporary imagine. The conceptual schema and the related empirical exercise were explicitly intended to embrace the two distinct categories of information content services which have provided the focus for so many theories of the contemporary. On the one hand, information society and other theorists have tended to stress the changing role of specialised producer (scientific, technical, economic) information or other types of instrumental (rational) knowledge. On the other hand, postmodernists such as Baudrillard and other cultural theorists have tended to stress the expanding economic role of the media and cultural industries, often pointing to the cultural 'freighting' of all economic and employment activities (Lash and Urry, 1994). Conceptually at least, these two dimensions or categories of information correspond quite closely to sub-sectors 2b and 2a in the typology of PIS industries proposed earlier. But as with most such innovative schema, it must be acknowledged that this match is less satisfactory in empirical application or operationalisation due to the limitations of the available datasets. Nevertheless, the main drift of the aggregate results (based on more detailed industry-level empirical research) can be taken as fairly robust and reliable guides to recent trends in the USA. As we have seen, they point to a relatively steady but slow overall growth of the primary information sector. But they also highlight that the industries supplying producer/instrumental information services experienced very significant growth since 1980. The findings underline the relatively rapid and continuing growth of such producer/instrumental and managerial information services, compared to the cultural/media information services. The former appear to be much more dynamic and significant than the latter, at least as measured with regard to their respective roles in the changing industrial division of labour.[9]

Notes

1   Of course, 'change' is one of the key distinguishing features of the capitalist development process as Marx and other classical theorists emphasised. It should also be emphasised again that in referring to long-wave movements as 'cycles' I am using the term in a manner that precludes any notion of precise or fixed, temporal or spatial rhythms.

2   This point has been well developed in some of the post-Fordist and labour process debates (Braverman, 1974). See also Rose (1991: 209–11) for a useful discussion of the origins of the 'industrial' society notion and of Babbages' stress on the division of intellectual labour.

3   This perspective on the apparent rise of information work was flagged and explored further in Chapter Three.

4   To some extent this might be qualified by adding 'adult' men and women since another feature of the post-war period has been the increase in the duration of average full-time education. This has meant that a certain proportion of students from upper and some middle class backgrounds, thanks to family income support, may defer their participation in the paid workforce and so enjoy a rather privileged, if temporary, reprieve from such economic imperatives. However the squeeze on the real value of middle range incomes combined with widening access policies seem to indicate that this proportion is declining.

5   The member states of the Organisation for Economic Co-operation and Development (OECD) do not comprise the totality of the global capitalist system, merely its core. They are the key sites of economic power and decision-making of the global system as well as directly acounting for the majority of the measured wealth, output and income generated by the global system. The OECD was constituted by a Convention signed by the original twenty member countries in 1960. Four other countries joined in the 1970s and Mexico in 1995. In 1996 membership was increased to twenty-nine with the accession of the Czech Republic, Poland, Hungary and Republic of Korea.

6   One notable exception here, is the study undertaken by the USA Department of Commerce (1999). I have only recently come across this study after the completion of my own research on the changing division of labour in the PIS sector (reported below). This US report is based on a much more restrictive definition of the primary information sector compared to the model adopted by this author.

7   It should be noted that such information-intensive 'business services' recorded very high rates of growth although they are here defined as excluding ICT software and computer services which are covered elsewhere [category 1b] in the adopted PIS typology.

8   This section has adopted a modified PIS model to describe and map selective aspects of the expanding 'new frontiers' of economic growth in the current long-wave downswing. I have described how this model was used to map recent changes in the industrial division of labour in the USA and some of the headline findings emerging from this empirical exercise. This model has also been used in similar fashion to map other dimensions of change, such as recent changes in PIS sub-sectors' rates of growth and shares of industrial output findings (and with broadly similar results). It should be noted too that this 'industrial' approach can be usefully augmented by a parallel exercise focused on the role of different types of occupations (the occupational division of labour). This permits an empirical analysis of change in various components of the secondary information sector, but for reasons of space, this work cannot be discussed here.

9   A fifth, if less satisfactory outcome to this mapping exercise may be worth noting briefly. As noted earlier, some of the debates surrounding competing conceptualisations of the contemporary have centred round a differentiation of the cultural realm into the separate spheres of science, morality and art. Some have identified this division as a key defining feature of modernity and one which may now be subject to significant transformation. When commencing this research project, I initially considered whether and how it might be possible to explore empirically the changing features of these particular forms/dimensions of 'information'. However, I found that this was not possible given the lack of appropriate data series.

CHAPTER EIGHT

POLARITIES: NEW MODES OF WORK, CONSUMPTION AND STATE REGIMES

'As in a flood, medieval constitutions and limitations upon industry disappeared, and statesmen marvelled at the grandiose phenomenon which they could neither grasp nor follow . . . Yet as machinery dwarfed human strength, capital triumphed over labour and created a new form of serfdom. Mechanization and the incredibly elaborate division of labour diminish the strength and intelligence which is required amongst the masses, and competition depresses their wages to the minimum of a bare existence.'

(Harkort, 1844, cited in Hobsbawm, 1969: 65–6)

'The net worth of the world's 200 richest people increased from $400 billion to more than $1 trillion in just over four years from 1994 to 1998. The assets of the three richest people were more than the combined GNP of the 48 least developed countries.'

(UNDP, 1999: 37)

MORE MATERIAL MATTERS: 'INFORMATION' WORK, EMPLOYMENT PRACTICES AND LABOUR PROCESSES

The empirical research reported in Chapter Seven indicated a rapid growth in the employment role of some core information and communication industries in the USA since 1980. But aggregate expansion in the employment role of the core PIS sub-sectors overall has been relatively slow or minor, at least when considered in the light of all the hype and excitement centred on new ICTs and the emergence of a revolutionary new 'information society' in more recent years. Taken together, the empirical trends indicate that only a surprisingly small portion of the changes in the industrial division of labour occurred in the core ICT and information/communication industries which have been celebrated so much in recent discourses. Here it should be stressed again that other non-PIS industries, especially those delivering direct person-to-person service functions in the fields of health, social services, shops and other retail outlets, hotels and catering services, as well as financial services, all also recorded significant employment growth in the last decades of the twentieth century. To a surprising extent, the key sites of job growth and general characteristics of change in the division of labour were in line with the trends identified by Mills in his 1940s *White Collar studies* (Mills 1956a).

This empirical work also indicates that the 'information sector' (embracing related communication activities) can be adopted fruitfully for the purposes of mapping and describing important contours of contemporary restructuring processes. Certainly, informationalisation can be taken as an important element in the long-run of shifts occurring in the division of labour and a useful indicator of the expanding new frontiers of employment and economic growth emerging from the prevailing gales of destruction. The empirical findings also suggest that the intensified industrial restructuring processes of the current downswing are not leading to any significant or radical *de-materialisation* of the economy. We are not on the brink of any fundamental shift to an economy of 'bits' versus that of 'atoms', let alone one that is post-capitalist. As with Mills' study of white-collar work in the 1940s, the emergence and continuing expansion of discrete information industries reflects changes in the division of labour. Whilst the economy may be increasingly 'cultural', the growth of such information industries is secondary to that of instrumental professional and managerialist services. Yet, the continued growth of all information services or occupations is central to, rather than external to, the changing economic logics or instrumental rationality of capitalist industrialism. It is dependent upon the ever-expanding output in industries supplying material functions such as food, clothing, buildings, and in sectors supplying other material infrastructures and services such as transportation, water, energy, and other utilities.

For example, all manufacturing industries have intense and complex inter-linkages with the inputs and outputs of the discrete information industries in the contemporary economy. They cannot be dismissed as atavistic or relegated to the 'rustbowl' category as proposed or assumed by many third-wave and information society theorists. Nor can manufacturing be adequately defined as 'a more roundabout way of producing services' (Lash and Urry, 1994). Indeed it might be usefully noted here that the share of manufacturing value added in total GDP has remained remarkably stable (around 20 per cent) in the USA and across the developed world in the 1980–97 period (UNIDO Industrial Statistics Database). Manufacturing industries directly accounted for a significant share of the total economic growth in the USA in the 1992–97 period (*Survey of Current Business*, November 1998). Even some of the more 'intangible' producer information services, such as public relations and management consultancy, depend on the manufacturing sector for more than half their revenues, at least in the EU region.

The analysis and empirical evidence so far underlines some more fundamental points: it suggests that the relative growth of core information industries has been fairly modest in recent decades, even in the case of the USA; the growth of many such sub-sectors is clearly dependent upon linkages with material production and distribution sectors and other non-(primary) information services activities; and it also reflects the continuous deepening of the technical, social and spatial divisions of labour. Such changes are important features of the contemporary, but they do not imply a shift towards a post-capitalist or post-industrial order. The production, distribution and control of most forms of information and knowledge is embedded in the logics of the capitalist industrial system to an increasing extent. It has been increasingly appropriated, rationalised and industrialised or commodified within capitalist property-ownership, control and market exchange relations. The available evidence on employment change in the US and elsewhere directly rejects the predictions of a radical shift towards 'prosuming' and home-working predicted by Toffler and other transformative theorists. Here again, C. Wright Mills' pioneering study of white-collar workers remains the more relevant prior strategic guide to contemporary developments.

However, it must be recognised that the growing categories of white-collar industries and occupations today are very different compared to those in the 1940s when Mills conducted his research. Certainly, it is widely argued that the emerging new forms of work imply radically new kinds of social relations in the workplace, especially in the case of 'information-intensive' industries and occupations. The basic idea is that the growth of industries and occupations, where knowledge or information is both the raw material and outcome/product, somehow leads to a significant shift towards post-capitalist labour processes and employment relations. This idea is far from new as we saw earlier. It is fashionable amongst the managerial élites controlling ICT information service industries, not least when justifying their frequently vehement opposition to employee membership of trade unions. But it also appears to be surprisingly seductive to other researchers and writers, including some whose work is otherwise quite distant from the claims of transformative theories.

For example, Lash and Urry tend to characterise the organisation and labour processes of the 'high-tech' ICT industries and information industries in terms of small-scale units with strong networking links with other firms involved in small batch production (1994). They suggest that this comprises an innovative milieu which is closer to a cultural institution (such as a university or film and TV production) rather than a unit of production. They further argue that these PIS industries and related occupations can be defined as a sort of post-industrial core based on a 'discursive reflexivity' where the production systems are 'to a large extent' expert systems and the majority of the workforce comprises professional or managerial employees, 'that is of experts themselves' (Lash and Urry, 1994: 94–9).

At best, such characterisations approximate to only a very small proportion of the firms, functions, occupations and employment conditions prevailing in the PIS sub-sector. They echo the now fashionable romance centred around 'flexible specialisation' and featuring a heroic role for the small high-tech, innovative and networking firm. As noted earlier, this vision tends to neglect the downsides of the competitive and market pressures involved in such enterprises and their consequences for working conditions and practices. The fashion is fed by focusing on the minority of success stories and tends to ignore the majority of 'heroic entrepreneurs' and small firms which do not realise the dream of rapid riches and/or which are engaged in highly asymmetrical 'networking' relationships with other firms or corporations. In a few cases, employees of high-tech firms involved in the supply of ICT systems and software can certainly enjoy the benefits bestowed by super-profits and (temporary) protections from market competition derived from (monopoly) technology rents. They may also benefit from share-ownership schemes and other incentives to maintain selective new knowledge clusters within the boundaries of corporate structures. In such cases, the higher-level technical and managerial employees may receive relatively privileged salary and other material benefits even if the owners and top managers receive much bigger shares. The same situation has long applied to a small minority of 'star' performers, writers, designers, directors and managers working within the media and cultural industries.

These particular groups may represent something like a new 'aristocracy of labour', but by definition any such aristocracy will remain a minority. Their special situation cannot be taken as typical of the working conditions or rewards system facing the majority of the workforce in the PIS service industries. For the latter, the fundamental social and power relationships in the workplace, as well as the levels of remuneration, are little different to those that prevail in other sectors of the economy. These conditions are broadly set by the complex of economic, industrial, social, and policy factors which apply in all other sectors of the capitalist economy. The precise definition of the status of different occupations or the relative skill/expertise levels of different industrial functions and associated forms of managerial control and labour remuneration is not pre-given. Nor can it be understood as some objective measure of knowledge or skill-intensity as I argued in Part Two of this book. In part at least, it is the outcome of supply and demand, distinctive industrial structures and traditions. It also depends on the conflicts and negotiation processes between employees and employers which may be conducted on an individual or collective basis. The fact that knowledge or information may be both the raw material and product of the labour or production process in an increasing number of industries has a minor rather than fundamental influence on these determinants. Besides, work organisation and labour processes in many institutions traditionally defined as 'cultural' (such as universities) have been re-orientated to more closely resemble the control and managerial logics of industrial production units. But what does make a material difference is the possession of specific clusters of ICT-related skills (usually in combination with other competencies) which are in relatively high demand globally. But again, this only applies to particular minority segments of the global workforce involved in the design, production and leading-edge applications of new ICT products or in the other primary information services sub-sectors.

These more general points can be illustrated by the case of call centres. These have been frequently identifed as one of the most important shiny new frontiers of both industrial and occupational growth associated with new ICT-based network developments. They have been declared 'the most remarkable employment phenomenon of the 1990s', one which has local development economic agencies 'fighting over every new centre looking for a home' in the belief that they bestow major economic benefit to the chosen locations (*Financial Times*, 23 April 1998). But important questions about the nature and significance of these developments lurk beneath the glossy surface of the consultancy reports and the enthusiastic embrace of local development agencies. In quantitative terms, many of the jobs involved are not new at all but simply transfers of jobs previously conducted in other corporate and locational settings. They often involve the application of 'high-tech' computing and telecommunication systems. But they often result from the specific restructuring processes of 'downsizing' or the 'contracting out' of specific functions previously conducted in-house. In more qualitative terms, many such call centre jobs simply represent the extension of Fordist mass production techniques and its detailed division of labour to the sphere of white-collar work rather than any shift to a post-Fordist mode. Much of the work in call centres is sales related, highly fragmented, repetitive and monotonous, not least because long hours spent communicating via the sole channel of the disembodied voice on the telephone are inherently stressful. Some recent empirical research on telesales work suggests that the supervision of employees is relentless, the targets unrealistic, and the constant collation of employee statistics 'utterly dehumanising' (*Sunday Business Post*, 22 November 1998). In some cases the working environment is 'more like a battery farm than some vision of a shining, twenty-first century future' (*Sunday Business Post*, 22 November 1998). Often employees are confined to tiny cubicles by the constant force-feeding of calls, the need to input data and intensive monitoring. The very locational mobility or flexibility of such operations as well as the increasingly global corporate 'cost-cutting' strategies which motivate them, all seem likely to ensure that managerial rather than worker orientated control strategies predominate.

As we have seen the majority of new jobs created in the USA and elsewhere in the 1980s and 1990s were not located within the primary information sector. Many of the new tasks and roles within the evolving division of labour have taken the form of low-status and low-pay jobs in other services sectors, including retailing, hotels, restaurants and other food outlets. Many have been part-time and marked by a distinctive set of 'flexible' contractual conditions, including fixed-term or temporary contracts and 'two-tier' wage systems which discriminate against new employees. All of these changes in work practices are designed to enhance managerial discretion or power and they explicitly by-pass the progressive kinds of job security norms that were achieved by the labour movement pressures in the earlier decades of the twentieth century. To some extent, the growth of part-time and flexible job arrangements have facilitated changes in gender roles and accommodate the increasing demands for women's participation in the paid workforce. But the norms and practices governing such flexible working schedules or rosters are often highly non-social in character and again reflect managerial efficiency calculus rather than the preferences of those employed. There is evidence to suggest that whilst the rise of part-time jobs has helped reduce the official statistical measures of unemployment levels, it does not satisfy the job preferences or income requirements of many workers involved. Besides, the remaining excess of labour of those workers confined to part-time jobs continues to put downward pressure on wages (Moseley, 1999).

However, even at the other end of the spectrum, the upper layers of the managerial and professional hierarchies are increasingly locked into a system of working and living conditions which are often far from a bed of roses. The upper ten per cent élite of 'symbolic analysts' and managers certainly derive disproportionate shares of the material rewards afforded by the capitalist system. But, more frequently than not, this is at the cost of dedicating their lives to a constant 'war-footing', not merely in the pursuit of corporate competition or financial performance, but also in protecting their position from an increasingly Darwinistic managerial culture of internal competition and continuous restructuring within the corporation.

According to many observers and other corporate heads, General Electric (GE) represents the 'new contemporary paradigm for the corporation . . . the model for the twenty-first century' (*Business Week*, 8 June 1998). GE's corporate model and managerial practices have delivered extraordinary growth, when measured by 'shareholder value', increasing market value from $12 billion in 1981 to around $280 billion in 1998 and this is widely predicted to exceed $500 billion by the end of the year 2000. By 1998, this business empire possessed $304 billion in assets and generated $89.3 billion in sales through the efforts of its 276,000 employees scattered in more than 100 countries around the globe. Approximately 27,000 of GE's employees, representing ten per cent of the total or one third of the corporation's professional and managerial workers, benefit from the company's share option scheme. The allocations of share options are strictly framed as incentives for improved performance from year to year. The distribution of such share ownership schemes remain heavily skewed towards the upper echelons of management, with less than one (approximately 0.43) per cent of GE's total employees owning share options worth more than $1 million in 1998. The corporation is widely admired in management circles for its apparent devolution of decision-making power to its component divisions and units. Such managerial 'freedom' applies as long as performance is in keeping with the relentless amplification of targets and goals for the various operating units established by the upper echelons, 'but the leash gets pulled very tightly when a unit is under-performing' (*Business Week*, 8 June 1998). No matter how many records are broken in productivity or profits, the approach of top management remains one of 'What have you done for me lately?'

Within this paradigmatic corporate model, workers and managers at all levels are under unrelenting pressure to out-perform their previous year's performance, even if there are major differentials in the levels of material reward. Compared to earlier managerial models, there is an increasing pressure on workers at all levels to dedicate ever more creative energy and time to the pursuit of corporate goals. This is merely a manifestation of the manner in which the broader structural shifts, in which contemporary corporate practices are embedded, actually serve to extend and amplify (rather than ameliorate or by-pass) the systemic features of the 'market-driven' logics of industrial capitalism. This is the dark side of the rise of a more 'reflexive' or information-centred division of labour which is masked by the descriptions offered by many of the prevailing theories of contemporary change. The result of the evolving new organisational paradigm for the majority of professional and managerial workers is a real and perceived sense of increasing 'stress', insecurity and pressures on time and energy resources. Apart from the still important differences in income and other material rewards, their situation may be little different to that of colleagues on the shop floor. Within the relentless, if partially reflexive, drive for expanded accumulation, it is not merely low status workers who are considered 'lemons', human actors eligible to be 'squeezed really dry' within the new corporate paradigm (*Business Week*, 8 June 1998).

POLARISED CONSUMPTION: SOCIAL INEQUALITY, CONSUMERISM AND EXCLUSION

'Personally, it doesn't bother me at all that Bill Gates's net worth ($46 billion) is larger than the combined net worth of the bottom 40 percent of American households ($37.8 billions excluding their cars).'

(Reich, 1998: 6)

Up to now my description of the long-wave downswing restructuring processes has largely focused on the sphere of production, but for reasons indicated earlier we must not neglect the consumption sphere in this particular analysis. Thus I will now highlight some of the most important trends in this latter sphere which are equally central to any adequate description of the contemporary condition and the prospects for a new SEP and more egal-itarian social order. Here I will focus on selective material or economic aspects and return to other aspects of consumption related to media and communication matters later.

One of the most striking shifts in the current downswing period has been an ever-widening gap or polarisation of incomes and hence of the material consumption capacities between different social groups or strata. This polar-isation process is particularly pronounced in the widening income gaps between those located at the upper and the lower levels of the evolving class system of capitalist industrialism. In essence, the winners are the élites in command of the ownership and control positions of the industrial system in capitalist economies and some 'top performers' in certain professional fields such as technology, finance, media, law and medicine. These minority élites have exerted their various competencies and powers in the present conjunc-ture to appropriate a major shift in the distribution of income in their own favour. For example, in 1974, the chief executive officers in command of the top 200 US corporations earned approximately thirty-five times the average income of production workers. But by the early 1990s, the annual earning of these executives had increased to almost $3 millon representing 150 times the annual income of production workers. Around the same time, it was also estimated that a very small minority of approximately 100 top lawyers in the USA had annual earnings in excess of $1 million (Frank, 1994).

The trends towards increasing inequalities of income and wealth were also evident within the shiny new frontiers of the primary information sector (PIS). Bill Gates, the CEO of Microsoft, had amassed a personal net worth of $46 billion by 1997. This represented a concentration of wealth that exceeded the combined net worth of the bottom 40 per cent of American households ($37.8 billion excluding their cars) (Reich, 1998: 6). Robert Reich, the former US Secretary for Labour, declared that that these facts about Gates' personal con-centration of wealth 'personally . . . [don't] bother me at all' but he does not say if they bother some or all of that bottom 40 per cent of American house-holders (Reich, 1998: 6). Nor have some of the more 'mature' PIS industries failed to play their role in the construction of a more polarised rewards system in which a handful of top managers or performers walk away with the lion's share of total rewards. In keeping with such trends, Michael Eisner, the CEO of Disney, received more than $50 million in salary and stock options in 1990. Indeed in many respects, the mature media and cultural industries may claim a dubious form of innovation award for pioneering 'the winners-take-all' rewards system. This kind of polarised rewards (payoff) structure has been common in entertainment and professional sports since the early twentieth century. But in recent years 'it has permeated many other fields – law, jour-nalism, consulting, investment banking, corporate management, design, fashion, even the hallowed halls of academe' (Frank, 1994: 104).

The trends towards increasing economic inequalities were not confined to the USA even if they appear to have taken a more extreme form in the society that is so often held up as the model or precursor of the future development of the 'information society' for citizens in Europe and much of the rest of the world. For example, in 1995 it was reported that income inequality in the UK had been growing since the late 1970s and had reached its highest levels since World War Two. Income inequality in Britain in the mid-1990s was reported to be 'growing faster than in any other developed country for which statistics are kept except New Zealand' (*Financial Times,* 10 February 1995).

In part at least, the trends in income and wealth polarisation are closely associated with the 'culture of greed' which was actively facilitated and encouraged by the neo-Darwinistic social philosophies underpinning neo-liberal state policy regimes. This was, perhaps, most clearly manifest in the case of the pioneering neo-liberal regimes established under Thatcher's leadership in Britain and that of Reagan in the USA. But even the traditional social democratic countries of Europe were not immune to these trends. Alongside the USA and UK, Sweden appears to have the dubious distinction of leading the league table for increasing inequalities in market income and disposable income between the early 1980s and 1990s (UNDP, 1999: 39). There is a dearth of standardised comparative international data on such trends compared to the availability of other economic and financial indicators. But even the existing partial data confirm a general pattern of increasing inequality of income and wealth across the capitalist industrial economies since the 1970s. There is evidence to indicate that, in most of the major OECD countries except France, market incomes have become less equally distributed over time, with the percentage shares going to low income groups falling and that going to the higher income groups rising.

In the case of total disposable income, the evidence is less clear-cut, but the general pattern is one in which the low income groups have lost out and the high income groups have gained. However, even in terms of total disposable income (reflecting the impacts of taxation and government transfer policies), the data indicate that inequality has increased in most countries over the past twenty-five years. In general, the distribution of disposable income was much more equal than the distribution of market income. The available international data indicate that the state (via the tax-transfer system) continues to play an important role in maintaining a more equitable distribution of income, as indicated by the shares of the total held by different income group categories with respect to 'total disposable income' compared to 'market income' (OECD, 1998: 51).

Second, although we are primarily focusing on the changing trends in consumption in the advanced industrial economies, these are embedded in a wider global context of marked inequalities. Here we may note that total world consumption (private and public) is estimated to reach $24,000 billion in 1998, twice the level of 1975 and six times that of 1950. But of this global total, 'approximately 85% of the expenditures for personal consumption

TABLE 8.1   Official data on distribution of income components across groups: selected countries, c. 1975–95

(Per cent, and changes in percentage points)

Country	Market income			Total disposable income		
	Three bottom deciles	Four middle deciles	Top three deciles	Three bottom deciles	Four middle deciles	Top three deciles
United States: 1995	7.6	32.8	59.6	11.5	35.0	53.5
– Changes 1974–95	–1.2	–2.6	3.8	–1.2	–1.4	2.6
Canada: 1994	6.0	33.4	60.6	14.0	35.9	50.1
– Changes 1974–94	–1.0	–2.9	3.8	1.2	–0.9	–0.4
Australia: 1993/4	4.7	33.6	61.7	13.8	35.1	51.1
– Changes 1975–94	–6.5	–2.8	9.2	–0.4	–1.0	1.4
Germany: 1994	8.0	34.2	57.8	14.8	36.1	49.1
– Changes 1984–94	–0.2	–0.8	1.0	–1.1	–0.1	1.2
France: 1990	11.6	32.8	55.6	15.3	34.6	50.1
– Changes 1979–90	0.1	0.2	–0.3	0.4	–0.2	–0.2
Sweden: 1994	7.7	35.1	57.3	17.0	37.7	45.3
– Changes, 1975–94	–0.7	–2.1	2.8	0.1	–0.2	0.1
Netherlands: 1994	8.3	36.1	55.6	16.0	36.8	47.3
– Changes 1977–94	–4.9	1.2	3.7	–1.8	0.3	1.5

Note:
Data are also available from this source for the distribution of different types of income sub-categories (e.g. labour, capital and self-employment income, government transfers, taxes).

Source: OECD (1998), Table 20, p. 52.

were made by 20% of the world's population whilst the poorest 20% consume only 1.3%' (UNDP, 1998: 12). Over the past twenty-five years, industrial countries have recorded an annual increase in consumption of 2.3 per cent, whilst the average African household today consumes 20 per cent less over the same time period (UNDP, 1998: 12).

Third, despite their disproportionate shares of global consumption expenditures, it should be noted when measured in relative terms, the available indicators suggest that poverty increased within the advanced industrial countries during the course of the current downswing. One recent UNDP survey estimates that between 7 per cent and 17 per cent of the population in the advanced industrial economies can be defined as 'poor' or in poverty 'by the prevailing national standards of living' (UNDP, 1998: 14). Amongst the advanced industrial economies, the USA registered the highest levels of human poverty although it ranked first in terms of average income (measured by purchasing power parity) (UNDP, 1998: 14). Nor were these problems confined to the unemployed. By the mid-1990s, it was estimated that the median wage earner in the USA was 'actually poorer now, in real terms, than he was fifteen years ago' and this was not simply due to the relatively slow rates of economic growth in the downswing period as the top earners in America 'have enjoyed spectacular growth' in income since the early 1980s (Frank, 1994: 99). During the long-wave upswing years between 1947 and 1973, the annual percentage change in median family income in the USA was approximately 2.7 per cent; but during the downswing years this annual rate of change has decreased, reaching 0.4 per cent between 1979 and 1989 and plunging to a negative annual change rate of –1.8 per cent between 1989 and 1993. Another indicator of increasing polarisation trends is the fact that, in real terms, the bottom 40 per cent of income groups in the USA experienced declining real incomes (negative income growth of between –4.6 per cent and –4.1 per cent) throughout the 1980s whilst the top 10 per cent enjoyed growth rates of between 15.6 per cent and 62.9 per cent in the same period. The official estimates of the growing shares of household income flowing to the top 5 and top 20 per cent of families in the USA over the 1970–96 period are indicated in Table 8.2.

TABLE 8.2 Estimated shares of family income received by each fifth and top 5 per cent, USA, 1970–96

Period	Lowest 5th	Second 5th	Third 5th	Fourth 5th	Highest 5th	Top 5 per cent
1970	5.4	12.2	17.6	23.8	40.9	15.6
1980	5.3	11.6	17.6	24.4	41.1	14.6
1990	4.6	10.8	16.6	23.8	44.3	17.4
1996	4.2	10.0	15.8	23.1	46.8	20.3

Source: USA Bureau of the Census (1998) Statistical Abstract of the US, 1998, Table 747.

Fourth, it must be stressed that the long-wave downswing since the 1970s has applied some brakes on the rapid increases in the real levels of household consumption which were characteristics of earlier decades. In real terms, average household incomes and living conditions in the USA remained stagnant or actually declined on a year to year basis throughout much of the 1980s and up to the mid-1990s at least. But beyond this average picture, the income and consumption purchasing power of the minority number of higher level income groups continued to expand in real terms as did the pattern of increasingly polarised income inequalities. A similar pattern has been recorded by one survey in the UK where real wages for the poorest 10 per cent of the male population declined by 17 per cent between 1979 and 1992, while middle incomes rose by 35 per cent and incomes rose by 50 per cent for those in the highest 10 per cent band. At the same time, income inequality grew between pensioners with occupational schemes and those who depended upon state pensions. In effect, the poorest 20–30 per cent of the population in Britain did not derive any benefits from the economic growth in the years preceding the survey (*Financial Times*, 10 February 1995).

One other key feature to be noted here has been the erosion of many forms of collective consumption provision, especially in European societies which were traditionally marked by a strong social democratic tradition and commitment to progressive 'welfare state' supports. The erosion, not quite yet dismantlement, of such collective forms of consumption has been a conscious and explicit concomitant of the shift away from Keynesian towards neo-liberal state policy regimes.

CONTINUITIES WITH OLDER ACCUMULATION TENDENCIES

These brief descriptions serve to emphasise how the long-wave downswing has produced significant shifts in the material dimensions of income trends and processes compared to those which prevailed in the decades prior to the late 1970s. The increasing polarisation in consumption power denotes a major change in socio-economic and political relations. The direct economic impacts are compounded by the drift towards an increasingly commodified social and political environment where 'the naked cash nexus' determines access to an ever greater range of informational and other goods or services. The extent and significance of such shifts are ignored or denied in the concepts of 'marginalisation' and 'poverty' which pervade contemporary policy discourses. They are also obscured and denied by the technocratic conception of 'exclusion' (usually defined as a potential 'threat' centred around differential access to new ICTs or information services) which has become a routine topic in national and international information society policy documents. The extent and significance of these shifts are also ignored in many recent sociological and cultural analyses which simply assume an extension of the kinds of individual and collective consumption practices which prevailed in the downswing. The same applies to theories which downplay the dynamic nature of consumption norms and the continuing relevance of material scarcity issues for large sections of the population (e.g. Beck, 1992).

This analysis serves to emphasise that recent shifts in the material dimensions of consumption processes and capacities are central to any adequate description or understanding of the contemporary social order. Taken together with other related trends, they point to very significant changes in the conditions of life and in the range of available consumption options and other 'life opportunities' for major sections of the working population.

Contrary to the assertions of some recent social theories, they indicate that, in many respects, life has become more precarious and 'risk'-laden precisely because of the continuing salience (rather than obsolescence) of material economic constraints for many in the working and lower middle classes. In effect, for large sections of the population, the intensified restructuring of the current downswing has amplified the salience of economic aspects of the threats to 'human security', welfare and well-being (UNDP, 1999: 36–7). These polarisation tendencies also pose significant questions concerning the new kinds of consumption norms which may be most appropriate for any new socio-technical paradigm centred around informational capitalism. The trends of change with respect to money-budget and time-budget norms point to potential structural deficits or barriers on the demand side of any new long-wave upswing where information commodities (products and services) are deemed to play the role of key 'driver' sectors.

What I want to flag here, most of all, is that the combination of these new trends points to the tendential establishment (or revival) of important *continuities* with certain trends that were more evident in much earlier stages of capitalist development. In many respects, they certainly seem to indicate a reversal of the kinds of prior developmental tendencies in capitalist industrialism which informed or underpinned much of the social theory produced in the middle decades of the twentieth century. I have in mind here many important works reflecting a broad spectrum of political values, ranging from conservative writers such as Schumpeter (1943) and Bell (1973) to critical theorists such as Habermas (1976). These were all underpinned by the perception that the secular path of capitalist development since the mid-nineteenth century had been delivering higher real wages and increased material living standards for the majority of workers. Viewed from that socio-economic context, capitalism also appeared to be capable of (and actually) delivering greater equality of wealth, income and life opportunities, based in part on the increasing influence of organised labour movements and the changing role of the state as a second steering mechanism beside the market. In this context, for example we find Schumpeter in robust and confident mode in his dismissal of any 'immerisation thesis' centred around elements of Ricardo or Marx's analysis of early capitalism (1943: 34–7).

However, as we have seen, much has changed in more recent decades. Whilst the average real wages of workers in the USA increased by 60 per cent between the mid-1940s and early 1970s, they declined by approximately 16 per cent between the mid-1970s and mid-1990s. The far from exclusively 'American' dream of ever rising living standards ceased to be a reality for many workers as 'for the first time in US history, many young workers fear that they will have a lower standard of living than their parents' (Moseley, 1999: 25–6). The changes in working conditions, labour markets and in the distribution of wealth and income described above are clearly linked to the strategies adopted to restore the general rate of profit and the conditions for renewed accumulation since the downturn of the mid-1970s. The main thrust of these struggles has not been confined to the construction of 'new frontiers' via technological innovation. Rather it has also sought to 'reduce the (real) wages of workers' via strategies targeting direct cuts in wages and benefits, the shifts towards 'contingent jobs', two-tier wage systems and the actual or threat of transfer of particular jobs to lower-wage locations abroad. The combination of these strategies with the increased levels of unemployment means that 'the decline of real wages since the 1970s is not an accident or a mystery' (Moseley, 1999: 29).

One can only speculate as to how Schumpeter would deal with these trends in real wages as they seem to run against the general thrust of his model of capitalist development and his upbeat treatment of the processes of creative destruction in advanced economies. His treatment of the crisis and restructuring process was attentive to the role of conjunctural economic, social and geographical developments, including the role of international markets. At the very least, the recent trends described here suggest that Schumpeter might have been somewhat premature in his totalising dismissal of Marx's claim that the accumulation of capital may be accompanied by the accumulation of poverty by the working class, at least with respect to the downswing phase of the long wave. The evidence above points to a flip side to the radical new technological innovations, expanding new information and communication services and extended consumerism for the upper middle class and wealthy élites. This downside is centred around a significant trend of increasing economic polarisation and social insecurity for major sections of the population, one which seems to merit the term 'immiserisation' in all its senses. These trends hark back to social conditions which prevailed in much earlier stages of capitalist development and, unless they are addressed and challenged, they point to an increasingly inegalitarian form (or paradigm) of future social development. They must be accorded a priority place in analyses of the contemporary and in social and political initiatives orientated towards a more just and participative social order.

A SELECTIVE 'HOLLOWING OUT' OF THE STATE AND POLITICS: FROM KEYNESIANISM TO NEO-LIBERALISM

'Despite these various upward, downward and outward shifts in political organization, a key role still remains for the national state as the most significant site of struggle among competing global . . . supranational, national, regional and local forces.'

(Jessop, 1994: 274)

If one US President (Eisenhower) could declare in the late 1950s that 'we are all Keynesians now', the ending of the long-wave post-war boom in the mid-1970s brought in its wake an uneven, but eventually pervasive, crisis of the Keynesian regime of state regulation. The crisis of the Keynesian state has been manifest not only in the almost universal abandonment of 'full employment' as the priority state policy goal in the advanced industrial world. It is also evident in a highly selective 'rolling back' of the state's role, especially in the areas of welfare, progressive taxation and income redistribution policies, industrial and spatial planning and a significant counter-current manifestation of 'strong-state' initiatives in other fields.

Clearly the changing role and characteristics of the state comprises a very important component of any description of the contemporary social order, not least because it represents the second key 'steering mechanism' of capitalist society – to borrow one of Habermas' more pointed and pithy terms. How then are we to describe and understand the origins and implication of the post-Keynesian state regulatory regimes and their linkages to the concurrent crisis and restructuring processes occurring in the economic and industrial system? The treatment here must be necessarily brief and operate a level of generalisation which neglects the complex of concrete political factors which have shaped political developments in specific societies. On the one hand, contemporary social science theory is generally suspicious of determinist linkages between the political and the economic realms and it regularly warns against any mechanical explanations of political developments as direct or automatic responses to the economic. On the other hand, the empirical evidence points to an almost pervasive abandonment of Keynesian state or governmental strategies throughout the capitalist world since the ending of the post-war boom and their replacement by (what is still best defined as) neo-liberal state policy regimes. In the context of this analysis, such widespread developments appear to suggest that the autonomy or separation of the political from the economic realms is somewhat limited or 'relative' in late capitalist industrialism, at least when it comes to economic and employment policy and some other key policy domains.

In seeking to understand the pervasive reshaping of state policy regimes, I have found the approach of certain post-Fordist political theorists particularly persuasive and suggestive. Such an approach suggests that the crisis of Keynesianism and the shift in state functions have been triggered more by the general slowdown in accumulation than any technological changes. In addition, the shift from a Fordist to a post-Fordist techno-economic paradigm and by internationalisation pressures have been very important (Jessop, 1994: 262). From the mid-1970s, the Keynesian state could no longer maintain the conditions for restoring Fordist accumulation. At this point 'economic and political forces alike' stepped up the search for a new state form that they hoped would be able to solve the deepening crises. This search process may be viewed as one of extensive trial and error experimentation involving various transitional political forms and policy measures. The still-developing product of this (continuing) search process may be described as a 'hollowed-out Schumpeterian workfare state' and one which marks a clear break with the Keynesian welfare state (Jessop, 1994: 263). In very general or abstract terms, the distinctive primary objectives of this emergent new state regime with respect to the domains of economic and social reproduction are quite clear-cut. It seeks to promote product, process, organisational and market innovation in open economies with a view to restoring capitalist profitability and growth rates. It is orientated towards strengthening the structural competitiveness of the national economy, largely by intervening on the supply side. It also clearly aims to subordinate social policy needs to 'the needs of labour market flexibility' and/or the constraints of international competition.

For some post-Fordist theorists, the increasing internationalisation of the economy has also played a significant and subtle role in the demise of the Keynesian state regime because even relatively large states have very little if any scope to act as if national economies were effectively closed or autocentric (Amin, 1994). For one thing, the national character of money is increasingly subordinated to the flows of international currencies. Secondly, because the internationalisation process tends to emphasise the character of wages as costs of production rather than sources of home demand, the basic domestic premises of Keynesian welfarism are put under further challenge. The major macroeconomic policies previously associated with the Keynesian welfare state lose their effectiveness with growing internationalisation, and so they must be replaced by other measures if key policy goals are to be secured. As a result, almost all states have become increasingly involved in supporting and managing the process of internationalisation itself. This strategy is pursued in the hope of minimising its harmful domestic repercussions, of securing a share of mobile investment and maximum benefit to each state's own home-based transnational firms and banks. Thus states in capitalist economies are increasingly drawn into the very process of internationalisation and into creating or managing the most appropriate frameworks for it to proceed. For some post-Fordist writers, this leads to the paradox that, as states lose control over the national economy, they are increasingly forced 'to enter the fray on behalf of their own multinationals' (Jessop, 1994: 262).

Some post-Fordist theorists emphasise that there is no single or dominant form of a post-Keynesian 'workfare state', not least because of the influence of specific political and social orientations in different countries. But scanning the thrust of national state policies in the advanced industrial world (as well as those of the European Union) it seems fairly clear that neo-liberalism is the particular form which has predominated over the 1980s and 1990s. It is important to note too that this applies irrespective of the particular colour of the ruling party in government as all the mainstream parties seem to be helplessly seduced by the single 'policy paradigm' of neo-liberalism. Indeed, in Britain, most of the 'new Labour' policy practices are but a repackaging of neo-liberalism with a big smile on the cover. Tony Blair's version of 'the third way' relies on the idea of an epochal shift to 'new times', one which stresses the new role of knowledge in an era of global competition. It also appears to rely on a curious 'cultural studies' vision of economics which suppresses questions of the increasing inequalities of income or wealth and whose conservatism is unable or unwilling to consider even Keynesian type policy strategies (Froud et al., 1999). Even the election of a majority of governments dominated by 'leftist' social democratic or labour parties in EU member states at the end of the 1990s has not resulted in any significant policy change to address mass unemployment or the polarisation of income and wealth, whether considered at the national or EU levels of policy-making. The traditional champions of full employment, welfare and collective consumption services, progressive taxation, income, educational and other egalitarian polices have abandoned the game. They seem either unable or unwilling to consider any more imaginative strategies or pro-active socially progressive policies other than spin-doctored versions of the orthodoxies of neo-liberalism.

Within the EU, much like most of the other major capitalist regions, the official levels of unemployment were averaging around 11–12 per cent in 1998. These levels are nothing less than 'gigantic' compared with an average of 3 per cent in the 1960s and early 1970s. They indicate that unemployment has become 'Europe's crucial economic and social problem', indeed one that may threaten the future of the EU project overall (Modigliani and La Malfa, 1998). Yet there is little sign of any distinctive 'social Europe' dimension in the EU's responses to this problem. Rather the general theme of the EU policy élite has been little different from that of the orthodox conservatives in the interwar years. The general refrain of the 1990s has been that unemployment is not a responsibility of the Union, but a task for each member state. Yet at the same time, the neo-liberal agenda guiding the EU's unification project has taken away from the member countries 'all the tools of demand management' (Modigliani and La Malfa, 1998). The 'technical rules' governing closer economic and monetary integration in the EU involve fixed exchange rates and full capital mobility preventing central banks from setting interest rates. Meanwhile narrow budget limits prescribed by the 'stability pact' make fiscal policy impossible. The EU's approach to unemployment, like its path to integration, involves the rejection of all demand-side policy tools and takes the view that unemployment is due mainly to the malfunctioning of the labour market. Thus the millions of unemployed and the many millions more affected by the threat of unemployment have the 'doubly wasted' opportunity of not only missing out on national demand management. They are also missing out on the vastly greater potential of a co-ordinated set of (neo-Keynesian) anti-employment policies on the part of the fifteen member states and a combined population of more than 300 million.

Thus, in important respects, the contemporary is also marked by what one might term *'a hollowing out of politics'* as well as a hollowing out of the state. Without subscribing to the nihilistic and rejectionist postures of some postmodern currents, it is important to register the absence of any significant political choices within mainstream politics in many countries. In my view, this development is not best or solely defined as a matter of the technocratisation of politics. Rather, its roots also lie in the structural changes and pressures linked to a long-wave downswing. At stake is the contemporary hegemony of a very specific form of 'political paradigm' which has significantly reshaped the priorities, contours and boundaries for what passes as 'legitimate' or acceptable policy issues or options and debate in the official political public sphere at the close of the twentieth century. The hegemony of neo-liberalism in the realm of political economy expresses the prioritisation of 'accumulation imperatives' on the part of the economic and political élites. It also marks a consequent marginalisation of distributional questions, welfare concerns and other specific social and cultural goals favoured by other social groups and interests. These shifts also appear to be linked to the increasingly hegemonic role of specific industrial interests. These include the financial sectors (e.g. witness the privileged role of finance sector spokespersons and analysts in media and other public discourses surrounding all areas of economic policy) and internationally orientated fractions of capital, not least those based in the new ICT and communication supply sectors.

THE SEDUCTIONS OF 'THE HIDDEN HAND': A DIGITAL META-NARRATIVE

The hegemonic neo-liberal policy 'paradigm' accords a very privileged role to technology and to the 'high tech' industrial interests involved in the supply and production of new ICT and other information-intensive products and services. This is manifest not only in the frequent resort to the old promise that the new sunrise technologies and industries will provide an abundance of new jobs to replace those lost in the processes of industrial restructuring. It is also evident in the key role of such industrial interests and élites in the construction of high-profile national, European and 'global' information society initiatives.

It is also manifest in the very content and orientations of the discourses surrounding such initiatives. Essentially these advance a common message that the extensive use of new ICTs and communication networks is both the means and end of ('information') society's development. At the same time these state-funded 'awareness-raising' initiatives do not merely augment the marketing functions and goals of the ICT supply corporations. They also embrace a very specific political or propagandistic orientation to the effect that the further development of new ICTs and/or the 'information society' is to be understood as fundamentally 'market-driven'. The users of new ICT and the constituent members of the 'information society' are configured as consumers, whose major influence on social development is to be exercised via individual choices in the marketplace of competing information goods and services. The result is that citizenship and other social or collective identities are eliminated or highly marginalised from any direct or indirect determination of the path of socio-economic or technological development (Preston, 1997a).

At first sight it may appear odd or strange that the discourses surrounding such state-funded initiatives seek to mask the potential role and influence of the state as a second 'steering mechanism' in guiding the form and pattern of technology-related developments, not least because of the continued importance of various forms of public funding in such fields. Yet this is perfectly in keeping with the selective 'hollowing out' of the state's role and the reshaping of the parameters of legitimate political concern and debate linked to the neo-liberal turn. It is also consistent with the political orientations of the most influential discourses surrounding new ICT, including the transformative theories discussed in Chapter Two. The dominant and common messages advance a celebration of the benign virtues of the 'hidden hand' of the market and competition which almost matches their enthusiasm for the technologies themselves. They assert that the new ICTs and related industrial innovation processes are intrinsically and inherently 'market-driven'. In addition, the further development and selection of alternative communication network configurations will be generally hindered rather than assisted by pro-active state initiatives or policies. Discussions of new ICT-based networks and related public communication processes are predominantly and explicitly configured around images of the individualised consumer and thereby imply an erosion of alternative social identities and potential political roles of related social movements (e.g. Negroponte, 1995; Toffler et al., 1996; Kelly, 1998). In essence, as Jameson notes, the old nineteenth-century romance of the autonomous market mechanism has been born again in many fields (1990, 1991). But, perhaps, nowhere has the seductive allure of the *hidden hand* of the market 'proved to be so sexy' than in the particular domains of discourse surrounding new ICT.

Despite (or precisely because of) the regular recent declarations of the death of 'terroristic' ideologies, the totalitarian sway in economic and policy discourses surrounding new ICT of the single meta-narrative (new ICT = the 'hidden hand' + market competition + entrepreneurship) is truly remarkable. The formula is centred around constructions of markets as autonomous and 'natural', whilst relevant socio-economic actors are defined as largely autonomous, calculating and risk-taking individual entrepreneurs or specialist knowledge-bearing workers. Users are defined as consumers roaming increasingly globalised and fragmented or individualised markets. The formula advances descriptions and prescriptions which erase away or marginalise the institutional (social and political) embeddedness of both markets and technology, not to mention the increasing role of corporate capital and oligopoly and monopoly structures within 'the market'. It denies the pro-active role of the state in extending intellectual property rights and globalisation processes. It also seeks to erase or marginalise the importance of social or political formations and identities, including those centred on citizenship, social class or gender position and so on, often selectively drawing on postmodern cultural theory to justify its particular descriptions and prescriptions of social development (e.g. Kelly, 1998).

In its celebration of individualism, competition, market forces and consumerism, the prevailing dogma represents a new ideology of 'market anarchism' which denies or represses the ever-growing power of private property rights, of monopolistic and oligopolistic economic interests, of the naked cash nexus over and against more socially or politically based interests – not to mention needs. Its romanticised celebration of the 'hidden hand' and competitive markets ignores not only the historical growth of monopoly power across the economy, but also the particularly intense forms of unequal 'competition' which prevail in technology and information-intensive sectors in the 1990s (Rohm, 1998). Its atavistic equation of all constraints and oppression with the state and of all freedom with the market and the hidden hand might be considered merely quaint if it was not so politically dangerous and socially disabling. In essence, this particular technocratic (or digital) meta-narrative seeks to deny or downplay the actual and potential role of the state as a 'second steering mechanism' guiding either technological or social development. In effect, if not in intention, it represents and expresses the vanguard or radical extreme of the neo-liberal view of the world. It not merely coincides with the general hegemony of neo-liberalism as the guiding model and practice of state policies but may also be defined as a specific and persuasively 'modern' (new technology-based) force which augments or reinforces its overall sway.

This particular meta-narrative may lay claim to some empirical grounding – but only if it is confined to very specific (minority) sub-sectoral niches or locational sites of the leading-edge ICT supply and application sectors in certain stages of the innovation process. In practice and ambition, this is certainly no mere 'local' theory confined to specific PIS sub-sectors and high-tech locational clusters. Nor has it been confined to particular social formations, such as the USA where, for various historical reasons, institutional conditions, restrictive social dimensions of citizenship rights, and so on have been different to those which have generally prevailed in western Europe. This particular meta-narrative has become hegemonic in a real sense, not merely because it is typically expressed in a mode and tone of address which is confidently linked to the clear commercial and economic success of the ICT sector (and its sophisticated networks of lobbyists and public relations experts). It appears to have successfully achieved the status of a hegemonic discourse or ideology that is every bit as imperial and universalising as the pervasiveness of the technologies to which it is linked. This meta-narrative is most pronounced in the discourses of the prominent techno-gurus of the late 1990s, such as Negroponte (1995) and Kelly (1998) and in the relevant ICT-based industry or trade publications. This includes the magazine *Wired*, which represents a sort of sacred text (or new Bible and Koran) for the global ICT industry élites and their many ideological bedfellows. But in important respects, this particular meta-narrative has also served as a prominent specific influence on the discourses surrounding new ICT and information society policies in Europe and elsewhere, as indicated earlier.

The recent socio-economic trends highlighted in this and the previous chapters provide important reasons to interrogate the ideology of market anarchism which seeks to deny the actual and potential role of the state as a 'second steering mechanism' guiding both technological or social development. For one thing, this particular 'digital' meta-narrative suffers from a selective amnesia which serves to deny the crucial role of various state subsidies, supports and policies in funding and shaping the successive streams of ICT developments in the past. This past role of the state is manifest in the development of key electronic components (from the transistor to the microprocessor), of computing, and satellite communications as well as the Internet (Hall and Preston, 1988). It advances a vision of the market as the sole or main source of ICT-based innovations which prescribes a minimal or marginal role to state policies. It therefore downplays and puts a very specific spin on the important present-day role of a plethora of state policies which subsidise or otherwise shape the development, application, marketing and consumption of new ICT based products, services and their markets. This selective spin also serves to deny the potential reorientation of state policies to pursue alternative future paths of technological as well as social development more generally. In essence, this highly specific meta-narrative adds up to a very powerful and persuasive ideological force. It takes sustenance from a selective account of new ICT-based innovation and industrial processes in order to advance a theory of social development and history which is potentially far more pervasive in its reach.

This new ideology directly undermines one key platform of ideas and practices which have been shared by very many liberal, socialist, social democratic and other progressive reformers and social theorists since the early stages of industrial capitalism. Despite other differences, they shared the general view that capitalist industrialism was a system capable of vastly increasing production and economic outputs based on a principle of private property and competition, but one which was also 'quite unfavourable to the individual or general happiness', as Robert Owen put it. However productive it may be, capitalism was seen by the early socialist Owen to 'produce the most lamentable and permanent evils', that is unless 'its tendency is counteracted by legislative interferences and direction' (Owen, 1815, cited in Hobsbawm, 1969: 66). Even liberals such as the German businessman and engineer, Fritz Harkot, recognised that capitalism's new machinery and its 'incredibly elaborate division of labour' was enormously productive but its market system would tend to create 'a new form of serfdom' and impoverishment, especially in times of economic crises (Harkot, 1844). These ideas and the lived experience of such conditions led the labour and other social movements to pressure for socio-economic and political reforms. From the mid-nineteenth century up until the 1970s, these served to greatly extend the role of the state as a 'second steering mechanism' shaping and framing the processes of capitalist development and ameliorating the conditions of everyday life at work and beyond for the majority of working people. The culmination of these developments was the post-war Keynesian welfare state regime which was centred around the notion of the 'mixed economy'. This was the consensus of ideas and practices which was taken as a core feature or platform in the analysis of contemporary capitalist industrialism advanced by a wide spectrum of political and social theorists. As noted earlier, even Daniel Bell's seminal theory of the information society was based on the assumption that the social role of the state would continue to increase and that of the market decline in relative terms (1973). This then provides some indication or measure of the profound social and historical implications of the digital élites' new-found romance with the 'hidden-hand' and the ideology of market anarchism.

The celebration of the 'hidden hand' of the market in public policy circles is the flip side of what I referred to earlier as *'a hollowing out of politics'* as well as a hollowing out of the state. It is linked to the persistent inability or unwillingness of both the traditional leftist or other socially progressive political parties (no less than their right-wing counterparts) to advance imaginative or socially progressive new policies which resonate with popular concerns and interests (in a manner similar to Keynesianism in the early post-war era). The current crisis of mainstream political culture may involve more than a failure of political imagination. But certainly its most obvious manifestations include the tendency to celebrate 'the hidden hand' and a renewed reification (or deification) of technology as some sort of universal panacea for pressing social and economic problems. The strategic alliance between such depthless politics and ICT industrial interests represents a new 'political-industrial complex' whose strategic vision is centred around new ICT-based innovations as both the end and means of future social development. In some senses, today's crop of politicians may be little different from their predecessors in the early nineteenth-century era of rapid capitalist development who 'marvelled at the grandiose phenomenon which they could neither grasp nor follow' (Harkort, 1844).

In other ways too, there are marked weaknesses and contradictions in the celebration of 'the market' within the currently hegemonic neo-liberal discourses and associated policy practices. I am suggesting that the changed role and direction of the capitalist state cannot be understood within the terms of its proponents' rhetoric. The restructuring of the state's role cannot be understood as some singular 'deregulation' process or rolling back of the state's role in the face of the asserted imperatives of either new technology, competitiveness or the intensification of globalisation processes. Instead the contemporary restructuring process involves a highly selective 'hollowing out' of certain aspects of the state's role accompanied by an expansion of other functions. The central and local layers of the state have been withdrawn from direct involvement in the maintenance of full employment, ownership of industry, progressive income redistribution, welfare and other policies which might favour the less wealthy and powerful social strata. But the state is more rather than less involved in establishing the general conditions favourable to private capital investment and profit-making and facilitating a new regime of accumulation favoured by the owners and controllers of capital in its various contemporary forms. What this amounts to is a significant redirection rather than any withdrawal of the role of this particular key steering mechanism with respect to the overall economic development process. But this redirection is far from neutral in its impacts on different strata of the social class system. Indeed, there are contradictions in the pervasive rhetoric and prescriptions proclaiming the essential virtues of a 'market-driven' approach to the so-called information society. It is more than ironic to note that for many years now, both national and supranational state bodies have been committing major resources to the technological, industrial and ideological investments deemed necessary to promote the alleged 'market-driven' application and diffusion of new ICTs.

Before closing this brief exploration of the changing role and features of the state, it is worth stressing a number of important implications for understanding the contemporary condition and assessing the alternatives as we enter the new millennium. This analysis suggests that the return of mass unemployment and growing social inequalities are not some natural or inevitable logic of a singular process of economic and technological development. Rather these must also be understood as the outcome of a fundamental shift and long-run restructuring of the political realm, especially with respect to the prevailing regimes or paradigms of state economic, employment and social polices. This is manifest in the now hegemonic doctrines of neo-liberalism, and associated neo-Darwinian economic and social theories. Compared to the Keynesian regimes of the post-war long-wave upswing era, these prescribe very specific directions and boundaries on the capacities of the state to regulate the process of capitalist economic development. They tend to favour a very narrow stratum of social class interests (e.g. the polarised redistribution of income, wealth and power) and reverse the more egalitarian thrust of state economic and social policies in previous decades. They do so in a manner that contains many echoes of the responses of the hegemonic economic and political élites to the first formu-lations of Keynes' theory, not to mention the concurrent demands of the unemployed workers' movements during the interwar downswing period. This is but one other specific aspect of the way in which we are confronted not merely with change but also with important continuities in key features of capitalist industrialism.

Friedrich Hayek, one of the high-priests of neo-liberalism, has drawn on certain strands of complexity theory in the natural sciences to support his particular brand of neo-Darwinian homage to the inevitabilism and univer-sal virtues of the 'hidden hand' and of the implicitly natural sway of market forces (Gillott and Kumar, 1995: 134–5). Forget about two hundred plus years of industrial and technological development, not to mention Bell's promise of the benign benefits of 'intellectual technology'. Forget about a reformed and marginally more accountable state pressured into playing a more progressive and egalitarian role, which, despite all its nasty warts and blemishes, has so utterly transformed the material base of economic life and the very fabric of everyday human social and cultural experience in so many ways. Despite all the shiny new technologies and information superhighways and material and informational abundance, we are now urged to think of the human social and economic world in the same terms as those governing the harsh inevitabilities and rough justice of evolution in the natural world. At the same time, we are pointed to an economic realm which is still governed by the imperatives of 'improvement' (the imperatives of increasing rates of profit, more growth in output and productivity). It is also one guided by a competitive game where only the 'leaner and meaner' are better or at least good enough to be eligible for a token share in material and symbolic rewards. For influential neo-liberal politicians like Margaret Thatcher, who often cited Hayek as her favourite economic theorist, the practical policy implications were clear-cut: we must adopt the TINA view of mass unem-ployment. Quite simply, 'there is no alternative'. This despite the (often forgotten) fact that the first Thatcher government was put into power in 1979 on the basis of an election campaign which was heavily centred around the promise to reduce unemployment – and whose key slogan was 'Labour isn't working'.

The shift towards neo-liberal politics and state regimes which accord a privileged place to new ICTs and 'information society' developments has been firmly established in many countries. Yet, it is important to note, the processes of experimentation and the search for some kind of consolidated 'post-Keynesian' state regime are not complete but still ongoing. The construction of a new 'mode of accumulation', with its attendant state policy reforms and other elements of a socio-technical paradigm capable of supporting a sustained new long-wave upswing or boom still remains an elusive goal at the beginning of the new millennium. That is especially the case if we define a 'boom' in terms of one that will bring an increase in material living standards, welfare and security for all sections of society. The adequacy of the neo-liberal state regime in this regard needs to be questioned, along with the possibility of alternative and potentially more progressive state policy strategies and other institutional innovations. Some of the requirements and possibilities involved here will be considered later.

SOME CONCLUSIONS AND IMPLICATIONS

In this and the previous chapter, I have sought to describe features of the interplay between socio-economic changes and continuities and to elaborate the long-wave model introduced earlier. I have indicated the continuing salience of material or economic factors in shaping the fabric and rhythms of everyday life of the majority of the population. I have also examined trends of change in the industrial division of labour in the leading information economy over the past two decades. The empirical findings point to a relatively steady but slow growth of the primary information sector, including the media and cultural industries. But they also indicate that the industries supplying specialised producer/instrumental information (rather than cultural/media) services experienced the most rapid rates of growth, in absolute and relative terms. In turn, these new managerialist and instrumental information services appear to be shaping capitalism towards ever more extended and intensified forms of economic growth.

The contemporary can be clearly characterised as a 'downswing' phase of the long-wave movement of capitalist accumulation, marked by relatively slow rates of growth in economic output and productivity. It is also marked by the return of high levels of unemployment, especially compared to the levels which prevailed during the upswing phase from the late 1940s to the early 1970s. Indeed, not only has unemployment risen to levels not experienced since the bad old days of the interwar years, but the downswing period has given rise to significant new economic and social cleavages. There has been an overall polarisation of incomes, consumption spending power, erosion of state welfare and collective consumption services and a very significant reorientation of the form and functions of state policy and political culture.

In this chapter, I have also sought to elaborate a more dialectical understanding of the complex processes and rhythms of technical, socio-economic and political change throughout the 1980s and 1990s. I have highlighted some of the downsides and continuities which necessarily lead to a relative neglect of the more positive features of the contemporary which are emphasised in the more dominant discourses. Yet, I am also mindful of the challenges and pitfalls in any 'real-time' analysis of contemporary socio-economic and political change. Looking back at contemporary analyses of the rise of industrial capitalism in the early nineteenth century, Henri Lefebvre stresses the difficulties and challenges involved in understanding any new socio-economic reality or era whilst it is unfolding (1974: 80–2). For example, he pointed out how land and space had been largely eliminated from conventional political economic analysis even though they remained central to economic activity and, indeed, have now become even more pressing issues at the beginning of the new millennium. In similar vein, we might suggest that material production and 'industry' often tend to be forgotten or marginalised in many of the contemporary economic and policy discourses centred on the changing role of new ICTs or an emergent 'information society'. The problems here are compounded by the recent fashions in academic discourses, not least the 'cultural turn' in social and human sciences, including tendencies to assume away questions of material production, scarcities and economic inequalities inherent in many of the consumption-orientated approaches to the contemporary.

For such reasons, this analysis of contemporary developments points to the importance of certain fundamental continuities of the capitalist industrial order alongside the development of new ICTs. This pertains despite significant changes in the division of labour, the role of technological knowledge and other information-intensive activities and the construction of new frontiers or sectoral sites for the production of commodities, profit and the employment of productive labour. Compared to many of the alternative models suggesting a shift to a radically new social order, this analysis emphasises a 'business as usual' approach. It points to the extended reach of the fundamental socio-economic relations and logics of capitalist industrialism into new spheres of economic activity as well as into the everyday life experience of increasing numbers of the population. The changes in the industrial division of labour suggest that, in some respects, it is valid to characterise the current order as an emergent era of 'informational capitalism'. But this does not imply any diminution but an extension of the essentially capitalist and industrial character of the production and labour processes. It also signals the continuing salience of old categories of social analysis such the division of labour, social class, gender and other inequalities.

In this era of expanding 'heritage' industries, it's not surprising to find that we now have a Henry Ford Museum which provides funding for historical research amongst other things. I don't know how this irony now sits with the original author of the industrial practices known as 'Fordism' – and who also authored the infamous line that 'history is bunk'. But, as both C.W. Mills and Fredric Jameson have argued, the tendency to annihilate history has been a striking feature of modern social and cultural analysis. The 'bunk' view of history appears to have been very much alive and influential throughout the 1990s and into the new millennium, and not only in the USA. Indeed, this particular view appears to have been reanimated or 'born again' in much of what passes for serious commentary on social, economic and cultural change processes in the contemporary ('post-Fordist') era (Jameson, 1991). Perhaps, this is nowhere more manifest than in the spate of recent analyses which, in late McLuhanite mode, reduce past historical change to a few major shifts or breaks in technological infrastructures. In sharp contrast, the long-wave approach adopted here is particularly attentive to the complexity of the historical processes of technological, economic, social and political change. It is also attentive to the relatively slow and complex processes involved in the intensified crisis in and restructuring of the economic and social order in downswing periods such as the present. What emerges is a complex mix of good news and bad news, of important changes as well as continuities with regard to the old tensions and inequalities of capitalist industrialism. It constructs a description of key contours of the contemporary condition which is quite different to the one-sided visions of the technological utopians and of the nihilistic postmodern dystopians discussed in earlier chapters. The approach also provides many challenges to the narrow – if glossy, technocratic – 'information society' visions advanced by the industrial and political élites.

CHAPTER NINE

'CONTENT IS KING'?: NEW MEDIA INNOVATIONS AND 'MATURE' MEDIA

'Although the rate of change is faster than ever, innovation is paced less by scientific breakthroughs . . . and more by new applications like . . . multimedia . . . The big changes in computers and telecommunications now emanate from the applications.'

(Negroponte, 1995: 76)

'Over the past two years "debate on media policy in Britain has undergone a profound change in emphasis. It has become focused on 'information superhighway', 'multimedia' and 'convergence' . . . There is a real sense in which a gradual accumulation of quantitative changes has now produced a qualitative transformation in the framework of media policy debate."'

(Goodwin, 1995: 677)

WHEN 'CONTENT IS KING': THE MEDIA AND PUBLIC COMMUNICATION

As we have seen, new ICTs are deemed to have particularly significant 'impacts' or implications for all forms of public and private communication processes, including the media and the sphere of public communication. In part, this is precisely because the dominant major new technology system of our era comprises a cluster of *information* and *communication* technologies. These are deemed to present an abundance of novel opportunities for 'downstream' product and process innovations, especially in 'content' sectors where the key resource and outputs comprise the production, distribution and handling of 'information' in its various forms. In particular, the widespread development and diffusion of the Internet and World Wide Web since the early 1990s is taken as a manifestation of the radically new communication possibilities suggested in the rhetorics surrounding the 'information superhighway' policy initiatives. The Internet is viewed as a radical new technical platform which will stimulate many novel application innovations, especially in media content and communication services. In addition, digital broadcasting innovations have also been hailed as a parallel set of developments which will stimulate rapid change in mature media sectors such as radio and television.

The fashionable slogan 'content is king' highlights how the new digital media and other information content services are now widely perceived to be significant sites for industrial innovation and dynamic economic growth according to contemporary ICT industry and related policy discourses. Certainly, both the established (mature) and new digital 'content' industries have been major sites for financial and other types of investment on the part of industrial and policy élites throughout the 1990s. For many critical theorists, these developments mark a significant further penetration of instrumental economistic logics into the realm of culture, whilst for others, they signal a further stage in the cultural freighting of economic processes.

In this and the following chapters, I will zoom in on some key dimensions of change in the established media and new digital 'content' services sectors, again paying attention to continuities as well as the specific ICT-based novel changes. These chapters will critically interrogate selected aspects of the dominant discourses focused on recent developments in these sectors, including competing conceptions of the key trends of change in the media and public communication services. In these chapters, I will pursue the dialectical and empirically grounded approach outlined earlier, viewing new ICTs as a disruptive force for change but one that is relatively malleable and essentially socially shaped in its origins, applications trajectory and implications. Here again, the approach will critically engage with the popular, technology-centred analyses which are so often laced by misleading, mistaken – and often downright silly – constructions of the implications of new ICT (and the changing role of information) for the reshaping of the sphere of public communication. For example, many of the influential transformative models as well as information society policy documents tend to emphasise or predict a complex set of radical new media products and forms. But such analyses or predictions are not confined to the more extreme utopian or dystopian theorists. Indeed, some of the more holistic and grounded social analysts seem to become intoxicated with an untypically heady cocktail of media-centric speculation, adopting an apocalyptic and determinist mode of address when it comes to unfolding changes in the media and communications realms (e.g. Castells, 1996).

Thus, this chapter and the next will examine recent trends of change in the role and characteristics of the media and communication sectors, paying attention to both the established media and new digital media developments in tandem. A key aim is to explore the forms and extent of *product* innovation in the communication sector whilst also addressing neglected but important *process* innovations associated with the widespread application of new ICTs in the production and distribution stages of the mature media industries. As we have seen, the exploding body of recent literature on new ICTs embraces an ever-growing number of specific claims concerning emerging or likely changes in the media, cultural industries and public communications services. Here I will focus on a grounded exploration of a small but key sub-set of the relevant developments and objects of recent research and debate. First, there is the widespread belief that new ICTs and/or changes in the information structures are leading to a significant quantitative growth in the overall economic and employment roles of the media and other communications services sectors. I will examine not only the quantitative but also the equally important qualitative aspects of the potential changes in the economic and social role of the media and sphere of public communication. Second, is the contention that there will be a rapid growth of radically new ICT-based content innovations (e.g. novel 'immersive' or 'interactive' digital multimedia products), especially those centred around the Internet, and a concomitant decline in the relative roles of the established 'mature' media of public communication. The analysis here will challenge such simplistic assumptions of the predominantly substitution effects of the new digital developments and will, instead, point to a much more complex set of interdependencies between the new and 'mature' media. Third, I will engage with the more general claim that new ICT is prompting or leading to a radical transformation in the overall nature, forms and power of media-based cultural (and political) expression or meaning-making.

TECHNOLOGY-CENTRED VISIONS: MEDIA EXPLOSION, SUBSTITUTION EFFECTS AND 'CONVERGENCE'

Let us first turn to some of the more pervasive claims in the 1990s concerning the role of innovative digital media and the trends of change in the overall economic and social roles of the media and cultural industries. As noted earlier, many of the 'information society' and related policy documents published by national governments and supra-national organisations, such as the European Commission and OECD, have tended to emphasise the rapid expansion of both the mature and new media sectors. Some have also emphasised the growth potential of many other new types of specialised or instrumental information 'content' services which will be delivered or distributed remotely along the new communication infrastructures or 'superhighways'. But most have tended to stress the rapid growth potential of both established and new media or 'cultural content' industries, measured in terms of economic output or turnover and in terms of their potential to provide many new 'high-level, grey-matter' jobs in the advanced industrial economies. Many such information society policy reports have also tended to extol the virtues of their particular local cultural traditions and creativity, celebrating their own particular strengths as a 'creative nation'. They also stress the presumed comparative advantages this bestows on the national economy in an era of new communication networks, expanding media and cultural industries markets (NTIA, 1988; Australia, 1994a, 1994b; Canada, 1995).

One typical example of the relevant 1990s policy literature is a key strategy paper published by the European Commission which explicitly linked new media developments to new ICT and the perceived emergence of an information society. This document emphasised the potential growth of film and television programming, suggesting that by the end of the twentieth century, 'the demand for audio-visual products will double in Europe', with expenditure on both audio-visual hardware and content growing from ECU 23 to ECU 45 billion (CEC, 1994a: 119). This document suggested that the rapid growth in content would be driven by new transmission technologies which are deemed to 'multiply and diversify the vectors for distribution'. It predicted that the number of TV channels in the EU region will increase 'from the present 117 to 500 by the year 2000' with an increase of TV broadcast hours from 650,000 to 3,250,000 over the same period whilst encrypted programming hours will increase by a factor of thirty (CEC, 1994a: 119).

Like many national information society policy documents in the 1990s, this report stressed that the audio-visual sector has a highly labour-intensive structure providing 'many high-level grey-matter jobs' such as script-writers, directors, technicians, performers and so on. It also suggested that the sector 'is thus potentially less vulnerable to competition from low labour cost markets' (CEC, 1994a: 119). Although it recognised the lack of reliable statistics, this report estimated that at least 1.8 million people were earning their living in the audio-visual services sector within the EU member countries. It furthermore stated that 'there is remarkable potential for job creation in this sector', that future job creation potential 'could be of the order of two million by the year 2000'. It suggested that if proper resources were deployed, 'it is not unrealistic to estimate that the audiovisual services sector could provide jobs, directly or indirectly, to four million people' by the end of 1999 (CEC, 1994a: 119–20). Like many of its counterpart national reports, this EC document emphasised that 'the stakes are high' as the audio-visual sector is no longer a marginal one in economic or employment terms. Indeed, on the contrary, it forecast that 'it will be one of the major service sectors in the twenty-first century, and should be given corresponding attention' in industrial, media and other policy fora (CEC, 1994a: 120).

The techno-gurus and industrial policy discourses in the late 1990s also tended to highlight the imminent emergence of radical new 'interactive' or 'immersive' digital media product innovations. But, once again, it must be stressed that there is nothing entirely new about this kind of claim. As indicated in earlier chapters, this is a now old and fairly familiar forecast. Ever since the 1980s, innovative media 'content' products have been regularly identified as a key downstream or 'killer' application with respect to successive generations of new ICTs. Transformative theorists and techno-gurus such as Alvin Toffler, as well as state industrial innovation policy discourses, have long pointed to the imminent development of radically new communication media. They have emphasised the emerging prospects for exciting new kinds of digital, 'interactive', 'intelligent', 'customised' and more immersive or multi-sensorial media formats and forms. The anticipated ready-made demand for such innovative media forms, especially of the entertainment variety, would finance the development of successive versions of the 'information superhighway', such as cable TV systems, broadband 'wired city' networks, ISDN or videotex systems in the 1980s. The frequent failure to realise such technology-centred visions in the 1980s did not deter the later enthusiastic speculation about radically innovative media products and services centred on subsequent new ICT platforms. By the early 1990s, CD-ROMs, CD-I and video-on-demand took centre stage as delivery platforms and multimedia became the dominant descriptors of the innovative new kinds of digital and interactive media content forms and formats that were expected to blossom and grow into real 'killer' applications. By the late 1990s, the Internet and WWW had somewhat displaced CD-ROMs and taken centre stage (alongside digital television) as the 'killer' delivery platform, even if some (especially European and Japanese) ICT industry and policy interests still harboured high hopes for CD-I and DVD platforms. But although the killer platforms may change (for example, the Internet displaced videotex), and even if the most prominent promotional prophets may also change (Negroponte displaced Toffler), the promise of vast new markets based on multiple downstream innovations or 'killer applications' in the shape of interactive, customised, digital/multimedia information 'content' products and forms remains remarkably constant as we enter the new millennium.

As noted earlier, for many contemporary pundits, investors, investment analysts and ICT/information society policy reports, 'content is king'. Not only are new ICTs offering ample new opportunities for the conception, design, development, and marketing of radically new multimedia content products and services.[1] It is also widely proclaimed that such content innovations will critically shape the future pace and direction of overall Internet-based developments. Alongside the other key application area of electronic commerce (or sometimes, transaction services), downstream innovations in the information content sector are defined as crucial in driving and financing the future growth of core Internet-based network developments. Such analyses also suggest that the multimedia and other content industries have a much greater potential to expand revenues and profits in the future than is the case with industries producing core ICT hardware products or software packages or those supplying telecommunications and computer services. This argument is frequently advanced by companies from these other sectors when embarking on investments in the media content sectors. In such cases, the reasoning is also often based on arguments stressing the logics of technological convergence (IDATE, 1997; PA Consulting Group, 1997; TechServ, 1998).

One other distinctive dimension of the widely predicted changes in the media and communication services sector should be noted in the present context. Here I am referring to the prediction (and prescription) that radically new ICT-based communication services are intrinsically more flexible, interactive and 'customisable' with respect to the information content requirements of individual users. Furthermore, it is also regularly predicted that such new media forms are likely to expand or diffuse very rapidly and thus replace or diminish the role of more established or mature forms of 'mass communication'. This particular claim has been a key theme in the work of transformative and other technology-centred analyses since the early 1980s at least (Toffler, 1980, 1983; Negroponte, 1995). Hence, this particular prediction long predates the mass diffusion of the Internet and related World Wide Web service developments since the early 1990s.

Although there is a long history of undelivered promises with respect to 'really innovative media' it may be claimed that the technical possibilities were somewhat limited until recently. Certainly, ICT-based developments since the early 1990s, not least relatively cheap home computers equipped with CD-ROMs and Internet-based multimedia platforms such as the WWW, are more technically advanced and widely diffused than was the case with videotex in the 1980s. Together with a cluster of related advances in digital technologies and significant improvements in the relative cost and functional capacities of electronic communication networks, the Internet can certainly be defined as a significant and disruptive radical innovation. But, as we will see later, there remain many grounds to challenge popular conceptions of its role as a stimulus to the emergence of radically new interactive and multimedia 'content' products, at least as these are defined within the technology-centred writings of digital beings and promotional pundits.

Writers such as Negroponte (1995) and Kelly (1998) have stressed the imminent prospects for radical multimedia innovations based on advances in, and convergences between, computing, mobile telecommunications and broadcasting technologies. They have pointed to the immediate possibilities of highly interactive informational and entertainment multimedia content products and services which are seen to combine textual, visual, audio and audio-visual texts in sophisticated and immersive new media forms and narrative structures. Such digital multimedia pundits also stress the flexible possibilities of Internet-based networks for broadcasting, narrowcasting and one-casting and the prospects for highly customised and individualised on-demand media content services. They also emphasise the democratic and participative potential of such new multimedia platforms alongside the reducing costs and increasing accessibility of video cameras, PCs and scanners and other content production technologies: 'on the Net, each person can be an unlicensed TV station' (Negroponte: 1995: 176).

Even the more sociologically informed and critical accounts often fall into this particular version of the 'powerful media' trap. For example, Manuel Castells emphasises the manner and extent to which the Internet and related ICT-based systems are actively 'revolutionizing the process of communication, and . . . culture at large' and shaping them towards more democratic and participatory modes (1996: 360). He suggests that the advent of digital multimedia 'is tantamount to ending the separation . . . between audio-visual media and printed media, popular culture and learned culture, entertainment and information, education and persuasion'. He adds further that such new multimedia forms construct an entirely new symbolic environment and 'make virtuality our reality' (Castells, 1996: 372). In addition, other academic commentators, including those more directly engaged with the communication and cultural studies field, have also tended to stress the transformative potential of digital multimedia content product innovations. Drawing on poststructuralist and postmodernist theory, Landow (1997) suggests that new modes of hypertextuality and interactivity afforded by the new digital technologies are effecting radical transformations in all moments of media-based communication processes.

As we saw in Chapter Two, Alvin Toffler was promising much the same kind of transformations some twenty years ago! But the now old idea of a relatively rapid growth of radically new ICT-based interactive media products and communication forms (and a concomitant decline in the scale or importance of mature media) appears to have become much more prominent within industrial and policy discourses in more recent years. It has featured as a key theme in the work of popular 1990s technology gurus such as Negroponte (1995) and in influential magazines such as *Wired*. It is also a key idea for policymakers and bureaucrats involved in the development and implementation of ICT and 'information society' related industrial policies in several European counties. This idea has certainly featured prominently in many of the technology-centred analyses of 'convergence' tendencies within the information sector.

Ever since the late 1970s, the belief that new ICTs are leading to various types of 'convergence' between previously separate communication services has been a major feature in successive generations of technology-centred analyses of change in the communication sector (Pool, 1983). Here, the basic idea is that the increasing shift towards a common digital mode at the level of information-processing or distribution technologies is leading to a significant erosion or blurring of sectoral boundaries between communication services or 'information' markets which were previously distinct. This concept has proved to be particularly resilient although it has been subject to much criticism from researchers in the communication studies field. The convergence idea is often invoked by industrial interests and élites based in the computer and telecommunications sectors when justifying their vertical integration strategies in pursuit of a firmer footing in the information 'content' industries.

It has also played a central role in a whole series of technology-centred new communication innovation initiatives and pilot projects which have proved to be unsuccessful in commercial terms. These range from the various optimistic initiatives around videotex services in the 1980s to the many subsequent 'interactive' services trials in Europe and the USA in the 1990s. The list here also included the many 'video-on-demand' initiatives in which the major telecommunications services operators invested so much hope and research funds in the early 1990s (Bouwman and Christoffersen, 1992; Preston, 1993, 1997c).

The convergence idea underpinned the public announcements of Microsoft and its CEO Bill Gates when justifying that company's major investments in new Internet-based information content services fields, especially in the 1995-7 period. The basic premise was that the company could utilise its dominant position in the areas of computer operating systems and applications software as leverage in establishing a prominent role in the emerging domains of on-line digital content services. But despite its vast investment resources derived from its monopoly position and related technology rents in the computer operating systems and software tools markets, even this major corporation was forced to revise its strategy rather dramatically. In the case of one major Internet-based content service, the corporation has not been able to successfully realise its particular take on the convergence idea in practice. The lessons of this particular experience seem to be that the boundaries between the various components of the primary information sector (identified in Chapter Seven) are not eroded by the trends towards digitalisation at the level of information engineering. The core competencies and distinctive industrial structures and organisational cultures which favour success in one domain of the primary information sector do not automatically translate into other domains. There remain many important barriers to the successful production and sale of new-ICT based multimedia services, however 'convergent', interactive or customisable these may seem at the level of technical delivery systems or technology-centred analyses (Preston and Kerr, 1998). Yet, despite the long history of such technology-driven visions of new media developments, the convergence idea remains very much alive and well as a core concept underpinning policy initiatives and analyses of multimedia content industries (e.g. Techno-Z FH, 1997).

In this context, I should briefly flag some initial grounds for challenging the reliability of 'forecasts' which highlight the imminent emergence of radical new digital media product innovations, however exciting or welcome the object of their analyses may be. First, they often rely on an essentially technology-centred model of media-based communication processes, one which tends to neglect the complex set of factors involved in the development of radically new media forms, codes and conventions in the domain of content services.

Second, such accounts tend to overlook the potential malleability of new ICTs with respect to their content applications, overemphasising radical product innovations whilst neglecting the potential role of process innovations. Third, they tend to neglect many additional potential brakes or barriers on the demand or consumption side. Attention to the latter suggests that if recent social trends (e.g. with respect to the distribution of income and patterns of consumer expenditures) are perpetuated into the new millennium, it seems likely that the promised new on-line multimedia product innovations will play only a minor (if growing) role within the cultural/consumer and the specialised PIS content sub-sectors. The overwhelming evidence on recent developmental tendencies in media markets, as well as in the time and money budget trends which influence overall consumption practices, all tends to point to a very limited role for novel media forms and content in the short to medium term future. Contrary to the confident expectations of many pundits, I want to stress how non-technical factors on the production and consumption sides suggest only a relatively limited range of digital media product innovations over the next decade. These factors also suggest that new multimedia content formats, products and services will play only a secondary (if growing) role compared to the established media and modes of information production and delivery within both of those PIS content sub-sectors, at least in the medium term.

THE FATE AND FUTURE OF THE 'MATURE' MEDIA

Before turning to a more empirical level of investigation of the fate and future of the mature media, a few additional theoretical and historical points are worth emphasising here. The continuing popularity of the belief, especially within influential industrial and policy élites, that the emergence and growth of new media will somehow lead to a decline and diminution in the role of mature media is itself quite a remarkable phenomenon of our digital times and its culture. It is based on the simplistic assumption that there is some intrinsic or necessary competition between established media and the new media. This assumption is fundamentally flawed in the light of the considerable body of theoretical work and historical research long available in the media and communications studies field. The ahistorical, technology-centred approach tends to automatically assume a substitution effect between the various mature media and the new digital media or modes of communication. It fails to take account of the possibility of complementary

TABLE 9.1   Employment in 'mature' media and cultural industries, USA, 1970–98

(Employment in 1,000s)[1]

SIC		1970	1980	1990	1995	1998
	TOTAL ALL INDUSTRIES	79,770	98,408	117,639	125,171	131,463
	Consumer Media/Culture Inds.					
27	**Printing and publishing**	**1,107**	**1,275**	**1,569**	**1,546**	**1,565**
271	Newspapers	373	420	474	447	443
272	Periodicals	75	90	129	131	138
273	Books	101	101	121	124	127
274	Miscellaneous publishing	38[4]	48	82	85	91
275	Other printing inds	520	616	763	759	736
78	**Motion pictures**	**202**	**225**	**405**	**506**	**573**
781	Motion picture production & services	66[4]	82	148	201	252
783	Motion picture theatres	127[4]	124	112	119	138
784	Video tape rental	n.a.	n.a.	134	146	165
483	**Radio and television**	**132**	**192**	**234**	**236**	**247**
4832	Radio broadcasting stns	72	107[4]	119	113	116
4833	TV broadcasting stns	58	103[4]	115	123	131
484	**Cable and other pay TV services**	**n.a.**	**100[3]**	**126**	**156**	**181**
79	**Amusement and recreation services[2]**	**472**	**795**	**1,119**	**1,519**	**1,601**
722	**Photographic studios [portrait]**	**42[3]**	**48[4]**	**64**	**74**	**60**
84	**Museums, botan/zoological gardens**	**n.a.**	**46[4]**	**64**	**85**	**93**
	Total Such Media/Culture Inds.	n.a.	2,588	3,586	4,122	4,320
	As percentage of Total Employment	n.a.	2.63	3.05	3.29	3.28

Notes:

1 The rows indicated in bold font refer to the major SIC categories. In some cases, these major categories include the employee numbers related to the sub-categories indicated in subsequent rows (printed in regular font). But not all the relevant SIC sub-categories are indicated in this table. In some cases, the data series is marked by a break in 1987/88 due to the changeover to the 1987 SIC system; for example, the SIC 483–4 data series is marked by a break in 1987/88, subsequently embracing cable, etc. pay TV services.

2 The 'amusement and recreation services' category (SIC 79) covers the following kinds of sub-categories: dance studios, schools and halls; producers, orchestras and entertainers; bowling centres; commercial sports; miscellaneous amusement and recreation services.

3 Author's estimate based on data in RUIT database and 'patchwork' tables.

4 Data cited are estimated from data for the year (in a few cases, two years) prior to that indicated at top of column.

Sources: Author's model and analysis. Based on data extracted from Co-Com and RUIT datasets, based on official data and estimates.

effects or the historical lessons of the complex interplay between substitution and complementary relations between different generations of media technologies, not to mention their 'content' applications and forms. Such an erroneous assumption would merit a 'fail' in an undergraduate essay in the communications studies field. Yet it underpins much of the analysis in certain bestselling books by authors widely hailed as gurus of the new digital technologies and their economic and policy implications! The ironies here are not lessened by recalling the truly amazing, but equally amusing, verbal acrobatics and contortions imposed on such 'digital beings' when seeking to justify the writing of a mere book to convey a thesis which declares that all such print-based media are redundant in this apparently post-information age! (e.g. Negroponte, 1995).

So how does the available empirical evidence on the changing economic role of the mature media measure up against the two, not quite exclusive, sets of analyses and predictions outlined above? Again turning to the model case of the USA, we find that the major mature media and other established cultural industries expanded their share of the overall division of labour between the 1970s and the late 1990s. The mature media industries have continued to experience considerable growth in the period since 1970, despite the emergence and diffusion of new communication technologies and related application innovations. In combination, the available indictors suggest that the mature media and other cultural industries provided employment for 2.59 million workers in 1980 and for 4.32 million in 1998 (see Table 9.1). The most rapid rates of employment growth occurred in the 'motion pictures' and amusement and recreation services, but even the more 'mature' print-based industries and radio broadcasting have experienced significant employment growth over the past two decades. Besides the absolute growth in employment numbers, these cultural industries registered an increasing share of all employment, accounting for approximately 2.63 per cent of total jobs in 1980 and 3.28 per cent in 1998.

The changing economic role of the mature media and cultural industries can also be considered in terms of changes in their shares of overall gross domestic product. Again turning to the USA, the available indicators suggest that, in combination, the relevant cultural industries have increased their share of overall GDP from 2.29 per cent in 1960 to 3.04 per cent in 1996 (see Table 9.2). These indicators suggest that the percentage share of print-based cultural industries declined somewhat over the past four decades whilst that of other media, especially radio and television broadcasting services, more than trebled over this same period. Indeed, according to some other industry estimates not shown here, the relatively old medium of radio broadcasting enjoyed the fastest rates of revenue growth of all media industries in the 1992–6 period. Meanwhile, worldwide revenues for US feature films (derived from the distribution and rental of films via cinema exhibition, television, home video and pay-per-view, etc.) increased from US$9,025 million in 1988 to US$21,178 million in 1997, suggesting that such media export earnings more than doubled over this period.

TABLE 9.2   Selected media and cultural industries:
estimated percentage share of GDP in USA, 1960–99

(Percentage shares of GDP, measured in current $US)

INDUSTRY/SECTOR	1960	1970	1980	1987	1987	1990	1995	1996
TOTAL ALL INDUSTRIES	100.0	100.0	100.0	100.0	100.0	100.0	100.0	100.0
CONSUMER MEDIA and CULTURAL INDs[1]								
Printing and publishing	1.354	1.259	1.172	1.331	1.331	1.286	1.170	1.184
Motion pictures	0.221	0.219	0.212	0.291	0.312	0.355	0.357	0.391
Radio and television	0.211	0.196	0.262	0.297	0.374	0.480	0.654	0.663
Amusement and recreation services[2]	0.505	0.459	0.507	0.557	0.581	0.680	0.774	0.797
TOTAL Such Media/Cultural PIS Services	2.292	2.133	2.153	2.476	2.598	2.801	2.955	3.035
Telephone/Telegraph 'connectivity' services	1.834	2.156	2.207	2.366	2.289	2.073	1.984	1.960

Notes:
1 In some cases, there are breaks in the continuity of this time series in 1987 due to the changeover to the 1987 SIC system in the USA; thus it is prudent to treat trends before and after this date as separate sets of indicators.
2 The 'amusement and recreation services' category (SIC 79) covers the following kinds of sub-categories: dance studios, schools and halls; producers, orchestras and entertainers; bowling centres; commercial sports; miscellaneous amusement and recreation services.

Sources: Extracted by author from Co-Com databases and US official statistics sources.

So much for the case of the USA which, in a global context, has long held a particular set of comparative advantages in the audio-visual and other mature media services markets. Unfortunately there are no comparable datasets available for the trends of change within the EU region which comprises fifteen member states and a major share of the global markets for media products and services. There are some partial data available for the media industries sector which indicate that, for example, the number of television channels in the EU region (excluding satellite channels) grew from 55 in 1980 to 213 in 1995. Meanwhile the number of permanent employees in the public broadcasting organisations within the EU15 region actually declined from 111,400 thousand in 1988 to 103,300 thousand in 1996. There are no comparable detailed data series for employment trends in the private television sector. But from the various estimates available for the major countries, it is certain that there was nothing like the doubling of employment in the media sectors (old and new) between 1994 and 1999 as predicted by the European Commission in 1994 (CEC, 1994a; European Audiovisual Observatory, 1998: 65).

The number of feature films produced in the EU area increased from 489 in 1992 to 531 in 1996 and local television drama and other programming also increased over the same period (European Audiovisual Observatory, 1998: 73; 193–4). But there was also a significant increase in the quantity and value of imports of films and television drama programming from the USA over this same period. The increased competition in the European television marketplace has been leading to rapid rises in the hourly costs of such imported programming – to the obvious benefit of the US-based film and TV production industries. From these and other available indicators on developments in the EU region, it seems safe to conclude that the optimistic predictions of a technology-driven rapid growth in employment in the media industries advanced by many European reports in the mid-1990s have failed to materialise. Certainly, this conclusion seems especially pertinent with respect to the much-celebrated doubling of 'high-level grey-matter' jobs located in the creative, 'content' or programming production segments of the media sector.

The empirical data for the USA clearly indicate that the established media have not been displaced by the new media developments. The data suggest that the overall scale of the mature media and cultural industries has continued to expand in recent decades, when measured in terms of employment and shares of GDP. The data certainly confirm that predictions of the decline or demise of the mature media industries seem somewhat premature. But as already flagged in Chapter Seven, these particular indicators also clearly suggest that the rates of growth have been relatively modest. This is certainly the case when compared to the growth of instrumental or producer information services. It is especially the case when the relevant empirical trends are considered in the light of the predictions and assumptions underpinning the analyses in much of the academic and policy literature reviewed earlier. In other words, these key cultural and symbolic information segments of the primary information sector still account for a relatively small share of the overall industrial division of labour in the advanced industrial economies. In addition, given their uniquely dominant position in global terms, it seems unlikely that the (relatively modest) rates of employment and turnover growth in the USA media industries over the past two decades have been matched in other countries and regions, such as the EU member states.

TV+ OR BEYOND THE TV AGE?: REREGULATING 'THE DOMINANT MEDIUM'

Having examined some of the quantitative aspects of the changing role of the established or mature media industries, it is now time to zoom in on trends of change in the organisation, industrial and regulatory structures of the major media of public communication. This section will therefore focus on television services and examine how recent changes imply an extension and transformation or transcendence of its prior role as 'the dominant new medium' of the post-war era.

The history of broadcasting alerts us to the fundamental limits of technology-centred analyses of the role and impact of new media based on what are presumed to be the inherent or universal technical characteristics of any particular medium. In the USA, the development of television very largely followed the predominantly commercial model adopted earlier for radio broadcasting. But in many other countries, especially in most of the countries now comprising the European Union, television was established within a 'public service broadcasting' institutional framework. Like radio in the 1920s, television in these countries was not constructed or treated as an ordinary economic sector as was the case in the USA. In brief schematic terms, its production structures and processes in Europe might be characterised as 'a sort of hyper-Fordist' combination of vertically and horizontally integrated hierarchies overlaid by external control through state or quasi-state bodies such as the BBC Board of Governors in Britain. The gradual introduction of two or more competing channels in the 1950s–70s period led to some change in the direction of specialisation, disintegration of production functions and segmentation of audiences.

However, by the early 1980s, there were increasing pressures from various interests seeking a more radical restructuring of television and radio broadcasting in Europe and other countries which did not initially follow the predominantly commercial and market-driven approach adopted in the USA. These pressures originated from industrial interests, including advertisers seeking lower-cost advertising platforms and investors seeking an opportunity to invest in new areas, as well as from politicians, film/programme makers (and 'wannabes') seeking a wider diversity of channels and greater scope for 'independent' programming and programme-makers. Of course technological developments also played a role, not least because they were also increasingly perceived to be reducing the limits imposed by spectrum scarcity, opening up significant new opportunities for multiple channel service provision and helping to reduce the costs of television programme production as well as of its distribution channels. Whilst multi-channel cable television expanded rapidly in the USA in the 1970s, it was much slower to take off in many of the larger European countries. Even by the end of the 1980s, cable and satellite-based multi-channel had made relatively little impact on the EU area as a whole, although it achieved fairly high levels of household diffusion in some of the smaller member states. The 1980s also witnessed the rapid introduction of video cassette recorders and players as a significant new media technology which afforded new time switching possibilities and led to a major new technical platform, revenue source and market for the distribution and exhibition of films and other programme content.

Nevertheless, despite these apparent lags in the diffusion of the then 'new media' of multi-channel cable or satellite television delivery in Europe compared to the USA, the 1980s marked a significant turning point. One key feature of change landscape of television since the early 1980s has been the relatively rapid growth in the number of national and regional terrestrial channels as well as satellite-based services within the EU area, especially when compared to the pace of change in the previous three decades of television services (see Table 9.3).

Table 9.3   Estimated growth of television channels in the EU15 area, 1980–95

	1980			1990				1995			
	Pub.	Priv.	Total	Pub.	Priv.	Total	Sat.	Pub.	Priv.	Total	Sat.
EU15 Region	40	15	**55**	43	80	**123**	38	53	160	**213**	403

Notes:
'Pub' = public channels; 'Priv' = private channels; 'Sat' = satellite.

Source: Author's estimates based on data in OECD (1997) *Communications Outlook, 1997, Vol 1*, Table 5.4, p. 72.

A major source of change in the EU context has been the efforts of the European Commission to construct an increasingly integrated 'single market', embracing an ever greater number of countries and industrial sectors as well as policy functions. As this overall integration project was developed, there were increasing pressures to construct a common regulatory framework for the television and film sectors within the EU area. The reasoning behind the Commission's push for an integrated 'audio-visual space' in the EU was largely in line with the economic logics applied to all other service industries. But it also reflected a certain belief that the increasing integration of media and cultural industries or 'markets' would serve to better cement the overall process of increasing integration. Amongst other policy shifts, the new 'television without frontiers' policies introduced in 1988 represented an initial but significant shift away from the highly specific and strongly national orientation of prior regulatory modes in European countries. These placed a strong explicit emphasis on expanding the role of the independent production sector. They also served to promote the development of more competitive television industry structures and regulatory regimes at the national level throughout the EU area. In combination, these policy shifts also opened up significant new opportunities for the expanded role of large integrated cross-media and transnational corporations in the television sector within the EU area. They have also reshaped the EU television sector as a particularly intense regional site for the kinds of globalisation processes occurring in the audio-visual sector more generally.

One other influential set of developments, in the EU context especially, were the policy innovations surrounding the introduction of a second commercial channel in Britain in the early 1980s. This new service, known as Channel 4, did not have its own studios, but was constructed around a 'publishing model' whereby the production of some of its content was subcontracted to the big TV companies but a large share of programming was sourced by commissions to the 'independent sector'. This contracting out model was explicitly designed to reduce production costs and has had important 'demonstration effects' on the organisation of the television programme production processes in other television channel services in Britain and elsewhere; one such effect has been the reduction of the direct workforce in other television companies and the expansion of short-term and other 'flexible' employment contracts.

These developments may be addressed in the light of post-Fordist analyses of industrial change in the audio-visual sector. As we have seen, many recent analyses of the contemporary have stressed a significant shift to new post-Fordist organisational and industrial structures, including tendencies towards vertical disintegration in many sectors of the economy. For example, some authors have argued that the flexible specialisation thesis may be particularly applicable to the film/cinema industry as a consequence of the rise of television and the decline of mass consumption markets for the cinema from the 1950s (Storper and Christopherson, 1987). This is said to have resulted in a reduction in transaction costs through the disintegration of cinematic production. With a smaller number of films being made (product frequency), it became economically efficient for the major film companies to reduce in-house facilities, hierarchies of functions, and other fixed overheads and to hire external labour and services on a film by film basis. Essentially, this has prompted the externalisation of production to small independent audio-visual producers (and associated clusters of small firms providing specialist support services) and a simultaneous externalisation of many aspects of the particular risks involved in the creative production processes. For some proponents of the post-Fordism thesis, this shift first led to flexibility via disintegration of the creative and high-profile functions and labour costs ('above-the-line' costs) such as film stars, directors, producers and writers. This was subsequently followed by the disintegration of 'below-the-line' labour costs and functions and it eventually led to the disintegration of facilities such as movie theatres, studios, film libraries, camera, sound and lighting equipment.

In line with Piore and Sabel's characterisation of the 'third Italy', some of the authors advancing the post-Fordist 'flexible specialisation' and 'reflexive accumulation' theses tend to describe the movie industry in terms of 'a transaction-rich network' of firms or individuals (Storper and Christopherson, 1987). They suggest that the audio-visual sector may be characterised as a transaction-rich nexus of markets linking a few large (often global) firms with many small firms (often comprising one self-employed person) offering a variety of relevant specialised services. They furthermore suggest a marked shift or tendency towards new decentralised spatial structures associated with the clustering of such activities in a variety of particular locations. In the hiring of specialised labour for pre-production, production and post-production stages, some emphasise that the process of hiring of relevant personnel is 'not a question of pure markets' because they are highly networked and because 'information and personal contacts are at a premium' (Lash and Urry, 1994: 115).

These post-Fordist accounts, emphasising trends towards vertical disintegration and territorial localisation in the audio-visual sector, have been highly influential in shaping national and local state cultural policy-making in Britain, Ireland and other EU countries since the late 1980s. But they may be criticised for 'heralding a benign post-Fordist era of flexible specialisation' and of overemphasising the autonomy and prospects of de-centralised 'cultural industrial districts' (Morley and Robins, 1995: 33). The adequacy of such post-Fordist characterisations of the unfolding production structures and processes in the audio-visual industry may be certainly challenged on a number of grounds. For one thing, they tend to neglect the fact that in the audio-visual industries, the key locus of power lies in access and control of distribution rather than in the production process. For another, the logic of disintegration of production is fully compatible with the logic of increasing integration of key control functions (Askoy and Robins, 1992). Thus, whilst disintegration and localisation tendencies may be important in the television industry no less than the audio-visual industry, in many important respects, integration and globalisation remain the dominant forces.

THE TV INDUSTRY AND ITS REGULATION IN THE USA AND EU

In several important respects, we can point to a rather striking set of convergences between the television landscape in the EU region and that of the USA at the end of the 1990s, especially if compared to the situation which prevailed in 1980s. But this has been more due to policy initiatives rather than technological innovations. There has been a rapid growth of competitive and multi-channel television services in most EU countries and a consequent fragmentation of the national audiences amongst the competing channels. Furthermore, in keeping with a marked policy shift towards treating television as a commodity service industry much like any other economic

activity, the vast majority of the new services are privately owned and supported by advertising and subscription revenues rather than by the licence fee.
Alongside such commodification shifts, there has also been a consequent
decline in the legitimacy and influence of the traditional 'European' public
service broadcasting approach and its particular orientation towards television services and their audiences. The latter tended to define broadcasting
services as primarily directed at distinctive sets of national communities of
political and cultural identities and to view television audiences as citizens of
distinct polities – rather than merely as consumers of commodified and competing information products or as essential prerequisites for the raising of
advertising revenues. In these respects at least, there appears to have been a
remarkable convergence centred around the kinds of television industry structures and regulatory practices adopted and advocated in US policy circles
since the 1970s and 1980s (e.g. Dizard, 1982; NTIA, 1988).

However, at the same time, there also remain some important differences
between the television industry landscape in the US and that of the EU area
at the start of the new millennium. For one thing, the latter is heavily dependent upon external imports of programming to feed the expanding appetites
of the multiplying distribution systems whilst the US television industry is
comparatively self-sufficient in this respect – indeed, it is the major source of
audio-visual imports to the EU region. For another, there is a peculiar lack of
congruence between the EU's increasingly large and integrated economic
space, on the one hand, and its political, media and cultural spaces on the
other hand. Unlike the USA, there remain many important and resilient barriers to an integrated political public sphere which embraces the diverse
national and regional boundaries and communities of identity within the EU
area. Indeed, it may be noted here that the EU case is particularly instructive
with respect to the severe limitations of the economistic, media-centric and
technology determinist approaches to the formation of meaningful social
spaces and political community (Lefebvre, 1974; Corcoran and Preston,
1995). In essence, despite the multiple efforts of the politicians, industrialists
and bureaucrats in crafting a new television order in the EU area, it is clear
that 'the media will not be the means to create the imagined community in
Europe' (Morley and Robins, 1995: 175).

Despite such differences between the USA and the EU as major world
regions and 'audio-visual spaces', there are some convergence tendencies
with respect to developments in the structure and regulation of television services. This key 'mature medium' has not only been marked by an expanding
economic and employment role in recent decades, but also by a rapid growth
in the number of channels available in most countries. This particular 'flow
technology' has become an increasingly prominent distribution platform for
the direct delivery of a continuously expanding quantitative flow of audio-
visual images into the homes of citizens and consumers in recent decades. At
the same time there has been an increasing fragmentation or segmentation of

audiences associated with the packaging or bundling of particular sets of programming directed at specific audience categories. Clearly, the ever expanding role of television and associated flows of audio-visual images have been strongly shaped by the investments and entrepreneurial initiatives of industrialists and by significant shifts in international trade, investment and intellectual property policies as well as in national and regional regulatory frameworks. But these developments have also been made possible by the application of previous generations of 'new media', such as cable and satellite delivery systems. The impending availability and diffusion of digital television seems certain to extend and amplify such trends even further as we enter a new millennium – as well as offering the, more distant, possibility of some additional innovative services.

Thus, contrary to the predictions of so many techno-centred gurus, we are clearly not arriving at the demise or decline of the 'TV age'. All over the world, people are watching more TV than ever, with the average viewer spending 200 minutes per day in front of the TV set. In the late 1990s, TV viewing varied from 150 minutes in Asia to 230 in North America whilst Europe's TV watching grew by nine minutes from 1995 to reach around 200 minutes a day in 1999. Indeed, with the further development of digital television, and the technical capacity of the Internet and other distribution systems, television is likely to expand and diversify its role as 'the dominant medium' in the next few decades. Television programming and audience viewing patterns are not declining even if they are becoming more fragmented than in the past as the delivery capacity of the digital networks – and the quantitative flows of programming and advertising delivered over them – increases significantly. But the evidence on evolving trends since the 1980s clearly suggests that the production of diverse and quality television programming (or 'content') will not match the impending expansion of delivery systems. The combination of technical advances in the ICT field and neo-liberal policy frameworks which privilege infrastructure development relative to downstream applications in the various programming content domains won't change matters. This combination does little to realise the greater potential for diverse and quality content production which so many commentators regard as an inherent characteristic of the new technical platforms.

NETWORK FOR A 'NEW FRONTIER': THE SHAPING AND RISE OF THE INTERNET/WWW

As we have seen, the 'information superhighway' metaphor achieved a particularly prominent position in policy discourses concerned with the implications of new ICTs for social and economic change in the mid-1990s. It has functioned as a key image in national and global information infrastructure policy initiatives or 'awareness campaigns' advanced by the high-tech industrial interests and policy élites seeking to promote even greater usage and consumption of new ICT products and services. It also served to highlight the tendential emergence of a radically new 'network of networks', comprising a complex set of interconnected broadband communication networks promising much-enhanced capacities to process and distribute diverse forms of information in a common digital mode. In some respects, the rapid development and diffusion of the Internet around the same time seems to have operated as a concrete manifestation (or prefigurative model) of the future promises and potential of the kinds of revolutionary new communication systems proposed by the NII and GII policy discourses.

The development of the Internet, including its offspring the World Wide Web, clearly represents a radically new and distinctive technological innovation in the history of communication systems. Like so many prior radical innovations in the ICT field, the Internet owes a lot to state-funded research, a point that is often obscured in more recent discourses celebrating 'the market' as the singular source of innovation. The emergence and growth of the Internet up to the early 1990s was largely dependent upon successive state military research initiatives and the combination of advances in a diverse range of specific ICT fields within a particular configuration of technical project design briefs and cultures (Winston, 1998). Given its present level of development and diffusion, together with the extensive range of research resources, industrial and policy investments now being mobilised to ensure its further development, it has already achieved a position which far exceeds that achieved by videotex in the 1980s, for example. It now certainly represents a radically new platform whose further development has the potential to provide a wide and flexible range of economically efficient communication functions. The Internet may be defined as a core sub-cluster of the overall set of radical new technological innovations which, in combination, comprise new ICT. Like the major new technology system of which it is both a product and crucial component, the Internet has a pervasive applications potential. In technical terms and features, the Internet is marked by a real, if quite specific, mix of technical features and functions which straddle computing, telecommunications and broadcasting fields (whilst also relying on advances in the core/enabling ICT fields such as semiconductors). Thus it may be defined as a novel technical platform which, potentially if not yet fully in practice, has the capacity to support the distribution of diverse forms of information in digital format and rapid one-to-one, one-to-many and many-to-one forms of connectivity.

The actual growth of the Internet over the past decade has been much celebrated by a continuing and ever-growing flow of bits and bytes in various old and new media. The Internet has been the subject of many competing analyses and speculations and often excited hype – concerning its historical significance, its distinctive characteristics and its implication for economic, social and cultural change. Indeed, it seems safe to assert that the quantity of words and images devoted to this particular technological innovation is without historical precedent. Also unique is the accumulation of hopes, aspirations and hype which have been invested in what is merely a new communication system. This is all the more remarkable given that this new communication platform is still in the early stages of its development. After all, when one moves from the realm of speculation and hype to that of practical use and implementation, the Internet (and World Wide Web) falls far short of meeting the promise of a seamless, fully integrated and interconnecting communication system offering 'instant access' to diverse forms of information. Even for long-time and intensive users, it is still riddled with many frustrating and time-consuming seams and breaks in the form of non-standardised interfaces, file formats and so on which make it far from user-friendly or fully broadband. These technical glitches mean that extensive use of Internet facilities still requires or assumes a certain hobbyist or 'geek' enthusiasm for technical problem-solving which has often been characteristic of the early or emergent stages of new technologies. But it certainly seems likely that these will be addressed by further research and development efforts in future years enabling the Internet to fully achieve the status of an instant, seamless or user-friendly multimedia communication system.

The mini information industry which has developed around analyses of the Internet in the 1990s has been marked by strikingly different constructions of its origins, significance and specificities as a communication system. For example, some accounts stress the military influences in shaping the Internet's design and architectural features, whilst other versions, including some advanced by participants in the early development stages, tend to deny or downplay military influences and instead emphasise the autonomous value orientations and design preference of the research teams involved. Whilst not denying the role of military funding, some other accounts place a great deal of emphasis on influence within the US computer industry and research community (and amongst early Internet user circles) of a very particular libertarian, political culture. Ironically enough given the ultimate sources of research funding, this particular 'California' brand of libertarianism is marked by a strong anti-statist ideology. Some commentators view it as marked by a utopian counterculture 'linked to the aftershocks of the 1960s movements'. This is deemed to have acted as a powerful counter to the commercial orientations of big business and the centralising and control tendencies of the Pentagon and 'big science' and to have strongly stamped the system with the characteristics of 'informality', pluralism and a 'self-directedness of communication' (Castells, 1996: 353, 357). But this culture might equally be defined as that of 'market anarchism' and besides, it seems prudent not to overstate the shaping role of an autonomous academic computer science agenda nor the influence of the early circles of users. For all that computer scientists and other early users played a role in making minor modifications to the developing computer network systems, the essential agenda-setting power, funding and other forces shaping the design, architecture and development of the Internet were 'still vested elsewhere' (Winston, 1998: 332).

To a remarkable extent, the important role of state, military and/or university-based research initiatives in shaping and developing the Internet has tended to be pushed into the background in more recent discourses. This rewriting of its history is occurring at a time when the commercial interests and commodification pressures and the ideology of market anarchism surrounding the Internet have grown throughout the late 1990s. The network is now frequently presented as emblematic of the innovative and creative potential of a competitive, 'market-driven' and private sector approach to the information society. There is a convenient amnesia concerning how the remnants of 'civilian freedoms' on the Internet are 'indebted to a tax-supported commons' even if one initially attached to the military-industrial nexus (Haraway, 1997: 4). This is but one dimension of the manner and extent to which contested versions of the Internet's history, origins and characteristics have become closely bound up with competing agendas concerning the future directions of economic and social development. Notwithstanding such contested histories, however, there is less uncertainty about the forces shaping future developments. The growing emphasis on the Internet as a platform for various forms of 'electronic commerce' and the more recent emphasis on 'business-to-business' communications within influential industry, financial and policy élites since the late 1990s seem to signal much about the likely orientation and forces shaping the further development of the Internet in the future.

THE INTERNET AS NEW PLATFORM FOR PUBLIC COMMUNICATION

The Internet is widely defined as a particularly flexible communication system that is relatively open or responsive to user-based downstream innovation and one that presents significant new opportunities for 'horizontal', non-commercial and more egalitarian forms of communication. So does the Internet promise to deliver some of the long-standing predictions advanced by 'third-wave' writers such as Alvin Toffler and other techno-enthusiasts such as Nicholas Negroponte, explored in Chapter Two? Certainly, as indicated earlier, some critical theorists, who explicitly state a concern to deflate much of the techno-hype in discourses surrounding contemporary change, also subscribe to such ideas. For example, Manuel Castells suggests that the Internet offers a unique basis for 'horizontal global communication' and a distinctive potential to embrace 'the peaceful coexistence' of various competing interests and cultures (Castells, 1996: 352; 355).

This optimistic vision appears to be supported by the development, operation and experience of various kinds of Bulletin Board Systems (BBS) and related new types of communication networking applications centred around specific interests and issues/topics or categories of user groups. Undoubtedly, these Internet-based developments represent new opportunities to create novel forms of Habermasian (political and cultural) public spheres centred around open access, egalitarian and transparent debate. Especially where such Internet applications manage to challenge and resist domination by commercial and other sectional interests, they may also be effective in operating as alternative and/or minority media for the exchanges of news and commentary on political and social developments which are marginalised in mainstream media and debates. For those with access to the necessary facilities, such Internet-based applications represent a more rapid, flexible, spatially extensive and efficient means of communication compared to the more traditional forms of 'alternative' or minority media, such as community presses or newsletters. As such they certainly represent a potentially important and novel means for sustaining, expressing and renewing minority cultural and political interest groups or identities.

Many optimistic accounts of the Internet emphasise its capacity to promote major shifts in cultural and political power structures, including new types of 'communities'. But it is necessary to challenge the more determinist views and suggest instead that new Internet-based communication networks are unlikely of themselves to create significantly new kinds of 'virtual' or other forms of community which challenge existing power structures. The history of past new communication developments suggests that entrenched economic and political interests may also equally, if not more readily, adapt and harness the Internet in line with élite interests. This eventuality does not require a conspiracy, simply a recognition of the supervening necessities imposed by the deep structural features of the particular context in which any new medium is embedded (Winston, 1998). If deemed necessary, the existing blocs of economic and social power interests may also utilise the myriad ways and various resources at their disposal to reshape their predominant communication modes, forms as well as content. Even the extended growth of new decentralised and alternative 'mini-public spheres' is likely to remain a fragmented secondary force in comparison to the increasingly centralised, commercially-orientated and global reach of mainstream information and communication systems. Indeed it is doubtful how far the much celebrated anti-commercial ethos of early Internet-based communication networking developments can remain insulated from the increasing influence of the political-economic and cultural context in which it is embedded.

Here I have in mind not only the privatisation of the original backbone and management facilities, but also the almost unanimous stress on the Internet as platform for 'Electronic Commerce' amongst influential industrial and policy circles in the late 1990s. The rapid colonisation of the Web by advertising hoardings and related marketing and sponsorship interests in such a short period of time is but one other sign of the powerful trends now shaping the future development of the Internet arena. So too are the increasingly frequent examples of commercial, marketing and other special-interest promotional 'messages' within academic BBS and e-mail list network applications. But then again, such electronic forms of marketing and junk mail may be taken as mere manifestations of the increasing penetration of marketing and promotional culture within the contemporary academic-publishing complex. In essence, it is clearly important to recognise and explore the potential of new Internet-based applications for establishing new communicational links to support alternative or minority political, social and cultural interests or identities. But it is also important to address and locate the potential for such developments in the wider matrix of communication institutions, social structures, economic interests and power relations in which they are embedded.

The core architectures and design of the Internet were framed and shaped by a very specific military research agenda which sought to construct a robust and 'fail-safe' communication system. Yet, as we have seen, one unintended spin-off from that original military project is the actual and potential use of the Internet as a new communication platform to support many new kinds of messaging, connectivity or even 'mini-public spheres' besides the 'e-commerce' which has dominated public discourse in more recent years. Consequently, many users and observers are committed to the view that the Internet can be harnessed in myriad ways to facilitate debate and information exchange between members of diverse interest communities, and it remains the case that the Internet is a relatively open and flexible new communication platform in many significant respects. However, it seems prudent not to overstate the significance of the actual or potential developments here.

Viewed overall, the emerging new public communications order is best defined as a case of 'business as usual' rather than any revolutionary shift toward more participative modes of public communication. This slogan certainly fits the overwhelming trends and evidence of the continuing dominant role of the mature media in terms of popular access and audience use and engagement with content. It is confirmed further by the paucity of 'really innovative' multimedia content development and the significant and growing role of the mature media in the public arena of digital content.

CONNECTIVITY MATTERS: ACCESS AND USE OF MATURE
AND NEW ICT FACILITIES

It is now time to consider some key issues related to the access and use of the overall portfolio of both new and 'mature' communication technologies and facilities. Much of the recent policy and academic discussion concerning access and use of communication and media technologies and related issues of information rich/poor cleavages have tended to focus on the newer media. As we have seen, this is a particular feature of many 'information society' policy documents which express concern about potential threats posed by new kinds of inequalities centred around access or exclusion from computing and Internet-based services. As a result, they ignore the kinds of fundamental socio-economic inequalities described in the previous chapters. They also tend to gloss over or ignore considerations of unequal access to mature communication technologies which continue to play a much more important role in the communication practices and everyday life experiences of most sections of the population. This section will now seek to address some of the key questions in terms of the overall matrix of available media and communication technologies and the broader social context in which they are embedded.

The mature media technologies of radio and television receivers have long reached almost 'universal' levels of access amongst households in the advanced industrial economies but much lower rates continue to prevail in low income countries. Of course, the past two decades have also witnessed the development and widespread diffusion of a wide range of new 'stand alone' information and communication technologies amongst household users in the advanced industrial world and beyond. The most prominent of these include video cassette recorders and cameras, the walkman, CD music systems, electronic games consoles, and, of course, personal computers. By 1996, approximately two thirds of households in the EU area were equipped with VCRs whilst the equivalent estimate for the USA was 90 per cent of households and 80 per cent in the case of Japan (European Audiovisual Observatory, 1998: 34). At the same time, of course, a number of on-line or over-the-air connectivity technologies have also diffused more widely over recent decades, including cable and satellite television as well as the 120–year-old technology of plain old telephone service (POTS), the fax and the newer offspring, mobile/cellular telephony.

In the accompanying table, I have sought to provide a summary of relevant indicators concerning the international levels of access and diffusion of some key communication technologies in 1996 (see Table 9.4). This table draws on data for a total of 206 countries with populations greater than 40,000. These are grouped into four major blocs or sub-categories, as follows: 50 high income countries where the level of per capita GDP was

TABLE 9.4   International communication access and connectivity indicators, 1996: country blocs by income group[1]

	World	50 'High income' countries	28 'Upper middle income' countries	65 'Lower middle income' countries	63 'Low income' countries
A) BACKGROUND INDICATORS					
Population (millions)	**5,778**	909	441	1,170	3,258
Density (per square km)	**43**	27	21	29	81
GDP per cap. ($US)	**5,104**	25,809	4,747	1,688	471
Number of households (millions)	**1,456.2**	340.3	105.8	273.3	736.7
B) TELEVISION INDICATORS					
TV receivers per 100 inhabitants	**23.8**	61.9	26.3	22.7	13.1
TV households as % of total h/holds	**66.0**	96[6]	80.2	73.3	47.4
Cable TV subscribers 1996 (millions)	**211.2**	131.0	10.2	18.9	51.1
Home satellite antennae (millions)	**50.6**	36.2	7.2	5.5	1.8
C) PLAIN OLD TELEPHONE SERVICE					
Main tel lines – per 100 pop. (1996)	**12.88**	54.06	13.36	9.710	2.45
– CAGR % 1990–96	**6.1**	3.6	9.0	8.5	28.5
Residential main lines per 100 h/holds	**39.9**	102.7	39.7	31.1	8.9
Public telephones per 1,000 pop.	**1.53**	5.17	2.68	0.91	0.56
Access/subscriptn. as % of pc GDP[2]	**8.6**	0.9	2.1	4.4	21.5
Outgoing intl.tel.call % growth 1990–96	**12.5**[3]	12.0	13.8	15.0	19.2
Outgoing intl.tel.call mins pc 1996	**12.3**[4]	62.7	13.0	4.1	0.8
Outgoing intl.tel traffic per subscriber	**94.4**	115.9	97.7	42.0	33.4
Faults per 100 main lines per annum	**22.3**	7	29	57	184
D) NEW(er) ICT-BASED COMMUNICATIONS					
Mobile subscribers per 100 pop. 1996[5]	**2.46**	13.17	2.00	0.53	0.23
Est. no. of fax machines, 1996 (millions)	**47.972**	44.479	1.839	1.031	0.620
ISDN subscribers, 1996 (millions)	**4.767**	4.714	0.039	0.014	< 0.001
Estim. PCs per 100 inhabitants, 1996	**4.65**	22.28	2.92	1.34	0.23
Internet hosts per 10,000 inhabitants	**28.14**	171.92	8.40	1.93	0.09
Est. Internet users per 10,000 inhabit.	**91.89**	498.73	55.87	19.00	0.89

Notes:
1   This table provides summary data for a total of 206 countries with populations greater than 40,000. These are classified into four major sub-categories, as follows: 50 high income countries with a per capita GDP of $US9,386 or more in 1995; 28 'upper middle income' countries with per capita GDP of $3,036–9,385; 65 'lower middle income' countries with per capita GDP of $766–3,035; and 63 'low income' countries with a per capita GDP of US$765 or less.
2   Access subscription costs calculated as per cent of GDP per capita.
3   Outgoing international telephone traffic/call growth 1990–96.
4   Outgoing international telephone traffic/calls, minutes per population, 1996.
5   Cellular mobile subscribers per 100 population in 1996.
6   Data from Co-Com 'Ir-Con5' and 'USicCon1' databases.

Sources: Abstracted and analysed by the author from data in various datasets.

$US9,386 or more in 1995; 28 'upper middle income' countries with per capita GDP of $3,036–9,385; 65 'lower middle income' countries with per capita GDP of $766–3,035; and 63 'low income' countries with a per capita GDP of US$765 or less. Section A of the table provides some general socio-economic indicators for each of the four blocs of countries and section B provides some indicators related to television. The table indicates that by 1996, there were almost 62 television sets per 100 inhabitants in the 50 countries with the highest average income levels whilst the equivalent figure for the group of 63 countries with lowest average incomes was only 13 sets per 100 of the population. It also shows that the estimated number of cable television subscribers in the 50 richest countries totalled 131 million in 1996, equivalent to approximately 38 per cent of all households, and the estimated number of home satellite antennae totalled 36 million suggesting an average household diffusion rate of approximately 10 per cent across the advanced industrial world. The expanding role of such multi-channel services underlines the trends towards increasing segmentation or fragmentation of national television audiences which were explored earlier. Within the 15 countries comprising the EU area, the estimated percentage of television households connected to cable services increased from 18 per cent to 26 per cent between 1991 and 1997, whilst the equivalent figures for the USA were 58 per cent and 62 per cent and those for Japan were 19 per cent and 29 per cent (European Audiovisual Observatory, 1998: 42).

Section C of the table provides indicators related to the diffusion of telephone technology. These point to generally very high levels of access in the richest bloc of countries where the number of telephone lines per 100 households reached a level of 102.7. This figure reflects the trend towards multiple telephone lines in some households within the advanced industrial countries alongside a very rapid growth of mobile telephony in more recent years. But it should also be noted that at the same time a significant number of households remain phoneless in many of the high income countries. This section of the table also indicates that the levels of access to the old technology of the telephone become progressively lower across the different blocs of countries ranked according to average income. To a large extent, this reflects the fact that the annual costs of a basic subscription to the telephone system in the top 50 income countries amounts to less than 1 per cent of average per capita GDP whilst this cost amounts to a staggering 21.5 per cent of average per capita GDP in the poorest bloc of 63 lowest income countries.

In many of the advanced industrial countries, the plain old telephone service (POTS) really only began to achieve something approaching 'universal' availability to household users in more recent decades. However, it should be noted that access to this particular technology has now become an essential prerequisite for effective participation in many areas of social and economic activity and average per capita rates of usage have grown considerably in recent years. Basic telephony may be defined as a component element of contemporary *consumption norms,* a status which places it outside the realm of discretionary consumer expenditures (Preston and Flynn, 2000). Yet despite increasing rhetorical emphasis on 'universal service' in the telecommunication policy discourses of the richer countries in more recent years, many households and citizens still remain excluded from access to basic telephony services. In the light of the growing disparities in income considered in the previous chapter, it is also significant that those lacking access are disproportionately concentrated in the lower income households. There has been a significant decline in the real cost of telephone services (e.g. as a share of average incomes), not least because of process innovations via the application of successive generations of new ICTs (Preston and Flynn, 1999). Despite such trends however, it must be stressed that access to POTS is still far from universal and that this particular mature technology merits a much more central place in contemporary debates concerning social or informational exclusion.

Let us now turn to the newer ICT-based connectivity services, where the questions of access to and usage of computers, advanced telecommunications and computer-based network services, especially the Internet, have featured most prominently. Within both the research literature and the mass media, one encounters a multitude of indicators emphasising the rapid growth of Internet access and usage, especially since the early 1990s. It should be noted here however, that many of the available measures are flawed by assumptions which tend to overstate the actual rates of diffusion and use. This is one reason why many analyses and claims concerning both the quantitative and qualitative aspects of the Internet's significance as a new system for public communication have been severely overinflated and require careful interrogation. A cautious and critical approach seems all the more important given the active role of highly partial marketing and industrial interests in the construction of some of the widely published sets of indicators. The problem is compounded by the trend towards proprietary enclosure and commodification of previously published data series which, in turn, are linked to the increasing commercialisation of the Internet since the mid-1990s. The paucity of reliable and impartial data sources concerning these and other important ICT-based developments is compounded by the lack of official statistics and other independent sources of information, in part due to the resource constraints and privatisation pressures exerted on official statistical agencies in many countries since the 1980s.

Despite this 'health warning' about many of the available indicators, it is certainly the case that the 1990s witnessed a rapid growth in access to and use of the Internet, not least when compared to the relatively small numbers of specialist users of its precursor networks in the 1970s and 1980s. This seems to be especially the case in the richer industrial economies such as those of North America and Western Europe where a significant proportion of households have acquired personal computers (PCs) equipped with modems, and have subsequently established access to the Internet over the course of the 1990s. Section D of Table 9.4 provides some basic indicators of the broad international patterns of diffusion and access to new ICT-based communication technologies. These data highlight some of the significant differences between the different blocs of countries ranked by levels of income, but it should be noted that the indicators refer to estimates of both home and business users.

Turning to the advanced industrial world, we find that, much like the mature media, the '[new] media are American'. Not surprisingly, the available data indicate that the USA held the predominant position in terms of international shares of PC ownership and Internet connections from the start. By 1996, the USA still accounted for almost half of all PCs in use and two-thirds of all Internet connections. At the same time, the 15 EU member states accounted for approximately 28 per cent of PCs and one quarter of total Internet connections. The purchase of PCs for both business and home use began to grow fairly rapidly in Europe from the early 1990s. The percentage of households with installed computers in the EU area increased from less than 0.5 per cent to approximately 8.0 per cent of homes between 1993 and 1996. In that year there were approximately 21 million PCs installed in US homes and about half that number in homes in the EU area. In 1996, the proportion of US homes with installed PCs was in the region of 20–21 per cent, suggesting a household computer diffusion rate which was approximately 2.5 times greater than that in the EU region (a 'diffusion gap' between the EU and the USA which almost exactly matched that for cable television). Amongst the EU member states, there are very large differences in the proportions of households connected to the Internet. The highest rates of home connection are found in the Scandinavian countries, where Finland recorded a rate of 24 per cent in 1998, Sweden a rate of 14 per cent, whilst the largest country, Germany, had a connection rate of approximately 8 per cent. But some of the other large EU member states such as Britain, France, Italy and Spain had much lower levels, recording between 2–4 per cent of households connected to the Internet in 1998.

In conclusion, the Internet and its downstream innovations in the form of the World Wide Web (and other multimedia related refinements) must indeed be recognised as a distinctive and important new communication system. It certainly represents a significant advance towards the construction of a flexible information highway or platform with respect to the communication of a variety of different media forms, types and formats. But the analysis of relevant data and trends above leads to the conclusion that its rate of diffusion has been rapid but the levels of access amongst households remains relatively low in the late 1990s. Hence, it must be concluded here that its role as a (potential) medium for public communication is likely to remain very minor for the foreseeable future. Indeed contrary to some of the more extravagant claims concerning the growth of the Internet, its levels of diffusion or access amongst households in some of the industrialised societies remains much less than that experienced in the first decade of previous new communication technologies such as radio and television receivers. This is not surprising given its costs and its still emergent status with respect to a seamless and user-friendly communication medium, compared, say, to the telephone for messaging or the TV for audio-visual content. Viewed in terms of access trends and developments, any emergent new public communications order will remain dominated by mature media and technology platforms for some time to come.

DIGITAL MEDIA AS TRANSFORMER: FROM VIRTUAL REALITY TO REAL VIRTUALITY?

So what about more qualitative changes in contemporary media culture, and the question of whether new ICT and related digital multimedia developments are leading to a radical transformation of public communication institutions and processes? In earlier sections we noted how so many recent authors have proclaimed a new communications order along with a profound cultural transformation arising from the development of the Internet and related digital technologies. For heuristic purposes, one may readily identify two crude but sharply contrasting sub-variants of such proclaimed transformations and their implications. In the more optimistic, utopian variant, new ICT based developments are leading to a much more open and egalitarian communication system and culture defined around greater individual freedom, reflexivity and expression. This is often linked to the perceived tendency of new ICTs and information structures to erode the hegemony of élite cultural forms and roles, and to foster a de-centralised, more participative or interactive and 'democratic' communications order. In this new frictionless capitalist culture, every digital being can be a broadcaster as class and gender and other social conflicts evaporate, and perhaps society itself (Negroponte, 1995; Kelly, 1998; Toffler, 1983; Dyson et al., 1996). The dystopian variants tend to stress the amplification of a flat, depth-less or meaning-less postmodern culture and associated disempowering or disabling political trends already deemed to be engendered by the mature 'mass' electronic and print media systems. The combination of new and mature information and communication structures is perceived to amplify the 'medium-is-the-message' effect or accelerate the vertigo and other disorientating effects of the flow of signifiers and so extend the 'void of information' and trends of communication or sensory overload (e.g. Baudrillard, 1998; Poster, 1995).

It is important not to overstate the contrast between these two schools, however, not least because some authors manage to combine elements of both perspectives in a single, if not always seamless, text. It could also be said that some authors in both camps often appear to rely heavily on the same cloudy crystal ball, to judge from content (the common hazy fog of hype and hyperbole which they seem to celebrate and generate) and method (an aversion to engagement in relevant empirical or historical research). In this particular niche of the commodified academic-publishing nexus, product differentiation is mainly established by a marketing strategy centred around cunning linguistic stunts and endless strokes with neologisms invoking the signs of cyber-this, hyper-that and post-everything. The result, too often, is a very particular form of thick description that is more depth-less surface and vacuous than any of the imaginary postculture it presumes to describe. More reflexively, it might be suggested that such analyses seem to apply less to the culture of everyday life than they do to the new and intensified forms of competition and commodification which are reshaping the culture of contemporary academic practices. Hence, despite their own declared mission, such authors seem to exemplify and secretly report the extension of capitalist modernism rather than any transcendence to a post- (-modern, -capitalist or -industrial) culture. In a way, then, the products of that particular niche in the academic-publishing complex may also exemplify the increasing salience of the commodification thesis. They manifest and express the sectorally peculiar modes of the deepening rationalisation and industrialisation of all forms of knowledge and information activities.

However, there are, mercifully, many exceptions to such irritating trends. For example, these include some stimulating and relevant analyses of the changing relations between the cultural and economic realms. Much of this work has focused on the changing role of the information and communication structures and the increasing dependence of the economy on various forms of symbolic and discursive knowledge. For some, this implies that, in significant ways, 'culture has penetrated the economy itself' and is thus tending towards potentially more open, flexible identities and lifestyles (Lash and Urry, 1994: 60–1). Whilst not convinced by the authors' claims concerning the extent and meaning of a shift towards a more 'reflexive mode of accumulation', their thesis certainly provides an interesting counter to notions of an autonomous, runaway and subversive culture and consumption sphere advanced by Bell and other neo-conservatives (Bell, 1973, 1976).

The present book's empirical analysis acknowledges the idea of an increasing but limited penetration of culture into the overall cluster of economic sectors and activities. But, my analysis suggests not only that such trends are more limited than others assume, it also points to a significant counter-trend of increasing industrialisation or commodification of culture as well as the more rapid growth of instrumental information services. This is marked by the growing commercial pressures and newer forms of capitalist industrial calculus (economic competition, performative instrumentalism) which now pervade the practices and discourses governing virtually all areas of the media and institutions of public communication. It is also manifest in the new kind of industrial and organisational structures within the media industries as well as the new kinds of ICT, communication and information policy strategies and discourses described above. These deepening commodification processes are evident in the declining role of public service broadcasting in the European context especially, and in the expanded role of advertising and sponsorship funding in the cultural industries realm. They also invade many of the non-media-based cultural and educational services, not least university-based research and teaching practices.

This book therefore points to the simultaneous tendencies towards both the limited penetration of culture into the economic sphere and a significant counter-trend of extended industrialisation and commodification of information and culture. Contrary to some other recent critical theorists (e.g. Lash and Urry, 1994), I am emphasising that there is no inherent conflict between the two tendencies or processes. I also suggest that the processes of deepening commodification of the cultural realm pose significant (old and new) challenges concerning the conditions of access, funding, diversity and quality of content in the realm of public communication as well as for audiences and users, defined as citizens as well as consumers. In a certain sense, commodification captures the essence of the old and the new in the unfolding new cultural, communication and social order. Commodification is not a new phenomenon in the cultural realm. But in the extent and mode of its expansion, this process certainly seems to capture some of the essential features of this latest stage of capitalist social and cultural development.

One notable feature of some recent culturalist versions of the contemporary is a rather hasty dismissal of the continuing salience of the concept of 'commodification'. This occurs alongside a dismissal of other conceptual elements of the critical cultural studies tradition (e.g. Baudrillard, 1998; Lash and Urry, 1994). In some cases, the relevant critical theorists seem to end up sharing much common ground with the neo-conservative Daniel Bell in their evaluation of the commodification thesis. A frequently adopted approach has been to treat the concept of commodification as crude or inappropriately totalising in scope and to characterise this critical studies tradition as anachronistic, or even somehow imply that it is intricately bound up with a fundamentalist Marxist materialism. Yet, ironically, some such critics of the commodification concept end up proposing a model of cultural developments or tendencies which is far more sweeping and totalising than anything that emerged from the Frankfurt tradition at its most apocalyptic.

We have also seen how some influential postmodernist accounts of contemporary cultural developments have a penchant for hyper-McLuhanite analysis of the cultural implications of new information and communication technologies. But the 'born-again' influence of such determinist accounts extends well beyond the (postmodern) media and cultural studies fields. One recent example of this influence crops up in Manuel Castells' impressive three-volume work. For the most part, *The Information Age* provides a compelling, persuasive and highly stimulating account of contemporary developments. In the chapter on multimedia and culture in the first volume, however, Castells seems to slip into a highly technology-centred mode of analysis which is out of keeping with that in most other sections. Here, he abandons his socio-economic perspective to shift significantly into a specific media-centric mode. He stresses the technical features of new Internet-based developments and celebrates their potential for more interactive communications. The analysis is poorly linked to the kinds of socio-economic developments addressed elsewhere in the same volume, and fails to engage with the growing commercial pressures surrounding the Internet and media sector more generally (Castells, 1996: Chapter 5). For example, at one point this former prominent theorist of urbanism suggests that the commercialisation of cyberspace will be closer to 'the historical experience of merchant streets that sprout out from vibrant urban culture, than to the shopping centres spread in the dullness of anonymous suburbs' (Castells, 1996: 355). In the concluding sections of the chapter, when summarising the key features of multimedia as a symbolic environment, some elements of Castells' analysis become a heady cocktail of neat McLuhan and Baudrillard.

Castells regards new digital multimedia systems as powerfully immersive and argues that they tend to absorb and transform traditional cultures (1996: 370). He proceeds to identify what he views as 'historically specific' about the new communication system, deemed to be organised around the electronic integration of 'all communication modes from the typographic to the multisensorial' (1996: 372). He argues that one of the core characteristics of the multimedia system 'is not its inducement of virtual reality but the construction of real virtuality' (1996: 372). Castells proceeds to further elaborate on the meaning of this in subsequent paragraphs, defining the essential feature of the new communication system as follows: 'it is a system in which reality itself (that is people's material/symbolic existence) is entirely captured, fully immersed in a virtual image setting, in the world of make-believe, in which appearances are not just on the screen through which experience is communicated, but they become the experience' (1996: 373).

To a remarkable extent, the approach and content of these sections of Castells' work seem severely out of line with the much more nuanced analysis of technology matters and their relation to socio-economic and political change which informs many other sections of this work. In terms of the accumulated body of communication studies research, it slips into a rather traditional 'strong' media or technology effects paradigm. But, this type of media-centric and strongly determinist approach is no more valid when applied to the new media systems than when applied to old media, even if it has been revived somewhat in some other more recent postmodernist work. It is merely the flip-side of the optimist 'dreamware' propounded by the techno-prophets or the promotional commandos of the ICT supply industry.

It harps back to the old strong-effect 'hypodermic' models of communication and flies against the prevailing currents of research on media reception and audiences. Such machinic analyses also by-pass the requirements for, or possibilities of, alternatives to the commodification trends and other forces shaping contemporary communication and cultural developments.

Rumours of the death of reality or 'people's material/symbolic existence' beyond the communication machine (of 'real virtuality' or any other linguistic variant) are not merely greatly exaggerated or highly premature. The analysis in this book provides theoretical and empirical grounds to reject this particular construction of the contemporary communication or cultural order. For sure, the (especially mature) communication systems and media have had a major place in the lived realm of production and especially consumption in the advanced industrialised and urbanised societies since the late nineteenth century. They have played an increasing role in re-framing the cultural/symbolic and political contours of the discursive spaces inhabited by all social groups since the first 'multimedia' revolution of the third long-wave era. But it is necessary to examine the continuing but changing role and features of the mature and new media systems in the wider socio-economic context and the daily experience of the interpretative communities in which they are embedded.

Thus, despite the considerable merits of other elements of his work, in this particular domain Castells' analysis lapses into a 'strong effects' view of media technologies. It adopts a particular form of the McLuhanite medium-is-the-message analytical mode which goes against the drift of accumulated research on the processes of media-based communication. In essence, it involves a too-rapid shift from (a selective reading of) the technical characteristics of the medium to the audience's 'experience', to the interpretative or meaning-making stages of the communication process. In the process, it ignores too many layers of intervening variables which shape the process of media-based communication practices according to the current state-of-the-art in the field of communication studies.

MATURE MEDIA BYTE BACK?

The Content . . . industry is still at an early stage of development, and is typified by concepts and trials rather than commercial services . . . Despite the high level of media 'hype' surrounding many of the content enabled multimedia consumer service opportunities . . . their development is still at a very early stage.'

(PA Consulting Group, 1997)

The 1990s have produced very little by way of radically new 'killer' product innovations in the field of multimedia content despite all the excited huffing and puffing of techno-gurus. Compared to many earlier forecasts, digital media innovations have been very limited relative to the major developments in new technological platforms, not to mention major programmes of private and public R&D investments in this field in Europe and elsewhere. Thus there remains a certain deficit gap between the hopes and expectations which underpinned much of the activity and investments in the multimedia content field since the late 1980s and the outcome so far. Most of the actual content productions fail to measure up to the pundits' visions of radically new interactive or 'immersive' media, textual and narrative forms – anticipated as 'killer applications' which would trigger a major expansion of new markets and demand patterns.

In the digital multimedia content field, the close of the 1990s witnessed some significant developments compared to the close of the 1980s, especially the use of the Internet as a new distribution system. In entering the new millennium, it still remains more a case of inflated gales of hype and hope rather than any Schumpeterian 'creative destruction' process. Perhaps the single biggest multimedia content success story of the 1990s (as in the 1980s) was in the area of electronic games, originally based on successive generations of specialised consoles and moving more to PC-based CD-Rom platforms and the Internet in the latter half of the 1990s. The 1990s witnessed many interesting and well-publicised trials and social experiments, in areas like interactive television, video-on-demand and on-line publishing, but most did not get beyond the trial stage (Preston, 1997c). In the first year of the new millennium, Wireless Applications Protocol has been elevated to the status of prime new 'killer application'. Targeted at the large user base of mobile phone users, WAP is unlikely to prompt much by way of media content innovations as it may only support very short, text-based content in the immediate future.

For sure, there have been a small number of commercially successful CD-Rom products but the most prominent of these have been tied into rather privileged distribution channels (linked to a monopoly position in neighbouring ICT markets). The majority of new media content initiatives and products based on CD-Rom formats have not been major success stories, whether measured in financial terms or in terms of the design and delivery of radically new media formats which trigger significant demand patterns or market developments (Preston, 1998a; Preston and Kerr, 1998). Indeed, it has been estimated that less than 10 per cent of all the CD-Rom content products which were published in the EU area during the 1990s generated a profit.

In terms of commercially successful new Internet-based services, the biggest single new content industry appears to be the sale and delivery of pornography. Yet, surprisingly enough, this particular 'killer application' does not feature prominently in the glossy market development analyses or relevant policy reports (apart from the quite specific content regulation issues related to child pornography). Besides pornography, the biggest success story in Internet-based applications in the late 1990s was Amazon.com, a company focused on the sale of good old 'stand-alone', but 'atoms'-based media products such as books. The on-line delivery of recorded music is widely regarded as offering one of the more promising prospects for commercially successful digital content services. But again, neither of these two particular Internet applications have much connection with the radically new forms of multimedia content envisaged and promised by the techno-gurus.

Apart from those examples, web (broad)casting is widely viewed as one other important Internet-based development which offers the promise of expanded new content-related innovations, not least in the light of potential future convergences with digital broadcasting services. Equally importantly, the established television companies (like newspaper publishers) have also launched new kinds of on-line ancillary services related to their existing portfolio of media-based content (e.g. radio and TV programmes). Web-based delivery of broadcast programming and additional ancillary services related to particular programmes or channels may also fail to qualify as an example of radical new product innovations or novel media form. Indeed, these might might be defined as an interesting sort of minor spin-off or secondary 'service innovation'. Yet this would be an inappropriate characterisation in my view. These developments represent significant types of process or service innovations on the part of the mature media organisations, which harness their own core competencies (not least, 'ready-made' audiences) to the new digital technologies. Such initiatives serve to widen audience access to established content products or mature media formats as well as opening up new potentially lucrative commercial opportunities to sustain and exploit 'ready-made' content and audiences in line with evolving marketing techniques. This development also parallels similar highly significant innovations centred around the on-line delivery of full-text or selected contents of newspapers and other print-based publications.

In combination, the growth and success of these Internet-based process or service innovations on the part of the established broadcasting and print (especially newspaper or periodical) publishing organisations is a significant but largely unexpected recent development in the digital public communication arena. Of course it upsets the technology-centred analyses and predictions – focused on radical product innovations – advanced by the pundits and expert consultancy reports over the years. But in my view, it highlights and expresses one of the most important and interesting developments in the multimedia content field over the past decade. Viewed within the overall context of established and new multimedia content industry trends at the close of the 1990s, these mature media-based initiatives amount to much more than minor or subsidiary 'spin-off' developments. They now represent a significant share of Internet-based flows of consumer-related content and public communication practices. In the process, they now signal a potentially commanding position for the mature media since they can readily provide content and access to significant audiences for on-line media content services in the immediate future.

In effect, these mature media industries have now positioned themselves to become the real masters of multimedia content markets as we march into the millennium. And they now also have advertiser-friendly audited audience data to prove it! This development has occurred via a sequential process of trial and error experimentation and learning-by-doing over a relatively short time span (c.1995–9). In the process, the mature media industries have managed to develop a much more effective (but still very much evolving) strategy for service and content development. They are well positioned with regard to the particular cluster of the competencies and resources required to exploit further new opportunity structures. Compared to would-be competitors from the more technology-based fields of computing and telecommunications, by the late 1990s, the mature media were poised to remain the real masters of the content domain within any 'new' communications order.

In economic terms, there are certainly some other real (as opposed to virtual or dreamware) developments in the media 'content' sectors in the 1990s. But in this case too, the core economic action and benefits lie with the mature media field, and especially the owners and controllers of mature (audio-visual) media content. As a direct result of policy rather than technical innovations, the continuing proliferation of television channels in Europe and elsewhere has caused demand for feature film and other programming rights to rise sharply throughout 1990s. This trend is continuing as the television market expands and demand and competitive bidding for film rights has escalated. One 1998 study estimated the present value of the film archives owned by the seven studios (Sony, MGM, Paramount, Warner Brothers, Twentieth Century Fox and Universal) at $40bn. Furthermore, the value of these content libraries was forecast to grow to nearly $55bn within five years when yet more new TV channels and digital services will have been launched. So, in this respect too, it appears that the mature media are the real masters of multimedia markets at the beginning of the new millennium. These developments usually fall outside the purview of the technology centred policy analyses and consultancy reports. Indeed, few could have imagined this in the 1950s when television first came on air. At that time the Hollywood studios counted themselves lucky to raise 'a couple of hundred dollars' in selling the broadcast rights for one of their classic feature films to a TV station (*Financial Times*, 30 April 1998). However, in a very short time, the 'mature' media moguls of Hollywood learned to just-love TV and adjust their business strategies to master the then new medium!

A ONCE AND FUTURE KING? EXPLAINING THE DIGITAL CONTENT DEFICIT

This particular mapping and reading of key trends in the realm of digital multimedia content developments over the past decade has highlighted the paucity of the much-heralded product innovations (radically new media forms and narrative/textual formats) on the one hand. But it has also pointed to the emergence of significant new, if largely unanticipated, process and spin-off innovations on the part of the mature media sectors, on the other hand. The reasons for the continued failure of the former to materialise, despite so much investment in research, technological and promotional resources in the 1990s, are complex. They certainly highlight the hazards and limitations of analyses and forecasts centred on the presumed technical characteristics, effects or potentialities of any set of technological developments. But it may be worthwhile here to outline some of the key factors for this gap between forecast and performance, at least as they appear from the long-wave perspective informing this book.[2]

For one thing, many excited pronouncements and forecasts concerning radically new interactive and immersive digital media content and forms are themselves based on restrictive and flawed assumptions about what is necessary or effective in media-based communication practices. Some are marked by a reliance on engineering or information science models of media-based communication processes. For example, these often seem to equate the process of effective communication (meaning-making) with a purely quantitative increase in sensory engagement. Such quantitative approaches cannot begin to apprehend that sometimes 'less is more' in many processes of media-based communication, as even McLuhan recognised in some of his distinctions between hot and cool media (e.g. poetry versus prose texts).

It may be suggested also that new digital/ICT media applications are based on what is still an emerging and rapidly changing major new technology system (one which is still at the relatively early stages of its potential development trajectory and thus marked by high levels of risk and uncertainty). Even at the technological level, digital multimedia comprises a cluster of interrelated radical innovations (of which the Internet/WWW is a major component element, alongside CD-Roms). The precise or effective integration, potential dynamic synergies and applications potential of this radical new technology sub-set are still poorly understood or developed with respect to the information content applications field (no less than in other ICT application sectors, for example, the continuing productivity paradox).

All this points to a high degree of uncertainty and incompleteness in terms of what constitutes digital multimedia as a technical platform level. Even if the Internet/WWW has replaced CD-Roms as the core platform since the mid-1990s, the former is still very much in its early stages and undergoing rapid change at the technical level. This poses many uncertainties and instabilities even at the level of technical tools and analysis. For example, some recent commentators still define its primary technical characteristics as those of an alphabetic medium (e.g. Levinson, 1999). Yet it is clear that the subsidiary stream of developments surrounding the WWW over the past three to five years have been mainly framed around visual, audio and audio-visual modes.

In addition, any radical new media form or content service requires a further, equally important and resource-intensive layer of radical innovations beyond the purely technical. This refers to the creative application layer of innovations focused on defining and developing the appropriate new mix (paradigm) of codes, grammars, conventions and textual strategies required for the authoring and design of effective new media forms and content. These must match the specific modalities and possibilities afforded by the new technical platforms as well as engaging with the prevailing portfolio of audience orientations, competencies and expectations related to media-based communication practices. The currently embryonic and rapidly evolving status of technical platforms such as the Internet/WWW amplifies the challenges involved in advancing this creative layer of innovations so essential for the development of distinctive new digital media forms and content services. The combined implications of these two essential layers of innovation suggest that the radical new digital multimedia content products (distinctive new MM forms and content) are still at a very early and embryonic stage of their potential development path (an analogy with the status of film/cinema around the 1900–05 era seems appropriate here).

In addition, I suggest that these barriers to multimedia product innovations have been compounded by the prevailing technocratic and economistic policy environment (in R&D and industrial innovation policy fields especially). Relevant policy initiatives and discourses continue to privilege purely technical research and to promote further platform or infrastructural developments. They tend to neglect the creative and other relevant multimedia competencies and expertise. Current policy aproaches to digital media are generally permeated by information-engineering based (and essentially quantitative) conceptions of communication processes. Thus they fail to understand cultural content production and consumption practices (e.g. alternative conceptions of 'interactivity'; the resource-intensive nature of effective media-based content production). Current policies usually fail to recognise the need for nuanced policy approaches which seek to embrace both industrial and cultural policy goals and hence fail to address the potential complementarities between them.

These broader conditioning factors mean that any specific Internet-based or other radical multimedia product innovation initiative remains a relatively expensive, high-risk 'heroic' venture. The production and design of effective media-based content is inherently resource-intensive. Contrary to the assumption of many engineering-based approaches, the production and design of digital or other forms of content cannot be readily automated; nor are they significantly speeded up by faster data delivery systems or faster data processing systems. Furthermore, the still emergent status of the technical and creative/applications innovation layers may be compounded by further policy constraints. These include the continuing failure to address and develop an appropriate cluster of social and institutional innovations (especially in the domain of consumption). These represent important components in any matching new socio-technical paradigm facilitating the wider diffusion of ICT based content service applications.

Notes

1 In terms of the PIS model proposed in the preceding chapters, it should be noted here that the 'content is king' slogan points to a particularly rapid growth in the overall scale and economic role of two distinct sub-categories. It points to a relatively rapid growth of both (a) specialised or producer media content (e.g. scientific, economic, financial) products/services directed at business or professional users, and (b) the kinds of digital informational, cultural, entertainment media products which are directed at final or household users. It furthermore suggests that innovative new-ICT-based multimedia content industries are poised to expand much more rapidly than those based on mature communication technology platforms. In line with the present chapter's main interest in media developments directly related to final users and the sphere of public communication, the following exploration is focused on the latter of these two categories of 'content' and media services.
2 Much of the following argument draws from the author's participation in an EU funded project: Social Learning in Multimedia (SLIM). For further details on this project, see the website: www.ed.ac.uk/~rcss/SLIM/SLIMhome.html

CHAPTER TEN

INFORMATION AS NEW FRONTIER:
COMMODIFICATION AND CONSUMPTION STAKES

'High Technology can distribute low culture: no problem. But high culture can persist at a low level of technology: that is how most of it was produced . . . In a period of what is certain to be major technical innovation in cultural production and consumption and in information systems of every kind, it will be essential to move beyond these old terms.'

(Williams, 1983: 128)

'NEW FRONTIERS': CULTURAL CONTENT
AND INFORMATIONAL CAPITALISM

The development and diffusion of new ICT and related shifts in the non-technical dimensions of the innovation process seem certain to involve a significant expansion in the role of information and communication services. This forecast is not only based on inherent technical characteristics or the incentive structures encoded in new ICT as the predominant major new technology system of today (as indicated earlier). The overwhelming drift of recent private sector investment strategies and public sector policies clearly indicate that information and communication services sectors have come to represent an important internal frontier to be exploited by the capitalist accumulation process in new ways. They have become the predominant target sites for the expansion of capital investment, accumulation and value added activities in the future. The reliability of this particular exercise in forecasting is further confirmed when key elements of the discourses favoured by influential sections of the industrial and political élites are considered (for example, those surrounding the 'information society' or 'e-commerce'). After all, the ideas of powerful élite groups can and do matter when the business at hand is one of prescription as well as description and when these future-orientated visions are accompanied by significant levels of financial and other forms of investment. This particular forecast also accords, of course, with the thrust of the analyses of many researchers in the communication and cultural studies fields which were reviewed in earlier chapters.

Indeed, to identify diverse knowledge, information and communication or media sectors as crucial frontiers or sectoral targets for economic exploitation and colonisation in any emerging new long-wave phase of capitalist development is neither novel nor severely 'risky' at this stage. Much more difficult and elusive are nuanced conceptual schema which address the complex set of challenges posed by these developments and the clusters of issues and stakes involved for different social interests. For example, up to now most of the long-wave literature has tended to concentrate on the diffusion and implications of major new technology systems as drivers of economic growth with reference to the manufacturing and other material production sectors. There has been a consequent lack of attention to the specific features and roles of information 'content' and communication services – other than specialised scientific and technical knowledge. In addition, much of this literature has been heavily economistic in orientation, tending to focus on efficiency concerns such as the factors shaping the trajectories of economic growth and development, with less frequent attention given to equity or distributional questions. The changing role of information and communication services in the contemporary restructuring process and the search for new paradigms has been recognised in a few recent contributions (e.g. Freeman and Soete, 1994: Chapter 3). But even here they tend to be treated in a manner which neglects the distinctive roles or the political and cultural aspects of the mass communication and cultural industries or the implications of expanded commodification of information for the public sphere.

Therefore, in this chapter I want to explore how any future expansion of the economic role of certain (cultural) categories of information and communication services poses very particular challenges which go beyond the traditional political economy concerns with the conditions of expanded economic growth or the distribution of its benefits. It will be necessary to augment the conceptual frames of existing long-wave approaches by explicitly drawing on concepts from other theorists, including those based in the political economy of communication and critical social and cultural theory fields examined earlier. I will also examine some potential flaws and barriers to an expanded new upswing of growth as imagined by the currently dominant discourses and practices surrounding new ICT and the information society.

The empirical research reported earlier indicated that the intensified restructuring processes in the current downswing period has led to some growth in media and cultural content services. But these growth trends have been limited when compared to many predictions or the actual growth of instrumental/producer information services measured in terms of changes in the industrial division of labour, etc. Both sets of information may be defined as 'leading-edge' (ICT application) sectors whose expanded role may be a central feature in the construction of any new long-run socio-technical paradigm in the contemporary period. Here in particular, I want to focus on the changing role of the media and cultural content services in the overall process of economic, social and cultural development, even if they remained secondary rather than core 'leading-edge' sites for the restructuring processes before now.

The identification of the media and cultural industries as important 'new frontiers' for a new phase of capitalist investment, accumulation and profit-making involves more than simply nominating and forecasting the 'leading-edge' sites of economic growth and development. These industries are very different compared to the kinds of 'leading-edge' industries in the past, such as those producing electrical goods or motor cars. They play very special roles in the social, political and cultural life in the modern world in a manner which does not apply to other past or current leading-edge sectors. Thus, some additional and quite specific conceptual adjustments to the established schema of neo-Schumpeterian theorists are needed in order to address the distinctive challenges and stakes involved in any such extended or intensified commodification of the mass communication and cultural industries. These are required to explicitly explore the further 'enclosure' of the information 'commons' and to address how the extended commodification of the public information sphere poses very specific challenges for research as well as for political strategies. For these purposes, I will selectively draw upon political economy concepts and research findings based in the communication and cultural studies fields, as indicated in Chapter Five. These are adapted to augment the basic institutional analysis of the neo-Schumpeterian model and address the very specific kinds of stakes and challenges involved in the potentially expanded economic role of the media and cultural industries as a new frontier. In brief, I will aim to do this along two overlapping dimensions of analysis.

First, the projected future expansion of the industrial or economic roles of such information services must be related to the economic, political and technological factors shaping the structures of control, access, and the types or diversity of media-based content. Second, any projected future expansion of this economic role can only be achieved by the further intensification of commercialisation and commodification processes. This tendency, as the past work of Habermas and many other communication and cultural theorists serves to remind us, will directly threaten the role and status of the public (information) sphere. The key stakes here are that the process of extended commercialisation may further undermine the cultural and political dimensions of the public sphere which has underpinned the democratic ideals and potential of the project of modernity since the late Enlightenment era.

CONCENTRATION, GLOBALISATION AND REGULATION IN MEDIA-BASED CONTENT INDUSTRIES

Few theorists of the contemporary, no less than most media audiences, would dispute the view that the media and cultural content industries are marked by high degrees of concentration and globalisation. Most would also agree with the view that the established media of public communication are structured around a high degree of centralised ownership and control on the production side, and by increasingly fragmented audiences on the consumption side.

For technology-centred analysts, both the causes of, and fixes for, this situation are generally located in the realm of the technical characteristics of particular communication platforms and systems. But for others, including myself, this is a highly mistaken view. For, although the constraints imposed by different technical systems of communications are real and material to any adequate explanatory framework, the most significant factors shaping the structure and control of the media of public communication lie in the economic and the political realms, rather than the domain of technology. Some of the reasons underpinning this particular perspective have been indicated earlier in my exploration of competing conceptualisations of the technology–society relation and so will not be rehearsed again here. Instead, I will focus on a number of economic or political economic arguments to support this position.

Turning to the more purely economic dimension, one can identify and describe a number of relevant factors without resorting to the technical jargon of the 'dismal science'. The processes of capitalist accumulation in all sectors of the economy are marked by an inherent tendency towards the concentration and centralisation of industry ownership and control functions. In other words, the very process of market-based competition itself prompts the tendency for many small capitals to be replaced by fewer larger capitals. This was one of the seminal contributions made by Marx's analysis of mid-nineteenth-century capitalism to the body of economic thought as even his sternest political critics acknowledge (Schumpeter, 1943). This tendency was captured by the concept of 'monopoly capitalism' which became current in the early part of the twentieth century to describe the emergence and dominant role of a few large corporations in one (or sometimes several) specific markets or industries.

These general tendencies towards the increasing concentration of ownership and control are especially prominent in the case of many information (content) as well as technology-intensive industries. Now it must be acknowledged that the precise reasons for this vary considerably according to the specific features of different information products and services (Preston and Grisold, 1995). But for the purposes of this necessarily brief treatment, let us take some of the most important economic factors which influence the tendency towards high levels of concentration in the media and cultural industries. One is that the products of these industries have very high first-copy costs and very low costs for the second and each subsequent copy. For example, imagine the relatively high costs of manufacturing the second or twentieth copy of a particular design of motor car compared to the low costs of making a copy of the second or tenth copy of a particular newspaper, film or TV programme. This characteristic provides the owners and controllers of any media firm with a particularly high profit incentive to maximise the circulation, sales or market share and audience reach for any specific book, newspaper or film. Second, the role of distribution (relative to production) functions plays a much more important role in ensuring the commercial success of these industries compared to others. Here distribution refers not only to the networks required for physically channelling the media content product to potential audiences. It also covers a range of more intangible competencies or resources to do with publicising, marketing and promoting the company's portfolio of content products. The control of such distribution functions has often been identified as one of the key factors which explain the dominance of the major Hollywood companies in global audio-visual markets since the 1920s (Garnham, 1990). It indicates how the centralisation tendency or argument may still apply even if the more risky production and difficult-to-manage creative functions are devolved to smaller media firms ('independents').

Third, it is often claimed (especially by owners and executives of the relevant industries) that media and cultural products are relatively 'high risk', and whilst a few successful artists, products or 'hits' may make a very large profit, only a small proportion end up being profitable compared to the situation which prevails in other industries. This is seen to provide a further economic incentive or justification for fewer large firms as they can spread risks and costs across a wide portfolio of products and artists. A fourth factor is that advertisers or their agencies play a distinctive intervening role in the relationship which is usually assumed (at least by mainstream economics) to prevail between the producers of products and their customers or audiences. In some senses (especially large) advertisers or their agencies may be defined as very significant or peculiar types of 'big customers' who can wield a disproportionate influence on media content and form compared to the many small and dispersed audiences in the case of most media markets. These advertisers or their agencies tend to favour dealings with large cross-media corporations who can most efficiently deliver the particular mix of target audiences required for advertising and public relations campaigns. For such reasons, some critical communication theorists have argued that commercial television should be defined as predominantly a vehicle for the delivery of audiences to advertisers rather than a medium of public communication. A fifth point which is closely related to (and amplifies the salience of) the first three factors, is that a relatively large home market helps to ensure success in external (international) markets for media content products.

These kinds of economic factors go a long way towards a non-technological explanation of the increasing concentration and centralisation of ownership and control functions within the media and cultural content industries. They suggest that the specific or peculiar characteristics of media-based products and markets provide powerful economic (profit-based) incentives towards increasing the concentration and centralisation of ownership and control compared to the conditions which prevail in many other industrial sectors.

So how does this claim about increasing concentration of ownership and control square with the quantitative growth in the number of radio and television channels (as well as print-based magazines) in the media markets of the USA and Europe over the past few decades? It is certainly the case that some of these new media outlets are owned and controlled by new kinds of firms, not least because state regulation and licensing policies may favour diversity of control when issuing new broadcasting licences. But in many other cases, the new outlets are owned in part or totally by established media organisations. Besides, these same economic factors favouring concentration kick into place after the licences are issued, often leading to the takeover of the newer smaller firms by the larger media corporations.

A separate but related question concerns the relationship between the increasing number of media channels and platforms (such as radio and television channels, or print magazines) on the one hand, and the actual degree of diversity or pluralism of content provided to the audience on the other. For analysts and policy-makers favouring the neo-liberal approach and the quantitative multiplication of media channels or outlets, the 'hidden hand' of the market is the best or sufficient guarantor that audience interests in particular types or forms of content are maximised (NTIA, 1988). More critical theorists emphasise the tendencies towards similar and standardised types of content even where competition exists (e.g. in the case of commercial radio stations). To support this position, they point to the empirical evidence and to the powerful influence of advertising interests and other economic factors in prompting a tendency toward homogeneous rather than heterogeneous media content and forms. They argue that only pro-active and ongoing state regulatory and other policies, drawing on concepts like the public sphere or public service broadcasting, can ensure the greater diversity or pluralism of media content and forms.

These specific economic characteristics of media products and markets are also taken to play a major role in explaining the increasing globalisation of the media industries, with respect to both ownership and control factors, as well as in terms of media-based culture, content and forms. The same powerful economic and profit-based incentives towards maximising market scale or audience reach apply at the international level as they do at the national levels. But clearly the manner and extent to which such economic benefits can be achieved at the international level will be strongly influenced by the nature and forms of state policies. The scope for realising the maximum audience or market for media content products at the international level will be strongly shaped by the polices of both the home government of the media corporation and of the government of the target market or audience. This same principle and consideration applies whether the content delivery platform is stand-alone or on-line.

Let us take the important example of the dominant role of the major Hollywood companies in large segments of global audio-visual markets since the 1920s. The above-mentioned economic factors, in combination with the role of state policies, go a long way towards providing a compelling explanation (albeit one which may be augmented by analysis of the actual audio-visual texts and forms involved). For example, the Hollywood majors' control over the distribution function and the consistent exploitation of its particular resources and advantages has been very important here. This particular factor has played a key role in its long-standing success in many external markets alongside the benefits of a relatively large home market. But a variety of state policies dating back to the end of World War One, including support from US government agencies located in other countries, have also played a major role in facilitating the long-run success of the Hollywood media content industries (Garnham, 1990).

Turning to more recent and 'information tempered times', we have seen how governments in many countries have placed an increasing stress on the economic and employment roles of the media and cultural industries since the advent of the downswing. The media and cultural content services have been identified and treated as (largely) undifferentiated components of a 'tradeable information' sector. Their anticipated rapid growth is assumed to follow from the maximum adoption of new ICTs and neo-liberal regulatory policies, including the reduction in production costs via the promotion of the independent sector. Such economistic visions of this sector have informed the drive towards a single integrated audio-visual 'space' or market in the European Union since the 1980s, as described in Chapter Nine. Here, media diversity issues and related policy supports have been accorded a marginal or tokenistic status. One of the key declared motivations and goals is to engender the same economies of scale and scope that have driven the integration project for steel and motor industries. At times, this was accompanied by elements of a rather crude technology-centred social engineering project aimed at constructing a new Euro-person identity to diminish or replace the established role of national identity formations. Not surprisingly, the economistic and technocratic vision underpinning this project has failed to deliver on both those counts, but it has been replicated in the EU information society initiatives in the 1990s. As in the area of unemployment policy, the significant potential opportunities for, and benefits of, an increasingly unified EU approach to policy formation has been missed, in this case due to a lack of a sufficiently nuanced approach to the specificities of media content and culture (a failure on the part of constituent national governments as much as the Commission).

This EU case again illustrates the important influence (both negative and positive) of policy factors in shaping media-based content developments. The case of the EU integration project can also be taken as a particularly intensified expression of the wider processes of globalisation trends over the 1980s and 90s which have been prompted by the initiatives of national state and supra-national policy organisations as much as by any technological logics. An important factor here was completion of the so-called 'GATT Uruguay Round' of negotiations in the early 1990s which greatly extended the concepts and practices of 'free trade' and free flow of international investment to the service sectors. In brief, this agreement has resulted in a new set of general rules which permit and require freedom of movement of capital, investment, and trade flows across national borders. It has also established the World Trade Organisation as a new body to promote and police the new codes and rules. In effect, it greatly expanded the parameters of the economic and political space open to large multinational corporations in the ICT, telecommunications and various other information services. This also applies to those involved in the production and distribution of media-based content. The extent to which the media and cultural industries were to be treated as special or exceptions to the general rules was one of the most hotly debated issues. The final agreement refused to affirm that the media and cultural industries were special or different to other services, but it fudged the issue somewhat in response to governments in favour of the exceptionality clause. More than any technological innovation (including the Internet) this political initiative, in which the USA and the old hegemonic power of the UK played a leading role, has greatly extended the scope for recent and likely future globalisation trends in the primary information sector overall. In many ways, it established new policy rules which eroded the significance of national borders for the operations of corporations in many information service sectors. This policy initiative has provided important prompts or prerequisites for the surge of international investments, mergers and take-overs which have subsequently occurred in the electronic communications service sectors.

Whilst it is important to recognise that the process of increasing 'globalisation' of economic, political and cultural affairs has been much heralded in recent decades, it must be addressed as an evolving tendency which has a long history. One of the key features of the capitalist industrial system as a distinct mode of production is the inherent tendency towards relentless self-expansion and this is manifest also in its increasing spatial reach or spread. Indeed, the history of capitalist modernity has been marked by successive forms of deepening internationalisation, or globalisation. But this process, whether through the formation of the system of nation states in the past or emerging new forms of globalisation today, cannot be reduced to the logic of particular communication systems (Lefebvre, 1974; Mandel, 1972). For sure, successive new transportation and communication systems have directly contributed to the 'annihilation of space by time'. They have significantly eroded the 'friction' of space by reducing the relative costs and time involved in transporting goods and people or communicating information. But again, these technological developments are not autonomous or singular in their application potential or implications for the reshaping of social space. They must be dialectically related to particular configurations of the social, economic and political contexts in which they are embedded. The same applies to the synergic implications of existing and new transportation and communication technologies for new forms of globalisation as we turn into the new millennium. The forms, extent and salience of an emergent new phase of globalisation will vary according to the specific industrial sector, type/form of information content, national and international regulatory regimes, as well as by particular configurations of social formation, social class, cultural and political community, and so on. For example, within the primary information sector, the form and extent of globalisation (in terms of both the production and consumption spheres) may be relatively high in the case of ICT hardware and software compared to that which applies to many kinds of culturally-laden information content services. Case study research indicates that national, linguistic and other bases of identity (interpretative communities) continue to play a major role in shaping the spatial structures governing the production and consumption of certain kinds of digital cultural content services compared to those which apply in the case of software tools (Preston and Kerr, 1998). Despite all the emphasis on the Internet as an inherently global system, the available evidence on traffic to and from sites registered by national domains suggests that the majority of it actually takes the form of intra-national communication.

This necessarily brief exploration serves to illustrate some of the political and economic stakes involved in the restructuring of the media and cultural industries. It also serves to support the more general points of my argument with respect to the following: a) the much-discussed increasing concentration and globalisation of the media owes more to political and economic forces than it does to purely technological factors; b) that state policies can and do matter when it comes to shaping the scale and forms of media or cultural content industries and markets; c) that, despite the fashion for market-driven approaches to new ICT and its content application sectors, it must be recognised that the 'hidden hand' very soon turns to a very 'visible hand' in the case of the media and cultural content industries; d) that the quantitative multiplication of media channels or outlets does not of itself ensure a diversity or plurality of content. It further implies that contemporary technology-centred discourses which celebrate the 'inherent' global scale or reach of the Internet (and its potential to deliver various forms of content) must be challenged with respect to the extent of their engagement with these kinds of political-economic factors.

Let us now turn to more cultural ('extra-economic') stakes and objections to the 'market-driven' economistic logics, with respect to the sphere of public communication and the issues of diversity and pluralism in the sphere of media-based 'content'. Here I will draw on a number of the intellectual resources already mentioned in Chapter Five.

Habermas' study of the emergence and transformation of the public sphere represents one seminal work in the field of critical communication studies (1992, 1962). Indeed, despite differences in foregrounded concerns, his approach shares many concerns with much of the critical cultural studies literature, including that of Raymond Williams and Pierre Bourdieu. All of these authors are very attentive to the historical role of public communications and its close connections with competing conceptions of democracy, political power and of the bases of ethnic and civic collectivities in modern societies (Williams, 1958: 13–48; 1961; Bourdieu, 1984, 1990a, 1993). In addition, many contemporary writers based in the field of communication and media studies have been keenly concerned with the implications of the commodification of the media and culture.[1] In this respect, they differ quite significantly from contemporary writers (and the hegemonic industrial and policy élites) who identify their intellectual base in liberal and neo-liberal theory traditions.[2]

Here I will borrow one of McLuhan's tools, the 'rear-view mirror', in order to glance backwards at earlier process of creative destruction in this arena for the purposes of exploring the future stakes involved in the extended commodification of the media and cultural industries. Up to the eighteenth century, the economic system was embedded in the social system in a manner which was parallel to the situation of literature and arts. In his account of 'the great transformation' Polanyi (1944) suggests that 'regulation and markets, in effect grew up together'. Before then, the self-regulating market was not only unknown but the very idea of self-regulation represented 'a complete reversal of the trend of development' up to that time (Polanyi, 1944). Thus Adam Smith's idea or image of the 'invisible hand' succinctly expressed the historical sundering of such relations with the dawning of capitalist industrialism and the emergence of the market as the increasingly dominant organising power in the economic sphere and beyond. The new idea and its associated practices declared that nothing must be allowed to inhibit the formation of markets or capitalism's inherent tendencies to replace all previous social bonds and identities with what Marx later called 'the naked cash nexus'. The idea of the 'invisible hand' of the self-regulating market is 'the very same principle' that Pope mocked in 'whatever is, is right' and that Swift ridiculed in 'the mechanickal operation of the Spirit'. Despite the confines of his later media-centric works, Marshall McLuhan occasionally recognised (more clearly than Daniel Bell's later information society thesis) the momentous changes in the role of knowledge and information that commenced from the late eighteenth century. From that time, 'the process of applied knowledge had reached such a momentum that it became accepted as a natural process' which must not be impeded, even though it involved 'an automation of consciousness' in many respects as the mechanical laws of the economy began to be applied 'equally to the things of the mind' (McLuhan, 1962: 268–70).

The emergence of a capitalist market as a new source of income (and a concomitant decline in direct dependency on wealthy patrons or the church) was closely bound up with the emergence of certain new sensibilities. These included notions of the autonomy or 'freedom' of individual expression within the fields of artistic and cultural production and in the political realm of the public sphere in the early stages of capitalist modernity (Habermas, 1992, 1962; Williams, 1958; McLuhan, 1962; Bourdieu, 1990a, 1993). As early as 1759, Oliver Goldsmith suggested in his *Enquiry into the Present State of Polite Learning in Europe* that the writers in England 'no longer depend on the Great for subsistence', rather they depend on 'the public . . . a good and generous master' (cited in Lowenthal, 1961: 75). The rise of capitalist industrialism and ideas about the self-regulating 'market' and specialised production (via the division of labour) entailed new kinds of relations between authors, artists, critics and other producers of cultural products, on the one hand and their audiences, readers and public on the other (Williams, 1958: 52–3). It also involved 'a new system of thinking' about the arts and culture more generally whereby artistic production became a special (if not superior) means of access to 'imaginative truth' and the writer or artist became defined as a special kind of person in many respects (Williams, 1958: 53; Habermas, 1983; Bourdieu, 1990a, 1993).

But as the capitalist market society began to define itself and the market-based 'public' became the patron, many subsequent writers and artists became increasingly critical of the commodification process and the particular forms of restraint and regulation that it imposed on artistic and literary expression (Williams, 1958, 1961). As literature moved into the role of consumer commodity and 'art reversed its role from guide for perception into convenient amenity' many voices and movements expressed their distaste and distanced themselves from the peculiar forms of constraint and incentive structures imposed by this particular dimension of commodification: 'hence-forth, literature will be at war with . . . the social mechanics of conscious goals and motivations' associated with ever-expanding capitalist produc-tion relations (McLuhan, 1962: 275).

Of course, the critique of the expanding hegemony of the capitalist market and associated ideas of individualised economic freedoms and forms of democracy was not confined to the spheres of literary and cultural pro-duction. The emerging new conceptions of economic and political collectivity based on individualised citizen, worker or consumer identities were actively questioned at the time. Conservative as well as radical writers stressed the virtues of particular community cultures and forms of civil soci-ety and expressed concern about the destruction of traditional forms of 'organic society' through the forces of political and economic modernisa-tion. The conservative Edmund Burke, for example, stressed that the 'spirit of the nation' or national culture is not a spontaneous 'individual momentary aggregation'. He argued that it had emerged from 'the peculiar circumstances, occasions, tempers, dispositions and moral, civil and social habitudes of the people, which disclose themselves only in a long space of time' (cited in Williams, 1958: 30). Burke focused his fire on new ideas of political democ-racy and citizenship even as the organic society he sought to defend was being steamrollered by the juggernaut of capitalist economic forces which largely fell outside his particular gaze. Political radicals like Cobbett focused their fire on the inequalities inherent in the new class system of capitalist industrialism, but also casting glances in their own 'rear view mirror', they joined the more literary voices of Wordsworth and others in stressing the virtues of traditional communal society against the expansive forms of eco-nomic individualism and the 'mechanickal' utilitarianism which was the driving philosophy of the new industrial order (Williams, 1958: 30–9).

Thus, ever since the industrial revolution, and long before the emergence of modern social and cultural theory – not to mention contemporary notions of an emerging new kind of 'information society' – many literary and artis-tic voices as well as critics and intellectuals have pointed to diverse tensions and antagonisms between the expanding hegemony of 'the market' and the idea of distinctive forms of 'culture'. They have vigorously resisted the unre-strained domination of artistic and cultural (and indeed political) forms of expression by the laws of the market or the mechanical processes of com-modification. They challenge attempts to define such expression as merely another form of specialised production which should be subject to much the same conditions as other forms of production. Cultural and political forms of expression have been largely defined as centrally concerned with imagi-nation, truth, beauty or the sublime, or moral and ethical matters of rights and wrongs, whereas the mechanical market and the expression of its spirit in orthodox political economy tended to exclude moral questions. The market mechanism itself, no less than the discourse of conventional economics which supported it, were both seen to 'know the price of everything but the value of nothing', to borrow Oscar Wilde's pointed quip.

Amongst cultural producers themselves, as novels, poetry and other forms of literature increasingly became an industry or trade alongside newspapers, there was a growing tendency to reject the legitimacy of market-based definitions of the public or popularity and to refuse these as measures of the standards of value, worth or truth. The concern of Pope and other writers was that 'language and the arts would cease to be prime agents of critical perception and become mere packaging devices for releasing a spate of verbal commodities' (McLuhan, 1962: 268).

This historical glance also touches upon some important questions about the appropriate conceptions of (social and cultural) collectivity or identities which are directly relevant to contemporary stakes surrounding globalisation and the changing role or extended commodification of the media and other institutions of public communication. It explicitly raises challenges and stakes which are neglected, if not totally ignored, in so much of the information society discourses. The older critiques of economic individualism and its tendencies to reduce social subjects to individualised agents (workers or consumers) in the competitive market-place rather than regarding them as members of distinctive social, cultural and affective (hermeneutic) communities and/or citizen members of distinct polities, all serve to remind us that, in some respects, nothing much has changed. They also remind us that many of the most important social and cultural bonds cannot be reduced to the mechanical or rational calculus of 'economic man' or individualised encounters in the market-place. They point to the complex, but essentially social and cultural (as well as reflexive) characteristics of individual identities in the modern world. Indeed they also underline the fact that, in many respects, communicative action and intersubjectivity does not derive from subjectivity, but the other way round (Giddens, 1991: 51; 1985).

The now old idea of culture as the historically grounded 'embodied spirit' of particular communities or peoples is still relevant to any considerations of the media of public communication, not least given their increasingly important role as platforms and conduits for the expression, maintenance and renewal of distinctive cultural communities and political mobilisation or social identities in modern societies. It is an idea which was central to the most pluralist, egalitarian and progressive strands of the late eighteenth-century Enlightenment movements. These sought to (a) accommodate collective aspects of the realms of 'feeling' and affective bonds as well as the more cognitive and abstract ideals of (individual) human rights, and (b) combine this with a respect for collective cultural pluralism whilst rejecting the supremacist rankings of specific cultural communities. Also, (c) they opposed imperialist dismissals (or annihilations) of alternative cultural traditions, whether in the name of 'progress' or a singular universal conception of 'modernisation' (Gibbons, 1998).

These particular historical, and indeed essentially political, glances in the rear-view mirror are very relevant to contemporary analyses of changes in the sphere of public communication. Now, more than ever, it seems important to recognise that communicative action and core identities are derived not from the market-based roles of economic agents (e.g. as individual consumers), but from what Habermas defines as the *life-world* or what Bourdieu terms *habitus* and Lefebvre calls 'everyday life' (Habermas, 1983; Giddens, 1985; Lefebvre, 1974). It is important to emphasise this because the predominant thrust of contemporary discourses centred around new information structures and communication networks seems to presume, describe and prescribe fundamentally individualised and a-social conceptions of 'virtual comminities'; networking and cyberspace. The latter are presumed to be constructed or inhabited by free-floating individual actors (productive or consumer) with autonomous and unique combinations of interests/identities. The exclusive focus falls on the individual who is presumed to be predominantly (if not fundamentally) disembedded from any significant bases of economic, social, affective or symbolic group loyalties or indeed any lived experience or life-world beyond the market and communication network (Kelly, 1998). This hyper-media-centric techno-sociology has many echoes with the extreme neo-liberal vision as encapsulated by Thatcher's infamous pronouncement to the effect that 'there is no such thing as society'.

Indeed, there is a strong convergence between neo-liberal discourse and many technology-centred analyses of the contemporary as noted earlier. Both tend to assume and assert that a market-based organisation of the production, distribution, and exchange of cultural and political information is the best, if not sole basis to provide for individual freedom of expression, pluralist flows of information and the satisfaction of 'consumer' requirements, whether in relation to artistic, literary or political communications (NTIA, 1988; Brittan, 1988; Negroponte, 1995; Kelly, 1998). Essentially, they invoke Adam Smith to assert that in 'commercial societies to think or to reason' (the production and distribution of knowledge) should be, 'like every other employment, a particular business' in line with the dictates of the self-regulating market. The function and orientation of the artist, no less than that of the intellectual, is to 'prepare for the market' their own particular 'species of goods' which will then be 'purchased, in the same manner as shoes or stockings' (Smith, cited in Williams, 1958: 52). But what this assertion assumes away is that an autonomous market-based commodification process could not function, as Polanyi put it, 'unless society' – and, one could add, cultural and communication processes – 'was somehow subordinated to its requirements' (cited in McLuhan, 1962: 270). Here as elsewhere, the 'self-regulating' market cannot be accepted as the realm of absolute (individualised) freedom as it too imposes its own constructions of identity, as well as constrictions or structuring forces which shape the very forms and content of cultural and political communication, even within an increasingly large range of public communication institutions.

As is the case with all such heuristic schema, Table 10.1 provides a rather crudely simplified summary of the positions held by the advocates of extremely polarised discourses. It highlights some of the major stakes involved in the extended commodification of the cultural and political dimensions of the public sphere, including the forms and orientations of its discursive spaces or, in other words, the space of public communication. In addition, it highlights some of the implications of the hegemonic neo-liberal discursive order. Here, 'the principle of non-interference' in the presumed natural order of the 'self-regulating' market has finally risen to become the universal or hegemonic dogma (or doxa), the 'paradoxical conclusion of applied knowledge', to borrow another fragment from McLuhan's 'rear-view mirror' perspective on the role of information in the early stages of industrial capitalism (1962: 270).

MEDIA, CONTENT AND THE NEO-LIBERAL 'WAY TO THE INFORMATION SOCIETY'

The surge of national and international information society projects and policy initiatives in the 1990s may be best defined as a very particular (if often, implicit) version of the search for elements of a new socio-economic paradigm. But it is one which reflects the interests, role and influence of a hegemonic alliance between powerful segments of the contemporary indus-trial and political élites. Even if not explicitly defined as such, these initiatives and their associated discourses (however chaotic) do carry some weight in this regard, especially when their proponents exercise control over the allo-cation of private and public sector investments in our technological and industrial futures. The discourses and ideas associated with the information society projects and related technology, trade and other policy initiatives of the 1990s certainly project a glossy bright vision of our social and economic futures, which more than matches the more optimistic third-wave theories reviewed earlier. They also present a highly limited view of the most pressing contemporary political and economic challenges (as noted in earlier chap-ters). Generally these recent discourses suggest that there are two essential keys to the realisation of this particular prescription for our social and eco-nomic futures: (i) the open and enthusiastic embrace of new ICTs on the part of all workers, citizens and consumers, and (ii) their equal embrace of the assertion that there is an intrinsic or necessary connection between new ICT and the essentialist 'market-driven' value systems of neo-liberal political economy.

TABLE 10.1   Models of commodification in public communication

	Liberal and neo-liberal theory	Critical communication and cultural studies
1) Ownership matters		
The commodity status of media-based information and communication	The (content neutral) 'invisible hand' of the market is the best mechanism for ensuring consumer welfare in media, etc. markets; Private ownership and distribution via markets is the best guarantee of media *freedom* and diversity; Pursuit of profit and market share means that owners are 'neutral' concerning media content (e.g. Brittan; Veljanovski; Friedman).	The commodity form broadly determines the meanings and content of the media; Capitalist ownership and control generally prioritises/selects content (values, ideology) in line with capitalist interests (e.g. Miliband; Schiller; Chomsky); Media organisations have important economic roles as direct sites/units of accumulation and profit.
Increasing concentration of media ownership	Large corporations: a) orientated to maximising market share and matching consumer demand; b) favour diversity and pluralism of content between the different media they may own or control for market share reasons.	Means enormous concentration of ideological and political power in hands of small (global) élites; Inevitable results of specific economic characteristics of commodified information; Extends ideological power of economic élites.
2) Role of the state		
Role/functions of the state with respect to mass media and public communication	Generally favour self-regulation by media organisations or trade associations; Favours a minimal role of state regulation (confined to areas such as protection of minors; controls on advertising of specific kinds of products); State ownership, subsidies or pro-active regulation viewed as inherently antagonistic to media and other dimensions of individual 'freedom'; Mainly focus on the state and political power as constraint/threat to 'freedom'; inequalities of economic power ignored or taken as legitimate; Social actors and interests defined primarily in individual and consumer terms; emphasis on competitive individualism; little attention to social or cultural collectivities or identities.	Two contrasting basic schools of thought: 1) Funding of media by state institutions (independent of direct political control) may provide important 'public service' communication function [e.g. PSB]; State subsidies for small or minority media organisations can play an important role in ensuring diversity of expression; Pro-active state regulation required to counter the power of economic élites; it may favour a greater diversity and better quality of media content/expression; 2) Capitalist state will generally serve to further the views and interests of hegemonic economic and cultural élites.

TABLE 10.1 *cont.*

	Liberal and neo-liberal theory	Critical communication and cultural studies
3) **Advertising matters**		
Functions and status of advertising (as aspect of public communication)	Reduces the cost of information or media access for final consumers; Advertising, sponsorship and PR may be defined as 'commercial free speech'.	Advertising media play a crucial indirect economic role in the overall process of capitalist commodity production; Media's role shifts from informing citizens to producing audiences for advertisers (Smythe); Advertising favours a trivialisation of politics.
Effects of advertising	Informs consumers of the range and characteristics of available products; Encourages consumers to buy but does not compel rational audiences to purchase anything.	A new form of regulation ('capture') or censorship of media content favouring commercial interests; Reshapes the parameters, forms and content of public communication; Generally promotes bland, trivial, non-controversial content; Advertising has strategic ideological and social impacts on audiences beyond the promotion of specific products.

Note:
This table is focused on work which addresses the production, distribution and exchange aspects of the media (including structures of ownership and control of media institutions); it does not address aspects of the considerable body of related work focused on audiences/consumption.

Source: Author

This is all very good news for the élites controlling the enterprises involved in the supply of new ICT products and services, as the message neatly complements the sales and promotional efforts of their own marketing divisions (not to mention the strategies of their 'human resources' divisions to exclude trade unions from their branches at home and abroad). But as an agenda for future social, political and cultural development, it is based on a very specific conception of the role and implications of new ICT, one where technology becomes both the means and the ultimate goal of social development. It also prescribes an impoverished vision of the parameters of any appropriate new socio-technical paradigm, not least in relation to the important roles of politics and state policy initiatives in the present and immediate future. In essence it is based on one specific conception of the characteristics of collective identities and the role of public communication and social bonds.

TABLE 10.2 Public communications and forms of collectivity: competing conceptions

Type of 'imagined' community	1) Affective national	2) Civic national	3) Postmodernist cultural	4) Global info society (neo-liberal version)
Conceptions of (predominant) identities and of the form of collectivity	Combination of political identity and particular cultural or ethnic identities; Distinct national, etc. civic and social formations.	Citizenship; Rational, critical members of a political community; Shared public sphere between members.	Active audiences; Collapse of national and other modernist social identities; Stress on indeterminate or multiple individual identities.	Consumers of media products in the market-place.
Key actors defined as:	Citizens and bearers of distinctive cultural or expressive identity.	Citizens.	Active audiences, or reflexive consumers; Sometimes: 'socially situated' audiences.	Consumers.
Typical/potential objections to extended commodification of communication	Globalisation threatens flows of public communication required for the maintenance and renewal of distinct expressive/cultural and social formations.	Commercialisation of media of public communication tends to distort or hinder: a) forms and flows of public info essential for rational/ critical citizenry and polity; b) Equal participation in political and cultural aspects of public sphere; Also: tends to trivialise or commodify the essence of politics.	None/Few; Supply or sources of mediated information is of little concern; Active and reflexive audiences 'subvert' and decode media messages or content; Audiences largely create their own meanings in the process of media consumption.	None; Stress on virtues of 'free market of ideas' and 'free flow of info' at national and global scales; Free trade principles and benefits of international division of labour apply to information as in any other market sector; Some propose idea of 'commercial free speech' (advertising).

Note:
This is based on abstract analytical ('ideal type') categories and predominant identity or value orientations; in practice, many discursive accounts and practices will combine different elements in complex ways.

Source: Author

244

The alternative approach proposed here also suggests that these global information society initiatives are marked by a restrictive neo-liberal vision concerning both the characteristics of information and knowledge and new ICTs on the one hand and the social actors involved in their use and consumption on the other. In the first place, they advance a very singular economistic vision of information and knowledge which privileges the potential economic development role of information and communication services. These are predominantly conceptualised as new sites or 'new frontiers' to be exploited for the purposes of economic growth and capitalist accumulation. These policy initiatives promote the expanded commodification of most types of information and communication activities on the part of private economic agents, including the 'enclosure' of the residual information 'commons' behind new property rights. Such crude economism fails to recognise the great diversity of information services, knowledge forms and their appropriate modes of communication. As we have seen, this reductionist view fails to distinguish the very particular cultural, political and social roles of certain information and communication services which are here deemed central to the expression and renewal of social and political communities (or affective and hermeneutic communities) in the modern world. Second, these extensive promotional and 'awareness-raising' publicity campaigns predict and prescribe that the future path of (information) society's development will/should be fundamentally 'market-driven' (excepting, of course, the allocation of large-scale state funding and other resources to promote and subsidise the production and maximum consumption of new ICTs).

Third, such perspectives also advance a very reductionist or one-dimensional economistic vision of the social actors involved in the use, exchange and consumption of information and communication services. By emphasising their role as consumers of increasingly commodified information and communications services, these discourses tend to privilege one dimension of the different identities of users as social actors. This is at the cost of denying or neglecting others, not least their identities as citizens and members of political and other types of communities which are quite distant from those of consumers in the market-place. Fourth, they are marked by an obsessive concern for the newest technologies and related application innovations. They sponsor the further development of new ICTs, as well as prioritise and promote the widespread purchase, application and use of such communication and media technologies. In addition, they predict, prescribe and emphasise the rapid expansion of innovative digital multimedia 'content' products and services.

Such prescriptions for future development paths amount to a qualitatively poor and knowledge-impoverished if quantitatively abundant 'information society'. In essence, they prescribe a society centred on producing and communicating (i) those forms of cultural and instrumental information which can and will be supplied by profit-seeking corporations and purchased by social actors defined as consumers in the market-place, and/or (ii) those forms of 'free' information produced by the expanding advertising, sponsorship and public relations activities of specific economic or other interests. These are the ultimate (or extreme) logics of the model which informs the dominant contemporary discourses and the related material investment and policy practices of the hegemonic economic and political élites. These tendencies point to an ultimate collapse or total reversal of all the principles and practices associated with the original 'ideal type' of bourgeois public sphere identified by Habermas. Conceptions of citizenship and the specific information and communication processes relevant to participation in civic or political community, or those related to other forms of affective and hermeneutic solidarities, are denied or at least greatly downplayed in favour of the all-dominant identity of social actors as consumers. Even at the level of consumer identity this is problematic, for these discourses repeat the old economistic assumption that all consumers are equally endowed with information or with the means to acquire information that is relevant to the effective exercise of their role as consumer. This is a misleading assumption with respect to the observable trends in everyday consumer information requirements and practices (Preston, 1997a).

At the extreme then, the dominant discourses and developmental practices point to a materially abundant but culturally impoverished and socially unequal 'information society'. This is built around a quantitative explosion of commodified information and other commodity products where all relationships, values and meanings between members of society are collapsed to the sway of the naked cash nexus. If realised, such tendencies would indeed take us a lot closer to Baudrillard's apocalyptic world of the total collapse of meaning. It would mark the further annihilation of the heterogeneous forms comprising the global store of instrumental, symbolic and often non-mediated knowledge which have been emphasised in the anthropological literature particularly. It would also mean the erosion of many diverse types of non-commodified cultures and information flows which were emphasised in the more nuanced information sector analyses of writers such as Machlup. In addition, the realisation of such tendencies would also take us much further away from the utopian visions of an increasing abundance of diverse forms of information and communication exchanges which were advanced by some of the original information society theorists.

It is important, however, to recognise the real if distant potential for counter-tendencies and barriers which may serve to render the practical implementation of such an apocalyptic vision far from inevitable. The path of future developments is not solely determined by managerial and organisational innovations nor by the initiatives of dominant interests in the economic realm any more than it is by technological factors. It is important to address the potential cracks, fissures and spaces for countervailing forces which might serve to shape a more imaginative, egalitarian and welfare-enhancing path of social and communication development. The alternative forces here include social and political movements and their potential to influence the direction of strategic change and innovation – whether in the economic spheres of production (e.g. labour or trade union movements) or in consumption or as citizens with respect to the second 'key steering mechanism' of the state (e.g. women's rights, environmental, ethnic and other minority rights movements).

There is one other essential prerequisite for any critical theory concerned to explore the spaces and counter-tendencies which may permit the realisation of a more egalitarian and progressive futures project. That is to critically deconstruct the disabling power of the two sides of the contemporary discursive 'iron cage': anti-statism and homage to the inexorable laws of the market and the powers of its hidden hand. The review of competing theories in earlier chapters suggested that anti-statism takes many forms and it is not monopolised by self-defined neo-conservative or neo-liberal theorists.[2] Many critical theorists have also increasingly abandoned the capitalist state as a potential site for progressive resistance or reforms, while the dominant forces of neo-liberalism have elevated the market to a distinctively new status as sovereign steering mechanism.

As indicated a little earlier, neo-liberal discourses advance a particular version of anti-statism, which is not only marked by the celebration of the superior virtues of a 'market-driven' road to a future information society. Despite their own rhetoric, many proponents of neo-liberalism can in practice also accommodate a highly selective extension of the role of the state, especially if it favours their own sectional interests. Yet for neo-liberal theorists, and the discourses advanced by many sections of the contemporary industrial and policy élites, the state is essentially viewed as an artificial and alien institution whose interventions disturb the presumed natural order and workings of the market. Attempts to apply the products of rational enquiry, the reflexive capacities of human experience and history for the purposes of planning a more just and equal economic or employment system are doomed to fail and make things worse. The market represents a natural and impersonal mechanism which can substitute for planning and replace the need for such human decisions and actions. In the present social and economic context of a long-wave downswing, anti-statism and the prevalence of neo-liberal policy orientations, the idea of the market now itself becomes a sort of 'Leviathan in sheep's clothing' and its ultimate impact is to restrict rather than to promote political freedom or cultural diversity (Jameson, 1990: 106).

A BOUNDED 'NEW FRONTIER'?: POTENTIAL LIMITS TO TECHNOLOGY
AND ECONOMISTIC LOGICS

The clashes between industrial innovation and economic development logics and other cultural and social policy goals, especially in the domain of the media and public communication, has a deep history which long predates those centred around contemporary ICT and information society issues. The actors directly involved in industrial development, investment decision-making and in information policy planning have been frequently criticised before for their lack of attention to cultural policy matters. But in turn, they may (and frequently do) argue that the more material matters of economic and employment growth tend to be neglected or dismissed as of little importance within academic and other discourses which focus on matters of the ownership and control of information, access to public communication and cultural diversity. At the very least, the existence of this particular divide poses distinct questions concerning the adequacy of current state policy strategies both in terms of industrial or economic development and cultural policy criteria (Preston, 1996c; 1996b).

Thus, at this point it may be instructive to consider some of the tendencies and developments described above in terms of their instrumental effectiveness as a basis for industrial policy, and for the creation of much needed new sources of employment in the advanced industrial world as well as more globally. For these purposes, I will refer to some of the concepts linked to the neo-Schumpeterian long-wave perspective outlined earlier. These point to the relatively high levels of risk and uncertainties involved in harnessing the 'gales of creative destruction' during the intensified and complex process of economic and social restructuring of the long-wave downswing periods. The shift from one mode of accumulation to another throws up a complex set of changes, challenges and uncertainties. These include technical innovation challenges related to the development and applications stages of a major new technology system and a cluster of economic, social and institutional innovations for the construction of an appropriate new socio-technical paradigm capable of supporting a sustained long-wave upswing of economic and productivity growth. This process requires multiple kinds of 'heroic entrepreneurs', entrepreneurship and high-risk radical innovations in many institutions and spheres beyond the technological arena. This applies with particular force to the multidimensional character of the process of search and social learning involved in the construction of a new socio-technical paradigm which best matches the new opportunity structures afforded by a major new technology system. Here the uncertainties and risk may be especially pronounced and the barriers and limits of any singular technology or economistic logics may be more apparent and pressing than in the technology supply and applications fields. But whatever 'heroic' innovators and pioneers we have had in the industrial domain, there has been remarkably little sign of heroic innovation or imagination on the political stage guiding the 'second steering mechanism' throughout the current downswing.

I have already examined the wider impacts and performative adequacy of various components of the prevailing neo-liberal state strategies and accompanying discourses which have dominated economic, employment policy and the polarisation of incomes over the downswing. As described earlier, these particular strategies and discourses have justified and fostered the return of mass unemployment and underemployment as well as significant other new patterns of inequality and social exclusions. But, after more than two decades, they may be deemed to have failed in delivering on their own priority goals of restoring the high levels of overall economic, employment and productivity growth which prevailed in the post-war long-wave boom.

The analysis of recent developments in the media and cultural content sector in the previous chapter also indicates that, here too, in terms of their own aims, predictions and assumptions, these neo-liberal strategies have failed to deliver. They have been marked by some major failures in terms of the declared goals of radical product innovation and industrial development, especially the digital and media content industries. Some of the reasons for this were indicated towards the end of the previous chapter. I suggested that, especially with respect to the EU area, a radical reorientation of state policy supports and subsidies may be required to realise the goals of many new 'high level, grey matter' jobs. This requires a major expansion or reorientation of existing R&D and industrial innovation policy supports toward digital content application areas, including support for process and service innovations. It would also require a radical policy shift at national and EU levels towards a firm commitment to the support of greater diversity and pluralism in cultural content in all media platforms, beyond the narrow range implied by the 'market-driven' vision. This would meet the criteria of a decent cultural policy, providing a wider platform of material opportunities for much greater numbers of creative and cultural workers to express themselves and their stories – an affordable option given the accumulating material abundance of industrial capitalism. It is also more likely to meet the policy goal of major increases in the levels of employment in the creative areas of media-based content production. It would provide a larger and more egalitarian flow of income to support the much larger numbers of society's members who have the skills and desire to work as authors, designers, musicians and artists, thereby going beyond the polarised and élitist 'winner takes all' logics of 'market-driven' culture industries – and thus reducing the secret structural forms of censorship on expression engendered by such economic logics.

This kind of radical reorientation towards a more meaning-full explosion of the cultural domain of advanced industrial or capitalist societies is materially possible but clearly beyond the imaginative reach of the hegemonic economic and political élites. But it could only be articulated and implemented as part of a much wider project for radical social change and development goals which would challenge the core values of the prevailing neo-liberal regime. The concluding chapter will address some of the conditions and possibilities of such a project. It also examines the implications with respect to the cluster of uncertainties, 'barriers', and challenges involved in the construction of an effective and appropriate new SEP, as well as the alternatives and social stakes and interests involved.

CONSUMPTION TRENDS AND NORMS: MONEY-BUDGET AND TIME-BUDGET MATTERS

'The question of "how to stimulate demand for new IT products and services", often defined as "revolutionary" rather than "evolutionary" has proved a central and elusive goal for many of the technological and utopian élites ever since the early 1980s.'

(Large, 1985)

The question of 'how to stimulate demand for new IT products and services' has been 'a central and elusive goal for many of the technological and utopian élites' ever since the early 1980s (Large, 1985). Since then there has been a growth of major new markets and patterns of demand for specific new ICT-based products and services, such as the personal computer, mobile telecommunications and other new broadcasting-related services. However, the 1980s and 1990s also witnessed many flops and failures compared to earlier expectations about one or other 'killer applications'. When viewed in terms of the enthusiastic expectations of the techno-gurus or the designers and suppliers of specific devices, there have been many 'technological titanics' which have simply sunk without trace even if developed and launched on the market.

In the closing years of the twentieth century, the Internet (and its offspring, the World Wide Web) was widely heralded as the most important and dynamic 'killer application' yet produced within the new ICT field. Between 1995 and 1999, demand and production trends in the industries directly surrounding the Internet were certainly 'growing and changing at breathtaking speed', due to a combination of new application innovations and falling real prices per communication function. These developments seemed to be having a very positive effect on the overall rates of growth in the US economy in this period (USA Department of Commerce, 1999). As noted in the previous chapter, the Internet is now widely seen as having opened up major new frontiers of electronic commerce ('e-commerce') including information content, financial, retailing, and messaging applications and transaction services. Contrary to many earlier forecasts, one of the most rapidly growing areas of the Internet applications turned out to be on-line retail sales of various stand-alone media products, such as books and records. By the end of 1998, the emergent but rapidly growing on-line ('e-commerce') sector accounted for a little under one per cent of the total retail sector in the USA (USA Department of Commerce, 1999).

The long-wave perspective adopted here suggests that fundamental change in the production sphere, such as the development and supply of a major cluster of pervasive new ICTs, does not automatically mean a parallel shift in demand patterns. The construction of a new socio-technical paradigm involves fundamental shifts in the sphere of consumption as well as production. In some important respects, the sphere of consumption enjoys its own relative autonomy and is the site of influential struggles and negotiation over the direction of long-run change within capitalist industrialism. In other words, the long-wave restructuring processes in the sphere of production must be accompanied by parallel changes in the sphere of consumption, recognising that the latter is not some direct or automatic reflection of (changes in) the former nor of some inexorable technological logic.

As Gramsci (no less than Alfred Sloan) recognised in the 1920s, 'Fordism' involved much more than new mass production techniques which lowered the cost per unit of output. It also implied entirely new kinds of marketing techniques, consumption practices and norms (expectations, demand patterns) alongside changes in consumer lifestyles. The subsequent more widespread diffusion of the motor car and the extension of Fordist labour process and organisational techniques in the 1940s–70s were key components of the production system which underpinned the fourth long-wave upswing. But the strong expansion of demand for the products of the car industry and other growth industries in the advanced industrial economies of that period cannot be simply explained by rising real wage levels. Rather it must be understood in terms of an accompanying interlinked web of new consumption norms and lifestyle changes such as the expanded role of the state, including its construction of new networks of highways and roads; these in turn facilitated the shift towards more spatially extended urban forms and suburban lifestyles, and later, the declining size of average households; finally, larger suburban homes helped stimulate new patterns of demand for a cluster of white goods as well as the browner electronic ones.

But these particular developments cannot be adequately understood in terms of the functionalism that sometimes marks the post-Fordist accounts (e.g. Aglietta, 1979). In important respects, the increasing mass production and consumerism which were central features of both the third and fourth long-wave eras were constructed around the structural shifts in consumption norms and patterns. These shifts were centred around the construction and diffusion of radically new kinds of money-budget (the improved purchasing capacities of the working classes) and time-budget norms. Again, to emphasise a point made in Chapter Six, the new consumption norms emerged as a result of the pressures exerted by the trade union, and other labour and social movements. In the late nineteenth and early twentieth centuries, labour movement and other progressive political pressures were explicitly concerned to address both time-budget and money-budget matters. The outcome in the industrialised regions of Europe, the Americas and elsewhere, was a significant shift in purchasing power (money budgets) and equally important reductions in the time spent in paid employment to match the prevailing consumption norms. These same social and political movements also explicitly sought to promote entirely new forms of collective consumption and social dimensions of citizenship. These latter shifts were more visible and pronounced in many European countries compared to the USA.

Besides such historical considerations, the innovation literature suggests that the invention and supply of any radical new communication technology or service (or many other innovative products) is only the first, perhaps easiest, stage of the overall innovation process in market economies. The real challenge lies in developing, packaging and marketing the technology-based application products or services to match new forms of demand amongst the target audience of users. With any radical new technology-based products this is a particularly risky business – even if the potential gains are relatively high for those who successfully manage the different moments of the innovation process. Even after apparently successful experiments and trials amongst small groups of users, there have been many new communication and other technical innovations which have failed to ignite consumer interest. Despite the enthusiastic expectations of the techno-gurus or the designers and suppliers of specific devices, there have been many 'technological titanics' which simply sunk without trace even though they had been developed and launched on the market. The risks are reduced when products are less rather than more technically innovative – one reason why the majority of new consumer products are simply a matter of packaging or marketing innovations and do not incorporate any new technical features at all.

At this point we may recall that some of the transformative theorists have pointed to possible elements of a new regime of consumption, but these were usually pitched at a very abstract and idealist level and viewed new consumption practices as some sort of automatic effect of technological change. Recent industrial and policy discourses have paid very little attention to the potential dynamic role and features of any emergent new consumption regime which might accompany or support a still-emerging new ICT-based production regime and help sustain any new long-wave upswing of sustained growth. The dominant assumption is that there will be a rapid growth of demand for new ICT-based products but that it is largely a case of 'business as usual' with respect to the consumption norms and structures.

The recent developments surrounding the Internet pose a number of challenging and difficult questions, even if they are assumed away in the dominant discourses. The first is the question of whether the rapid spate of recent developments and investments surrounding the Internet mean that this is now the key dynamic radical innovation (within the family/cluster of ICT innovations) which will help promote an economy-wide long-wave upswing in the early years of the new millennium. Second, will it support a significant array of 'killer applications', giving rise to significant new industries, especially in the area of information content services? Will it prompt a spate of significant new downstream industries producing new information products which 'plug in' to the new on-line networks and infrastructures similar to those that grew on the back of the (on-line) electrical power networks which emerged at the close of the nineteenth century?

Third, even if these questions can be answered in the affirmative, they give rise to a further set of questions concerning structural changes in the sphere of consumption, and I want to focus on these particular issues here. Assuming such (above-mentioned) changes are possible and likely in the production sphere or supply side, what kinds of changes do they imply with regard to matching shifts in the structural patterns of demand by final or household users? In other words, assuming that the Internet (and other new ICTs) gives rise to a significant 'new frontier' for investment, profit-making and job creation in the shape of commodified information services, what kinds of 'matching' innovations are likely or required on the demand side? What kinds of radical new 'matching' social and institutional innovations might be expected or required with respect to consumption norms and practices if information content services are to become a major new 'driver' sector in any future long-wave upswing?

Here, of course, we must again fully acknowledge the malleability of any major new technology system, respecting the variety of forces and factors which will shape its future path of development and applications, and fully recognise the relative openness and unpredicatability of any new socio-technical paradigm. With respect to the key questions posed here – emergent and future consumption trends related to an expanded economic role for information and communication services – it may be fruitful to by-pass the extreme uncertainties of technology-centred speculations via the route of a material and grounded analysis centred on relevant socio-economic trends. The focus will fall on the strategic issues of consumption norms linked to user communication practices and time- and money-budget issues (related to the consumption and use of various information 'content', media and communication services) within the household setting or spheres of everyday life.

In particular, I want to address the issues of how the main trends of change in the consumption of (or access to) ICT and IC goods or services relate to the wider patterns of social and material inequalities (especially the increasing polarisation of income and consumption power and its implications for new forms of social stratification or exclusion). In terms of my own political values and norms, it should be clear by now that I strongly object to the dominant drift of socio-economic trends in recent years, not least those related to the polarised redistribution of wealth and income. But in this case too, it may be instructive to explore some contradictions and 'internal' tensions in neo-liberal policy analyses and in the dominant discourses surrounding new ICT and the information society which have been favoured by the industrial and policy élites in recent times. Thus, taking these models as given, for the moment, I will here focus on their potential contradictions and major tensions in the realm of consumption. I will focus on two specific potential barriers to a major upswing of economic and employment growth based around the expectation that commodified information services will be the major 'driver' or leading-edge sector.

The first relates to the polarisation trends in the distribution of wealth and incomes over the 1980s and 1990s. Clearly, this trend has been leading to significant parallel increases in consumption inequalities over the same period. As indicated in Chapters Seven and Eight, this shift in differential access to consumption opportunities is clearly linked to significant changes in unemployment levels, social power relations in the sphere of production as well as in the regulatory role of the state. This means that the issues of increasing forms of inequality centred around access and uses of new ICT and Internet-based communication or information services (the so-called 'info rich/poor cleavage') are clearly important. But they must be redefined and understood in this wider context of social change. They can only be addressed fully if they are clearly related to the new trends in the polarisation of income and general inequalities of consumption power over the downswing period. These trends include a very small or non-existing rise in the real wages of large sections of the working population in countries such as the USA or UK for much of this period. There are two main points that must be stressed here. First, any new upswing centred around a wave of new additional services in the form of commodified information services will require significant improvement in the money budgets at the disposal of the majority of the population if they are to be matched by adequate levels of demand. They will require matching new consumption norms in the form of a generalised increase in real purchasing power for large sections of the population (i.e. a radical reversal of recent trends). Second, these recent income polarisation trends cannot be addressed in terms of some kind of distinct 'information' or 'digital' rich/poor cleavage. They can only be addressed and tackled adequately if located in the older categories of social class, gender and ethnic inequality structures and the broader framework sketched out in earlier chapters.

The second barrier on the consumption side concerns time-budget matters. If there is one thing that we know about active user engagement with most media and information content services, it is that their consumption is highly time-intensive. This is likely to be the case with the newer digital media, especially those where users are paying a premium charge for access. Indeed, in this respect, they are very different to many of the innovative consumer goods in the previous eras. For example, in the past, the then new goods such as motor cars, electrical washing machines, fridges, freezers and vacuum cleaners could be marketed on the basis that they had a (domestic) labour and time-saving bias. This claim cannot be applied to many of the new kinds of information and communication services which are deemed to comprise the major new-wave of consumer-orientated goods and services in the immediate future. On the face of it then, if commodified information services are to play a major role as a 'key driver' sector in a new long-wave upswing (as now widely expected in industrial and policy strategies), this will require greater availability of non-work time. The successful marketing of an information-intensive wave of new consumer goods would seem to point to the reshaping of consumption norms in a direction which will expand the general levels of time budgets available for user engagement in such time-intensive activities.

Yet, at the same time we find that the general drift of socio-economic trends does not point to any restructuring of consumption norms in this direction. For sure, there is a significant minority of the population who have been projected into the enforced time-abundant leisure zones of unemployment or short-time working, but they also end up in the zone of low incomes and purchasing power. For the majority of the population tied up in the full-time paid-work economy of capitalist industrialism, there has been no significant reduction in average working hours in recent decades, as noted in Chapter Seven. Some trade unions, especially in Europe, have continued to negotiate some minor reductions in working hours in the 1990s, but in general time-budget matters have been relegated to a much more minor role in the industrial relations arena compared to the decades before and after 1900. Yet, in recent times, the lived experience of many full-time workers and especially parents, has been one of an increasing sense of time pressure and stress.

This is a very brief analysis of these two inherent tensions or contradictions on the consumption side. But it serves to highlight the extremely short-sighted vision and aspects of 'the imaginative failure' which underpins the current hegemonic discourses and practices surrounding new ICT and the politics of social development. At the same time, it offers some hints or concrete examples of the kinds of challenges which must be addressed urgently by any radical alternative strategies aimed at constructing a more socially inclusive, human-centred, welfare-enhancing and culturally progressive path of social development. In combination with the accumulated productivity-enhancing potential of past changes in the realms of technology and the division of labour, new ICT may render that path now more possible than ever as we enter the new millennium. But this potential cannot be realised or achieved, or even imagined, by those peddling the neo-liberal version of the digital dream and the accompanying baggage of increasing social division and cultural impoverishment.

Notes

1 Examples here include Williams, 1958, 1961, 1983; Habermas, 1962, 1992; Smythe, 1983; Garnham, 1990; Mosco, 1996; Schement and Curtis, 1995; Venturelli, 1998.

2 The pervasiveness of anti-statism in recent social and cultural theory is quite remarkable; it ranges from postmodernists such as Lyotard to the more political economic analyses in Manuel Castells' *The Information Age* (1997). The latter in particular seems to embrace the populist neo-liberal idea that statism is inimitable to technological innovation and development (despite the Internet/WWW example). Similar tendencies to abandon the capitalist state as a site for resistance to current trends are also evident within communication and cultural studies (Mosco, 1996; 144, etc.)

Part 4

ALTERNATIVE PROSPECTS AND POSSIBILITIES

CHAPTER ELEVEN

BEYOND TECHNOLOGICAL FETISHISM: TOWARDS A NEW SOCIAL AND MEDIA ORDER @Y2K+

'There is no want of knowledge respecting what is wisest and best in morals, government, and political economy, or at least what is wiser and better than what men now practice or endure. But . . . we want the creative faculty to imagine that which we know; we want the poetry of life; our calculations have outrun conception; we have eaten more than we can digest.'

(P.B. Shelly, *A Defence of Poetry*, cited in Williams, 1958: 59)

MAPPING A NEW MILLENNIUM: THE 'ROAD AHEAD' IN THE REAR-VIEW MIRROR

It's wrap-up time. In this book, I have sought to interrogate key features of new communication technologies and information systems and their role in reshaping the contours of contemporary social, economic and cultural developments. To a striking extent the issues have moved to the forefront of popular media concerns and political discourses in the 1990s compared to the past. In part, this has been a response to genuinely novel technical developments such as the World Wide Web and other ICT-based innovations. Yet many of the influential accounts which deal with the perceived radical, social, economic and cultural impacts of these new information systems and communication networks are much less innovative or novel than they presume or the technologies they invoke. As we have seen in the early chapters, many merely recycle similarly exaggerated ideas of social change and the same failed predictions that have been advanced by earlier techno-gurus since the 1970s. In contrast, the empirically grounded analysis of social and economic trends in this book points to many fundamental *continuities* amongst the *changes*. Indeed, some of the recent socio-economic trends can best be characterised as continuities with those which prevailed in much earlier periods of capitalist industrialism.

Hence, the key concern of this book has been to move beyond the excited techno-hype and technocratic discourse which surrounds these matters in the media and influential élite circles. It seeks to reinsert the social and political back into the analysis and process of social development. This exploration has been committed to a certain type of social holism in order to avoid the pitfalls of technology-centred or media-centric analyses of the contemporary. It aims to address socio-economic and political as well as technological developments, by relating changes in the sphere of public communication to broader sets of social and cultural change. But for reasons of space, the selection of potential topics has been necessarily curtailed, with the focus on the advanced industrial regions of the world. Many important issues surrounding new forms of international social and cultural relations, privacy and surveillance deserve more attention than has been possible here.

BALANCING CONTINUITIES AND CHANGES

In large part, this book adopts an orientation which focuses on observable social, economic and communication trends rather than on speculative 'dreamware' based on particular readings of the perceived characteristics or 'effects' of new technology. It addresses the development of major new technologies and significant changes in the industrial division of labour, while pointing to some important shifts in the economic role of different categories of information services which challenge many influential ideas. This book therefore ends up with an analysis of the dominant drift of social and communication trends over the recent past which is fundamentally different to the rose-tinted visions of the techno-gurus and the technocratic discourses favoured by the high-tech industrial élites and related policy-makers. It presents a very different portrait of the role of changes compared to the continuities with respect to the dominant drift of socio-economic, political and informational developments over the course of the current long-wave downswing. In essence, the closing decades of the twentieth century were marked by some important changes in economic and social structures, including a marked polarisation of wealth, income and life opportunities. But this analysis suggests that it is the continuities rather than the breaks with the past which are more predominant. The unfolding changes do not imply any shift to a fundamentally new post-industrial or post-capitalist 'information society'.

The empirically-grounded analysis in the preceding chapters has focused more on social, economic and communication trends than the more technology-centred issues. It also recognises some important changes in the ICT field and in the social and technical divisions of labour, as well as in industrial structures – including the expanding role of various forms of specialised information as economic resource, input and output across most sectors of the economy. The empirical analysis points to a certain quantitative growth in the economic and employment role of the primary information sector and communication services in recent times, plus a proliferation of various new ICT-based innovations such as the Internet. Most emphatically, the recent trends do not undermine the essential political, economic and social features of the capitalist mode of production as a distinct social and economic system as it has been defined by classical social theorists or indeed more recent accounts (Mills, 1956a; Giddens, 1995). Rather, many of the recent developments represent a deepening of many fundamental features of the capitalist system, expressing the inherently expansive character of this mode of production. The expanded commodification of information, for example, comprises an extension of trends and tendencies which have been evident since the early modern era. Even if we are heading towards an increasingly information-intensive economy and society, the predominant drift of recent trends certainly points to a much more intensively capitalist and industrialised social and economic order. In other words, this analysis recognises and maintains the important distinction between changes in surface form and more fundamental structural features.

HOW TECHNOLOGY MATTERS: LINKS BETWEEN MATURE AND NEW INFRASTRUCTURES

If technological factors are not foregrounded much in this particular analysis, it fully acknowledges the importance of the current cluster of new information and communication innovations. These comprise a major new technology system with a pervasive application potential which is historically rare. There is little doubt that new ICT provides novel incentives for important shifts in the capitalist industrial system, such as those prompted by innovative information infrastructures and related broadband communication networks and devices increasingly capable of delivering all types of information in a common digital mode. Of course, new clusters of radical technologies such as new ICT are socially shaped or constructed. But their development does present certain new disruptive impacts and possibility structures, not least in the economic realm (for example, prompting but not determining shifts in productivity thresholds, in industrial structures, divisions of labour and so on).

This analysis also fully acknowledges the cumulative role of successive waves of past technologies, alongside the deepening division of labour and other forms of instrumental knowledge (as a sort of visible hand). These have facilitated the forward march of industrial capitalism's productive capacity, as indicated in Table 11.1. This is manifest in the secular increase in per capita real income since the industrial revolution. But as we have seen, the general rise of income and purchasing capacity has not been the inexorable or inevitable result of the logics of technology or industrial capitalism. Indeed the two periods of most rapid growth in average income per head (the third and fourth long-wave upswings) were precisely those where social and political movements played a major role in reshaping the key norms and institutional features underpinning production and consumption practices.

TABLE 11.1   Estimated long-run rates of growth in average income
per person, 1500–1996[1]

Period	Average income growth per person
1500–1800	0.2 %
1820–70	0.6 %
1870–13	1.3 %
1950–73	2.9 %
1974–96	1.2 %

Note:
1 Estimated long-run rates of growth in average income per person, in the advanced industrial economies.

Source: OECD (1999) The Future of the Global Economy, p. 10.

At this point, it may be useful to locate the significance of new ICT-based information networks and systems in relation to other more mature (material) infrastructures and utilities which have facilitated the modern urban and industrial revolutions since the early nineteenth centuries – and indeed which continue to sustain economic and everyday life in the new millennium. For, despite the dreams of some would-be digital beings or others lost in the void of information, the increasing role of information technologies and services does not eliminate the salience of the material or physical world – such as land and water as increasingly scarce and finite resources in relative terms. Hence, it is now timely to turn to one key, if usually neglected issue: how do we relate new ICTs to the significant clusters of prior developments in building, transportation, energy, utilities and related technologies which enabled – and continue to underpin – the massive shifts from rural to industrial and (sub)urban 'ways of life' over the past two centuries? How do these 'mature' technological infrastructures compare to the more recent and much-heralded developments in communication technologies, networks and information services? For example, how significant are the new ICT 'super-highways' or communication networks compared to the complex mosaic of networks and utilities which, since the nineteenth century, have provided ready and reliable supplies of water, energy and sanitation to urban and rural populations and which have played such a major role in reducing health hazards and mortality rates?

Notwithstanding his own role as prophet of an emergent information or post-industrial society, Daniel Bell acknowledged that there is much confusion concerning the social implications of the role of knowledge and technology. He identified the initial problem as the pace of change in these two variables but added that it was also because 'few people have ever been able to define exactly *what* is changing' (1973: 42). Indeed, he suggested that, in terms of technology, probably more substantial change was introduced in the lives of individuals in the nineteenth century by the railroad, steamship, electricity and telephone, and in the early twentieth century by radio, automobiles, motion pictures, aviation and elevators, compared to television or computers, 'the main technological items introduced in the past twenty-five years' (Bell, 1973: 42).

Future developments may well indicate that this 1970s evaluation underestimates the subsequent spread of computing and the ever-growing fields of its application and diffusion, the still-unfolding patterns of new ICT and related communication networks. But it is worth mentioning this neglected aspect of Bell's analysis in the present context for a number of reasons. First, it provides an instructive counter to the explosion of excited hopes and hype subsequently generated by the technology-centred or media-centric conceptualisations of new ICTs, especially constructions of ICT as an independent or autonomous lever for radical socio-economic or cultural change. It certainly poses questions concerning the quite extraordinary levels of emphasis which have been placed upon a mere cluster of new communication technologies in recent times. This particular cluster of technological innovations is certainly important in providing a new infrastructure and set of opportunity structures for economic, social and cultural change, as I argued in Chapter Six. But in the broader scheme of things, new ICTs do not merit the historically unprecedented levels of emphasis, investments of imaginative hopes and other resources which they have been accorded, not only by influential political and economic élites but also by a wide range of symbolic analysts in the sphere of public communication. These more recent phenomena amount to a clear case of 'overkill', however interesting the technologies for specific purposes. In contrast, the above-mentioned observation of Bell's – and indeed, his general analysis of post-industrialism – seems relatively sober and subdued.

Second, this comment also underlines a point made in the previous chapter to the effect that new ICT-based networks and facilities will be laid down over those prior technology systems and infrastructures (rather than displace them). Indeed, the long-wave approach suggests that, in general, the interactions between major new technology systems and the prior, established infrastructures or systems may be complementary rather than competitive (i.e. involving processes of supplementation rather than substitution).

Third, it draws attention to the fact that the development and diffusion of new ICT-based communication networks (including the potential expansion of Internet-based developments) and the general growth of the primary and secondary information sectors do not imply any absolute diminution of material/goods production or in the levels of people/goods transportation services. In other words, it challenges the idealist claims that such new ICT and information developments will provide a fix for, or diminution in, the growing problems of environmental overload arising from the global trends in the production, distribution and transportation of agricultural, manufacturing and extractive products and in the construction sector.

GAPS AND CRACKS IN THE SUPERHIGHWAY: THE SPACES BETWEEN THE PROMISES AND THE REAL(ISED)

This book's empirically grounded description of polarisation as the dominant trend in socio-economic and political change over the 1980s and 90s seems a long way removed from the trajectory of developments or the implied agenda of current political issues highlighted in the glossy technocratic versions of an unfolding 'information society'. But are these developments inevitable or unstoppable? Can these trends of growing political-economic inequalities, the return of mass unemployment, the polarisation of social and consumption power, and increasingly commodified information and communication structures be challenged, modified or reversed?

Clearly, the trends described above cannot be explained or reversed by any inherent technological characteristics or autonomous logics imposed by new ICTs. The transition between one long-wave downswing and a new upswing period involves an intensified or strategic long-term restructuring of the overall web of economic, technical, social and political processes. In the past, the major costs of the crisis and restructuring processes were borne by the working classes. This is a generic sociological term for the majority of men and women excluded from ownership and control of productive capital and who depend on the sale of their labour power to meet their material needs within the increasingly differentiated and urbanised social framework of capitalist modernity. Allowing for changes in the social and industrial divisions of labour over time, not least the growth of diverse kinds of 'white collar' or 'information' jobs, it is precisely the same social groups who are bearing the brunt of the present crisis and restructuring process. Indeed, the evidence reported in previous chapters suggests that the burden of the down-swing is not being shared by all social groups. There has been a significant redistribution of income and wealth, and all its attendant benefits, from the poorer sections of the population to the already wealthy and powerful top strata of the class structure.

The adopted long-wave approach stresses that technology should not be considered as a single or major determinant of the unfolding trends of socio-economic change. By extension, there is no ready-made remedy or salvation to be found in a 'technological fix', however benign or seductive the various 'characteristics' of new technology systems may appear in certain optimistic readings. Neither can we rely on a resolution based on 'knowledge is power' or any alternative form of 'information-determinism' such as that implied by Lyotard's proposal to 'open up the databases', or indeed the promises of ever-growing 'abundance' for all proposed by some of the more idealist versions of information society theory. As we have seen, the latter variant tends to stress certain inherent or intrinsic characteristics of information (e.g. its non-exclusivity in consumption). It proceeds to extrapolate socio-economic impacts via an idealist analysis which abstracts from the actual political-economic context in which information is actually embedded. This is a polite way of saying that such analyses simply 'ignore' or 'deny' the increasing pen-etration of capitalist property rights, market calculus, bureaucratic instrumentalism and monitoring systems into all areas of information pro-duction, distribution and exchange. They simply end up ignoring or effectively denying one of the key features of political economic change since the late 1970s: precisely the expanded role of information as a source of profit, the growing business of 'making a business of information' (ITAP, 1983).

Within the changing social and technical division of labour, a certain small group of 'high-level grey-matter' occupations or 'symbolic analysts' may possess some distinctive forms of discretionary autonomy (e.g. authors, directors of audio-visual programming, university researchers – especially the [declining] percentage with tenured posts). But even for these relatively privileged occupations, the key decisions shaping work project agenda-setting, strategic manoeuvres, and implementation strategies are not immune from the wider trends of change in information structures. The changing roles of primary and secondary information sectors and related occupations certainly point to important changes in the nature of what is produced, and how. But such shifts in the composition of output or in the division of labour do not change the fundamental social relations or fea-tures of industrial capitalism as a distinct mode of production. In any fundamental sense, knowledge or information activities can only be imag-ined as having an independent influence if they were somehow extracted (rather than abstracted) from their base in capitalist economic social relations or the rational/instrumental structures of the state. But to an increasing extent, especially since the nineteenth century, the trend has been in the opposite direction as all forms of knowledge and information have been enclosed, commodified and produced within the nexus and logic of capitalist social relations.

What about the second key steering mechanism of the state and the official arena of electoral politics and parties? We have seen that the downswing period has been marked by an abandonment of the Keynesian mode of state regulation and a growing hegemony of neo-liberal ideas and related policy practices. The transition to a neo-liberal state has involved a highly selective 'rolling back' of state functions in some fields and an extension in other respects. It has been far from a neutral force with respect to the drift of key developments described above, ranging from the abandonment of full employment as a priority policy goal to the dilution of progressive taxation and income redistribution policies and cutbacks in various forms of collective consumption. Although shaped and modified by specific local institutional and social factors, this has been the general trend in most of the advanced industrial societies. The rapid diffusion of the electoral 'choice' politics of tweedledum/tweedledee and the shift from political content to surface spindoctoring in Western Europe has little to do with any specific media-system effect. It has much more to do with the ending of the post-war upswing and the political failure of the former social democratic parties (especially) to deliver any alternative to the inegalitarian and divisive politics of neo-liberalism.

The shift from governments dominated by conservative to former social-democratic parties in the EU area in the late 1990s has not been accompanied by any significant shift towards more 'social Europe' policy practices, for example. The same neo-liberal state regime has conjured up a spate of ICT and information infrastructure/society policies, often in close collaboration with industrial interests based in the ICT supply industries. These state initiatives manage to combine glossy visions of a technology-based march of social progress and highly conservative economic, social and cultural policies. The *Good* [info] *Society* now becomes the one where the population develops, applies and, especially, consumes lots of shiny new ICT-based technologies and products. In its Green Paper on 'social' dimensions of the 'information society', the supra-national state version developed by the EC proved unwilling to incorporate the relatively modest 'social' agenda proposed by its appointed 'high level group of experts'. These national and supra-national policy strategies generally combine major state expenditures in the further development of new ICTs and in promoting maximum application, use and consumption of new ICT-based products – but in the process also explicitly prescribe a selectively minimalist role for state policy in shaping the path of social development (Preston, 1996a; 1996d).

(A SPACE FOR) SOCIAL INNOVATIONS AND MOVEMENTS?:
NOT QUITE DIGITAL BEINGS

So current state strategies and the official political establishment are hardly ready-made independent candidates either to reverse the inegalitarian trend of socio-economic developments or to provide a more 'social' as opposed to technology-centred vision of a new socio-technical paradigm. The historical evidence suggests that the state, as the second 'key steering mechanism' remains an important potential conduit through which alternative forces for change or reform may be asserted. But, it appears that this will only happen if some external social movements are mobilised to exert and assert a powerful shift in the direction of state policies as well as challenging the power of the currently hegemonic economic élites. Clearly the socio-economic and communication trends identified earlier are driven by a powerful combination of economic and political (the state) rather than technological forces. The question still remains: are there any potential and viable forces which might be mobilised to counter these trends and provide the necessary push for more egalitarian future social and economic development programmes as we embark on a new millennium?

Scanning the horizon from the western edge of the European Union, the only possible alternative forces for such change comprise the various 'mature' and new social movements, including trade unions, unemployed workers' organisations, the green/environmental movement, the women's movement, and ethnic and other minority rights movements, as well as various non-governmental organisations and pressure groups. As noted earlier, the labour movement played a critical role in reshaping important components of the production and consumption regimes associated with the distinctive long-wave socio-technical paradigms in the past. For example, in the closing decades of the nineteenth century (especially in industrialised Europe), the mobilisations and pressures from various strands of the labour and socialist movement played a key role in effecting increases in real levels of wages (income), and reducing working hours for large sections of the working population. These movements initiated a set of reforms which had major impacts on the socio-technical paradigm that characterised the third long-wave era. The role and impact of these movements in shaping production and consumption systems as well as the state policy frameworks are as important as any technological developments for a rounded understanding of the first emergence of a mass production/consumption regime in this period of capitalist development. In the case of the post-war regime of accumulation, the origins and central role of the Keynesian welfare state regime can only be adequately understood or explained by reference to the particular configuration of political and social forces in the closing years of the war and those immediately following it. In the British case in particular, the core components (full employment as a priority policy goal; an expanded welfare state) were not novel policy demands on the part of the traditional reformist labour movements. But they were only successfully asserted as legitimate and adopted as a new consensual norm by all the official political parties because of the changed balance of social power, itself largely occasioned by the national mobilisation and conditions of the second 'total war' . Whilst intellectuals and their ideas might have indeed played a role (e.g. Keynes' theory of unemployment), these were very minor compared to the shifts in the balance of social and political power as well as the wider climate threatening more radical political change should there be any return to the mass unemployment and social conditions of the pre-war years.

So rather than technology, information, the market, or the neo-liberal state regime, this analysis is pinning its main hopes for a potentially more egalitarian and progressive social formation on politics, on the mobilisation of a cluster of social movements. For sure, each of these movements has formed around very specific interests, legitimate claims and political pursuits which cannot be readily subsumed within one another. This is not a single cohesive movement and therefore remains only a potential constellation of diverse forces. But it comprises interests with a potential to construct a more equitable and inclusive new socio-technical paradigm for a sustained phase of development. This alternative is not based on an anti-technology agenda, more an agenda with technology allocated its appropriate place.

However, the trade union, socialist and other alternative labour movements are generally much weaker now in terms of social and political power than they were in the 1960s and 1970s. It is notable that they frequently do not feature in contemporary discussions of social movements at all, especially those strongly focused on identity politics and which imagine the demise of the social for reasons other than the technological determinists. For sure, new computer industries, like some other ICT sub-supply sectors, pro-actively discourage workers from exercising the civic rights to trade union membership, no doubt sharing Toffler's view that unions belong only to the 'rustbowl' industries. But no more than their old media counterparts, the 'mature' social movements representing labour interests have not disappeared from the stage of relevance or history. Indeed, it might be argued that, in the general EU area at least, the labour movements may not be as weakened today as in the interwar years, especially after the rise of fascism. The percentage of workers in Western Europe who are members of trade unions declined slightly from an estimated 38 per cent in 1970 to 34 per cent in the mid-1990s; this decline is more marked in the case of male workers where the unionisation rate fell from 44 per cent to 37 per cent, whilst the unionisation rate of women workers actually increased from 25 per cent to 30 per cent over the same period. There is obviously a close affinity of interests between the trade union movement and the unemployed workers' movements, but as was the case in the interwar years, this objective affinity of interest has not often been matched by co-ordinated action and mobilisations in practice. Organisationally the latter are more sporadic and fragmented, and they lack the potential power leverage associated with a base in the sphere of production. But as in interwar Britain or France in the late 1990s, public demonstrations or other protests by the unemployed workers' movements can occasionally mobilise particularly strong waves of political attention and interest.

Since its re-emergence in the 1960s, the women's movement has clearly become an important force for political and social change. It encompasses different strands, and it is marked by distinctive organisational forms and culture and an agenda centred around the multidimensional forms of gender inequalities. For these and other reasons its agenda and approach often conflicts with, or by-passes, that of the traditional trade union movement. But there some important areas of common interest, such as those centred around low pay, part-time workers' social citizenship rights and improved health, childcare and other welfare services, especially when viewed in the light of the recent trends of socio-economic development described earlier. The green and environmental movement again comprises many separate strands and perspectives, not least those focused on questions of the role of technological change, the global (and essentially public interest) consequences of ever expansive 'private'-sector or 'market-driven' economic systems, the waste of material and human resources associated with ever shorter product life-cycles (built-in obsolescence) and the expansion of marketing and advertising influences associated with 'the growth illusion' (Douthwaite, 1992). In some EU member states, elements of the green movement seem to have established a closer affinity with the aims and interests of independent trade union movements, especially with the conversion of the former social democratic parties to neo-liberal orthodoxies and the politics of spin-doctoring. Some strands, at least, are highly attuned to questions of 'how economic growth has enriched the few, impoverished the many' in addition to having endangered the planet (Douthwaite, 1992). The green movement frequently encompasses a strong, anti-imperialist spirit and international perspective which has resonances with that of the most progressive strands of the early labour and socialist movements.

The list of relevant groups here also includes a cluster of the civil, voluntary, and non-profit organisations (and networks of such organisations[1]) explicitly concerned with communication issues, such as the regulation and content of the mass media and the commodification of the public communication sphere, including Internet-based services. It is less easy to assume a fundamental commonality of interests or a single 'public interest' in this particular cluster of groups. Not surprisingly perhaps, given the highly cultural and value-loaded nature of the object of concern, this sub-category of groups is marked by pronounced ideological and political differences (concerning fundamental questions of regulatory approaches, definitions of standards of content and so on). On the other hand, it may be deemed likely that a significant sub-set will find sufficient common interest to link up with the first category of social movements. In part this is because some of the key issues surrounding unequal access to communication services are closely bound up with the wider patterns of social polarisation. This is also likely because many specific alternative communication-related policy goals are only likely to be expressed and implemented if linked to broader platforms of more public concern.

I fully recognise that this very brief and crude sketch goes against the grain of much recent analysis, which assumes that we have reached the 'end of history' and that there is no alternative to the unfolding direction of industrial and technological trajectories and attendant social development. This is not confined to the subtle political prescriptions inherent in the visions of 'friction-free capitalism' or individualised 'libertarian' consumerism propounded by the ICT promotional gurus. It also informs certain strands of self-defined critical studies which stress the demise of the social whilst highlighting increasing individualisation, elastic and flexible identities centred around media consumption. These also stress the inherent differences or conflicts between the various new and 'mature' social movements. In contrast, I am suggesting that there is no end of history and that furthermore, despite growing consumerism in all its forms, the essentially social and cultural basis of cognitive and affective identity remains paramount. Here I also reject the tendency in certain quarters to stress differences and conflicts between the different social movements, and have emphasised instead the considerable common interests between these quite distinct social movements. I believe that this is especially the case when the orientations and interests of such movements are viewed in the context of the recent trends of increasing social inequalities, unemployment and commodification. They offer the only real hope of rescue from a shallow political-economic culture focused on competitiveness, 'winner-takes-all' markets, and a distinct tendency to treat technology as the end of social development rather than the means. And after all, even recent history is not without examples of the kind of unifying but socially progressive broad-front approach suggested here, as was demonstrated so clearly at the WTO's Ministerial Conference in Seattle in November of 1999.

I would not presume to predict the precise forms or directions such constellations of social movements might take, for that would be more hazardous than predicting technological trajectories – and we have already seen that the landscape is amply littered with miserable failures of that sort. But it might be helpful to offer an example of the kind of possibilities and requirements imaginable here. Some of the common interests shared by these movements appear to converge around specific immediate and pressing demands such as the reduction of high unemployment, a radical programme of income and wealth redistribution (to reverse the polarisation of incomes and associated consumption power), plus an expanded but less bureaucratic system of welfare support for the ill, the increasing number of elderly and those unable to work. They also clearly converge around a radical reorientation of the mature and new digital media trends towards a more pluralist and culturally rich communication order.

Again in example mode only, I can also indicate potential common interests in the construction of a more radical and innovative programme which would link these demands to a significant reduction in the standard working week/year. This particular component of a radical reform programme could serve to (a) extend rights and career opportunities for women workers with children and accommodate the changing culture of gender roles, not least with respect to parent–child relations; (b) engage with some strands of green politics posing challenges to the hegemonic competitiveness 'imperative' and 'the growth illusion' and the huge portion of collective social labour and time that is wasted on ever shorter product life cycles; (c) address the growing sense of stress surrounding time availability and enhance the opportunities for real (as well as virtual) sociability and communication in everyday life; and (d) last but not least, serve to restore an important but forgotten component from the rich tradition of the 'mature' labour movements (in Europe, especially), one which placed a strong emphasis on 'time-budget' matters rather than simply 'money-budget' issues (Preston, 1996d).

The effective organisation and implementation of such a programme would require various forms of visible public as well as institutional mobilisation. For one thing it would only be effective if the mobilisation was genuinely participative and social in form; it could not be realised or real if it was merely centred around an alternative version of the political establishment's spin-doctoring. Yet, at the same time, it would be important to fully harness the communicational opportunities and benefits of the new and mature media systems. In particular, because of their continuing position in popular public communication, this would mean taking the mature media of television, radio and print very seriously indeed. As regards the dominant medium of television and radio, (a) gaining significant access would require imaginative public mobilisations and other appropriate tactics, and (b) it would also mean taking the grammar, forms and styles of the broadcast media seriously and consciously harnessing them for an alternative politics. For there is nothing intrinsic to these systems which necessitates depthless or superficial political content – a more significant problem lies in the failure of established economic interests and power structures, and political culture to explore the alternative possibilities. This includes the persistent imaginative failure of mainstream politicians and media professionals to offer relevant political content: radically new goals, ideas, and values as well as practices which might inspire support from the majority of their constituents. For sure, the management style and formats of many channels in the new competitive environment do not help. But the possibilities have not been totally foreclosed as the (admittedly minority) of quality 'public service' orientated programming serves to demonstrate. The strategy would also include making maximum appropriate use of the Internet-based media and networking; these would be likely to prove particularly helpful for internal organisational and communication purposes.

NEW CONSUMPTION NORMS AND COMMODIFICATION

In addition (this time, admittedly within the soundbite-unfriendly frame of a 'socio-technical paradigm'), this kind of a social movement mobilisation and programme raises another possible scenario. The demand for a significant reduction in standard working-time could link up with certain structural features of informational capitalism's continuing failure to construct a socio-technical paradigm for a new long-wave upswing. Here I have in mind the context where: (a) new (especially consumer) information and communication services are expected to provide a major new frontier for economic growth (analogous to the motor car and its related industries in the post-war upswing); and yet (b) there has been a major product-innovation gap between the promises of multiple radical downstream/application innovations in the multimedia fields and the actual paucity and slow realisation of such developments to date. Now one thing we certainly know about 'the work of consumption' is that it often takes a lot of time, and this is especially so in the case of information products and services. In addition, we know that the average time spent on the consumption of all information-content/communication media has not been changing very much, despite the major expansion of different delivery platforms and distribution systems in recent decades. Indeed it might be argued that, media apart, the majority of new technologies which entered households over the past two long-waves (especially white goods) had an inherently labour-saving bias. In contrast, the imagined future expansion of new ICT-based information services could be defined as inherently time-intensive in consumption terms. In this light, the demand for a major reduction in the standard working week might even begin to offer some appeal to even some of a more technocratic or economistic bent, especially amongst the expanding army of post-Fordist consultants and reformist social engineering experts! (This demand clearly draws on historical lessons arising from the late nineteenth-century labour movement where reformist demands were centred around both time-budget as well as money-budget issues.)

Inevitably, in the context of an increasingly internationalised system of social labour, markets and political processes as well as communication flows, any alternative strategy (similar to that tentatively sketched above) must embrace appropriate forms of the 'act locally, think globally' approach. An alternative programme of social development centred around a constellation of social movements (similar to that tentatively sketched above) would also be attentive to the potential commonality of interests across the globe. Certainly, compared to the prospects for an extension of the unfolding informational capitalism regime it points to a potentially significant redistribution of the expanding material 'wealth of nations' in favour of the majority of men and women engaged in paid work. It would also favour the ranks of the unemployed and those currently engaged in the non-paid but important work of childcare and support of the elderly and less able. In contrast, the regime of informational capitalism offers merely the prospect of some relatively minor changes within an essential continuity of the historical patterns of spatially uneven industrial development and the attendant locational dynamics of 'high-tech' and other kinds of paid work. Such an imaginable constellation of social movement currents could also offer the real prospect of a more equitable and meaningful new global communications order, especially if based on the principles of the best Enlightenment traditions. Such principles would go beyond the merely abstract level of formal citizenship rights to address the grounded social, economic and political dimensions of such rights. They would embrace not merely notions of individual rights, they would also address collective social and cultural rights (respect for 'collective others' or communities based on distinct cultural and social traditions).

In sketching this imaginable or possible counter-movement to the unfolding trends of informational capitalism, I do not underestimate the difficulties even whilst stressing the possibilities and desirability of such alternatives. The obstacles are very considerable in the European Union context. Yet, here the increased scale of an integrated market and financial system would seem to offer much untapped scope for progressive policies and initiatives not possible in a single national context. However, the prevailing neo-liberal and technocratic political style has been singularly lacking in the imaginative capacities to envision any radical set of alternative possibilities. Even with new governments and atttendant (highly post-Fordist) expert systems, the would-be 'statesmen' have again not merely 'marvelled' but worshipped phenomena which they seem to 'neither grasp nor follow' (Harkort, 1844). Little is offered beyond the tired old emphasis on economies of scale leading to increased competitiveness and extremely conservative economic dogmas of neo-liberalism combined with a shallow technocratic vision of a future social development programme primarily focused around the maximum use and application of new ICT.

The constellation of social movements and interests sketched out above, and the attendant package of proposals (including that for a significantly reduced standard of full-time working hours) would be more economically feasible to implement in the EU than in any single national context. Such proposals also point to the more creative forms of political content which might well resonate with popular interests and affinities and thus provide a more genuine sense of engagement with a meaningful programme of EU integration. But the challenges of a project to construct an appropriate EU-wide social movement constellation should not be underestimated, especially in the light of the continuing hegemony of neo-liberalism in the official political arena and the absence of a shared EU-wide public communication space.

This imagined modest menu for the millennium, (rather than manifesto!) points to the need for, and possibilities of, a more egalitarian, inclusive and *social* 'information society' compared to the drift of social development trends under the sway of neo-liberalism. It asserts that whether this alternative to informational capitalism is brought into being is not essentially a question of technology, or knowledge or information, but of political will and social mobilisation.

NOT THE LAST WORD(S): CONCLUDING COMMENTS

This book is essentially based on a value position which objects to the fundamentally unequal and polarisation thrust of the unfolding new social and communication order of informational capitalism. It also acknowledges the relative openness of the economic and social restructuring possibilities associated with both the development and application of new ICT as a major new technology system and the changing features of instrumental and symbolic information. It points to the high levels of uncertainty and risk associated with the construction of a new socio-technical paradigm. It also indicates that the neo-liberal project for a specific type of informational order, centred around the extended sway of capitalism and the attendant inequalities of a 'market-driven' approach to an 'information society', has not yet proved successful in its own terms. For sure, this project has made a few people much more wealthy and powerful. But, as in the last downswing, this development is not any 'chance excrescence of an otherwise harmonious system', but one that is the 'logical and inevitable goal of a capitalist system, with its keynote: production for profit' (Anon, 1936: 4). For the vast majority, the unfolding regime of informational capitalism has not succeeded in delivering on its promises of a sustained phase of rapid employment, economic, or productivity growth. Despite some interesting new technical platforms, this project is marked by a persistent 'innovation deficit' with respect to the realisation of the major cluster of radically new downstream information industries which were promised by its proponents over the past 10–20 years (e.g. radically new multimedia content industries and associated 'high-level, grey-matter' jobs). Like in the interwar downswing period, there are many gaps between the *potential* and the *achieved* application of new knowledge and information with regard to a more equitable and participative path of social development. Although some of the spoils won by the winners in this broad restructuring and redistributional process 'may have been "ploughed back" as it were, into industry re-investment', as in the 1930s, 'the toll of vested interests . . . in cramping and distorting development remains considerable' (Anon, 1936: 4).

It should be stressed once more that the book is not proposing an anti-technology agenda. On the contrary, it points to a political strategy or programme which treats the production and use of new ICT (and its potential cluster of downstream process and product innovations) as one of the facilitating infrastructures or *means*. But it rejects the idea that ICT is the *goal or end purpose* of future social and cultural development. The latter vision might deliver goodies in the form of ever more profit, wealth and power to the élites in the ICT industry-policy nexus or in the communication services sector. But it will hardly meet the needs, interests and visions of the majority of final users (citizens as well as consumers) or even producers. The producers of new ICT are not merely the few 'heroic entrepreneurs' who own the technological patents or copyrights or other forms of industrial capital and who are so celebrated in contemporary discourses. These new technological facilities are produced by an increasingly integrated international system of collective male and female labour that is stamped by typically capitalist internal cleavages of power and economic inequalities and agenda-setting. The final users of ICT-based products and services are citizens with substantive social and civic rights, as members of distinct civic and cultural (cognitive and affective) communities or social formations, not merely consumers in an increasingly global market-place. As we have seen, it is not appropriate to talk about growing information rich/poor cleavages in isolation from the wider patterns of social inequalities in which they are embedded.

In Chapter One, I set out a rather ambitious agenda of issues to be addressed in this book. The key concern throughout has been to move beyond the constricted visions imposed by excited techno-hype which surrounds these matters in many popular discourses and influential élite circles. The aim has been to arrive at a more grounded understanding of the nature and extent of continuities as well as changes in the social and communication order in the advanced industrial societies. I fully recognise that the extent and nature of the treatment of many important specific issues has been highly selective, but for the most part, I would also suggest, this has been necessarily so within the confines of a single book.[2] With this caveat, I must now leave it to readers to assess the merits of this venture and decide on the success or failure of its implementation.

1 One example of the relevant networks is the Cultural Environment Movement. Another is The Culture Jammers Network, which can be contacted at the web address: *http://adbusters.org/information.html*.

2 For one thing, this has often meant dealing with generalisations ('the European Union' or 'the advanced industrial world') which ignore or neglect very important institutional, political and cultural specificities prevailing in different social formations. For another, it has resulted in highly generalised descriptions of social and communication inequalities and a consequent relative neglect of important specific trends and issues (e.g. the distinctive dimensions of inequality related to gender, ethnic minority and other kinds of social exclusions). In some respects at least, it has been a corollary of my attempt to construct a story and menu which points to the commonalities rather than highlights differences between the vast majority of social interests negatively impacted by the trends within informational capitalism.

ACARD (Cabinet Office – Advisory Council for Applied Research and Development) (1980) *Information Technology*. London: ACARD.

Aglietta, M. (1979) *A Theory of Capitalist Regulation*. London: New Left Books.

Aldrich, Michael (1982) *Videotex: Key to the Wired City*. London: Quitter Press Ltd.

Altenpohl, D.G. (1985) *Informatization: The Growth of Limits*. Dusseldorf: Aluminium Verlag.

Amin, Ash (ed.) (1994) *Post-Fordism: A Reader*. Oxford: Basil Blackwell.

Anon ('A Group of Economists, Scientists and Technicians') (1936) *Britain Without Capitalists: A Study of What Industry in a Soviet Britain Could Achieve*. London: Lawrence and Wishart.

Askoy, Asu and Robins, Kevin (1992) 'Hollywood for the 21st century: global competition for critical mass in image markets', *Cambridge Journal of Economics*, 16 (1): 1–22.

Australia (Government of) (1994a) *Creative Nation: Commonwealth Cultural Policy*. Canberra: Dept. Of Industry, Science and Technology.

Australia (Government of) (1994b) *Commerce in Content: Building Australia's International Future in Interactive Multimedia Markets*, Report by Cutler and Company for Dept. Of Industry, Science and Technology, CSIRO and Broadband Services Expert Group.

Babe, Robert E. (1995) *Communication and the Transformation of Economics*. Boulder, CO: Westview.

Banks, Marion (1992) 'Is more less?: the dynamics of the information industry', in Kevin Robins (ed.) *Understanding Information: Business, Technology and Geography*. London: Belhaven. pp. 61–73.

Bannon, L., Barry, U. and Holst, O. (eds) (1981) *Information Technology: Impact on the Way of Life*. Dublin: Tycooly International Publishing.

Barthes, Roland (1967) *Elements of Semiology*. London: Jonathan Cape.

Baudrillard, Jean (1981) *For a Critique of the Political Economy of the Sign*. St. Louis, MO: Telos Press.

Baudrillard, Jean (1983) *Simulations*. New York: Semiotext(e).

Baudrillard, Jean, (1988) *Selected Writings*. Ed. Mark Poster. Cambridge: Polity Press.

Baudrillard, Jean (1998) 'The end of the millennium', *Theory, Culture and Society*, 15 (1): 1–11.

Beck, Ulrich (1992) *Risk Society*. [Original German edition, 1986] London: Sage.

Beck, Ulrich, Giddens, Anthony and Lash, Scott (1994) *Reflexive Modernization: Politics, Tradition and Aesthetics in the Modern Social Order*. Cambridge: Polity Press.

Bell, Daniel (1960) *The End of Ideology*. New York: Glencoe.

Bell, Daniel (1973) *The Coming of the Post-Industrial Society: A Venture in Social Forecasting*. New York: Basic Books.

Bell, Daniel (1976) *The Cultural Contradictions of Capitalism*. New York: Basic Books.

Bell, Daniel (1980) 'The social framework of the info society', in T. Forester (ed.) *The Microelectronics Revolution*. Oxford: Blackwell.

Bell, Daniel (1989) 'The third technological revolution and its possible socioeconomic consequences', *Dissent*, Spring 1989: 163–76.

Beniger, J.R. (1986) *The Control Revolution: Technological and Economic Origins of the Information Society*. Cambridge, MA: Harvard University Press.

Bennington, Geoff (1988) *Lyotard: Writing the Event*. Manchester: Manchester University Press.

Bijker, Wiebe E. (1995) 'Sociohistorical technology studies', in S. Jasanoff, G.E. Markle, James C. Petersen and T. Pinch (eds) *Handbook of Science and Technology*. Thousand Oaks, CA: Sage Inc. pp. 229–56.

Bohme, Gernot (1997) 'The structures and prospects of knowledge society', *Social Science Information*, 36 (3): 447–68.

Boulding, Kenneth E. (1971) 'The economics of knowledge and the knowledge of economics', in D. Lamberton (ed.) *Economics of Information and Knowledge*. London: Penguin. pp. 21–37.

Bourdieu, Pierre (1984) *Distinction: A Social Critique of the Judgement of Taste*. Cambridge, MA: Harvard University Press.

Bourdieu, Pierre (1990a) *In Other Words: Essays Towards a Reflexive Sociology*. Cambridge: Polity Press.

Bourdieu, Pierre (1990b) 'Social space and symbolic power', in *In Other Words: Essays Towards a Reflexive Sociology*. Cambridge: Polity Press. pp. 123–39.

Bourdieu, Pierre (1993) *The Field of Cultural Production; Essays on Art and Literature*. Cambridge: Polity Press.

Bouwman, Harry and Christoffersen, Mads (eds) (1992) *Re-Launching Videotex*. Amsterdam: Kluwer.

Braman, Sandra (1997) *The Information Economy: An Evolution of Approaches*. Paper to the ICA Conference, Montreal, 22–26 May 1997.

Braman, Sandra and Sreberny-Mohammadi, Annabelle (eds) (1996) *Globalisation, Communication and Transnational Society*. Hampton, NJ: Hampton Press.

Braverman, H. (1974) *Labour and Monopoly Capital: The Degradation of Work in the Twentieth Century*. New York: Monthly Review Press.

Brittan, S. (1988) *A Restatement of Economic Liberalism*. London: Macmillan.

Brittan, S. (1987) 'The Fight for Freedom in Broadcasting', *Political Quarterly*, 58: 3–20.

Bryant, A. (1988) 'The info society: computopia, dystopia, myopia', *Prometheus*, 6 (1): 61–77.

Burck, Gilbert (1964) 'Knowledge: the biggest growth industry of them all', *Fortune*, Nov: 128–31, 267–70.

Burnham, D. (1983) *The Rise of the Computer State*. New York: Pantheon.

Cairncross, Frances (1997) *The Death of Distance: How The Communications Revolution Will Change Our Lives*. London: Orion Business Books.

Callinicos, Alex (1985) 'Anthony Giddens: a contemporary critique', *Theory and Society*, 14.

Callinicos, Alex (1987) *Making History*. Cambridge: Polity Press.

Canada (1995) *Connection, Community, Content: The Challenge of the Information Highway. Final Report of the Information Highway Advisory Council*. Ottawa: Industry Canada.

Carey, John (1995) *The Faber Book of Science*. London: Faber and Faber.

Castells, Manuel (1996) *The Information Age, Vol. 1: The Rise of the Network Society*. Oxford: Blackwell.

Castells, Manuel (1997a) *The Information Age, Vol. 2: The Power of Identity*. Oxford: Blackwell.

Castells, Manuel (1997b) *The Information Age, Vol. 3: The End of the Millennium*. Oxford: Blackwell.

Cawkell, A.E. (ed.) (1987) *Evolution of an Information Society*. London: ASLIB.

Cawson, Alan, Haddon, Leslie and Miles, Ian (1995) *The Shape of Things to Consume*. Aldershot: Avebury.

CEC (Commission of European Communities) (1994a) *Growth, Competitiveness and Employment – Challenges for entering in the 21st century*. (White Paper, colloquially called 'the Délors Report'). Luxembourg: EC.

CEC (1994b) *Europe and the Global Information Society: Recommendations to the European Council*. ('Bangemann Report'). Brussels: CEC. 26 May.

CEC (1994c) *Strategy Options to Strengthen the European Programme Industry in the Context of Audiovisual Policy of the EU*. (Green Paper). Brussels: EC (COM, 94. 96 Final, 6.4.1994).

CEC (1996a) *Building the European Information Society for Us All: First Reflections of the High Level Group of Experts*. Brussels: EC, DGV.

CEC (1996b) *People First: Living and Working in the European Information Society*. Luxembourg: Bulletin of the European Union, Supplement 3/96.

CEC (1997) *Green Paper on the Convergence of Telecoms, Media and IT Sectors and Implications of Regulation: Towards an Info Society Approach*. Brussels: EC. December 1997.

CEC (1998) *Industrial Aspects of the Information Society: ICT Investment in the Intangible Economy*. Luxembourg: OOPEC. (Authored by Clark Eustace and Jorgen Mortensen, for DGIII/A–5.)

Cerf, Vinton G. (1996) 'Foreword', in Mark Stefik (ed.) *Internet Dreams: Archetypes, Myths and Metaphors*. Cambridge, MA: MIT Press.

Cherry, Colin (1978) *World Communication: Threat or Promise? A Socio-technical Approach*. Chichester: Wiley.

Chesnais, François (1986) 'Marx's crisis theory today', in C. Freeman (ed.) *Design, Innovation and Long Cycles*. London: Pinter. pp. 186–94.

Chomsky, Noam and Herman, E.S. (1992) *Manufacturing Consent: The Political Economy of the Mass Media*. London: Vintage.

Clarke, Colin (1940) *The Conditions of Economic Progress*. London: Macmillan.

Clarke, S. (1990) 'New utopias for old: Fordist dreams & post Fordist fantasies', *Capital and Class*, 42: 131–53.

Collins, R. (1990) *Television: Policy and Culture*. London: Unwin Hyman.

Connor, Steven (1989) *Postmodernist Culture*. Oxford: Blackwell.

Corcoran, Farrel and Preston, Paschal (eds) (1995) *Democracy and Communication in the New Europe: Change and Continuity in East and West*. Creskill NJ: Hampton Press Inc.

references

Crook, S. (1998) 'Minotaurs and Other Monsters: everyday life in recent social theory', *Sociology*, 32 (3): 523–40.

Curran, J., Smith, A. and Wingate, P. (eds) (1987) *Impacts and Influences: Media Power in the Twentieth Century*. London: Methuen.

Curran, J. and Seaton, J. (1988) *Power Without Responsibility: The Press and Broadcasting in Britain*. London: Routledge.

Debons, A., et al. (1980) *Manpower Requirements for Scientific and Technical Communication: An Occupational Surrey of Information Professionals*. Pittsburg, KS: University of Pittsburg.

De Certeau, M. (1984) *The Practice of Everyday Life*. Berkeley: University of California Press.

De Jonquières, Guy (1985) 'Confounding Orwell's predictions', *Financial Times*, 2 January.

Dizard, W.P. (1982) *The Coming Information Age: An Overview of Technology, Economics and Politics*. New York: Longman.

Dosi, G., Freeman, C., Nelson, R., Silverberg, G. and Soete, L. (eds) (1988) *Technical Change in Economic Theory*. London: Frances Pinter.

Douthwaite, Richard (1992) *The Growth Illusion*. Dublin: Lilliput.

Downing, John, Mohammadi, Ali and Sreberny-Mohammadi, Annabelle (eds) (1995) *Questioning the Media: A Critical Introduction*. London: Sage.

Drake, William (ed.) (1995) *The New Information Infrastructure: Strategies for US Policy*. New York: Twentieth Century Fund Press.

Drucker, Peter F. (1968) *The Age of Discontinuity*. New York: Harper and Row.

Drucker, P. (1985) *Innovation and Entrepreneurship*. London: Pan Books.

DTI Communications Steering Group (1988) *The Infrastructure for Tomorrow*. London: HMSO.

Dunlop, C. and Kling, Rob (eds) (1991) *Computerization and Controversy: Value Conflicts and Social Choices*. Boston, MA: Academic Press.

Dutton, W.H. (1996) *Information and Communication Technologies: Visions and Realities*. Oxford: Oxford University Press.

Dyson, Esther (1998) *Release 2.1: A Design for Living in the Digital Age*. London: Penguin Books.

Dyson, Esther, Gilder, George, Keyworth, George and Toffler, Alvin (1996) 'Cyberspace and the American dream: a Magna Carta for the knowledge age', in *The Information Society*, 12 (3): 295–308.

Elam, Mark (1994) 'Puzzling out the post-Fordist debate', in Ash Amin (ed.) *Post-Fordism: A Reader*. Oxford: Blackwell. pp. 43–70.

European Audiovisual Observatory (1998) *Statistical Yearbook 1998*. Strasbourg: European Audiovisual Observatory.

Evans, Christopher (1979) *The Mighty Micro: Impacts of the Computer Revolution*. London: Gollancz.

Featherstone, Mike (1991) *Consumer Culture and Postmodernism*. London: Sage.

Ferguson, M. (1986) *New Communication Technologies and the Public Interest: Comparative Perspectives on Policy and Research*. London: Sage.

Feyerabend, P. (1988) *Farewell to Reason*. London: Verso.

Finnegan, R., Salamon, G. and Thompson, K. (eds) (1987) *IT: Social Issues*. London: Hodder & Stoughton.

Forester, T. (ed.) (1980) *The Microelectronics Revolution*. Oxford: Blackwell.

Forester, T. (ed.) (1985) *The IT Revolution: The Complete Guide*. Oxford: Blackwell.

Foster, F.G. (ed.) (1981) *Informatics and Industrial Development*. Dublin: Tycooly International Publishing Ltd.

Frank, Robert (1994) 'Talent and the winner take-all society', *The American Prospect*, no. 17, Spring: 97–107.

Frankel, Boris (1987) *The Post-Industrial Utopians*. Oxford: Blackwell.

Freeman, C. (1982) *The Economics of Industrial Innovation*. (2nd edition) London: Pinter.

Freeman, C. (ed.) (1984) *Long Waves in the World Economy*. London: Pinter.

Freeman, C. (1985) 'Long waves of economic development', in Tom Forester (ed.) *The IT Revolution: The Complete Guide*. Oxford: Blackwell.

Freeman, C. (ed.) (1986) *Design, Innovation and Long Cycles in Economic Development*. London: Pinter.

Freeman, C. (1987) 'The case for technological determinism', in R. Finnegan (ed.) *IT: The Social Issues*. London: Hodder & Stoughton.

Freeman, C. (1994) 'The economics of technical change', *Cambridge Journal of Economics*, 18 (5): 463–514.

Freeman, C. (1995) 'The "national system of innovation" in historical perspective', *Cambridge Journal of Economics*, 19 (1): 5–24.

Freeman, C. (ed.) (1996) *Long Wave Theory*. Cheltenham: Edward Elgar.

Freeman, C. and Perez, C. (1988) 'Structural crises of adjustment', in G. Dosi et al. (eds) *Technical Change and Economic Theory*. London: Pinter. pp. 43–64.

Freeman, C. and Soete, L. (eds) (1987) *Technical Change and Full Employment*. Oxford: Blackwell.

Freeman, C. and Soete, L. (1994) *Work for All or Mass Unemployment?* London: Pinter.

Froud, J., Haslam, C., Jahal, S., Leaver, A., Williams, J. and Williams, K. (1999) 'The third way and the jammed economy', *Capital and Class*, no. 67: 155–65.

G7 (Group of Seven) (1995) *General Conclusions of the G7*. Brussels: EC. February. Document accessed via Internet.

Gandy, Oscar H. Jnr (1993) *The Panoptic Sort: A political economy of personal information*. Boulder, CO: Westview Press.

Garnham, Nicholas (1979) 'Contribution to a political economy of mass communication', *Media Culture and Society*, 1 (1): 123–47.

Garnham, Nicholas (1981) 'The information society is also a class society', in L. Bannon, Barry, U. and Holst, O. (eds) *Information Technology: Impact on the Way of Life*. Dublin: Tycooley International Publishing. pp. 284–92.

Garnham, Nicholas (1990) *Capitalism and Communication*. London: Sage

Garnham, Nicholas (1994) 'Whatever happened to the information society?', in R. Mansell (ed.) *Management of Information and Communication Technologies: Emerging Patterns of Control*. London: ASLIB. pp. 42–51.

Gates, Bill (with N. Myhrvold, P. Rinearson?) (1995) *The Road Ahead*. London: Viking.

Gerbner, George, Mowlana, Hamid and Schiller, Herbert (eds) (1996) *Invisible Crises: What Conglomerate Control of Media Means for America and the World*. Boulder, CO: Westview.

Gershuny, J.I. and Miles, I. D. (1983) *The New Services Economy: The Transformation of Employment in Industrial Societies*. London: Pinter.

Gibbons, Luke (1998) 'Alternative Enlightenments', in M. Cullen (ed.) *1798: Two Hundred Years of Resonance*. Dublin: Irish Reporter Publications.

Gibbons, Michael, Limoges, Camille, Nowotny, Helga, Schwartzman, Simon, Scott, Peter and Trow, Martin (1994) *The New Production of Knowledge: The Dynamics of Science and Research in Contemporary Societies*. London: Sage.

Giddens, Anthony (1985) 'Reason without revolution? Habermas's *Theory of Communicative Action*', in Richard J. Bernstein (ed.) *Habermas and Modernity*. Cambridge: Polity Press. pp. 95–124.

Giddens, Anthony (1991) *Modernity and Self-Identity: Self and Society in the Late Modern Age*. Cambridge: Polity Press.

Giddens, Anthony (1995) *A Contemporary Critique of Historical Materialism*. (2nd Edition.) Houndmills: Macmillan Press.

Gillott, John and Kumar, Manjit (1995) *Science and the Retreat From Reason*. London: Merlin Press.

Gitlin, Todd (1989) 'Postmodernism: roots and politics', in I. Angus and S. Jhally (eds) *Cultural Politics in Contemporary America*. New York: Routledge.

Godelier, M. (1986) *The Mental and the Material: Thought, Economy and Society*. London: Verso.

Godwin, Mike (1996) 'Foreword' in Peter Ludlow (ed.) *High Noon on the Electronic Frontier: Conceptual Issues in Cyberspace*. Cambridge, MA: MIT Press.

Golding, P. and Murdoch, G. (1980) 'Theories of Communication and Theories of Society', in C.G. Wilhoit and de Bock, H. (eds) *Mass Communication Rev. Yearbook: Vol. 1*. London: Sage.

Golding, Peter and Murdoch, Graham (eds) (1997) *The Political Economy of the Media*. (2 vols). Cheltenham: Edward Elgar.

Goldsmith, Oliver (1759) *Enquiry into the Present State of Polite Learning in Europe*. Cited in Leo Lowenthal (1961) *Popular Culture and Society*, Englewood Cliffs, NJ: Prentice Hall. p. 75.

Goldsmith, Oliver (1759) *Enquiry into the Present State of Polite Learning in Europe*. Reprinted in 1985 in *The Globe Edition: The Miscellaneous Works of Oliver Goldsmith*. London: Macmillan. pp. 419–46.

Goodwin, P. (1995) 'British media policy takes to the superhighway', *Media, Culture and Society*, 17 (4): 677–89.

Gore, Al (1994a) 'The global info infrastructure: forging a new Athenian age of democracy', *Intermedia*, 22 (2): 4–7.

Gore, Al (1994b) 'Plugged into the world's knowledge: how global information systems will aid development', *Financial Times*, 19 September.

Gregory, Derek (1994) *Geographical Imaginations*. Cambridge, MA: Blackwell.

Groom, Brian (1998) 'Call centres become a jobs phenomenon', *Financial Times*, 23 April.

Guback, Thomas (1969) *The International Film Industry: Western Europe and America Since 1945*. Bloomington: Indiana University Press.

Guback, Thomas (1979) 'Theatrical Film' in B.M. Compaine (ed.) *Who Own the Media?* New York: Harmony Books.

Guback, Thomas (ed.) (1993) *Counterclockwise: Perspectives on Communication – Dallas Smythe*. Boulder, CO: Westview Press.

Gudeman, S. (1986) *Economics As Culture*. London: Routledge.

Habermas, J. (1976) *Legitimation Crisis*. London: Heinemann.

Habermas, J. (1983) 'Modernity – an incomplete project', in Hal Foster (ed.) *The Anti-Aesthetic.* Port Townsend, WA: Bay Press. (Reprinted in 1985 as *Postmodern Culture.* London: Pluto.)

Habermas, J. (1985a) 'Psychic Thermidor and the rebirth of rebellious subjectivity', in Richard J. Bernstein (ed.) *Habermas and Modernity.* Cambridge: Polity Press. pp. 67–77.

Habermas, J. (1985b) 'Neoconservative culture criticism in the United States and West Germany', in Richard J. Bernstein (ed.) *Habermas and Modernity.* Cambridge: Polity Press. pp. 78–94.

Habermas, J. (1992) *The Structural Transformation of the Public Sphere.* Cambridge: Polity Press (originally published in German, 1962).

Hall, Peter and Preston, Paschal (1988) *The Carrier Wave: New Information Technology and the Geography of Innovation.* London: Unwin Hyman.

Hamelink, Cees, H. (1994) *The Politics of World Communication.* London: Sage.

Haraway, Donna, J. (1997) *Modest_Witness@Second_Milennium.* New York: Routledge.

Harkort, F. (1844) *Bemerkungen uber die Hindernisse der Civilisation und die Emancipation der unteren Klassen,* cited in E. J. Hobsbawm (1969) *Industry and Empire.* London: Pelican. pp. 65–66.

Harvey, David (1989) *The Condition of Postmodernity: An Enquiry into the Origins of Cultural Change.* Oxford: Basil Blackwell.

Hatt, Paul and Foote, Nelson (1953) 'On the expansion of the tertiary, quaternary and quinary sectors', *American Economic Review,* May, cited in Bell (1973).

Heap, Nick, Thomas, Ray, Einon, Geoff, Mason, Robin and Mackay, Hughie (eds) (1995) *Information Technology and Society: A Reader.* London: Sage.

Herschman Leeson, Lynn (ed.) (1996) *Clicking In: Hot Links to a Digital Culture.* Seattle, WA: Bay Press.

Hertz, J.C. (1997) *Joystick Nation.* London: Abacus.

Hobsbawm, E.J. (1969) *Industry and Empire.* London: Pelican.

Hollinger, Robert (1994) *Postmodernism and the Social Sciences: A Thematic Approach.* London: Sage.

Howell, David (1994) 'The skills myth', *The American Prospect,* 18: 81–90. [http:// epn.org/prospect/18/18howe.html]

Hughes, Tom P. (1983) *Networks of Power: Electrification in Western Society, 1880–1930.* Baltimore, MD: Johns Hopkins University Press.

IDATE (1997) *Electronic Publishing in Europe: Competitiveness, Employment and Skills* (Flash Presentation of the Electronic Publishing Sector). Report commissioned and published by EC, DG XIII/E. October.

ILO (International Labour Office) (1997) *The Economically Active Population, 1950–2010.* (Five Volumes). Geneva: ILO.

Innis, Harold A. (1950) *Empire and Communication.* London: Oxford University Press.

Innis, Harold A. (1951) *The Bias of Communication.* Toronto: University of Toronto Press.

Innis, Harold A. (1956) *Essays in Canadian Economic History.* Toronto: University of Toronto Press.

Inose, H. and Pierce, J.R. (1984) *Information Technology and Civilisation.* New York: Freeman & Co.

International Labour Organisation (1997) *The Economically Active Population, 1950–2010*. (3 vols) Geneva: ILO.

International Labour Organisation (1998) *World Employment Report*. Geneva: ILO.

ITAP (IT Advisory Panel, Cabinet Office) (1983) *Making a Business of Information*. London: HMSO.

Ito, Yoichi (1981) 'The "Johoka Shakai" approach to the study of communication in Japan', in G. C. Wilhout and H. de Bock (eds) *Mass Communication Yearbook Vol. 2*. Beverly Hills, CA: Sage.

Ito, Y. (1991) 'Johoka: a driving force of social change', *KEIO Communications Review*, 12: 33–8.

Itoh, Makoto (1997) 'Ernest Mandel, 1923–1995', *Review of International Political Economy*, 4 (1): 248–55.

ITU (International Telecommunication Union) (1988) *World Telecommunication Development Report*. Geneva: ITU.

ITU (1995) *World Telecommunication Development Report*. Geneva: ITU.

Jameson, F. (1984) 'Postmodernism or the cultural logic of late capitalism', *New Left Review*, 146: 53–92.

Jameson, F. (1988) 'Postmodernism and consumer society', in Hal Foster (ed.) *Postmodern Culture*. London: Pluto Press. pp. 111–25.

Jameson, F. (1990) 'Postmodernism and the market', in R. Miliband and J. Saville (eds) *Socialist Register 1990: The Retreat of the Intellectuals*. London: The Merlin Press.

Jameson, F. (1991) *Postmodernism or The Cultural Logic of Late Capitalism*. London: Verso.

Jasanoff, Sheila, Markle, Gerald E., Petersen, James C. and Pinch, Trevor (eds) (1995) *Handbook of Science and Technology*. Thousand Oaks, CA: Sage Inc.

Jessop, Bob (1994) 'Beyond Fordism and the state', in Ash Amin (ed.) *Post-Fordism: A Reader*. Oxford: Blackwell. pp. 251–79.

Jhally, Sut (1991) *The Codes of Advertising, Fetishism and the Political Economy of Meaning in the Consumer Society*. New York and London: Routledge.

Karunaratne, Neil D. (1986) 'Issues in measuring the information economy,' *Journal of Economic Issues*, 13 (3): 51–68.

Katz, James E. and Philip Aspden (1998) 'Internet dropouts in the USA: the invisible group', *Telecommunications Policy*, 22 (4/5): 327–39.

Kearney, Richard (1991) *Poetics of Imagining: From Husserl to Lyotard*. London: HarperCollins Academic.

Kellner, Douglas (1989) *Jean Baudrillard: From Marxism to Postmodernism and Beyond*. Cambridge: Polity Press.

Kelly, Kevin (1998) *New Rules for the New Economy: Ten Ways the Network Economy is Changing Everything*. London: Fourth Estate.

Kennedy, N. (1989) *The Industrialisation of Intelligence*. London: Unwin Hyman.

King, D.W., Roderer, N. and Olsen, H. (eds) (1983) *Key Papers on the Economics of Information*. New York: Knowledge Industry Publications.

Kling, Rob (1994) 'Reading "All About" computerization: how genre conventions shape non-fiction social analysis', *The Information Society* 10 (3):147–72.

Kubicek, H., Dutton, W.H. and Williams, R. (eds) (1997) *The Social Shaping of the Information Superhighways: European and American Roads to the Information Society*. New York: St Martins Press.

Kuhns, William (1971) *The Post-Industrial Prophets: Interpretations of Technology.* New York: Weybright and Talley.

Kumar, Krishan (1996) *From Post-industrialism to Post-modern Society: New Theories of the Contemporary World.* Oxford: Blackwell.

Lamberton, D.M. (ed.) (1971) *The Economics of Information and Knowledge.* London: Penguin.

Landow, George P. (1997) *Hypertext 2.0: The Convergence of Contemporary Critical Theory and Technology.* Baltimore, MD: Johns Hopkins University Press.

Large, Peter (1985) 'Information age needs realism', *The Guardian*, 9 September.

Lash, Scott (1990) *Sociology of Postmodernism.* London: Routledge.

Lash, Scott and Urry, John (1987) *The End of Organised Capitalism.* Cambridge: Polity.

Lash, Scott and Urry, John (1994) *Economies of Signs and Space.* Lond on: Sage.

Latzer, M. and Thomas, G. (eds) (1993) *Audiotex Services in Europe and the USA.* Amsterdam: Kluwer.

Lefebvre, Henri (1974) *The Production of Space.* (English translation, published 1984) Oxford: Blackwell.

Lefebvre, Henri (1991) *Critique of Everyday Life.* London: Verso.

Levin, Charles (1981) 'Introduction', in Jean Baudrillard, *For a Critique of the Political Economy of the Sign.* St. Louis, MO: Telos Press. pp. 5–28.

Levinson, Paul (1999) *Digital McLuhan: a Guide to the Information Millennium.* London: Routledge.

Lowenthal, Leo (1961) *Popular Culture and Society.* Englewood Cliffs, NJ: Prentice Hall.

Ludlow, Peter (ed.) (1996) *High Noon on the Electronic Frontier: Conceptual Issues in Cyberspace.* Cambridge, MA: MIT Press.

Lukacs, G. (1971) *History and Class Consciousness.* Cambridge, MA: MIT Press.

Lyon, D. (1988) *The Information Society: Issues and Illusions.* Cambridge: Polity Press.

Lyotard, Jean-François (1984) *The Postmodern Condition: A Report on Knowledge.* Manchester: Manchester University Press.

Machlup, F. (1962) *The Production and Distribution of Knowledge in the United States.* Princeton, NJ: Princeton University Press.

Machlup, F. (1980) *Knowledge: Its Creation, Distribution and Economic Significance. Vol. I Knowledge and Knowledge Production.* Princeton, NJ: Princeton University Press.

Machlup, F. (1983) 'The economics of information: a new classification' *Intermedia* 11 (2).

Machlup, F. (1984) *Knowledge: Its Creation, Distribution and Economic Significance. Vol. III The Economics of Information and Human Capital.* Princeton, NJ: Princeton University Press.

Machlup, F. and Mansfield, Una (1983) *The Study of Information: Interdisciplinary Messages.* New York: John Wiley.

MacKenzie, Donald and Wajcman, Judy (eds) (1985*) The Social Shaping of Technology: How the Refrigerator Got its Hum.* Milton Keynes: Open University Press.

Maddox, Brenda (1972) *Beyond Babel: New Directions in Communications.* London: Andre Deutsch.

Maffesoli, M. (1996) *The Time of the Tribes.* London: Sage.

Mandel, E. (1972) *Late Capitalism.* London: NLB/Verso.

Mandel, E. (1982) *The Second Slump.* London: New Left Books.

Mandel, E. (1984) 'Explaining Long Waves', in Chris Freeman (ed.) *Long Waves in the World Economy*. London: Pinter. pp. 195–202.

Mandel, E. (1995) *Long Waves of Capitalist Development: A Marxist Interpretation* (2nd revised edition). London: Verso.

Mandel, E. (1996) 'The international debate on long waves of capitalist development', in Christopher Freeman (ed.) *Long Wave Theory*. Cheltenham: Edward Elgar. pp. 608–31.

Mandela, Nelson (1995) 'Towards a world-wide information society', *Intermedia* 23 (6): 46–7.

Mansell, R. (ed.) (1994) *Management of Information and Communication Technologies: Emerging Patterns of Control*. London: ASLIB.

Mansell, Robin and Silverstone, Roger (eds) (1996) *Communication by Design*. Oxford: Oxford University Press.

Marshall, T.H (1950) *Citizenship and Social Class*. Cambridge: Cambridge University Press.

Martin, James (1978) *The Wired Society*. Englewood Cliffs, NJ: Prentice Hall.

Marvin, C. (1988) *When Old Technologies Were New: Thinking About Communications in the Late Nineteenth Century* New York: OUP.

Marx, Karl (1973) *Grundrisse*. (Tr. Martin Nicolaus.) Harmondsworth, Middlesex: Penguin.

Masuda, Yoneji (1980*) Managing in the Information Society: Releasing Synergy Japanese Style*. Oxford: Basil Blackwell.

Masuda, Yoneji (1982) 'Vision of the global information society', in L. Bannon, U. Barry and O. Holst (eds) *Information Technology: Impact on the Way of Life*. Dublin: Tycooley International. pp. 55–9.

Masuda, Yoneji (1985) 'Computopia', in T. Forester (ed.) *The IT Revolution*. Oxford: Blackwell.

Mattelart, A. (1979) *Multinational Corporations and The Control of Culture: The Ideological Apparatuses of Imperialism*. Sussex: Harvester Press.

Mattelart, A. (1991) *Advertising International: The Privatisation of Private Space*. London: Routledge.

Mattelart, A. (1996) *The Invention of Communication*. Minneapolis: University of Minnesota Press.

Mattelart, A. and Mattelart, M. (1998) *Theories of Communication*. London: Sage.

McBride Commission (1980) *Many Voices, One World* (Report for UNESCO). London: Kogan Page.

McLuhan, Marshall (1951) *The Mechanical Bride*. Boston, MA: Beacon Press.

McLuhan, Marshall (1962) *The Gutenberg Galaxy: The Making of Typographic Man*. Toronto: University of Toronto Press.

McLuhan, Marshall (1964) *Understanding Media: The Extensions of Man*. [Reprinted, 1987] London: RKP/Ark.

McQuail, D. (1987) *Mass Communication Theory: An Introduction*. London: Sage.

McQuail, D. and Siune, K. (eds) (1998) *Media Policy: Convergence, Concentration and Commerce*. London: Sage.

Melody, William H. (1985) 'The Information Society: unveiling some contradictions', Special issue of *Media, Culture and Society*, 7 (3).

Melody, William H. (1996). 'Towards a framework for designing information society policies', *Telecommunications Policy*, 20 (4): 243–59.

Melody, William H. (ed.) (1997) *Telecom Reform: Principles, Policies and Regulatory Practices*. Lyngby, Denmark: Technical University of Denmark.

Melody, W.H., Salter, L. and Heyer, P. (eds) (1981) *Culture, Communication and Dependency: The Tradition of H. A. Innis*. Norwood, NJ: Ablex.

Miege, B. (1989) *The Capitalisation of Cultural Production*. New York: International General.

Miles, Ian (1988) *Home Informatics: IT and the Transformation of Everyday Life*. London: Pinter.

Miller, D. (1987) *Material Culture and Mass Consumption*. Oxford: Basil Blackwell.

Mills, C. Wright (1956a) *White Collar: The American Middle Classes*. New York: Oxford University Press.

Mills, C. Wright (1956b) *The Power Elite*. New York: Oxford University Press.

Mills, C. Wright (1959) *The Sociological Imagination*. New York: Oxford University Press.

Mitchell, William J. (1995) *City of Bits: Space, Place and the Infobahn*. Cambridge, MA: MIT Press.

Modigliani, Franco and La Malfa, Giorgio (1998) 'Perils of unemployment', *Financial Times*, 16 January, 1998.

Mody, Bella, Bauer, Johannes M. and Straubhaar, Joseph D. (eds) (1995) *Telecommunications Politics, Ownership and Control of the Info Highway in Developing Countries*. Mahwah, NJ: L. Erlbaum Associates.

Moody, F. (1996) *I Sing the Body Electronic*. London: Hodder & Stoughton.

Moore, Nick (1996) 'How the State, not the market drives info industry policy in East Asia', *Intermedia*, 24 (3): 26–9.

Morley, D. and Robins, K. (1995) *Spaces of Identity: Global Media, Electronic Landscapes and Cultural Borders*. London: Routledge.

Mosco, V. (1996) *The Political Economy of Communication*. London: Sage.

Mosco, V. and Wasko, J. (1988) *The Political Economy of Information*. Wisconsin: University of Wisconsin Press.

Moseley, Fred (1999) 'The US economy at the turn of the century: entering a new era of prosperity?', *Capital and Class*, 67: 25–45.

Mowlana, Hamid (1997) *Global Information and World Communications: New Frontiers in International Relations*. London: Sage.

Mulgan, G.J. (1991) *Communication and Control: Networks and the New Economies of Communication*. Cambridge: Polity Press.

Mumford, Lewis (1934) *Technics and Civilization*. New York: Harcourt Brace.

Murdoch, G. (1993) 'Communication and the constitution of modernity', *Media, Culture and Society*, (15): 521–39.

Murdoch, Graham and Golding, Peter (1974) 'For a political economy of the mass communication', in R. Miliband and J. Saville (eds) *The Socialist Register, 1973*. London: Merlin Press. pp. 205–34.

Negrine, R. (ed.) (1989) *Satellite Broadcasting: The Politics and Implications of the New Media*. London: Routledge.

Negroponte, Nicholas (1995) *Being Digital: The Road Map for Survival on the Information Superhighway*. London: Hodder & Stoughton.

Negt, Oskar and Kluge, Alexander (1993) *Public Sphere and Experience: Toward an Analysis of the Bourgeois and Proletarian Public Sphere*. (Tr. by Peter Labanyi) Minneapolis: University of Minnesota Press.

Noble, David F. (1977) *America by Design: Science, Technology and the Rise of Corporate Capitalism*. New York: Knopf.

Noble, David F. (1984) *Forces of Production: A Social History of Industrial Automation*. New York: Knopf.

Noble, David (1998) 'Selling Academe to the Technology Industry', *NEA Higher Education Journal*, Spring: 29–40.

Nora, S. and Minc, A. (1980) *The Computerisation of Society: A Report to the President of France*. Cambridge, MA: MIT Press.

Nordenstreng, K. and Schiller, H. (eds) (1993) *Beyond National Sovereignty: International Communications in the 1990s*. Norwood, NJ: Ablex.

Norris, Christopher (1990) *What's Wrong with Postmodernism: Critical Theory and the Ends of Philosophy*. Baltimore MD: Johns Hopkins University Press.

NTIA (National Telecommunications and Information Administration, US Department of Commerce) (1988) *NTIA Telecom 2000: Charting the Course for a New Century*. Washington: US Goverment Printing Office.

OECD (1981a) *Information Activities, Electronics and Telecoms Technologies: Impacts on Employment, Growth & Trade (Vol. 1)*. Paris: OECD: ICCP Report No. 6, Vol. 1.

OECD (1981b) *Information Activities, Electronics and Telecoms Technologies: Impacts on Employment, Growth & Trade (Vol. 2)*. Paris: OECD: ICCP Report No. 6, Vol. 2.

OECD (1986) *Trends of Change in the Information Economy*. Paris: OECD: ICCP Report No. 11.

OECD (1989) *New Technologies in the 1990s: A Socio-Economic Strategy*. Paris: OECD (PPh).

OECD (1997) *Global Information Infrastructure-Society (GII-GIS): Policy Recommendations for Action*. Paris: OECD (ICCP Committee Reports).

OECD (1998) *OECD Economic Outlook* 62. Paris: OECD.

OECD (1999) *The Future of the Global Economy*. Paris: OECD.

OECD (2000) *The Service Economy*, (OECD Business and Industry Policy Forum Series). Paris: OECD.

PA Consulting Group (1997) *Opportunities for Content and Service Provision*. Final version of report commissioned by the UK government's Department of Trade and Industry, April, 1997. London: DTI.

Pendakur, M. (1992) *Canadian Dreams and American Control: The Political Economy of the Canadian Film Industry*. Detroit: Wayne State University Press.

Perez, Carlotta (1983) 'Structural change and the assimilation of new technologies in the economic and social systems', *Futures*, 15: 357–75.

Perez, Carlotta (1985) 'Microelectronics, long waves and world structural changes: new perspectives for developing countries', *World Development*, 13(3): 441–63.

Piore, Michael and Charles Sabel (1984) *The Second Industrial Divide*. New York: Basic Books.

Plant, Sadie (1997) *Zeros + Ones – Digital Women and New Technoculture*. London: Fourth Estate.

Polanyi, Karl (1944) *The Great Transformation*. New York: Farrar Strauss.

Pool, Ithiel de Sola (1983) *Technologies of Freedom: On Free Speech in an Electronic Age*. Cambridge, MA: Belknap Press/Harvard University Press.

Pool, Ithiel de Sola and Inose, H. (1984) *Communication Flows: A Census in the USA and Japan.* New York: North Holland.

Pool, I. de Sola, Inose, H., Takasaki, N. and Hurwitz, R. (1984) *Communication Flows: A Census in the US and Japan.* Tokyo: University of Tokyo Press.

Porat, M.U. (1976) *The Information Economy.* Stanford, CA: Stanford University (PhD Thesis).

Porat, M.U. with the assistance of Rubin, M. R. et al. (1977) *The Information Economy: Definition and Measurement.* Washington DC: US Govt Printing Office (9 Vols).

Porter, Vincent, Garnham, Nicholas and Askoy, Asu (1987) 'Measuring and Classifying the Information Economy', Supplement 2 to 'PICT Report on the Information Sector and the ISIC'. London: ESRC/PICT (mimeo).

Poster, Mark (1990) *The Mode of Information: Poststructuralism and Social Context.* Cambridge: Polity Press.

Poster, Mark (1995) *The Second Media Age.* Cambridge: Polity Press.

Preston, Paschal (1984) *Innovation in Information Technology: Defining IT and Related Job and Wealth Creation Potential.* Innovation in IT Project Working Paper 2.1.

Preston, Paschal (1986) 'The Tradeable Information Sector: Review of Definitional, Measurement and Data Issues'. London/ESRC (PICT CCU Working Paper, mimeo).

Preston, Paschal (1987) 'Technology waves and the future sources of employment and wealth creation', in M. Breheny and R. McQuaid (eds) *The Development of High Technology Industries: An International Survey.* London: Croom Helm.

Preston, Paschal (1989) *Measuring the Information Economy: Proposals for Updating the ISIC.* Oxford: Economic and Social Research Council/PICT, ESRC/PICT Policy Research Paper, No. 6.

Preston, Paschal (1993) 'The Diffusion and Regulation of Audiotex Services in Ireland', in M. Latzer and G. Thomas (eds) *Audiotex Services in Europe and the USA.* Amsterdam: Kluwer.

Preston, P. (1994) 'Neo-liberal regulation and the smaller and peripheral economies: an institutionalist perspective', in H. Williams and M. Borman (eds) *Telecommunication: Exploring Competition.* Amsterdam: IOS Press.

Preston, Paschal (1995) 'Information and citizenship in a European context: competing conceptions and definitions', paper presented at EU DGXIII Conference on 'Information and Citizenship', Luxembourg, October 1995.

Preston, Paschal (1996a) 'Technology, space and cohesion: an Irish perspective on "Europe's Way to the Information Society",' in Special theme issue of *Telematics and Informatics*, 13 (2/3): 123–40.

Preston, Paschal (1996b) 'Content matters: a strategy for the "content" industries in the Irish information economy', Commissioned consultancy report (unpublished).

Preston, Paschal (1996c) 'Multimedia convergences or divergences?: the uneasy encounter between industrial innovation logics and the cultural/media spheres', paper presented to 4S/EASST Conference. Bielefeld, Germany, 10–13 October 1996.

Preston, Paschal (1996d) 'Democratic and cultural issues along "Europe's way to the information society"', paper to OGK conference 'Time After Media', Schloss Hagenburg, near Linz, 1–3 March 1996.

Preston, Paschal (1997a) 'The info superhighway and the less developed regions/smaller entities', in H. Kubicek and R. Williams (eds) (1997) *The Social Shaping of the Info Superhighway: European and American Roads to the Information Society.* New York: St Martins Press. pp. 277–98.

Preston, Paschal (1997b) 'Information for citizenship: the Ireland case', in Jane Steele (ed.) *Information for Citizenship in Europe.* London: Policy Studies Institute. pp. 108–46.

Preston, Paschal (1997c) 'The key challenges for TE's "information age town" project: context, challenges and prospects', paper to conference 'On Ireland in the Information Age: Developing a National Strategy', Dublin City University, 19 September 1997.

Preston, Paschal (1998a) 'The media, public communications and "Europe's way to the information society"', in theme issue of *Kurswechsel Journal*, 2: 101–116.

Preston, Paschal (1998b) 'Social science knowledge and "Europe's way to the Info Society"', Paper to conference on 'The role of the Social Sciences in the Making of the European Union', organised by the Austrian Ministry of Science on the occasion of Austria's Presidency of the EC, Vienna, 10–12 December 1998.

Preston, Paschal and Grisold, Andrea (1995) 'Unpacking the concept of competition in media policy making: the case of Ireland and Austria', in F. Corcoran and P. Preston (eds) *Democracy and Communication in the New Europe.* Hampton, NJ: Hampton Press. pp. 67–96.

Preston, Paschal and Lorente, Santiago (1995) 'Competing visions of information superhighways: implications for users', PICT International Conference on Social and Economic Implications of New Information and Communication Technologies, Queen Elizabeth II Conference Centre, London, 10–12 May 1995.

Preston, Paschal and Kerr, Aphra (1998) 'Multimedia, technology and the nation state: cultural dimensions of multimedia "content"', paper to Twenty-first Conference of International Association for Media and Communication Research, Glasgow, 26–30 July 1998.

Preston, Paschal and Flynn, Roderick (1999) 'The long-term performance and utility of national telecoms systems: a case study of Ireland, 1920–1998', *Telecommunications Policy*, 23 (5): 437–58.

Preston, Paschal and Flynn, R. (2000) 'Overhauling universal service: citizenship, consumption norms and the telephone', *The Information Society*, 16 (2): 91–9.

Ramirez, Rafael (1998) 'Unchaining value in a new economic age', *Financial Times*, 12–13, (Special Supplement on 'Mastering Global Business').

Reich, Robert (1998) 'My Dinner with Bill,' *The American Prospect*, 38: 6–9.

Rice, R.E. & Assoc (1984) *The New Media: Communication, Research and Technology.* London: Sage.

Robins, Kevin (ed.) (1992) *Understanding Information: Business Technology and Geography.* London: Belhaven Press.

Robins, K. and Askoy, Asu (1990) 'Hollywood for the twenty-first century? Global competition for critical mass in image markets', paper to ICA Conference, Dublin.

Rogers, Everett M. (1983) *Diffusion of Innovations* (Third Edition). New York: Free Press.

Rogers, Everett M. (1995) *The Diffusion of Innovations* (Fourth Edition). New York: Free Press.

Rogers, E.M. and Kincaid, L. (1981) *Communication Networks: Towards a New Paradigm for Research*. New York: Free Press.

Rohm, Wendy Goldman (1998) *The Microsoft File: The Secret Case Against Bill Gates*. New York: Random House.

Rorty, Richard (1998) Interview in *Times Higher Education Supplement*, 16 October 1998.

Rose, Margaret A. (1991) *The Post-modern and the Post-industrial*. Cambridge: Cambridge University Press.

Rosenberg, Nathan (1982) *Inside the Black Box: Technology and Economics*. Cambridge: Cambridge University Press.

Roszak, T. (1986) *The Cult of Information: The Folklore of Computers and the True Art of Thinking*. New York: Pantheon Books.

Rubin, M.R. and Huber, M.T. (1986) *The Knowledge Industry in the United States, 1960–80*. Princeton, NJ: Princeton University Press.

Salvaggio, J.L. (ed.) (1989) *The Information Society: Economic, Social and Structural Issues*. New York: L. Erlbaum.

Sayer, Andrew (1989) 'Post-Fordism in question', *International Journal of Urban and Regional Research*, 13: 666–95.

Samarajiva, Rohan and Shields, Peter (1997) 'Telecommunications networks as social space', *Media, Culture and Society*, 19 (4): 535–56.

Schement, J.R. and Lievrouw, L.A. (eds) (1988) *Competing Visions, Complex Realities: Social Aspects of the Information Society*. Norwood, NJ: Ablex.

Schement, Jorge R. and Curtis, Terry (1995) *Tendencies and Tensions of the Information Age*. New Brunswick, NJ: Transaction Publishers.

Schiller, H.I. (1981) *Who Knows: Information in the Age of the Fortune 500*. Norwood, NJ: Ablex.

Schiller, H.I. (1986) *Information and the Crisis Economy*. Norwood, NJ: Ablex.

Schlesenger, P. (1991) 'Media, political order and national identity', *Media, Culture and Society*, 13 (3): 297–308.

Schor, Juliet (1991) *The Overworked American: The Unexpected Decline of Leisure*. New York: Basic Books.

Schramm, W. (1964) *Mass Media and National Development: The Role of Information in the Developing Countries*. Stanford, CA: Stanford University Press.

Schumpeter, Joseph (1939) *Business Cycles*. New York: McGraw Hill.

Schumpeter, Joseph (1943) *Capitalism, Socialism and Democracy*. London: Unwin Hyman.

Schumpeter, Joseph (1954) *History of Economic Analysis*. New York: Oxford University Press.

Shapiro, Carl and Varian, Hal (1998) *Information Rules: A Strategic Guide to the Network Economy*. Cambridge, MA: Harvard Business School Press.

Shillingford, Joia (1996) 'Middle-sized companies most at risk in digital future', *Financial Times*, 6 March 1996.

Silverstone, Roger and Hirsch, Eric (eds) (1992) *Consuming Technologies: Media and Information in Domestic Spaces*. London: Routledge.

Sinclair, J., Jacka, Elizabeth and Cunningham, Stuart (eds) (1995) *New Patterns in Global Television*. New York: Oxford University Press.

Singelmann, J. (1979) *From Agriculture to Services*. Beverly Hills, CA: Sage.

Slack, J. and Fejes, F. (eds) (1987) *The Ideology of the Information Society*. Norwood, NJ: Ablex.

Sloterdijk, P. (1989) *Critique of Cynical Reason*. London: Verso.

Smith, Adam (1776) [1981] *An Inquiry into the Nature and Causes of the Wealth of Nations*. Indianapolis: Liberty Press.

Smith, A. (1980) *The Geopolitics of Information*. New York: Oxford University Press.

Smith, Merritt Roe and Marx, Leo (eds) (1994) *Does Technology Drive History? The Dilemma of Technological Determinism*. Cambridge, MA: MIT Press.

Smythe, D. (1981) 'Communications: blind spot of economics', in W.H. Melody, L. Salter and P. Heyer (eds) (1981) *Culture, Communication and Dependency: The Tradition of H.A. Innis*. Norwood, NJ: Ablex.

Smythe, D. (1983) *Dependency Road*. Norwood, NJ: Ablex.

Soja, Edward (1989) *Postmodern Geographies*. London: Verso.

Sokal, A and Bricmont, J. (1998) *Intellectual Impostures*. Berks: Profile Books.

Sorensen, Knut and Berg, Anne-Jorune (eds) (1990) *Technology and Everyday Life: Trajectories and Transformations, Report No. 5*. Trondheim: NTU.

Sparks, Colin (ed.) (1996) Special issue on 'electronic democracy', *Media, Culture and Society*, 18 (2).

Splichal, Slavo, Calabrese, A. and Sparks, C. (eds) 1994) *Information Society and Civil Society: Contemporary Perspectives on the Changing World Order*. West Lafayette, Indiana: Purdue University Press.

Stanback, T.M. Jnr (1979) *Understanding the Service Economy: Employment, Productivity, Location*. Baltimore, MD: Johns Hopkins University Press.

Stanback, T.M. Jnr and Knight, R.V. (1980) *The Metropolitan Economy*. New York: Columbia University Press.

Stanback, T.M. Jnr et al. (1981) *Services: The New Economy*. Totowa, NJ: Allanheld & Co.

Stevenson, Nick (1995) *Understanding Media Cultures: Social Theory and Mass Communication*. Sage.

Stevenson, R.L. (1988) *Communications, Development and The Third World*. New York: Longman.

Stonier, T. (1983) *The Wealth of Information*. London: Thames Methuen.

Storper, M. (1989) 'The transition to flexible specialisation in the US film industry: external economies, the division of labour and the crossing of industrial divides', *Cambridge Journal of Economics*, 13: 273–305.

Storper, Michael (1993) 'Flexible specialisation in Hollywood: a response to Askoy and Robins', *Cambridge Journal of Economics*, 17 (4): 479–84.

Storper, Michael (1994) 'The transition to flexible specialisation in the US film industry', in Ash Amin (ed.) (1994) *Post-Fordism: A Reader*. Oxford: Basil Blackwell. pp. 195–226.

Storper, M. and Christophersen, S. (1987) 'Flexible specialisation and regional industrial agglomerations: the case of the US motion picture industry', *Annals of the Association of American Geographers*, 77 (1): 104–17.

Strachey, J. (1956) *Contemporary Capitalism*. London: Victor Gollancz (Facsimile Reprint, 1994. London: William Pickering).

Strange, Susan (1994) *States and Markets*. London: Pinter.

Strange, Susan (1996) *The Retreat from the State*. Cambridge: Cambridge University Press.

290

Streeter, Thomas (1996) *Selling the Air: A Critique of Commercial Broadcasting Policy in the USA*. Chicago: University of Chicago Press.

Survey of Current Business (1998, November issue) Washington DC: Bureau of Economic Analysis.

Sussman, G. and Lent, J.A. (eds) (1991) *Transnational Communication: Wiring the Third World*. London: Sage.

Taylor, J., Kramarae, Cheris and Ebben, M. (eds) *Women, Information Technology and Scholarship*. Urbana, IL: Center for Advanced Study.

Techno-Z F.H. (1997) *The Content Challenge: Electronic Publishing and the New Content Industries*. Research report commissioned and published by CEC, DG XIII/E, October 1997.

TechServ (1998*) The Future of Content: Discussions on the Future of European Electronic Publishing*. Research report commissioned by EC, DG XIII/E. Luxembourg: TechServ.

Thompson, E.P. (1963) *The Making of the English Working Class*. London: Vintage Books.

Thompson, John B. (1995) *The Media and Modernity: A Social Theory of the Media*. Cambridge: Polity Press.

Toffler, Alvin (1970) *Future Shock*. London: Pan Books.

Toffler, Alvin (1980) *The Third Wave*. London: Pan Books.

Toffler, Alvin (1983) *Previews and Premises*. London: Pan Books.

Toffler, Alvin and Toffler, Heidi (1995a) *Creating a New Civilization: The Politics of the Third Wave'*. Atlanta: Turner Publishing Inc.

Toffler, Alvin and Toffler, Heidi (1995b) 'Getting Set for the Coming Millennium', *Futurist*, 29 (2): 10–15.

Toffler, Alvin and Toffler, Heidi (1995c) Interview (by Sam Whitmore) in *PC Week Executive* 12 (15), 17 April 1995, E4–5.

Toffler, Alvin, with Dyson, Esther, Gilder, George and Keyworth, George (1996) 'Cyberspace and the American dream: a Magna Carta for the knowledge age', *The Info Society*, 12 (3): 295–308.

Tomita, T. et al. (1975) 'The volume of information flow and the quantum evaluation of media', *Telecommunications Journal*, 42 (6): 339–49.

Tyler, C. (1997) 'Darwin Still Gets Under the Skin', *Financial Times*, 15 February 1997.

UK (1982a) *There's No Future Without IT*. London: Ministry for IT, Department of Industry.

UK (1982b) *Information Technology: The Age of Electronic Information*. London: Ministry for IT, Department of Industry.

UNDP (1998) *Human Development Report, 1998*. Oxford: Oxford University Press.

UNDP (1999) *Human Development Report, 1999*. Oxford: Oxford University Press.

USA-NII (1994) *The National Information Infrastructure: Agenda for Action – Executive Summary*. Washington DC.

USA-NTIA (1988) *Telecom 2000*. Washington: NTIA.

USA Bureau of the Census (1996) *Statistical Abstract of the US, 1996*. Washington DC: US Bureau of the Census.

USA Bureau of the Census (1998) *Statistical Abstract of the US, 1998*. Washington DC: US Bureau of the Census.

291

USA Department of Commerce (1999) *The Emerging Digital Economy, II.* Washington DC: Department of Commerce. Report obtained online from: *WWW.ecommerce.gov/ede/report.html*

Veljanovsky, Cento (ed.) (1989) *Freedom in Broadcasting.* London: Institute for Economic Affairs.

Venturelli, Shalini (1998) *Liberalising the European Media: Politics, Regulation, and the Public Sphere.* Oxford: Oxford University Press.

Wasko, Janet (1994) *Hollywood in the Information Age: Beyond the Silver Screen.* Cambridge: Polity Press.

Wasko, Janet, Mosco, Vincent and Pendakur, Manjunath (eds) (1993) *Illuminating the Blindspots: Essays Honoring Dallas W Smythe.* Norwood, NJ: Ablex.

Webster, F. and Robins, K. (1986) *Information Technology: A Luddite Analysis.* Norwood, NJ: Ablex.

Webster, Frank (1995) *Theories of the Information Society.* London: Routledge.

Weizenbaum, J. (1976) *Computer Power and Human Reason.* San Francisco, CA: Freeman.

Williams, Raymond (1958) *Culture and Society: Coleridge to Orwell.* London: Hogarth Press.

Williams, Raymond (1961) *The Long Revolution.* London: Chatto & Windus.

Williams, Raymond (1974) *Television, Technology and Cultural Form.* London: Fontana/Collins.

Williams, Raymond (1983) *Towards 2000.* London: Chatto & Windus.

Williams, Robin and Edge, David (1996) 'The social shaping of technology', *Research Policy*, 25: 865–99.

Winner, Langdon (1977) *Autonomous Technology: Technics-out-of-control as a Theme in Political Thought.* Cambridge, MA: MIT Press.

Winston, Brian (1996) *Technologies of Seeing: Phototgraphy, Cinematatography and TV.* London: BFI.

Winston, Brian (1998) *Media, Technology and Society: A History.* London: Routledge.

Wired (1996) 'The *Wired* Manifesto'. *Wired.* October 1996: 42–7.

Wood, Ellen M. (1996) 'Modernity, postmodernity or capitalism', *Monthly Review:* July-August, 21–40.

Wood, Ellen Meiksins (1997) 'Modernity, postmodernity or capitalism?', *Review of International Political Economy*, 4 (3): 539–60.

Woodward, K (ed.) (1980) *The Myths of Information: Technology and Post-Industrialist Culture.* London: Routledge & Kegan Paul.

Wright, Marc (1983) *Tevolution: The Evolution of TV, Cable and Satellite.* London: Pear Publications.

INDEX